The Liberal De

Manchester University Press

This book is dedicated to Professor Ron Johnston (1941–2020), who was the greatest boss, supervisor, friend and mentor to both Dave and Andrew. He instilled our love of detail and nuance but primarily made us acknowledge that geography matters.

The Liberal Democrats

From hope to despair to where?

David Cutts, Andrew Russell and
Joshua Townsley

Manchester University Press

Published by Manchester University Press
Oxford Road, Manchester M13 9PL

www.manchesteruniversitypress.co.uk

British Library Cataloguing-in-Publication Data
A catalogue record for this book is available from the British Library

ISBN 978 1 5261 2781 5 *hardback*
ISBN 978 1 5261 2783 9 *paperback*

First published 2023

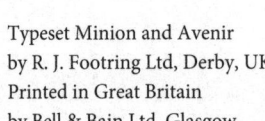
Typeset Minion and Avenir
by R. J. Footring Ltd, Derby, UK
Printed in Great Britain
by Bell & Bain Ltd, Glasgow

Contents

Figures

Tables

Acknowledgements

There are so many colleagues, friends and acquaintances who have generously contributed their time and have been instrumental in getting this book over the line. We are particularly grateful to Peter Allen, Matthew Goodwin, Tim Haughton, Paula Keaveney, Paul Kennedy, Alia Middleton, Jon Tonge and Paul Widdop for their insight and longstanding support.

We are grateful to David Denver and Justin Fisher for giving us full access to the survey of election agents and their wider encouragement. We wish to thank the British Election Study (BES) team, as well as members of the Elections, Public Opinion and Parties Group of the Political Studies Association and the British Politics Group of the American Political Science Association, who have repeatedly improved draft versions of our work.

We would like to thank every party member, activist, councillor and politician who spoke to us about our work over the years and all those who encouraged us to keep going when the prospects for another account of the Liberal Democrats seemed as uncertain and as bleak as the party's national fortunes. We are particularly grateful to Mark Pack and Duncan Brack, who have always been extremely supportive and helpful. We hope that our endeavours have been worthwhile. Naturally all mistakes remain ours.

We particularly want to thank Emma Brennan and all of the team at Manchester University Press for their patience, advice and professionalism on seeing this project through to the final stage.

Dave and Andrew. We are deeply indebted to Charles Pattie and Ed Fieldhouse, who have always been great friends, colleagues and instigators. We thank all our colleagues and students at Birmingham and Liverpool respectively (and prior to that at Bath and Manchester) who have listened to seminars and given wise counsel about the state of the Liberal Democrat party in the last few years.

Dave. I would like to thank Anna for her love, understanding, advice and support. I could not do what I do without her. I would like to thank Cerys and Evan, who have brought me untold happiness and joy. Thank you for being an inspiration to me. To my dad (Geoffrey) for his unfailing support, wisdom and political chats and lastly my mum (Jacqueline), who sadly passed away over the course of writing this book. Thank you Mum for your love and everything you did for me.

Andrew. Family has been the greatest love as always and I would like to thank Jackie, Huw, Rhydian and Beth for being superstars each and every day. Becoming

Grandrew to Isla, Imogen and Jacob has been the joy of my life. I am indebted to the marvellous professionals at the Manchester Royal Infirmary, Manchester Children's Hospital, Salford Royal, the Christie NHS Foundation Trust and the Brain Tumour Research charity for their inspiring, unending devotion to my family – and so many others – whenever required.

Josh. I would like to thank Gina for her unceasing support and love, and Edith. Edith – while you didn't enter the world until after the full draft was finished, it was your arrival that spurred me on to finish the book on time. Welcoming you into the world has been the joy of a lifetime. I would also like to thank my mum (Lesley), step-dad (Iain), brother (Oliver) and dad (Richard) for everything they have done for me. My family and friends are a constant source of support and strength for me – thank you.

Introduction: structure, agency and an identity crisis

Since their foundation in 1988, the Liberal Democrats have faced a political identity crisis. As the third party in a predominantly two-party system, they struggle to translate support into seats, overcome weakness in their social and political base, build an infrastructure and an activist base capable of challenging the major parties, develop a distinctive identity which can mobilise the electorate, build credibility so that electors are willing to set aside concerns that the Liberal Democrats are a wasted vote, compete against parties with greater human and financial resources, and get the national media to give them airtime so that their messages reach a wider audience. Faced with such a predicament, should the Liberal Democrats adopt quick-fix solutions in an attempt to join the top table of British politics or should they play the long game and deal with the underlying issues that have hampered the growth of liberal politics for 100 years? The quandary for the party is that neither the short nor the long game guarantees success. The former seeks to exploit the biorhythms of politics, strategically placed to benefit from dissatisfied Labour or Conservative party supporters as the electoral climate fluctuates. On the downside, when the popularity of the leader wanes and the party brand becomes discredited, the softness of the party's support is exposed, and Liberal Democrats cease to become the destination for protest voters. The latter approach presents an opportunity to shape a distinctive identity and build social and political heartlands of support, but it risks the prospect of banishment to the electoral wilderness. It requires an ideological magnet on which policy programmes can be built and that voters can be drawn towards. Getting the balance right is extremely difficult as tempting short term political and electoral opportunities arise. Both approaches are vulnerable to events and shocks which can change the political climate in an instant. How a party and its leader respond to such events can shape the political narrative for decades and in the worst-case scenario can expose the underlying weaknesses that agency can mask. In the face of such toxicity, this scenario can reduce the party from key player to bystander and even call into doubt their future viability.

The purpose of the book

This book represents an effort to analyse the fortunes and prospects of the Liberal Democrats, from its clear rise to dramatic fall, with now every possibility still open to the party, from evaporation to rehabilitation. Yet the party is severely under-researched in both British and comparative contexts. The rise of the party from the margins to threatening to break the mould of British politics, from clinging onto representation in the geographic periphery of the country to being a party of national government during the 2010–2015 coalition, was far from inevitable and this book covers gaps in our collective understanding. The fall from grace after the coalition years seemed irresistible but was far from inevitable. Since 2015, the prospects for the party's recovery have often seemed both compellingly obvious but tantalisingly elusive. This book is a compelling analysis of the party's electoral and ideological reality, its strategic dilemmas as a third party constantly defined not by itself but by its relationship to others. It should be essential for those who wish to understand challenger political parties in general, the contemporary political scenario in particular and the peculiarities of the tradition of British liberalism.

Over the last 40 years, the Liberal Democrats have played a prominent role in British political life. Nevertheless, there have been few comprehensive studies on the party. The most authoritative academic account of Liberal Democrat politics in Britain is *Neither Left Nor Right?*, published in 2005.[1] Between its publication and the time of writing the present volume (2022) there have been five general elections and massive fluctuations in Liberal Democrat fortunes. The Liberal Democrats reached a high watermark at Westminster in 2005, experienced an incredible surge in apparent popularity in the 2010 election with 'Cleggmania', and entered coalition government with the Conservatives for five years.

After its involvement in national government, the party faced a real battle for survival under the leadership of Tim Farron, Vince Cable and then Jo Swinson. In 2015, it was close to electoral wipeout and remained in a fragile state in 2017 following Brexit and the return to two-party politics. In 2019, it continued to be relatively unpopular, with one-third of the vote, and fewer than one-fifth of the representation of a decade earlier. Nevertheless, it saw off the threat of a new centre party, won by-election seats, and performed well in local contests and in the 2019 European election (in which the UK participated before Brexit was implemented). The implosion of the Conservatives since the Covid-19 pandemic has suggested an apparent way back for the party and under Ed Davey the Liberal Democrats have looked like a viable national party once more.

In light of the Liberal Democrat rollercoaster ride, this book takes stock of the party's role in British politics. It analyses why public sentiment towards the Liberal Democrats fell so dramatically after 2010 and explains how key political shocks, combined with poor political agency, failed to overcome longstanding structural problems and shaped an anti-Liberal Democrat shift in public mood. We examine the nature and distinctiveness of Liberal Democrat support: how it was built, where it went and the prospects for recovery. We address whether the Liberal Democrat toolkit for building support is fit for purpose and assess how the failure to build an enduring political identity was shaped by internal decisions, national events and an inability to deal with fundamental structural flaws. Lastly, we highlight dangers and opportunities, and discuss whether the Liberal Democrats must address fundamental questions about their continued role in British politics, either as a vote-maximising, office-seeking party or as an agenda-setting movement inside and outside Westminster.

This book has the following objectives:

- to provide a wide-ranging and reflective account of the Liberal Democrats in modern British politics;
- to explore the longstanding difficulties confronting the Liberal Democrats in its battle for a political identity and distinctiveness in the British political arena;
- to provide a comprehensive account of how and why the Liberal Democrats became politically and electorally 'toxic' among swathes of British voters;
- to examine public sentiment towards the Liberal Democrats and the difficulties facing the party in netting new supporters and recapturing old ones;
- to explore how events and political shocks shaped the fortunes of the Liberal Democrats in British politics;
- to assess whether the Liberal Democrats' community-based ethos of person-alised grassroots activism is still fit for purpose in twenty-first-century British politics;
- to examine the short- and long-term challenges facing the Liberal Democrats in post-Brexit, post-Covid Britain.

There are seven interrelated themes that run throughout our analysis, and these are set out before the contents of the book are outlined below.

1. The credibility gap is the biggest obstacle to Liberal Democrat electoral success

How can third parties convince voters in majoritarian systems that voting for them is not a waste of time? This has been the essential struggle for the Liberal Democrats, and their predecessors, since the advent of universal suffrage. Like most third parties in majoritarian systems, the Liberal Democrats get squeezed out (known as Duverger's law) as voters are drawn towards the two largest parties. Overhauling the inbuilt disadvantage that the Liberal Democrats face as a challenger party is always likely to be a struggle. Bridging the electoral credibility gap is vital, as credibility needs to be forged at both national and local levels. Until 2010, the Liberal Democrats built locally, using targeted campaign activism. Local election gains and council representation became a platform from which the Liberal Democrats could garner support and position themselves as the viable alternative to the incumbent. Using this blueprint, the Liberal Democrats were able to build reputational capital and establish themselves as the main opposition in specific places, thereby simultaneously strengthening partisanship ties and ensuring they were the main recipients of borrowed or tactical support.

We show that after 2010 the destruction of the Liberal Democrat local councillor base and the limitations of place-based campaigning in defensive scenarios combined to remove local credibility in seats the party once held or was extremely competitive in. However, national credibility also impacted local credibility. A third party that is trailing or declining in the polls, is suffering from lukewarm public ratings, and has an unpopular or non-connecting leader will see its wider electoral viability diminish. Voters are less willing to lend their votes and seek alternatives or they simply stay with the main parties. Here we stress how the coalition shock and its legacy not only wiped out the party's credibility in many seats but damaged it so badly that it has struggled to re-establish itself as the main competitor. The longer the Liberal Democrats remain unviable nationally, the more difficult it will be to build credibility on the ground, to bridge this gap to voters in places that matter to secure representation. The credibility conundrum remains an essential problem for the Liberal Democrats.

2. Quick-fix policy solutions have masked longstanding structural deficiencies and exposed a vacuum in the political identity of the Liberal Democrats

Our analysis shows that the pre-coalition Liberal Democrats used quick-fix policy positions to capitalise on shifting public support against incumbent governments on both flanks. As traditional sources of support began to dry up, the party used issues such as tuition fees, hypothecated taxation and opposition to war to develop a radical and distinctive edge. Such policy positions were designed to transform the party's image and to counter accusations that it did not have a distinctive political identity. However, such stances often masked internal tensions over party direction, despite affording media opportunities and crucial airtime to communicate to voters. Strategically, the party recognised the correlation between representation at Westminster, and in other elected parliaments, and offline media profile. In many ways the strategy worked: first, to win seats and reduce the geographical evenness of the Liberal Democrat vote while at the same time boosting local credibility through increasing representation in councils; second, to build national vote share so that credibility could be built in the public's mind.

However, there was a severe cost to this approach. The strategy for rapid growth required the building of tactical alliances and securing support that was borrowed rather than owned. It presented a misleading picture about the stability of the Liberal Democrat vote and meant that the party was chameleon-like in its message and tactics, which it changed to suit the electoral context in particular places. Consequently, the party's core identity was blurred.

As an electoral strategy, segmenting specifically targeted sections of the electorate and built tactical alliances for the Liberal Democrats as a transactional activity. As such, it was always built on sand and fog, exposing the soft underbelly of party support and the likely fluidity of tactical supporters. The obvious difficulty was keeping different sections of support onside, especially when the key principles of the Liberal Democrats were not wholly connected with the values of the targeted voters.

The effect of coalition – the abandonment of policies and reversal of manifesto commitments – exposed the underlying weakness of the Liberal Democrats' quick-fix strategy. Indeed, the coalition was not only a missed opportunity for the party to own the policy arena and develop an identity with the electorate, but also led to disillusionment internally as party policy-making processes became largely redundant as a means of influencing decisions made in government. The Liberal Democrats' long-term problems were then precisely highlighted in the aftermath of the 2016 EU referendum. Despite the dominance of Brexit in the campaign discourse of the 2017 and 2019 general elections, which provided the Liberal Democrats with the potential to develop a long-desired distinctive identity, the party was unable to capitalise. The coalition legacy contributed to a failure to capture the public mood on Brexit (and the 2019 revoke policy backfired spectacularly). Moreover, the inability to package liberal, cosmopolitan, internationalist values across the policy arena outside the European question and to push the party as their protector against nativist lurches to the right was a notable mistake. It reflected the quick-fix tendency, which is still innate within the party and among its leaders. Almost four decades after the formation of the Liberal Democrats, few voters know what the party stands for. Given the 'hollowing out' of the centre and the crucial political questions now facing Britain in a post-Brexit, post-pandemic world, the failure to address this could continue to consign the Liberal Democrats to bystander status.

3. Agency is crucial to Liberal Democrat electoral fortunes

We focus on how agency – the impact of individuals – and its interplay with structure are crucial to the Liberal Democrats' electoral viability. Twenty-four-hour media coverage of leader visits, rallies and speeches has somewhat overshadowed traditional local campaigns, especially in key seats. With growing electoral volatility, voters have become less politically entrenched and few are fully informed of policies across all parties. Voters therefore increasingly use leaders as a heuristic short-cut to make decisions on who to vote for when issues are too complicated. For a third party to punch above its weight in modern British politics, the leader is more important than ever. Given their relatively small numbers of partisan supporters, the Liberal Democrats often have to walk a political tightrope of appealing to different sides of the political spectrum to build coalitions of support in order to win parliamentary seats. Leaders, through their personal qualities and communication skills, play a pivotal role in securing this support and enhancing credibility. Yet, as our analysis shows, for third parties, popular leaders get them so far but are unable to overcome the longstanding structural issues facing challenger parties in majoritarian systems. Importantly, leader effects seem to be a one-way street. The unpopularity and political baggage of its post-2010 leaders (bar Vince Cable) have significantly harmed the Liberal Democrats' electoral fortunes. Making Nick Clegg the centre-piece in 2010 almost worked (height of 'Cleggmania') but backfired thereafter as he symbolised the toxic nature of the coalition, inextricably linked with austerity policies, u-turns and, for some, electoral betrayal. We show how Jo Swinson's overly presidential campaign of 2019 suffered the same fate, for similar reasons.

Agency matters in other ways too. We stress how since 2015 the Liberal Democrats have been weakened by a lack of parliamentary representation. This has knock-on consequences for winning seats and building a national media profile. The relative lack of airtime means that the Liberal Democrats struggle to cut through to voters. Previous election results also frame and restrict future performance. With few representatives, the party is effectively bound over. The pool of talent is limited and, given the lack of turnover, inextricably tied to the coalition era, and therefore individuals have fewer opportunities to build a public persona and reputation among the electorate. It also has consequences for party positioning. The same people who were responsible for party policies in the past remain influential, which has somewhat hindered the possibility of any large-scale positional shift given their own political preferences and reputational baggage. In the post-2015 era, the rump of politicians left in Westminster have adhered to an economic liberal/pro-coalition narrative which has reinforced the aversion of swathes of voters. The party has looked stale, bereft of ideas and of new faces.

4. The coalition and its legacy have significantly damaged the Liberal Democrats' reputation with British voters

This is a constant refrain throughout the book. Going into coalition was never without risk but it represented an opportunity for the Liberal Democrats to forge a distinctive identity, rubber-stamp their credibility credentials and ultimately weaken the structural shackles that had restricted their electoral growth for more than 80 years. However, they simply got the coalition wrong, from the agreement and portfolios to messaging and misreading the politics. Furthermore, they amplified the problem through a series of misjudgements and mistakes while in coalition and during the 2015 general election campaign as they fought for survival. The legacy of Liberal Democrat participation in the coalition government has reshaped how voters view the party. Among many, it soiled their reputation, led to a loss of trust and explains why the party capitulated in 2015 and has largely failed to recover since. The legacy of coalition hampered the party's efforts to rebuild credibility; scuppered electors' trust in its post-2015 policies; damaged leaders' campaigns; restricted access to airtime and wider media exposure; weakened the party brand and identity; and exposed the gaps in its campaign armoury. The coalition shock and its legacy still shapes how the party is perceived.

5. The 'coalition shock', enduring structural barriers and self-inflicted errors prevented the Liberal Democrats capitalising on any Brexit realignment

A core theme of the book is how the Liberal Democrats' pro-European credentials did not result in the conversion of 'Remainers' to party supporters and how this represented a missed opportunity. Our analysis stresses how political agency and enduring structural barriers combined to diminish the prospect of the Liberal Democrats gaining political capital from Brexit. Although their longstanding pro-European stance gave the Liberal Democrats the chance to fight Brexit on ground where they had a track record and political identity, the legacy of coalition weakened the party's brand and countered policy ownership. Through the coalition shock, the Liberal Democrats suffered reputational damage that undermined their electoral credibility. The Liberal Democrats were not viable nationally because they were not credible as a party, and not viable locally because in the vast majority of seats they were simply uncompetitive.

The Leave–Remain cleavage tapped into the growing significance of liberal–authoritarian values in British elections through attitudes to immigration and the cultural backlash. This divide cuts through socio-demographics. If these value dimensions remain salient (or if there is a longstanding realignment of some kind along the Leave–Remain axis) it opens up a viable avenue of potential support for the Liberal Democrats, but this is dependent on the party breaking completely free from the self-inflicted wounds of the coalition and bridging the credibility gap generally. Structure and agency problems have meant Brexit has largely passed the Liberal Democrats by so far and even in a post-Brexit arena capitalising on these political fault lines is likely to be a struggle.

6. The Liberal Democrats have lost their competitive campaigning advantage as rivals have appropriated and adapted their practices

Recent electoral travails of the Liberal Democrats have exposed the much-heralded party campaign machine as a myth. For a long time, the modes, tactics, targeting strategies and intensity of the Liberal Democrats' ground campaign were the ace up the party's sleeve. Yet while the coalition shock exposed just how effective rival parties' campaigning had become, we illustrate that the Liberal Democrats' competitive advantage had begun to wane even before the party entered coalition. Like other parties, the Liberal Democrats' campaigning is multifaceted and joined up, integrating the national and the local together with a range of different offline and online modes. Yet they lack the resources of other parties and, as such, volunteer labour and intensive grassroots campaigning are an integral part of how the Liberal Democrats bridge the electoral credibility gap. The legacy of coalition laid bare the fragility of the ground campaign and the limitations of the party's community politics ethos. It also suggests that the party had been 'flat track bullies' – campaigning was highly effective when they were on the offensive during the 2000s but could not stop the party haemorrhaging votes when they were defending. We note how the party lost a huge chunk of its local base, including experienced campaigners, activists and councillors – foot soldiers who basically knew how to run and win campaigns. For a party built on local/grassroots politics this has proved hugely damaging, stripping the Liberal Democrats of valuable know-how in their road to recovery. To make matters worse, it is evident that their rivals learned lessons from their previous success. Worse still, both main parties have an online presence that dwarfs the Liberal Democrats', and have adapted and integrated online and offline tools in a far more effective and sophisticated manner. We explore this narrative in some depth and detail just how crucial it is for the Liberal Democrats to reduce this gap if they are to rebuild their electoral fortunes.

7. The Liberal Democrats remain reliant on the fortunes of others

Throughout this book we note a constant theme running through the Liberal Democrats' political history: they are not masters of their own fate. With too few fresh faces to turn to and little traction in the media, the Liberal Democrats appear somewhat stuck, unable to overcome their structural shortcomings and still in the process of mending bridges with scores of voters. The party seems adrift in a post-Brexit, post-pandemic, polarised political world. They remain reliant on the failures of others – a party voters may turn to if they are exhausted with the chief protagonists. More than ever, they lack a distinctive selling point or political identity that can cut through in the post-Brexit environment. Longstanding credibility issues continue to cause significant damage and, notwithstanding political openings, will always put a ceiling on the party's electoral growth.

Nevertheless, there are reasons for optimism. Labour under Keir Starmer provides challenges to the Liberal Democrats but also opportunities. Bedevilled by Boris Johnson's character failings and the catastrophe under Liz Truss, the Conservative party's brand is seemingly trashed and reliant on Rishi Sunak to rescue its economic reputation in an unprecedented cost-of-living crisis to save them from an electoral drubbing. Once again, an opening has appeared for the Liberal Democrats and, as we show, Ed Davey, by abandoning a political stance of equidistance between the two main parties, that is, by taking a vocal anti-Conservative line and building new informal progressive alliances with Labour and others, has offered the party an opportunity simultaneously to reconnect with centre-left voters and to win over disillusioned Conservatives.

For the Liberal Democrats this is a window of opportunity to start a process of renewal by rethinking their long-term political strategy and identity, embracing a socially liberal agenda which breaks from the recent past. The political and economic fallout from the pandemic is likely to dominate political discourse for the foreseeable future. Traditional left–right debates about the role, size and funding of the state will come to the fore and the Liberal Democrats need to be clear on these post-pandemic, cost-of-living questions. Expressing a clear direction of travel and generating distinctiveness in core policy areas could allow them to connect with voters and to become politically relevant in the contests they need to win. The 2019 general election showed that even when the Liberal Democrats had recovered their relevance, they still found it hard to be popular. How the party defines and positions itself in the post-pandemic era could dictate its viability and long-term future.

Outline of the book

The book is in three parts. Part I, 'The road to government', focuses on the pre-coalition period. Chapter 1 details how the Liberal Democrats' political and electoral strategy worked in tandem to tackle the embedded structural obstacles head on. It explores how the Liberal Democrats provided a viable alternative by tearing up its traditional equidistance stance and simultaneously offering high-profile policy positions and credible, distinctive leadership, in contrast to its competitors, and therefore profited when their rivals floundered. It examines how the party successfully translated votes into seats through assiduous targeting, building local platforms, tailoring messages to suit the electoral context and intensive grassroots activism. Chapter 2 notes that despite the Liberal Democrats' high electoral watermark in 2005, structural flaws such as the weak partisan base and the borrowed nature of their vote remained prominent. Moreover, significant cracks were appearing in the campaign machine and ideological battles placed key actors at odds with members and large swathes of its voters. Amidst the euphoria in 2010 of entering government for the first time since the early 1920s, the warning signs and weak fundamentals were ignored. The seeds of electoral collapse were already sown.

Part II, 'The coalition years: from government to obscurity', examines the coalition period and the subsequent destruction of the Liberal Democrats' local infrastructure and political support. Chapter 3 examines whether the Liberal Democrats' electoral disaster after the coalition was inevitable. Using coalition theory, it stresses that avoiding electoral damage was always unlikely but became unavoidable because the Liberal Democrats got the coalition badly wrong. It details the failings – from the coalition agreement and the distribution of portfolios to presentation and coalition messaging. The chapter demonstrates how the Liberal Democrats lost control of events and the wider political narrative, and how the party inflicted further self-harm through avoidable mistakes and errors of judgement. Chapters 4 and 5 detail the consequences. The former details how going into coalition betrayed a sizeable number of those who voted for the party in 2010, who almost immediately left, exposing the deep structural weaknesses in the party's support. High-profile policy u-turns and support for austerity then reinforced this sense of duplicity and deception, from which the Liberal Democrats could not recover. The latter examines what happened to the local base and the much-vaunted Liberal Democrat campaign machine. Despite being severely weakened during the coalition period, the chapter shows that the party's local infrastructure probably saved the Liberal Democrats from extinction. Nevertheless, the aura of invisibility associated with Liberal Democrat campaigning unravelled, partly reflecting the party's own failings and the electoral situation it faced; more worryingly, its rivals were outgunning the party and leaving it behind.

Part III focuses on the post-coalition era through to the 2020s. Chapter 6 looks at the post-2015 period and covers the party's battle for survival. It details how the coalition legacy smothered any prospect of revival but also how the 'hollowing out' of the centre ground reinforced by the rise of Corbynism and the decision to Leave the EU left the party adrift despite its longstanding pro-European track record. The chapter then explores how familiar structure and agency issues combined to dampen electoral prospects in 2019. The final section of that chapter briefly examines the party under Ed Davey. Freed somewhat from the shackles of the coalition legacy following Labour's lurch to the centre, it shows how Davey's repositioning of the party within an informal anti-Conservative progressive alliance could bear fruit, albeit within the confines of longstanding structural constraints. Chapter 7 examines why the Liberal Democrats have struggled to rebuild and break through since 2015. It assesses how the coalition legacy and the weaponising of austerity weakened the Liberal Democrats' recovery and explores why Brexit proved not to be the lifeline the party hoped for. It also addresses agency and how the failings of Farron and Swinson neutered any prospect of growth. Chapter 8 explores the changing electoral geography from 2010 onwards and how the coalition shock exacerbated the longstanding problem of translating votes into seats. It also details how the referendum in Scotland and the consequences of Brexit laid bare structural weaknesses and redrew the geography of Liberal Democrat support in Britain. The final section of that chapter assesses whether the green shoots of recovery and resilience in so-called 'Southern Crescent' seats can act as a catalyst for electoral momentum across the 'Blue Wall'. Chapter 9 examines whether Liberal Democrat campaigning post 2015 has been left behind by the party's rivals and whether the ethos of community politics and place-based campaigns can still make a difference. Using the 2019 general election as a benchmark, it assesses whether the party was showing signs of winning back its campaign advantage. Finally, the concluding chapter provides a summary of the key issues raised and returns to the underlying themes and core objectives of the book. We discuss whether the party has resolved the fundamental contradictions of being an office-seeking party in the Westminster system. As such, we outline the way forward for the Liberal Democrats and possible trajectories for the party.

Methods

The research reported in the book combines quantitative and qualitative methods. We use a range of data, at both the individual and the aggregate levels: the British Election Study (BES) survey series 1964–2019; the British Election Panel Study

(BEPS), 2014–2020; general election results (1922 onwards); local election data (1992 onwards); census data (1991 onwards); and constituency-level data (1979–2019). We also conducted interviews with figures at the national, regional and constituency level.

Summary

The Liberal Democrats face a set of existential challenges in the aftermath of the 2015, 2017 and 2019 general elections and the referendums of 2014 (Scottish independence) and 2016 (Brexit). This book seeks to outline the reasons for these crises and the room for manoeuvre for the party in the post-Brexit, post-pandemic environment of British politics. The party's post-coalition fortunes have fluctuated between hope and despair because of an inability to solve the obstacles caused by structure and agency. The way forwards is far from easy but, in order to set themselves on the right path, the Liberal Democrat party should acknowledge and address its own existential questions.

Part I. The road to government

In Part I we detail how the Liberal Democrats partially overcame the structural barriers against them along the road to government with the Conservatives in 2010. Chapter 1 explores how the Liberal Democrats' political and electoral strategy worked in sync to circumvent these structural obstacles. The first section details how the abandonment of equidistance proved pivotal to the Liberal Democrats rise As a third party in a two-party system we stress how the Liberal Democrats do not control their own destiny and are reliant on exploiting the weaknesses of other parties when they occur. With the removal of the equidistance shackles, we show how agency mattered. Policy distinctiveness on salient high-profile issues were presented through the personalised lens of the party leader, and this boosted his popularity. This allowed the party to cut through traditional alignments and exploit the policy mistakes of the two main parties. In Chapter 1, we show how translating votes into seats was dependent on an electoral strategy that built credibility through intensive grassroots activism. We critically examine how the so-called 'Rennard strategy' catapulted the party to a record parliamentary high, by assessing its influence and adaptability to the electoral context. We detail how the electoral strategy evolved post Rennard, noting continuity and revisions in 2010.

Chapter 2 begins by bringing together the stories of agency and structure before looking beneath the surface of the great electoral strides made by the Liberal Democrats from 1992 until 2010. Despite cementing itself as the third party of British politics, we reveal just how weak the fundamentals were and illustrate the Liberal Democrats' inability to tackle underlying problems in spite of short-term success.

Policy distinctiveness, popular leaders and 'winning here'

How did the Liberal Democrats partially circumvent the two-party squeeze and the structural barriers against it to become a potent third force in British politics? In this chapter we address how the party's political and electoral strategies worked in sync and propelled it to government. The first half of the chapter examines the political strategy. As a third party in a majoritarian system the Liberal Democrats were not masters of their own fate and, as such, we argue that electoral progress was determined by three factors. Firstly, the policy errors of other parties, particularly the incumbent. This provided political space through which the Liberal Democrats could pursue an alternative narrative and exploit opponents' weaknesses. To do this they abandoned equidistance, which ensured they could adapt and position themselves to the political context. Secondly, the party adopted popular, high-profile but distinctive short-term policies on issues where the public perceived the two main parties to be similar. Thirdly, it embraced the importance of agency: having a popular leader (or leaders) allowed the party to reach out to people and create goodwill towards the party brand. The goal was to intertwine the party leader with salient, distinctive policy stances to enhance perceived personal ownership among the public, thereby boosting leader trust, credibility and visibility. This enabled the Liberal Democrats to brand themselves as the 'go-to' choice for voters who were fed up with their natural party and build coalitions of support, which broadened its electoral appeal. Nevertheless, if the party was to translate votes into increased representation at Westminster, it needed to tackle the structural barriers from the majoritarian system head on. To do this, the party needed a viable electoral strategy to boost its credibility. In the second half of the chapter we examine how credibility was built through intensive place-based campaigning and how the so-called 'Rennard strategy' used tactics and targeting, stressed the pivotal role of the 'local' as a platform for parliamentary success and used one-off local and parliamentary by-elections as vehicles to build credibility and maximise electoral advantage. We also assess how the party adapted its strategy through the application of different messages to suit the electoral context and target new areas to build new coalitions of support. Finally, with the Liberal Democrats' comparative 'ground campaign' advantage increasingly under threat post Rennard, we examine how the electoral strategy evolved in the run-up to the 2010 general election.

The Liberal Democrats' electoral conundrum

Why individuals vote the way they do has been a focus of scholarly debate for 70 years or more. These have commonly been divided into two camps: socio-logical and instrumental explanations. The former encompasses the importance of socio-demographic characteristics (the so-called 'Columbia model') and party identification conceptualised through a psychological attachment to a party (the 'Michigan model') which, once acquired, remains intact throughout the lifetime of the individual.

Instrumental explanations, meanwhile, question the validity of this long-time attachment in light of on-going partisan change in response to cumulative evalu-ations of party performance. Such performance-based explanations (the 'valence model') stress that while individuals agree on the policy outcomes they desire, they differ on which party or leader will be best able to deliver them. Leaders are seen as crucial decision-makers and their capabilities, image and responsive-ness are utmost in voters' calculations. Valence issues such as the economy are deemed pivotal. Voters will either seek to reward the party and leader whom they deem most accomplished at managing the economy or, if they ascribe personally experienced prosperity to the incumbent government, they will seek to preserve how things stand and continue to support it. Alternatively, within the instru-mental camp, a prominence is given to issue positions and the proximity between parties and voters on these issues (the 'spatial model'). According to advocates of this model, voters rationally select the party closest to them on issues that they hold most dear. Alongside these voting camps, cross-cutting explanations based around the electoral context have also been put forward as influencing individual decision-making. For instance, candidate-specific factors or external shocks – such as MPs' expenses in 2010 – may arise at a particular election which temporally shapes voting preferences. The nature of the constituency contest and the likelihood that their preferred candidate cannot win locally may lead to tactical voting for a 'second preference' party in order to stop that voter's least favoured candidate or party winning. Moreover, sometimes an issue arises at a specific election which dominates the politics both prior to and during the campaign. The consequences can lead to mass individual switching which in turn can shape the outcome of the election.

As a third party in a majoritarian system, the extent to which sociological explanations drive Liberal and subsequently Liberal Democrat support has been somewhat contested. Aside from the weakening historical connection with Nonconformism in the 'Celtic fringe', the lack of a distinct social base of support to match that of Labour and the Conservatives has been a longstanding sore. Yet, an examination of the party's social base from 1974 to 1997 suggests that if it did have a natural electoral heartland, 'it was among the thinking middle classes' (Russell and Fieldhouse, 2005: 93). Weakening class loyalties, rising electoral volatility and increasing social mobility driven by the expansion of university education provided the Liberal Democrats with a political opportunity. Building on support from those with degrees and appealing to new types of voters who were more like Labour in social status but sympathetic to liberal values opened up the real possibility of electoral lift-off. Overcoming structural barriers and being perceived by these individual voters as a credible alternative to the two traditional parties remained major hurdles, however.

From a reward–punishment perspective, the Liberal Democrats have always been unlikely to form a government outright and therefore could not be judged on the management of the economy or the delivery of other valence issues like its opponents. Yet they could still reap the benefits. If an incumbent government started to haemorrhage support and the Liberal Democrats represented the main opposition in a constituency contest, disgruntled voters might have been more likely to lend their support. More widely, if voters were dissatisfied with the governing party and the Liberal Democrats garnered more credibility among voters than the main opposition (as in the late 1990s and early to mid-2000s), then there was an opportunity for the party to make electoral ground across the country. For the Liberal Democrats to build electoral support, they were (and are) reliant on the failures of and general disenchantment with their opponents. They are not in control of their own destiny.

The road to electoral success: abandoning equidistance

Whether this was by design, political opportunism, reflective of the electoral strategy or simply Paddy Ashdown's misguided faith in the 'Project', the decision to abandon equidistance was an implicit recognition that the Liberal Democrats were somewhat reliant on the policy mistakes of their competitors. Furthermore, it was this approach (which remained largely intact until the formation of the coalition) that kick-started the Liberal Democrats' revival. It made political sense to adapt to the electoral context and position the party so it could exploit opponents' weaknesses when they arose. This also had important ramifications for tactical switching and became a focal point of the party's political and electoral strategy.

The soundness of this approach is strengthened by the largely static but favourable public perception of the party from 1997 to 2010, which contrasts with the wild fluctuations in feelings towards its rivals. In 1997, 40 per cent of all voters either favoured or strongly favoured the Liberal Democrats. This figure remained remarkably consistent across the three general elections that followed: 39 per cent in 2001, 44 per cent in 2005 and 41 per cent in 2010. From 2001 to 2010, roughly a third of the electorate were against or less favourable towards the Liberal Democrats. Over the same period, favourable feelings towards the Conservatives increased from less than a quarter in 2001 to 46 per cent in 2010. For Labour, it dropped from 52 per cent in 2001 to 36 per cent by 2010. While the main parties' favourability fluctuated during this period, the Liberal Democrats were generally viewed as a viable alternative.

Abandoning equidistance also provided voters with a steer that the party had a closer affinity with one of the main parties than with the other. Past evidence suggested that if anything the Liberals were closer to the Conservatives than Labour, though by 1992 there was some indication that this perception was waning (Russell and Fieldhouse, 2005). Yet, as the John Major government faltered, and the Liberal Democrats' official anti-Conservative stance took hold, voters for all three main parties began to pick up on the closer affinity between the Liberal Democrats and Labour. In 1997, nearly 60 per cent of Liberal Democrat voters claimed the party was closer to Labour, increasing to 68 per cent by 2001. Less than 30 per cent of Liberal Democrat voters disapproved of Labour in 2001, while more than two-thirds provided a negative assessment of the Conservatives. Similar trends existed when analysing the second-choice party of Labour and Conservative supporters. The evidence suggested that the Conservatives were more sympathetic to the Liberals before 1997 (Russell and Fieldhouse, 2005) but in both 1997 and 2001 more Labour voters (65 and 70 per cent respectively) claimed they would vote for the Liberal Democrats as their second choice (rather than for the Conservatives).

During the 2000s, closer affinity with Labour started to wane. In 2005, 52 per cent of Liberal Democrat voters claimed the party was closer to Labour, but the figure had fallen to 40 per cent in 2010. Crucially, however, prior to entering coalition, more Liberal Democrat voters felt the party was closer to Labour than to the Conservatives – albeit marginally. In 1997 and 2001 the Liberal Democrats were more positive towards Labour than the Conservatives, but less anti-Conservative than Labour supporters. In 2005 and 2010, Liberal Democrat voters became far more positive towards the Conservatives. The strength of the relationship between Liberal Democrat supporters and Labour barely changed across these four general elections, reflecting the party's desire to reap maximum electoral rewards. Average proximity positions (absolute distances between respondents' locations and per-ceptions of parties' locations) on the left–right continuum also confirm this trend. Across the three elections from 1997 to 2005, the Liberal Democrats and Labour were close to each other, but between 2005 and 2010 the proximity scores for the Conservatives declined as that party gradually relocated towards the centre ground (Whiteley *et al.*, 2013).

Exploiting two-party convergence and indifference

According to conventional spatial explanations, the Liberal Democrat vote should be squeezed when the main parties have increasingly similar policies, or, when seeking to occupy the centre ground, the Liberal Democrats should push Labour and the Conservatives to more divergent positions. Existing evidence suggests that the Liberal Democrats would gain from occupying the 'vacated centre', when the two major parties diverge (Nagel and Wlezien, 2010) and that the Liberal Democrats presence and third party vote gains in prior elections motivates two-party policy divergence, known as the 'occupied centre' hypothesis (Adams and Merrill, 2006; Nagel and Wlezien, 2010). Yet from the mid-1990s, reflective of partisan dealignment and a growing consensus around previously contentious economic issues, the ideological space among the British electorate narrowed (Green, 2007). With the incentive for party divergence weakened, there was also evidence of depolarisation between the two main parties as perceived by BES survey respondents (Adams et al., 2012; Green and Hobolt, 2008) and reflected in Comparative Manifesto Project scores of party positions (Bara, 2006). However, over the same time period, voters also perceived the Liberal Democrats as a party at the centre (Green, 2015). Given the competition from the two main parties, how did the Liberal Democrats manage incrementally to increase its national vote and get a historically high number of MPs in Westminster?

On one level, a number of factors were in play. Abandoning equidistance allowed the Liberal Democrats to be flexible and adapt to the electoral context. Even in the run-up to the 2001 election, the party leadership was increasingly dissatisfied with Labour. Like the anti-Conservative alliance forged during the mid-1990s, this tied into the party's electoral strategy, which sought to make ground against Labour while holding off any Conservative resurgence in those seats where the Liberal Democrats had made gains. Before, but particularly after 2005, those from the economically liberal wing of the party were starting to gain prominence in shadow cabinet and spokesperson roles. This shaped the political discourse emanating from the leadership, which became more hostile to Labour. However, these factors do not wholly explain how, according to conventional expectation, the Liberal Democrats avoided being squeezed in an increasingly crowded centre. Research on third parties, however, does suggest that if voters find it difficult to distinguish between the two main party alternatives then such parties can convert proximity votes on cross-cutting policy dimensions by nurturing the importance of these additional dimensions (Callandar and Wilson, 2007; Rapoport and Stone, 2005). Other research stresses that indifference can result in voters turning to other issues and alternative voting criteria such as leader evaluations rather than simply abstaining, which can assist third parties (Green, 2015). Across the first three elections of the 2000s, Green (2015) found that the Liberal Democrats gained votes either because individual voters observed the Conservatives and Labour to be similar on policy, or because these perceived similarities led to stronger issue voting or a focus on the competencies of the leader, which benefited the third party. Simply put, instead of penalising third parties, two-party policy convergence opens up an opportunity for a third party like the Liberal Democrats to enhance its support by pushing alternative policies, leadership competence and candidate qualities (Green, 2015; Nagel and Wleizen, 2010). This became the focus of the political strategy.

The struggle to build a distinctive identity

Prior to 2005, the Liberal Democrats' electoral strategy yielded significant seat gains but not large-scale increases in national vote share. The political opportunities to push forward with alternative policies were somewhat scuppered by Tony

Blair's and New Labour's dominance of British politics. That is not to say that the Liberal Democrats were not offering something different. Since its formation, the Liberal Democrats had known that electoral survival depended on their ability to create an identity distinct from that of the Conservatives and Labour. From the 'Our Different Vision' manifesto to the emphasis on the five 'E's (Europe, Environment, Electoral and constitutional reform, Education and Economic policy), the strategy of concentrating on a core group of key issues reflected a desire to establish ownership or policy primacy. In both the 1997 and 2001 general elections, the Liberal Democrats' policy platform stressed continuity with the past, with an emphasis on maintaining their distinctive identity. Aside from its pro-European outlook and a holistic approach to constitutional reform, including a commitment to proportional representation, the party sought to stress its social liberal agenda. During the early Kennedy years there was a renewed attempt to restate its commitment to social liberalism (based on revisionist Liberals such as Hobhouse and Hobson) as a means of developing the party's identity and distinguishing itself from New Labour. With the principle of individual freedom at its heart, the Liberal Democrats emphasised the importance of decentralised decision-making and a commitment to using the state (albeit in a non-collectivist manner, thus stressing its difference from Labour) to challenge social injustice (Brack *et al.*, 2007; Grayson, 2007). As part of this social liberal agenda, one clear issue of distinctiveness was its pledge to increase the tax burden (specifically, a 50 per cent top rate of tax on earnings of over £100,000 in 2001) to pay for education and health provision. Further, the party's commitment to hypothecated taxation (one penny on the basic rate of income tax) was a cornerstone of its manifestos from 1992 to 2001. Following the introduction of tuition fees by the Labour government in September 1998, the Liberal Democrats sought to distinguish themselves from the Conservatives and Labour through a commitment to their abolition in the 2001 manifesto (entitled 'Freedom, Justice and Honesty'). On health provision, the party pledged to increase funding in 1997 to cut waiting lists, with additional revenue earmarked to the NHS from raising the price of cigarettes by 5p (the 1997 manifesto, 'Making the Difference'). In 2001, a similar promise to increase health spending by as much as £3 billion was made, for cutting waiting times by recruiting more nurses and doctors, retaining more staff by increasing pay, providing an additional 10,000 beds, abolishing fees for dental and eye checks, and stopping elderly and long-term patients having to pay for personal care costs. Alongside public service provision, the Liberal Democrats sought to stress their environmental credentials, by prioritising a carbon tax to reduce pollution in their 1997 manifesto and stressing a green dimension for every policy pledge in 2001. With additional promises to increase the top rate of income tax, stop rail privatisation and reintroduce benefits for asylum seekers, come the 2001 general election, a *Guardian* leader proclaimed, 'Step forward the Liberal Democrats, now Britain's left-wing political party' (*The Guardian*, 2001). But while there is evidence that at the 2001 general election the proximity of Labour to the Conservatives enabled the

Liberal Democrats to gain votes at the expense of Labour (Green, 2015), sympathy among a pool of voters for the Liberal Democrats' policy stances was not enough. As Russell and Fieldhouse (2005: 124) noted, in 1997 the Liberal Democrats won less than a quarter of those voters who shared their policy position on issues ranging from hypothecated tax for education spending to proportional representation for Westminster elections. On the big social agenda items, the Liberal Democrats battled for distinctiveness against Labour, who already had credit in the bank on the NHS, schools and equality rights. The trend continued in 2001: 'Liberal Democrat voters were liberals but liberals were not necessarily Liberal Democrats' (Russell and Fieldhouse, 2005: 129). Despite the electoral breakthrough in 1997 and incremental success in 2001, sympathy did not convert into mass support at the polls. For the Liberal Democrats to cut through, the party needed high-profile but distinctive policy stances on issues where the Conservatives and Labour were perceived to be similar, positive public evaluations of the leader and for the other parties (particularly the incumbent) to make policy mistakes so it could capitalise and win over voters.

Policy distinctiveness and popular leaders

During the 2000s, the political context began to change. New Labour under Tony Blair began to falter as sleaze, spin, policy errors and general public disquiet about the pace of social and political change began to emerge. The Conservatives remained unelectable for much of the decade but their electoral transformation started in earnest after 2005, following the election of moderniser David Cameron. Between Labour's efforts to maintain a stranglehold over the centre ground and the Conservatives vying to replace Labour there, the Liberal Democrats – despite increasing representation after the 1997 and 2001 general elections – faced a challenge to be distinctive and electorally credible to swathes of the electorate.

Post 2001, high-profile policy stances undoubtedly gave the Liberal Democrats a distinctive platform – raising the top rate of tax to 50 per cent (in 2001 and 2005); imposing higher eco taxes on airline flights (2010); no like-for-like replacement of the Trident missile system (2010); increasing the tax-free threshold to £10,000, to be paid for by a 'mansion tax' of 1 per cent on properties worth over £2 million (2010); tax relief on pensions at the basic rate (2010); opposing the war in Iraq in 2005; and scrapping university students' tuition fees in 2001, 2005 and 2010. From the very beginning the Liberal Democrats stressed that military action in Iraq should only be taken as a last resort following irrefutable evidence of the existence of weapons of mass destruction and only with the mandate of a second UN resolution.[1] On 18 March 2003, the Liberal Democrats (aside from one MP who abstained) voted against a government motion approving the invasion of Iraq. However, in line with its qualified stance, it also proposed an amendment to that motion (which was defeated) stating that the case for war had not yet been met and military intervention had not obtained UN authorisation. Of the three main parties, the Liberal Democrats were the only one to oppose the government motion (without the amendment). Thus the party had clear policy distinctiveness on a salient high-profile issue. What proved to be critical though was Charles Kennedy's personal ownership of the issue, despite unease among a number of senior colleagues. For Kennedy, the pivotal moment occurred on 15 February 2003, when he spoke at the 'Stop the War' rally in Hyde Park, London, in front of an estimated one million people. Kennedy reiterated the party's qualified anti-war stance: 'without a UN second resolution based on the authority and facts from the weapons inspectorate, I can assure you there is no way, in all conscience, that the Liberal Democrats either could, or should, support a war and we will not'.[2] The symbolism of speaking at the rally proved more valuable. Kennedy's presence cemented a public perception – that the Liberal Democrats, and more importantly Kennedy, was the leader(s) of the opposition to the war.

In contrast to the Liberal Democrats' policy stance on the war in Iraq, the party's position on tuition fees was longstanding. However, like opposition to the war in Iraq, public perception of the party's stance was hugely influenced by the actions of their leaders. Following the introduction of tuition fees under Labour in 1998, the Liberal Democrats almost immediately signalled their intention to oppose them. Ahead of the 2001 general election, Kennedy reaffirmed the party's commitment to abolishing them, and called their introduction 'one of the most pernicious political acts' ever (Scott, 2001). Four years later, the abolition of tuition and top-up fees remained a key plank of the party's policy platform and was distinct from the policies of both the Conservatives and Labour. For Kennedy (and the Liberal Democrats), the policy was symbolic of the party's commitment to education and equality of opportunity. It also made strategic sense, as it appealed to a section of the electorate which could deliver electoral gains.

Like opposition to the war in Iraq, Kennedy became personally committed to, and associated with, the policy – so much so that he vehemently opposed efforts (now as a backbench MP) to dump the commitment prior to the 2010 general election. As the election neared, senior Liberal Democrats, mainly from the 'Orange Book' wing of the party, began to question whether the policy was credible and financially deliverable. Party leader, Nick Clegg, initially concurred that the policy was unaffordable but his attempts at a compromise faced a backlash from the party's Federal Policy Committee, prominent Liberal Democrat MPs (including Kennedy) and party members. Despite hostility to a compromise proposal at conference, the policy was watered down. Clegg (and his team) managed to argue that it should not be a headline proposal in the manifesto or policy in the election campaign. The reality proved rather different after Clegg recorded a YouTube video for the annual conference of the National Union of Students (NUS) less than a month before the election in which he pledged to abolish fees within six years and scrap them immediately for final-year students (in England only). He also signed an NUS pledge to vote against increasing tuition fees. With Cleggmania in full throttle and the party leader actively courting the student vote, Clegg became the public face of opposition to tuition fees.

The party also began to carve out a distinctive electoral platform on tax and spending. Unlike the two main parties, the Liberal Democrats were not afraid to propose tax increases to pay for more spending on public services such as education and health. While the commitment to fund education through a penny on income tax was partly longstanding (under Ashdown, and then Kennedy in 2001), the drive to 'own' the progressive agenda and a fairer stance on tax and spending was taken to a new level under Kennedy's leadership (e.g. proposing a 50 per cent top rate of tax, replacing the council tax with a local income tax). In 2005 the Liberal Democrats directly linked changes to the top rate of tax to higher spending on education (scrapping tuition fees) and health (free personal care for the elderly). While Clegg distanced himself from increases to the top rate of taxation, the party in its 2010 manifesto stressed that 'fairer taxes' was one of its four key themes. The headline policy was scrapping income tax on earnings up to £10,000, to be paid for by a 'mansion tax', while spending commitments such as the 'pupil premium' to help disadvantaged children reinforced the party's redistributive and progressive credentials.

Under both Kennedy and Clegg the promotion of the leader and the party were intertwined – 'a new kind of politics' based on fairness, honesty and keeping promises. The party leader not only became the face of the policies but used them to enhance personal credibility, trust and profile. These policy stances also hurt the incumbent Labour party and paralysed the Conservatives in opposition, who broadly supported the incumbent stance (in favour of the war; approved tuition fees; against higher taxes for high earners) and therefore could not benefit from voter disillusionment. Critically, these issue stances enabled the Liberal Democrats to target support in new areas, and among sections of the electorate that hitherto were reluctant to support the party as a first option. Yet, did these leadership traits and policy positions directly boost the Liberal Democrats' electoral prospects? And/or were they largely indirect effects aiding the wider reach and popularity of the leader which in turn influenced Liberal Democrat support?

Kennedy and Clegg

Leader images are now widely regarded as a major driver of vote choice, with voters using them as a shortcut to acquire information and as a helpful cue when issues or polices are too complicated (Clarke *et al.*, 2004; Green and Jennings, 2017). Voters judge political leaders on a wide range of traits, such as competence, being to decisiveness/strong, likeability, responsiveness, stick to principles and trustworthiness. For third parties, leader visibility and profile are a crucial part of 'cutting through' to the public and building party and issue identity. According to BES pre-election and post-election data, Kennedy and Clegg enjoyed personal support and were generally well liked as party leaders (though the latter only

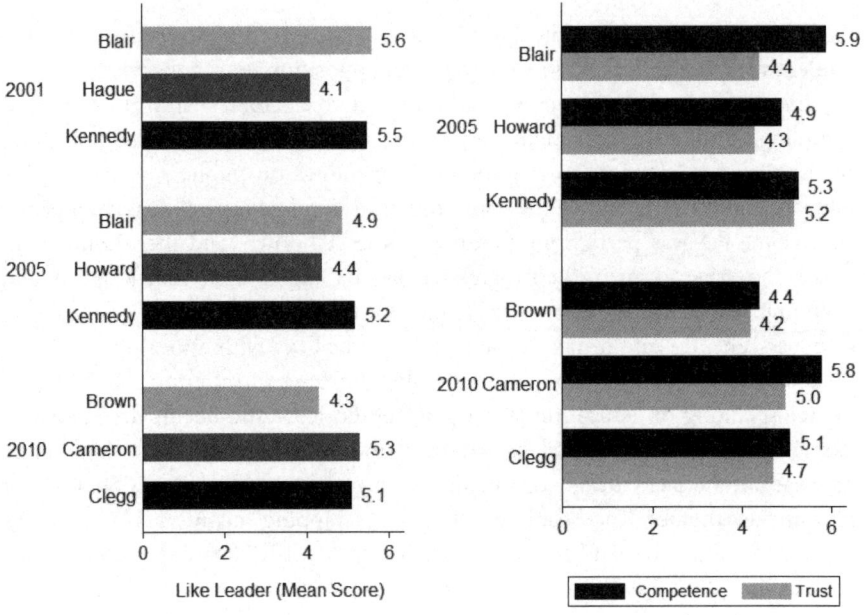

Figure 1.1 Leaders' ratings (mean scores) for likeability, 2001–2010 (left), and competence and trust, 2005–2010 (right). *Source*: 2001–2010 British Election Study

in 2010). While Blair's leadership likeability scores worsened between 2001 and 2005, buoyed by his straightforward, personable style, Kennedy was liked and trusted more than both his opponents (Tony Blair and Michael Howard) in 2005 (see Figure 1.1). On competence, Blair still enjoyed a healthy advantage although Kennedy saw his rating improve during the 2005 election campaign. Previous evidence that most voters regarded Kennedy as the most likely leader to stick to principles and keep promises was likely to have been enhanced by his stance on Iraq (Clarke *et al.*, 2004). In 2005, this personal popularity transferred to views about the party, with 57 per cent stating that the Liberal Democrats kept their promises compared to just under a quarter for Labour and just under 30 per cent for the Conservatives.

When Clegg replaced Menzies Campbell in December 2007 as leader, few outside of the 'Westminster bubble' knew very much about his leadership capabilities, style and personality. Up until the 2010 election campaign, his 'best Prime Minister' rating barely achieved double digits and lagged well behind Kennedy's ratings during his tenure as leader. On the eve of the official (and short) campaign period, only 10 per cent of respondents in a YouGov poll (5 April 2010) felt that, of the party leaders, Clegg would make the best Prime Minister. Ten days later, the leadership dynamics completely changed following the first ever televised leadership debate. The presence of a Liberal Democrat leader on the same platform as the two established main party leaders gave the party and the leader instant credibility and a national stage from which to present a new, fresh alternative. It required Clegg to perform strongly, and this he duly did, emerging as the clear victor. With both Gordon Brown and David Cameron repeatedly endorsing Clegg's opinions during the debate, 'I agree with Nick' became not only the catch-phrase of the election but embodied change and a 'new kind of politics'. While Clegg failed to reach the heights of the first debate in the two subsequent encounters, his leadership poll ratings surged and even at some stages of the campaign surpassed those of Kennedy before him.[3] Clegg outshone his two rivals during the campaign with large increases in likeability and competence ratings, although his 2010 post-election mean scores were still lower than Cameron's on every metric (see Figure 1.1). Additional information from the 2010 BES post-election wave of the campaign panel does, though, indicate that Clegg enjoyed an advantage over Cameron and Brown on other leader traits. While there was little difference between the leaders on knowledge, Clegg was seen as being more inclusive and having the interests of others in mind. However, it was honesty where Clegg had a clear lead over his rivals and this undoubtedly reflected his pitch – 'I believe it's time to do things differently … I believe it's time for promises to be kept I believe in a new kind of politics, where politicians keep their promises'.[4] Simply put, other parties could not be trusted and would say anything to get into power. While scholarly opinion is sceptical about the direct effect of these leadership debates on 2010 vote choice (Whiteley et al., 2013), the indirect boost to leaders' image and its potential role as a vehicle for transmitting details of party policies and positions on salient issues suggest that it may bear electoral fruit, particularly for third parties and their leaders.

War in Iraq

Public opinion on the war in Iraq from the very beginning proved to be volatile and divided. Early on, polls found as many as 50 per cent were opposed (The Guardian, 2002). By the start of the conflict in the third week of March 2003, opinion had flip-flopped, with approval ratings topping 50 per cent and around 30 per cent opposed (The Guardian, 2003). However, after the invasion, key events such as the suicide of British weapons inspector Dr David Kelly and growing disbelief about the legitimacy of the claims regarding weapons of mass destruction (which had previously bolstered public support for the war) led public opinion to become increasingly negative (more than 60 per cent disapproving in October 2003). Politically, a consensus grew that Blair was to blame. Evidence from the 2005 BES suggested that evaluations and emotional reactions to the Iraq war did not have a significant direct effect on Labour support. Instead, they indirectly eroded support for Blair, part of which was then transmitted to the party, which in turn significantly lowered the likelihood of voting Labour (Clarke et al., 2009). There is some circumstantial evidence that disapproval of the Iraq war cultivated support for the Liberal Democrats. Among all respondents on the 2005 BES, 65 per cent disapproved of British involvement in Iraq. But, opposition increased to 78 per cent among 2005 Liberal Democrat voters and 79 per cent among those who switched to the Liberal Democrats (indeed, among the latter group, 45 per cent strongly disapproved. Emotional reactions to the Iraq war also illustrated the strength of negative feelings. When respondents were provided with a list of four positive (happy, hopeful, confident and proud) and four negative (angry, disgusted, uneasy and afraid) words to describe their feelings towards the Iraq war, more than 80 per cent of BES pre-election respondents chose negative words (Clarke *et al.*, 2009). The negative feelings were much higher for those who voted Liberal Democrat (87 per cent) and those who switched support to the party (88 per cent). While most respondents regarded the Iraq war as a failure, negative feelings were greater among those who supported the Liberal Democrats and switched to them in 2005.

Tuition fees

Descriptive evidence on other Liberal Democrat policy stances is more difficult to assess. Specific questions on student top-up and tuition fees were not asked in either the 2005 or the 2010 BES. However, there is anecdotal evidence that the party's stance on this issue generated support in new places and among different types of voters. There was a moderate ($R^2 = 0.10$) positive bivariate relationship ($\beta = 1.75^{**}$) between Liberal Democrat support in 2005 and those constituencies with larger numbers of people working in education (see Figure 1.2). A similar relationship was found in 2010 ($R^2 = 0.10$; $\beta = 1.81^{**}$). The Liberal Democrats also won over students in greater numbers. Evidence from the 2005 and 2010 BES suggest there was a significant positive association between being a student and voting Liberal Democrat and this was also mirrored at the constituency level in both elections – and these relationships hold when analysing vote change from 2001 to 2005: at the constituency level, there is a clear positive bivariate relationship ($R^2 = 0.09$; $\beta = 0.34^{**}$) between living in areas with large numbers of students and Liberal Democrat 2001-05 vote change. A smaller but nonetheless significant relationship is evident for those living in seats with greater numbers working in education ($R^2 = 0.03$; $\beta = 0.42^{**}$).

This supports the scholarly evidence linking education and voting for the Liberal Democrats in 2005, based primarily on the party's position on student top-up fees, with some estimates suggesting that it was worth as much as 10 extra seats to the Liberal Democrats at the election (Fieldhouse *et al.*, 2006). Yet despite Clegg signing the NUS pledge, our evidence suggests that 2005 may have been the highwater mark in terms of attracting additional support from these groups. There was no relationship between those living in seats with large numbers of students or working in education and Liberal Democrat vote change from 2005 to 2010. While the Liberal Democrats maintained their strong level of support among students

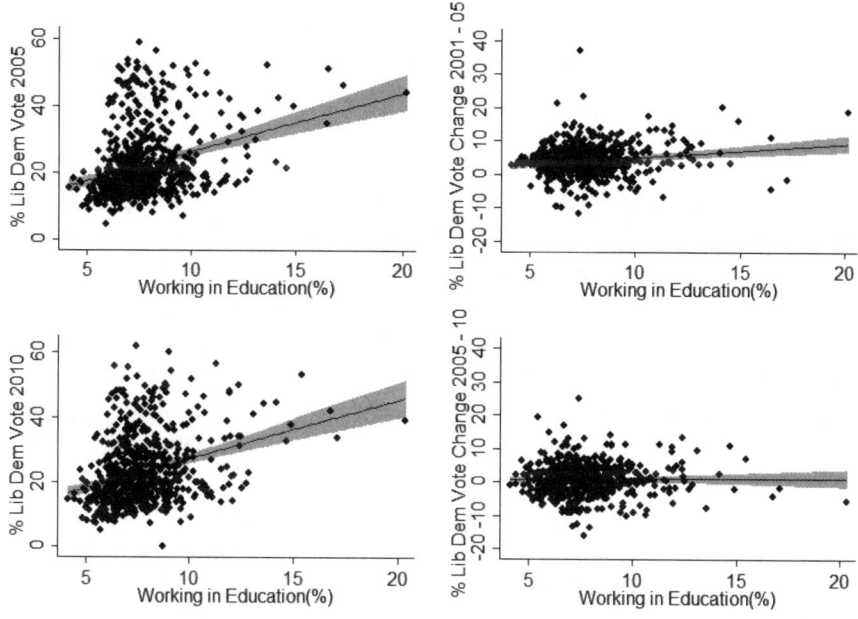

Figure 1.2 Percentage 2005 and 2010 Liberal Democrat vote and 2001–2005, 2005–2010 vote change by percentage working in education. *Source*: 2001–2010 British Election Study

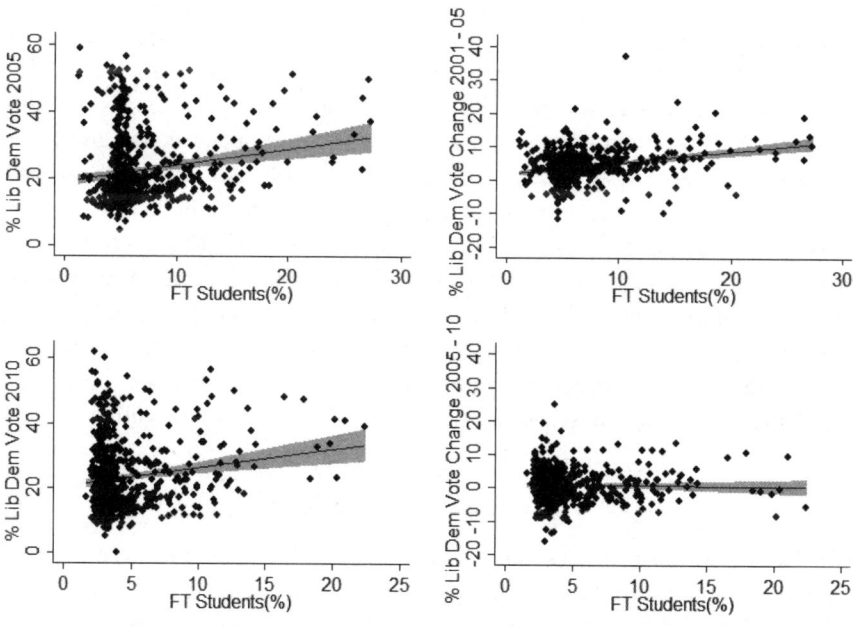

Figure 1.3 Percentage 2005 and 2010 Liberal Democrat vote and 2001–2005, 2005–2010 vote change by percentage full-time students. *Source*: 2001–2010 British Election Study

and those living in university towns in 2010, it seems that they were unable to convert additional voters living in these areas to their cause (see Figure 1.3).[5]

Fairer taxes

Spatial models of political competition – wherein voters establish where competing parties stand on certain issues and calculate the distance between parties' issue positions and personal 'ideal' stances on these issues and then vote for the party closest to them – is a longstanding explanation of electoral behaviour (Downs, 1957; Adams *et al.*, 2005). Aside from the conventional left–right scale, both the 2005 and 2010 BES surveys included issue 0–10 scales on taxation reduction (coded 0) versus increases in spending on public services (coded 10). By examining respondents' mean scores on this issue scale and the absolute difference between their own positions and their perceptions of the parties' locations on the taxation–spending, it is possible to assess how popular the Liberal Democrats' policy stance on increasing tax to pay for increased spending was with the electorate compared with its competitors. On tax–spend, the Liberal Democrats were closest to the electorate than their rivals in 2001 and 2010 and only two-tenths and one-tenth of a point more than Labour in 1997 and 2005 respectively. They enjoyed a considerable spatial advantage over the Conservatives, although this diminished considerably post 2001. By 2010, there was little difference between the three main parties. In 2010, the Liberal Democrats' two headline tax policies – raising the tax threshold (exempting the first £10,000 of earnings from tax) and the mansion tax (on property worth £2 million or more) – proved hugely popular with the public. While more than four-fifths were supportive of raising the tax threshold, evidence from the 2010 BES campaign panel shows that this increased to more than 90 per cent among Liberal Democrat voters and those who switched to the party in 2010. Similarly, three-quarters of respondents agreed with a mansion tax, a figure that increased to 86 per cent among switchers. On other distinctive policies, such as limiting tax relief on pensions and eco taxes on airlines, the Liberal Democrats were less vocal and levels of support were much lower among the public. Clegg's tough talk on honesty around tax and spending and the need for 'fairer taxes' positioned the party as dependable, reasonable and trustworthy on the economy. On a number of these distinctive policy proposals, they had a great deal of public support.

Impact of policy stances on support for Kennedy and Clegg

Did distinctive policy stances impact support for Kennedy in the 2005 and Clegg in the 2010 general elections? To answer this question, we specify OLS regression models where feelings towards the leaders (Kennedy in 2005; Clegg in 2010) as measured on a scale of 0–10 are the dependent variable.[6] The 2005 OLS model includes a variable measuring disapproval with British involvement in the Iraq

Table 1.1 OLS regressions: Feelings towards Charles Kennedy in the 2005 general election and Nick Clegg in the 2010 general election

Variables	Model 1: Kennedy		Model 2: Clegg	
	β	SE	β	SE
Constant	3.19*	0.37	3.19*	0.20
Fairer taxes	–		0.26*	0.03
Eco taxes	–		0.07*	0.02
Trident renewal	–		0.20*	0.02
Disapprove of Iraq war	0.07*	0.03	–	
Closeness to Lib Dems on tax–spend	0.18*	0.03	0.08*	0.01
Approve of EU	0.45*	0.11	0.15*	0.02
Education most important issue	0.15	0.23	0.05	0.22
University towns	−0.03	0.04	−0.06*	0.02
Student	0.04	0.39	0.26	0.15
Socio-economic variables				
Male	−0.05	0.11	−0.21*	0.05
Age	0.00	0.00	0.00	0.00
Degree	0.39*	0.13	−0.05	0.06
Professional/managerial class	0.22*	0.10	0.15*	0.06
Work in public sector	0.11	0.16	−0.06	0.05
Non-white	−0.12	0.20	−0.10	0.12
Economic prospects				
Personal economic expectations	0.13*	0.05	0.16*	0.02
Political				
Liberal Democrat partisanship	1.07*	0.20	1.21*	0.09
Labour partisanship	−0.15	0.23	−0.41*	0.07
Conservative partisanship	−0.34	0.21	0.13	0.07
Other partisanship	−0.33	0.23	−0.63	0.12
Lib Dems best on the economy	0.86*	0.25	1.14*	0.09
Tactical voting	0.28	0.26	−0.09	0.08
Model fit				
R^2	0.14		0.24	
N	2,596		10,466	

*Significant $p < 0.05$. 2005 validated voters only. BES pre–post-election survey – post-election weight used); 2010 voters only – BEPS (post-election weight used). Both models include robust clustered standard errors (at the constituency level).

war, while the 2010 regression model includes attitudes to Liberal Democrat policy stances on a mansion tax, increasing the tax threshold and limiting tax relief on pensions (included as one factor)[7] and separate questions on an eco tax on airlines and not renewing Trident. Both models also include other predictors to assess distinctive Liberal Democrat policy stances: closeness to the Liberal Democrats on tax and spending, and approval of EU membership. As neither survey contains a direct measure of attitudes towards tuition fees, we include a couple of proxies: whether the respondent is a student or not, and an aggregate variable 'university towns' (which is essentially a factor derived from two components – percentage working in education and percentage of full-time students). Whether individuals regard education as the most important issue is also included, with the expectation that the party's high-profile policy stance as articulated by the leader may have had a positive impact on feelings towards Kennedy and Clegg. We also include partisanship, 'Liberal Democrats best on the most important issue', personal economic expectations, tactical voting and socio-demographic variables (age, class, public sector employment, education, ethnicity and gender) as controls.

The results shown in Table 1.1 reveal that feelings towards Kennedy and Clegg were significantly affected by a number of variables, including partisanship, perceptions of Liberal Democrat competency on the economy and personal economic expectations. Demographic characteristics also mattered, with those from a professional/managerial class positively disposed to both Kennedy and Clegg. Those individuals with a degree tended to like Kennedy, while women were more supportive of Clegg than men. After taking account of other factors, disapproval with Britain's involvement in the war in Iraq had a significant positive effect on feelings towards Kennedy. Likewise, those who were supportive of increasing the tax threshold, implementing the mansion tax, limiting tax relief on pensions, putting an eco tax on airlines and not renewing Trident were significantly positively disposed towards Clegg. Those who approved of the party's position on Europe and were close to the Liberal Democrats on taxation and spending also tended to have positive feelings towards both Kennedy and Clegg. After controlling for all these evaluations, there is little evidence that being a student or living in a university town had a positive impact on feelings about either leader.

Impact of policy stances and leadership on voting Liberal Democrat

Did these distinctive policy stances directly affect voting Liberal Democrat in 2005 and 2010 or did they primarily influence party support indirectly, through the popularity of the leader, or did they have both a direct and an indirect effect on support? We address this question using a series of logistic regression models. These are run in two stages. Model 1 includes all the same predictors as used in the leadership models above, while model 2 builds on this through the addition of party leadership evaluations. All the results are shown in Table 1.2.

Those who believed the Liberal Democrats were best on the economy were significantly more likely to vote for the party, while opposing partisans were not. Demographic characteristics had no significant effect on the voting Liberal Democrat but distinctive policy stances did matter. Those who disapproved of the war in Iraq were more likely to vote Liberal Democrat, while party-issue proximity on tax and spending also proved to be an important driver. There is also some indication that the party's position on tuition fees may have enhanced Liberal Democrat support in 2005.

Table 1.2 Logistic regression of 2005 and 2010 Liberal Democrat (LD) vote

Variables	Model 1: LD 2005 vote		Model 2: LD 2005 vote		Model 1: LD 2010 vote		Model 2: LD 2010 vote	
	β	SE	β	SE	β	SE	β	SE
Constant	−3.37*	0.78	−3.52*	0.83	−3.64*	0.32	−4.15*	0.37
Fairer taxes	−		−		0.29*	0.04	0.21*	0.05
Eco taxes	−		−		0.01	0.03	0.00	0.04
Trident renewal	−		−		0.30*	0.03	0.23*	0.03
Disapprove of Iraq war	0.13*	0.06	0.02	0.07	−		−	
Closeness to Lib Dems on tax–spend	0.19*	0.06	0.16*	0.06	0.09*	0.02	0.09*	0.02
Approve of EU	0.27	0.22	0.21	0.23	0.11*	0.03	0.09*	0.03
Education most important issue	−0.22	0.33	−0.28	0.33	−0.45	0.36	−0.46	0.35
University towns	0.18*	0.06	0.18*	0.07	0.05	0.04	0.06	0.04
Student	0.34	0.44	0.34	0.53	−0.01	0.25	−0.18	0.27
Socio-economic variables								
Male	0.22	0.15	0.21	0.16	−0.05	0.07	−0.02	0.07
Age	0.01	0.00	0.01	0.00	0.01*	0.00	0.01*	0.00
Degree	0.38	0.20	0.25	0.19	0.15	0.08	0.16	0.09
Professional/ managerial class	0.14	0.16	0.05	0.17	0.10	0.07	0.05	0.08
Work in public sector	0.47	0.29	0.43	0.30	−0.00	0.07	0.03	0.08
Non-white	−0.29	0.33	−0.26	0.38	0.22	0.17	0.36*	0.18
Economic prospects								
Personal economic expectations	−0.08	0.12	−0.06	0.12	−0.00	0.04	−0.01	0.04
Political								
Liberal Democrat partisanship	2.13*	0.25	1.88*	0.25	1.74*	0.12	1.40*	0.12
Labour partisanship	−1.49*	0.23	−1.34*	0.25	−1.24*	0.10	−1.25*	0.10
Conservative partisanship	−2.20*	0.27	−2.20*	0.31	−1.98*	0.12	−1.90*	0.13
Other partisanship	−0.67*	0.34	−0.70*	0.34	−1.33*	0.16	−1.31*	0.17
Lib Dems best on the economy	2.20*	0.55	2.11*	0.64	2.06*	0.15	1.60*	0.16
Tactical voting	0.84	0.54	0.77	0.53	1.02*	0.12	1.04*	0.13
Leadership								
Kennedy/Clegg	−		0.30*	0.05	−		0.34*	0.02
Blair/Brown	−		−0.15*	0.04	−		−0.09*	0.02
Howard/Cameron	−		−0.08	0.05	−		−0.13*	0.02
Model fit								
Chi-square (P = <0.05)	689.27*		668.32*		1,672.05*		1,637.76*	
Log likelihood	−801.04		−765.39		−3,638.35		−3,428.36	
McFadden's R^2	0.38		0.40		0.42		0.45	
AIC	1,642.08		1,576.77		7,320.70		6,906.73	
N	2,469		2,469		10,466		10,466	

*Significant p < 0.05. 2005 validated voters only. BES pre–post election survey – post-election weight used); 2010 voters only – BEPS (post-election weight used). Both models include robust clustered standard errors (at the constituency level).

Once leadership evaluations are added to the model, the party's policy stance on Iraq proves insignificant after controlling for other factors. Disapproval with the war in Iraq did boost support for the Liberal Democrats in 2005 but indirectly – through personal support for Kennedy and dislike of Blair. To ease interpretation, we estimate the change in probability of voting for the Liberal Democrats when a significant independent variable is varied over its range, in the case of continuous variables holding them at their means and for dummy variables at their minimum (zero). The changes in probability of voting Liberal Democrat (range from zero to one) are multiplied by 100 for ease of interpretation. As feelings about Kennedy moves from negative to the positive end of the 0–10 scale, the probability of voting Liberal Democrat increases by 48 points, while the feelings about Blair changes the probability of voting for the party by 26 points (Figure 1.4). Issue proximity effects are large with proximities to Liberal Democrats enhancing the likelihood of voting for the party by 21 points. Those who believed the Liberal Democrats were best on the economy altered the likelihood of voting Liberal Democrat by 46 points. The party's stance on tuition fees also seemed to pay dividends. Given issue proximity and partisanship also operated indirectly through increasing support for Kennedy, it seems that these predictors have both direct and indirect effects on Liberal Democrat voting.

Turning to the 2010 Liberal Democrat vote model, notwithstanding strong positive effects for partisanship (which increases the likelihood of voting for the party by 31 points) and evaluations of Clegg, there is evidence that the party's high-profile policy stances drove support (Figure 1.5). Those who supported fairer taxes and the party's position on Trident increased the likelihood of voting Liberal Democrat by 17 and 19 points, respectively. Issue proximity and strong approval of EU membership also enhanced the probability of voting for the party, by 11 and 6 points after controlling for other predictors. Given that all these policy stances drove support for Clegg and that positive feelings towards Clegg increased the likelihood of voting Liberal Democrat by 48 points, our evidence suggests that these high-profile policy positions had both an indirect and a direct effect on party support in 2010. However, we find little evidence that students, those living in university towns or individuals who felt that education was the most important issue in the elections were more likely to support the Liberal Democrats. This seems to play down the effects of the party's tuition fees policy on driving the Liberal Democrat vote. Such an assumption does though require caveats. Firstly, we do not have a direct measure of attitudes to tuition fees. Our measures are indirect proxies, although the insignificant findings for students and those living in university towns are noteworthy and surprising. Secondly, these effects may have been picked up in the issue proximity measure or fairer taxes variable, given that attitudes to tuition fees may be correlated with these variables. Thirdly, we did find some effects in 2005. While Clegg's signing of the NUS pledge was a memorable campaign moment, the opposition to tuition fees was longstanding, so it may be that the party's stance on the issue in 2010 just emboldened existing support.

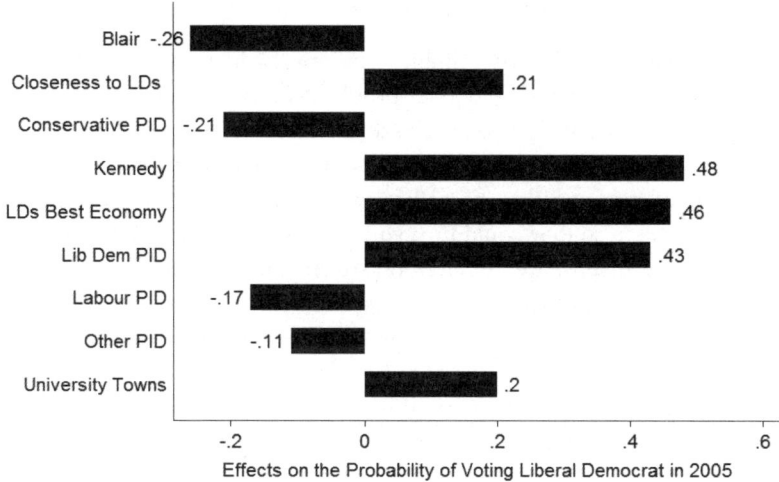

Figure 1.4 Effects of significant predictor variables on the probability of voting Liberal Democrat in the 2005 general election. *Source*: 2005 British Election Study

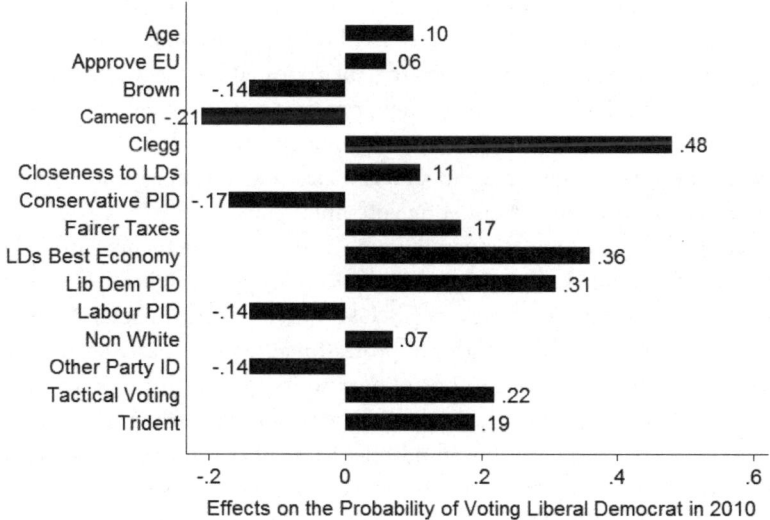

Figure 1.5 Effects of significant predictor variables on the probability of voting Liberal Democrat in the 2010 general election. *Source*: 2010 British Election Study

The electoral strategy: how the party started 'Winning Here'

The Liberal Democrats gained visibility and policy identity through agency: combining popular leader(s) and high-profile distinctive policies. Aside from creating goodwill towards the party brand, the Liberal Democrats were able to become a focal point for discontented voters. But to tackle these electoral credibility challenges head on, they needed to overcome the structural barriers that worked against them so they could turn votes into seats. Central to the upturn in Liberal Democrat fortunes was an electoral strategy masterminded by the party's first Director of Campaigns and Elections and then latterly Chief Executive, Chris Rennard. The main goal was to adapt the strict targeting approach that had been traditionally used by the Liberal party at the local level and to apply it at Westminster elections using place-based intensive party campaigning. Winnable key seats would be identified and resources would be targeted to support campaign activity overseen by the central campaign operation run by Rennard. An emphasis was placed on building a strong local government base through continuous local activism and using this as a platform for success in Westminster elections (Cutts, 2006a, 2006b, 2014). By-elections were also a viable means by which the party sought to bridge the 'credibility gap' and translate votes into seats. They served as unique, one-off opportunities to establish a presence from which the Liberal Democrats could build support. Often the Liberal Democrats were adept at exploiting opposition party weaknesses and offering voters a credible vehicle to express discontent. Once loyalty to the main two parties had been broken, it was felt that protest voters would become naturalised Liberal Democrat identifiers (find a natural home as opposed to once willing to protest always willing to protest!). This would strengthen and broaden the party's loyal base. Developing a political strategy that focused on key issues also enabled the party to combine and mobilise existing support with new voters which together boosted the party's credibility in certain seats. Of crucial importance, though, was the party's reputation for fighting highly organised, ruthlessly competent and sophisticated local campaigns, which for a long time gave the Liberal Democrats an electoral advantage and ultimately proved to be a key weapon in translating votes into seats.

With Ashdown's backing, Rennard became instrumental in turning around the culture towards national elections and professionalising the Liberal Democrats' approach to campaigning (Pack, 2014).[8] Like other parties, Liberal Democrat activism became far more joined-up and professionalised with party headquarters and key figures operating greater control over strategy. Rennard took control of how target seats were selected, the evaluation criteria used, staffing to oversee the key-seats operation, installing the mind-set of sustained campaign activity and performance, determining the tactics employed and party messaging. While the autonomous nature of the campaign operation post 1997 and the influence of Rennard on party strategy sat uneasy with some, they were deemed necessary to deliver results. But just how efficient and effective were the key facets of the Liberal Democrats' electoral strategy under Rennard?

Targeting and place-based (local) campaigning

During the 1990s, the electoral status of the constituency – in particular, whether or not the seat had been targeted by a party – led to considerable place variations in the intensity of party activism. All parties began to categorise target seats into those it had a possibility of winning where it was challenging or losing if it was the incumbent. Parties would direct their spending and wider resources – which increasingly were centrally managed – alongside intensive local activism at such seats. Safer seats were not monitored as carefully and left to a small band of local party activists while parties began to put up token efforts in non-winnable constituencies. While the acme was Labour's key-seats operation in 1997, the Liberal Democrats under Rennard's stewardship became equally ruthless. The party was not blessed with the resources of the two main parties. When Rennard became Campaigns Director, aside from pockets of strength, the Liberal Democrats did not have strong local organisations or activists to counteract this imbalance. Unable to match its competitors' campaign machines, the party quickly recognised that if it was to reap electoral rewards, it needed to target resources in specific seats using place-based tactics and to tailor a variety of modes to suit the local electoral context.

Data derived from surveys of party electoral agents[9] and local party campaign spending for the three main parties from 1997 to 2005 consistently show that the Liberal Democrats had the least active campaign (Denver and Hands, 1997; Fisher and Denver, 2008; Pattie and Johnston, 2009). Yet, campaign intensity was noticeably more comparable with the other main parties in target seats, suggesting that the party was adept at using its resources efficiently to maximise its chances of electoral success (Fisher et al., 2006a, 2006b). The Liberal Democrats spent substantially more in their marginal seats than in non-winnable seats. Moreover, there was also a clear twin-based strategy of the party spending heavily and campaigning most in seats it held, even in its safest seats, as well as in winnable marginal seats where it was the main challenger. To build an electoral base, Rennard knew that the party needed to hold onto what it had. Also, the Liberal Democrats not only used traditional campaign methods more in target seats than in other seats but their use was more intense in their target seats at each of the three elections over the period than was the case for its competitors. This is unsurprising given the party's emphasis on community-based politics, operationalised through continuous grassroots activism. Traditional tools such as 'Focus' leaflets, resident surveys and doorstep canvassing in safe and target seats were an integral part of the party's electoral strategy (Cutts, 2006b). However, this was not at the expense of other tools. Electoral agent data clearly show how the Liberal Democrats, like all parties, increasingly used modern methods – direct mail and telephone canvassing – in both target and non-target held seats to remain competitive. There is clear evidence that the electoral strategy adapted to changing electoral circumstances. Take 2005, as Conservatives intensified their efforts, Liberal Democrat activism rose – even in non-target held seats – as the party became wary of holding onto what it had as well as making electoral ground. Meanwhile, with Labour on the back foot, the electoral strategy was adapted, with far more intensive campaigning in those Labour seats which were most vulnerable to the party. Even so, campaigning in its safest seats still remained more intense than that of its rivals. The Liberal Democrats were ruthlessly efficient in how they used resources, but this did not mean they always operated in a purely rational manner.

Despite the target status of many seats changing from 1997 and 2005, the party performed best in those seats where it placed most resources. On average, Liberal Democrat support increased by more than four percentage points in these target seats at both elections. The more intense the Liberal Democrat campaign or more money spent, all things being equal, the better the party performed (Cutts, 2006a; Denver and Hands, 1997; Fisher and Denver, 2008; Johnston and Pattie, 2006; Whiteley *et al.*, 2006). Evidence from a model using a latent measure of campaign effort also found that not only did Liberal Democrat activism have the largest impact on the party's own performance when compared against rival campaign effort, but Liberal Democrat campaigning also had a negative impact on their rivals (Labour) which was not reciprocated on Liberal Democrat performance (Fieldhouse and Cutts, 2009). Incumbent candidates also performed strongly, strengthening existing evidence that once the Liberal Democrats had gained credibility they were effective at retaining support (Fieldhouse *et al.*, 2006). Rennard's twin strategy of campaigning intensively in competitive seats and securing the seats they held seemed to bear fruit.

Thus, place-based intensive campaigning was an integral part of the Liberal Democrats' electoral strategy and played a key role in the party's electoral revival. Yet while local campaigning was the vehicle, the need to build a local platform and to target by-elections to offset inbuilt structural barriers was also vital. Then, from 2005, targeting specific groups of voters in new types of places became a pivotal part of the Liberal Democrats' electoral advance.

Building a local platform

Winning in local elections had long been a means through which the Liberal Democrats had sought to bridge the electoral credibility gap. However, an emphasis on community politics and the local took on much more of an electoral focus during the 'Rennard' era. Liberals have a longstanding attachment to the local. Nothing illustrates this more than the party's enduring commitment to the vision and application of community politics. Officially adopted by the Liberal party at its 1970 Assembly, the ethos of community politics stresses the empowerment of individuals and communities. Through the dispersal of power, individuals are able to protect and enhance their own interests, which in itself boosts participation and promotes mobilisation, thereby not only making individuals aware of the problems that exist around them but also encouraging people to seek (and take) power themselves (Cutts, 2014; Greaves and Lishman, 1980). Tensions between those in the party who regarded community politics as a 'unique ideology' and those who saw it as a way in which the party could make electoral advances have been ever present since the 1960s and 1970s (Copus, 2007; Greaves and Lishman, 1980). Although not envisaged or promoted as a technique for winning local elections, but seen as a means to an end, its proponents acknowledged that, for community politics to become a reality and achieve the social transformation desired, local campaign tools and techniques would have to be devised and operationalised (Greaves and Lishman, 1980). Even leading Liberals of the 1960s and 1970s (Jo Grimond and Jeremy Thorpe) used local elections to promote the rhetoric of community politics. Not only did it stress the importance of the local but it concurred with their vision of how politics should be done. From an electoral standpoint, it was also seen, even then, as a means of building the party's national identity and providing the foundations for achieving representation at the parliamentary level (Russell and Fieldhouse, 2005). On the formation of the Liberal Democrats, community politics became one of the sacred tenets of their vision and activity (Meadowcroft, 2001).

Under Ashdown, Rennard drove the integration of local campaign techniques and community politics across all contexts, from local to parliamentary elections. At the local level, a new concerted attempt to gain control of local councils was designed to stress the governing ability of the party. Faced with the perennial problems associated with being a third party, the Liberal Democrats knew that it could counter electors' suggestions of inexperience by running more local governments. By now, the ideological spirit of community politics espoused by Grimond and others had become subverted as the party promoted the means – grassroots and community-based campaigning – to serve electoral ends (Copus, 2007). The use of *Focus* leaflets to provide details of the party's policies and highlight local issues placed the Liberal Democrats as local guardians, rooted in community concerns and wider local activities. Such local engagement contrasted clearly with the perceived remoteness of the two main parties and was used successfully by the Liberal Democrats to shape local support, promote a distinctive party image, acquire activists and local candidates, and build personal reputations and profiles (Cutts, 2006a, 2014; MacIver, 1996).

Reviving community-based politics and placing an emphasis on winning locally were therefore not mutually exclusive, as reaching out to what residents were concerned about and addressing the needs of the people required the development of campaign techniques, skills and new approaches to win public support and get people more engaged in local communities. By 1996, the Liberal Democrats had amassed the strongest local electoral base in their history: roughly 5,000 seats and control of more than 50 councils. As the second party of local government, the Liberal Democrats reaped the benefits, as they more than doubled their representation in Westminster a year later. For example, in 1997, in no fewer than 24 of the 30 seats the party captured from the Conservatives, the Liberal Democrats were the largest party on the local council (Russell and Fieldhouse, 2005: 151). During the 1990s, voters living in wards neighbouring Liberal Democrat held seats were more likely to vote for the party mainly because the party was seen as a credible electoral force. The party's electoral strategy built on winning local wards and then using them as a base camp to attack vulnerable neighbouring wards was also shown to be highly effective (Dorling *et al.*, 1998: 65). Spatial proximity was more important for the Liberal Democrats than social proximity with parliamentary constituencies neighbouring Liberal Democrat held seats where local growth had occurred appearing to be at most risk from a Liberal Democrat advance. Examples at the constituency level include parts of the south-west of England and south-west London in 1997 and the early 2000s where intensive campaigning across contiguous seats underpinned by the strength of the party in local government was given as the most likely reason for the patterns of support (Russell and Fieldhouse, 2005: 153). A different picture emerged in 2005 as the party made gains in new types of places. Nevertheless, even in these 'new seats' it would be wrong to dismiss the role of the local base on party support, as the Liberal Democrats still retained control of a sizeable number of local councils and even saw some growth prior to and immediately after the 2005 general election.

One study found that local Liberal Democrat grassroots campaigning not only had a significant impact on its own vote in 2010, even after taking account of rival parties' campaigning, but increasing their local representation through winning council seats played a vital role in boosting Liberal Democrat performance indirectly through campaign effort (Cutts, 2014). The indirect effect was roughly twice that of the direct effect illustrating just how crucial local election success is to the party's constituency campaign effort and its effectiveness in enhancing Liberal Democrat performance. The total effect of local success on party performance was much larger and far more important for the Liberal Democrats than for Labour or the Conservatives (Cutts, 2014: 376). Not only was local success pivotal to the electoral health of the party but any weakening in its local base was likely to have severe long-term consequences for the party at the parliamentary level.

The role of by-elections

Parliamentary by-elections arguably play to the Liberal Democrats' strengths. Often they provide an opportunity for voters to vent frustration with the government, when electors look for an appropriate party through which to record such disillusionment. Given its historic appeal to protest voters, the Liberal Democrats has often been that party of choice. Also, because by-elections are one-off events, third parties like the Liberal Democrats are able to match the resources of the main parties. Targeting voters through place-based intensive campaigning is often crucial. Turnout is generally much lower, so the role of grassroots activism in identifying, persuading and then mobilising supporters comes to fore. The Liberal Democrats (and its predecessors) have regarded by-elections as critical opportunities to build representation; moreover, given the emphasis on the local, targeting and ruthless place-based campaigning, post 1992 they became an integral vehicle for countering the structural electoral barriers against them.

The Liberal Democrats have enjoyed memorable by-election successes turning around huge incumbent party majorities on more than one occasion. Since 1945, the Liberals/Liberal Democrats have won 39 parliamentary by-elections – from Torrington March 1958 to (at the time of writing) Tiverton and Honiton in June 2022. They have proved to be critical signposts for Liberal revivalism in the case of Orpington in 1962 and of growing Liberal momentum in the cases of the Isle of Ely in 1973, Crosby in 1981, Newbury in 1993 and Brent East in 2003. Of the 39, parliamentary by-election victories, five of these seats (including the void election in Winchester in 1997) were elections where the party was defending the seat and held it. Of the remaining 34 parliamentary by-election gains, 26 have been from the Conservatives with eight from Labour. Twenty-four of these 26 seats occurred when the Conservatives were in government, with only David Steel's victory in 1965 – Roxburgh, Selkirk and Peebles – and Sandra Gidley winning Romsey in 2000 the exceptions. Three of the eight seats gained by the Liberal Democrats from Labour occurred when Labour was in opposition: Rochdale in 1972, Bermondsey in 1983 and Greenwich in 1987.

But just how vital have Liberal Democrat parliamentary by-election gains proved in bridging the credibility gap and acting as a stepping stone for subsequent general election success? Of the 34 parliamentary by-election gains (i.e. excluding the five seats that they successfully defended at a by-election) 14 of these seats were won at the subsequent general election: nine from the Conservatives and five from Labour. Yet there is some evidence that since the formation of the Liberal Democrats, the party has struggled to convert by-election gains into success at general elections. Of the 16 by-elections won by the Liberal Democrats since 1989 (excluding Winchester), the party has successfully defended only five of these seats – Newbury, Eastleigh (gained in 1994), Romsey, Brent East and Cheadle – at the subsequent general election. Nevertheless in two cases – Eastbourne and West Aberdeenshire and Kincardine (formerly Kincardine and Deeside) – the Liberal Democrats did win them in future elections, suggesting that earlier by-election success did establish party credibility with voters. Parliamentary by-elections therefore provide a key gateway for the Liberal Democrats to translate votes into seats but the protest element involved has meant that around 50 per cent of party successes have been short lived and not led to long-term Liberal Democrat representation in the seat. Nonetheless, they proved to be a pivotal part of the 'Rennard strategy' with high-profile wins providing visibility, credibility and representation which ultimately edged the party closer to the top table of British politics.

'New types' of seats and targeting specific voters

The Liberal Democrats' electoral strategy was both offensive and defensive. On the one hand, it would actively target winnable seats, and tailor tactics and intensive campaigning to the electoral situation. On the other hand, it heavily resourced seats it held – even its safest seats – to ensure it secured its electoral base. Under Rennard, the party also adopted neighbourhood targeting strategies, identifying areas of strength for mobilisation and other places where the local party needed first to persuade voters to lend their support to remain competitive and then mobilise them to get over the line. Cutts (2006a, 2006b) stressed that intra-constituency targeting, often by street within wards, was commonplace, with the party engaging in continuous activism (where resources allowed) and employing tactics and tools to suit the different stages of the campaign cycle. Increasingly, though, the Liberal Democrats also sought to target specific types of voters – those who were more amenable to high-profile policies and the values the party espoused. At the national level, this became more visible under Kennedy, when the Liberal Democrats' strategy shifted to winning over Labour voters in competitive Labour–Liberal Democrat seats. 'Wedge issues' such as the war in Iraq allowed the party to promote an identity that was distinct from the two main parties and this proved attractive to specific types of voters. The party then actively targeted these groups through intensive campaigning in winnable seats to supplement the existing core vote.

Evidence from the British Constituency Campaign studies in 1997, 2001 and 2005 (where questionnaires were sent to the electoral agents of all candidates from parties standing in the election) suggests that the Liberal Democrats put more effort into targeting specific groups in their key target seats with comparable effort scores noticeably higher than those of their main rivals in 2005 and higher than the Conservatives in all three elections (Fisher and Denver, 2008). In 2005, nearly 60 per cent of Liberal Democrat campaigns targeted specific groups with local leaflets; 35 per cent of these local campaigns contacted postal voters and just shy of 30 per cent targeted first-time voters. Direct mail was used to contact specific groups in around half of Liberal Democrat campaigns. Around 28 per cent of the 2005 party's local campaigns used leaflets to target students in constituencies with a high student population. Only 14 per cent of local Liberal Democrat campaigns specifically targeted anti-Iraq war voters, though, suggesting that such messages were largely part of the national 'air war' and tied with the Liberal Democrats' political positioning and Kennedy's leadership on the issue.

In 2005, there was also some indirect evidence from the BES that the Liberal Democrats enjoyed increasing support from new types of voters. Among students, 45 per cent supported the Liberal Democrats in 2005 compared with 46 per cent for Labour. For those under 25, 31 per cent supported the party while the Liberal Democrats also won 34 per cent of Muslim voters, which is sizeable given the group's historic partisan affinity with Labour. Despite this, just shy of a third of those who strongly disapproved of the Iraq war actually supported the Liberal Democrats. This not only points to the loyalty of the two main parties voters but the perennial Liberal Democrat problem of converting a seemingly popular high profile position into votes at the ballot box.

Individual-level data provide some evidence (albeit not conclusive) that the Liberal Democrats' electoral strategy of targeting specific voters did bear fruit.

Such conclusions, though, need to be tempered by the caveat of small samples. By contrast, examining the aggregate picture provides a clearer picture even after accounting for 'ecological fallacy' arguments (Fieldhouse *et al.*, 2006). Three major points stand out. First, there was a visible 'education' effect. In 2005, Liberal Democrat support increased significantly in places with large numbers of degree holders. The party gained eight of its 16 successes in these places. Five of these eight gains were also university seats, where both students and those working in education (staff at universities and in further education, and secondary school teachers) exceeded 10 per cent of the population. Overall, the party gained seven and eight seats respectively in seats where 10 per cent or more of the electorate were students or those working in education (six where there were both). Evidence from 'change' score models indicate a discernible 'education' effect in 11 of the 62 seats won and in seven of the seats gained (Fieldhouse *et al.*, 2006: 90). Here the 'ground war' clearly complemented the party's vocal national push on topics such as top-up fees. Second, Liberal Democrat support jumped by more than eight points in those seats with significant numbers of Muslim voters and this contributed to the party gaining two seats. However, it was hamstrung by low base levels of support in many of these constituencies and by other parties, such as Respect, heavily targeting the Muslim vote on an anti-Iraq war platform. Third, the party's shifting electoral strategy post 1997 was evident in the gains made and the improving performance in Labour-held seats irrespective of their vulnerability. Here, anti-Labour tactical switching was on the rise but tactical unwind was beginning to happen where the Liberal Democrats were fighting the Conservatives. In those tight contests where the Liberal Democrats were defending the seat, there was clear evidence of their inability to squeeze the Labour vote any further. Targeting specific voters worked in particular types of places, predominantly where Labour was the incumbent but the old anti-Conservative alliance was starting to unravel. This targeting predicament for the Liberal Democrats is an inherent consequence of the party fighting against the structural barriers of the electoral system. The danger of such an approach in the long term is that the party will be perceived by the electorate as chameleon-like, targeting different messages and selling different policies to similar groups of people in different places.

There is little doubt that the ruthless targeting of specific places and groups within the electorate was part of a holistic electoral strategy to join up the party's national distinctive political positioning on high-profile issues with highly effective local operations to maximise seat gains. The Liberal Democrats' approach should be viewed in the context of the increasing professionalisation and centralisation of campaigning that emerged in Britain during the 1990s and which had become pivotal to all parties' electoral strategy by the end of the 2000s. Nonetheless, it did represent an important break from the past for the Liberal Democrats. Under Rennard, the local platform remained key and part of the answer for gaining credibility and building representation at Westminster. Nevertheless, it was not the only route. Garnering support from different groups in the electorate through distinctive policy positions opened up new opportunities for electoral success and building a credible base of support over the long term.

The electoral strategy since Rennard

Rennard's replacement, for the 2010 general election, as party Chief Executive, Chris Fox, and the new Director of Campaigns, Hilary Stephenson, did not drastically change the campaigning style. There was much more of an integrated strategy at the national level, with key figures in central headquarters (Cowley Street) responsible for the 'air war' and 'ground war' working far closer together than in previous elections.[10] A special unit was in place at the national level to deal with key target seats at the election which interacted with regional campaign officers and highly trained campaign organisers in these specific target seats. Elsewhere, the centralisation and increasing professionalisation of campaign strategy continued apace.

National party headquarters was responsible for organising regional phone banks across the country to target voters in key seats (with a downloadable system available for local parties to use in their own constituencies), setting templates and style options for leaflets in targets, overseeing digital campaigning, conducting local constituency polling, undertaking centralised direct mailing and national mailings for postal votes, alongside general encouragement to get people to help out in target seats. The selection of target seats was based on marginality and a track record of winning (with a strong emphasis on local elections), as well as candidate quality. It was predominantly carried out well in advance of the election (at least two years) and continued to be dependent on key performance indicators (KPIs), based primarily on the volume of activity. Seats that did not meet these KPIs would face the sanction of losing 'target seat' status, which meant funding and assistance from the centre. Ultimately, though, some contention over this issue remained, as long-standing incumbents who had not necessarily met these local campaign performance criteria still received help and funding from the national campaign. Visits by the leader and other key party figures were controlled by the centre through a series of interlocking tours, while former leaders (Kennedy, Ashdown and Campbell) were also used to visit constituencies to muster support and increase party morale.

Crucially, ruthless targeting and intensive activism remained a key part of the Liberal Democrats' strategy in the 2010 general election. There was also a focus on targeting electors under 30, although there was no specific national targeting of students. This was primarily left to the ground campaigns, although there was national targeting help in the form of messages tailored to attract student support where this looked favourable and intensive activism was evident. The same applied for Muslim voters, with national and local campaigns working in unison in specific seats, which led, for example, to Sarah Teather holding onto Brent East. Simply put, the targeting of non-traditional Liberal Democrat areas and specific types of voters endured in 2010. The digital campaign (a post-Rennard innovation) was also a notable success, with the national website the most visited of all the parties' (1.6 million hits) and 200,000 downloads of the Liberal Democrat manifesto. Twitter and Facebook were heavily used, as the central campaign team worked with local parties and candidates (certain candidates were more active than others – e.g. Mark Williams, Lynne Featherstone and Tessa Munt) to encourage a presence on these social media platforms and provide advice on what to put up on tweets and Facebook updates.

On the face of it, campaign tactics had evolved, but the key elements of the Rennard era remained intact. Like its rivals, the campaign became increasingly joined up with greater prominence given to the 'air war' alongside the 'ground war'. However, the latter remained critical to the Liberal Democrats' prospects, with strict targeting strategies of seats and specific voters alongside intensive place-based activism prior to the 'long campaign' period and during the official campaign at the core. The party also sort to exploit digital platforms as a gateway to target specific voters. In 2010, building support in Labour areas remained the goal while simultaneously holding off an electoral squeeze from the Conservatives. Yet, the Liberal Democrats still faced the age-old problem of 'tight targeting'. In simple terms, the party had a number of seats to defend with small margins while the majority of held seats were not safe enough to neglect. At the same time, the Liberal Democrats had the possibility of making gains but in reality they were just too far behind to make the large-scale electoral breakthroughs to take them to the next level (Cutts *et al.*, 2010). Strategists were somewhat in a bind. Offensively they had little room for manoeuvre, and defensively a Conservative surge led to an often repeated phrase, 'there is no such thing as Liberal Democrat safe seat' (Fox, 2010). Ultimately, the Liberal Democrats struggled to overcome a strong Labour defensive effort and hold a Conservative offensive push. They were unable to squeeze Labour voters in close contests against the Conservatives and failed to mobilise enough of the Conservative vote where it was weakest in close battles with Labour. While the Liberal Democrats broadened their base of support across the country, these were not in the right places to convert into seats.

Summary

As the third party in British politics the party knew that any electoral advancement required rival parties to falter. Yet, when this occurred the Liberal Democrats needed to be a viable alternative, offering a policy platform and leadership distinctive from their competitors to take advantage. This required the party to tear up its traditional equidistant stance, develop its identity and distinguish itself from New Labour.

By reasserting its commitment to a social liberal agenda under Kennedy, high-profile policy platforms became a key part of the Liberal Democrats' sell, enabling the party to promote a distinctive agenda as both the two main parties battled for the median voter. Central to this political strategy was the leader. It provided a route by which third parties could cut across structural barriers by articulating salient policy positions and personal stances to an increasingly volatile electorate. The Liberal Democrats' policy positions proved popular but were more effective when they contrasted with unpopularity of those put forward by their rivals. Blair paid a personal price for the war in Iraq, which indirectly contributed to Labour's faltering performance in 2005. Kennedy's personal stance positioned the Liberal Democrats as the main beneficiaries, which indirectly and directly influenced the party's performance in the 2005 general election. The political strategy also paid dividends in 2010, as high-profile policy positions and Clegg's personal popularity following the first leaders' televised debate worked in sync to have direct and indirect influences on voting Liberal Democrat. Here the succinct policy messages and portrayal of the leader were effective at appealing to waverers and the increasing numbers of voters who had become less tribal.

Agency mattered by offering viable alternatives to its rivals and their political failings. However, converting sympathy into votes was dependent on the party being credible at both the national and local level. Overcoming embedded structural barriers required an electoral strategy that could translate votes into seats. Through its emphasis on the local to build electoral credibility and the vehicle of intensive, highly targeted place-based campaigning the party began to do just that. The Liberal Democrats also capitalised on one-off by-election opportunities by unleashing their ground game tactics and targeting, which their rivals found difficult to compete against. As the electoral context evolved, the party reached out to Labour heartlands, tailoring its distinctive policy messages to specific groups of voters in target seats and places where it could cultivate long-term support. This had some knock-on consequences. Both campaigning and the local platform remained highly effective in winning over voters but the latter started to diminish from the heady heights of the mid-1990s. By 2010, the party had reached a ceiling in these new types of areas where it had made ground five years earlier. Despite the problem of 'tight targeting', the joined-up electoral strategy in 2010 still proved influential, although there was increasing evidence that the party overstretched its resources, misdirected support late in the day and was complacent about certain seats which were vulnerable (Fisher et al., 2011; Pack, 2014). The Liberal Democrats were both overly ambitious and overly cautious.

More worryingly though for the Liberal Democrats, the 2010 election revealed early-warning signs of electoral retreat, a diminishing 'ground campaign' advantage and an electoral strategy which did not have the same potency in defensive situations as it did in places where the party was on the front foot. Despite the salience of agency and high-profile polices, the fundamentals still seemed shaky. The party elites' drift away from social liberalism also seemed at odds with its voters and activists. These emerging fragilities and embedded weaknesses are explored in the next chapter.

'Cowley Street, we have a problem': the false political and electoral dawn

In many ways, the goals of the political and electoral strategy had been achieved. The Liberal Democrats had become the undisputed third party of British politics. The party was kingmaker in the hung parliament, and ultimately returned to government for the first time since the First World War. Yet beneath the surface, the electoral and political warning signs were flashing brightly – but went unheeded. We divide this chapter into three main sections. The first examines whether the political and electoral strategy addressed the longstanding weaknesses in the party's vote. We evaluate whether the Liberal Democrats were still reliant on lent votes and fragile voter coalitions, and whether its short-term appeals on specific issues undermined its ability to build and retain loyal support. We also assess if appeals to specific groups of voters exacerbated the tactical nature of its vote. The second assesses whether the effectiveness of the party's grassroots activist strategy had started to wane as rival parties adopted similar campaign techniques. Finally, the third section explores just how important the signs of friction were between the centre-right, small-state liberalism espoused by key figures in the party leadership and those who traditionally hailed from the social liberal wing of the party. While the factions had peacefully coexisted for much of the twentieth century, the repositioning of the party under Clegg led to internal battles that became visible in terms of rhetoric and policy platform, ultimately culminating in the decision to go into coalition with the Conservatives. Most importantly, we examine whether the leadership's shift away from social liberalism was at odds with its voters and members. Was there now a mismatch between how 2010 Liberal Democrat voters perceived the party and the political direction of its leadership? We conclude by discussing the Liberal Democrats' reluctance to dwell on these electoral and political warning signs and consider just how vulnerable this made the party.

The Liberal Democrat voter: still more lent than loyal?

The lack of a distinct social base of support has been a longstanding problem for the Liberal Democrats and their forerunners. Aside from a historic link with Methodism, predominantly concentrated in rural Nonconformist communities known as the 'Celtic fringe', the Liberal party sought to distance itself from the notion that it stood for a particular social group or class interests. Instead, it always claimed that it was about values. Yet while the Liberals did not enjoy longstanding class backing, the party regularly secured more support from middle-class, especially well-educated, voters than the working class (Heath *et al.*, 1985). This prompted Curtice (1996: 194) to claim that while 'it is perhaps doubtful whether the Liberals ever were a truly "classless" party ... the Liberal Democrats certainly do not seem to be'. Russell and Fieldhouse (2005) also concluded that educated public sector professionals who were traditionally disinclined to vote Labour had emerged as the core social base of Liberal Democrat support.

There are strong reasons why we might expect the Liberal Democrats to have developed a stronger, more coherent social base than its predecessors. Over the past 30 years, social change in Britain has led to the decline of class voting, and this has coincided with the expansion of a more affluent and educated middle class. Increasing social mobility, driven by the expansion of university education since the late 1990s, accelerated the weakening link between class and political attachment. While rising electoral volatility has made securing loyal support harder, these social changes have opened up political opportunities for the Liberal Democrats among certain groups who are more likely to possess sympathies for liberal values and ideals. In the 1990s, the profile of the typical Liberal Democrat voter was someone who looked like a Conservative in social status but was closer to Labour attitudinally (Russell and Fieldhouse, 2005). However, the size of this portion of the electorate is limited, which has hampered the party's efforts to consolidate a social base of support. However, the number of graduates increased steadily throughout the 2000s, totalling 12 million in 2013. This trend, particularly among individuals from working-class backgrounds, provided a unique opportunity for the Liberal Democrats.

First, through policy appeals it could add depth to a longstanding association with degree holders. Second, it could increasingly pitch to new types of voters, who were more like Labour supporters in social status but had become detached from the class- and place-based party loyalty that had dominated British politics for 50 years. For the Liberal Democrats, marrying these two types of voters could consolidate a social base of support more robust to fluctuations in the political and electoral context. The Liberal Democrats sought to tackle the loyalty problem by building partisan identity among these groups through selling itself as a progressive force in British politics. The party was successful post 1997 in building support and representation in Westminster. But did this translate into stronger attachment to the party among its voters? Did these Liberal Democrat identifiers now vote for their 'natural party' or was retaining its vote still a major problem?

Partisanship, loyalty, retention and recruitment

Table 2.1 reports the levels and strength of party identification at each of the 10 general elections from February 1974 to 2010, based on the BES. The data show that identifying with a particular party declined considerably from its heyday in the 1950s and 1960s. Yet while both Labour and the Conservatives no longer enjoy anywhere near the same levels of partisan identity now, party identification still endures and remains an important buffer in times of electoral volatility. Previous evidence has consistently stressed that one of the major reasons for the 'soft' Liberal vote was its weak partisan base (Crewe, 1985; Heath et al., 1985). Looking at recent elections, it is noticeable that the proportion of voters who identify with the Liberal Democrats remained fairly stable since 1987. Indeed, despite electoral success under Kennedy and Clegg, there is little evidence that party loyalty grew. While the party under Clegg more than matched the performance of the Alliance in 1987, the proportion of voters identifying with the party was actually slightly lower. There is little evidence that the Liberal Democrats built a strong loyal base during the 2000s. The Liberal Democrats are not alone in recording a drop in identification, but Labour and the Conservatives still had either double or triple the proportion of very strong party identifiers. In sum, there is little evidence that the political and electoral strategy pursued by the Liberal Democrats post 1997 had tackled the loyalty problem or indeed closed the gap between themselves and their rivals.

Historically, not only have the Liberals/Liberal Democrats suffered from a smaller partisan base, but there has also been a tendency for a sizeable number of their 'natural supporters' to vote for their rivals. Figure 2.1 reports how Liberal identifiers actually voted across the 10 elections from February 1974 to 2010. Around 30 per cent of Liberal identifiers voted for rival parties in 1979, while four years later the figure was half that (Russell and Fieldhouse, 2005). In 1997, around one-fifth of Liberal Democrat identifiers voted for either Labour or the Conservatives, though the figure has since declined somewhat. Under Clegg, 88 per cent of Liberal Democrat identifiers voted for the party in 2010 – the highest figure across the 10 elections. However, there is no clear discernible trend.

Table 2.1 Party identification and strength of identification, 1974–2010 (%)

	1974 (Feb.)	1974 (Oct.)	1979	1983	1987	1992	1997	2001	2005	2010
Party identification										
Lib Dems	13	14	11	17	16	12	12	13	13	13
Conservatives	35	34	38	36	37	42	28	26	26	29
Labour	40	40	36	31	30	31	42	47	37	30
None	7	8	10	11	11	10	12	10	17	17
Strong party identification										
Lib Dems	12	14	14	12	10	9	6	7	4	7
Conservatives	32	28	24	26	23	22	15	14	13	13
Labour	41	36	29	28	26	25	24	16	14	21

BES 2010. $N = 3,075$ (pre- and post-election face to face with post-election weight).
BES 2005 . $N = 4,161$ (post-election cross-section, GB weight).

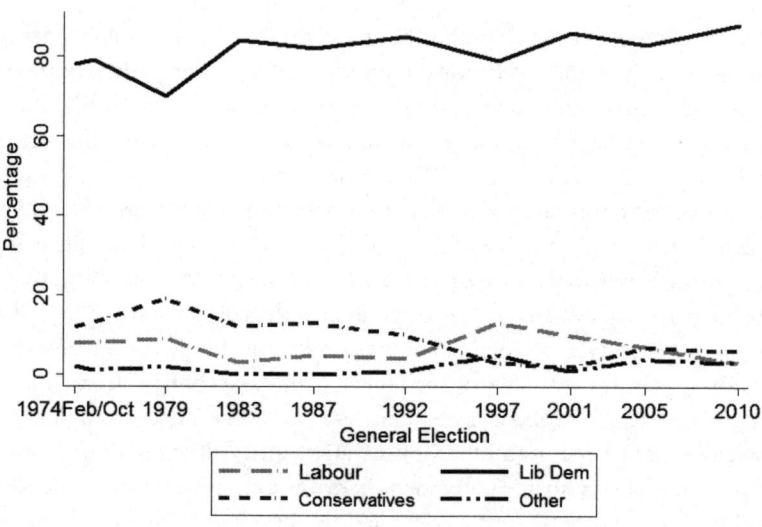

Figure 2.1 Votes of Liberal/Liberal Democrat identifiers, 1974–2010 (%). *Source*: February 1974–2010 British Election Study

Identifiers were seemingly less committed in 2005 than in 2010, 2001 or 1992, but more likely to vote for the party than in 1997 or in 1987 under the heights of the Alliance. Overall, there is little evidence that the party improved its ability to mobilise its core supporters irrespective of the electoral context. Despite efforts to shore up their vote during the 2000s, questions remained about the softness of Liberal Democrat identifiers and their willingness to support the party through 'thick and thin'.

Another longstanding Liberal weakness has been the ability to retain their vote. As noted by Crewe (1985), Liberals were the most likely of the three main parties' supporters to switch to other parties between elections. The high points came in 1983, when the party retained just over fourth-fifths of its prior vote, and in 2001, when it retained 75 per cent. Large-scale voter defections in 1979 after the Lib-Lab pact and in 1997, when nearly a third of 1992 Liberal Democrats switched to Labour, demonstrated its vulnerability and the 'lent' nature of its vote (Russell and Fieldhouse, 2005).

Tellingly, the Liberal Democrats struggled to retain supporters despite increasing party support and the implementation of strategies designed to cement their vote post 2001 (see Figure 2.2). In 2005, the Liberal Democrats retained only 63 per cent of support from 2001, representing its third lowest retention rate since February 1974. In part this reflects the Liberal Democrats' inability to retain Conservative support that it had gained in previous elections, which in many ways was offset by increasing support in Labour areas. Indeed, Labour's own retention rate dropped considerably in 2005 (reflecting the party's decline in vote

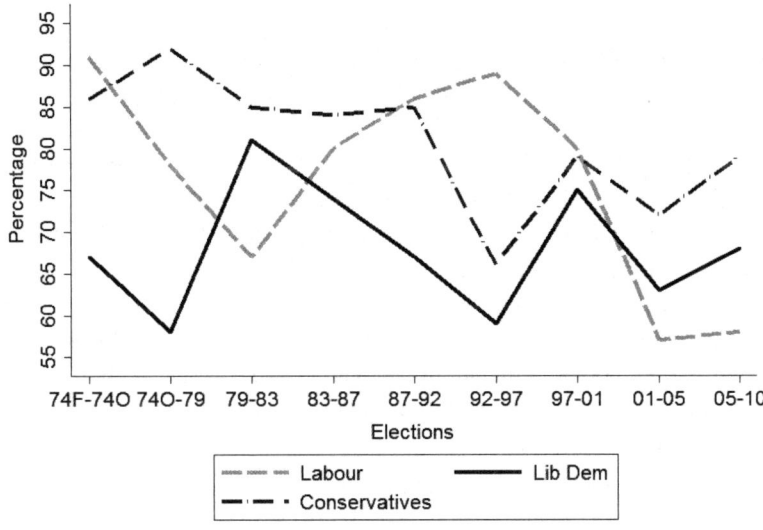

Figure 2.2 Retention rates, 1974–2010 (%). *Source*: February 1974–2010 British Election Study

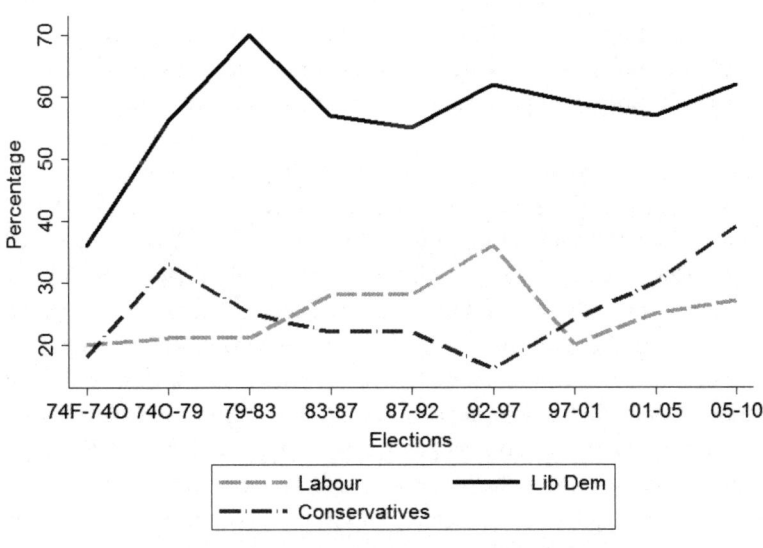

Figure 2.3 Recruitment rates, 1974–2010 (%). *Source*: February 1974–2010 British Election Study

share despite winning the election) and failed to recover in 2010. Yet even in 2010, when the Liberal Democrats were expected to capitalise from a faltering Labour party, they were able to retain only just over two-thirds of their vote from five years previously. Data on the actual flow of the vote for the 2005 and 2010 general elections using the BEPS[1] suggests a similar story, with 71 per cent of Liberal Democrat voters remaining loyal, compared with 82 per cent of Conservative voters and around 58 per cent of Labour supporters. Of the Liberal Democrat defectors in 2010, 12 per cent went to the Conservatives and only half that went to Labour, which is unsurprising given the pressure from the Conservatives in Liberal Democrat held and marginal seats. That said, there is no discernible upward trend post 1992, with notable fluctuations in retention from one election to the next. Simply put, the Liberal Democrats had not remedied their retention problem.

The Liberal Democrats have constantly needed to offset their low retention rates by attracting new voters. Given the historic issues of credibility and the lack of visibility in the media, much of the recruitment effort was undertaken by the grassroots activism of local parties. After the 2001 general election, there was an expectation that recruitment rates would remain relatively high as the Liberal Democrats sought to entice specific voters (students, university graduates, etc.). Higher retention would ensure less volatility in the long term, and allow the party to reach the levels of voter stability generally enjoyed by Labour and the Conservatives.

In their analysis of Liberal/Liberal Democrat recruitment from February 1974 to 2001, Russell and Fieldhouse (2005: 104–105) illustrated the temporary nature of the party's support. Recruitment was highly dependent on the electoral context and voter discontent with the main parties. With retention rates fluctuating from one election to the next, the party continued to heavily rely on recruitment through the 2000s to counteract any switching to its rivals. In 2005, 57 per cent of Liberal Democrat support came from new recruits, according to the BES, with the figure rising to 62 per cent in 2010 (see Figure 2.3). But where did Liberal Democrat recruits come from post 1997? In addition to retaining around two-fifths of its vote at each of the 2001, 2005, and 2010 elections, the largest proportion of recruits (around a quarter) came from those who voted Labour in the previous election. This reflects the party's political and electoral strategy of building support in Labour heartlands and exploiting the gradual decline in Labour support first under Blair in the mid-2000s and then under Brown. The Liberal Democrats also began to win over non-voters (a sizeable proportion of these were ex-Labour supporters) and first-time voters. However, they began to struggle to win over Conservative voters post 2001 as that party started to poll better. This typifies the quandary of a third party that relies on profiting from its rivals' woes. Moreover, failing to retain and win the 'softer' Conservative vote in seats it was defending resulted in losing seats to the Conservatives in 2005 and 2010.

Across the 57 seats the party won in 2010, the Liberal Democrats retained 62 per cent of its vote from 2005, recruited 22 per cent from Labour, but recruited only 6 per cent from the Conservatives. Even in those critical Liberal Democrat–Conservative contests in the south-west of England that the Liberal Democrats won in 2010, the pattern was remarkably similar: 64 per cent of the Liberal Democrat vote was retained from 2005, 22 per cent came from 2005 Labour voters, and only than 6 per cent came from prior Conservative voters.[2] The longstanding retention and recruitment problems remained unsolved. By 2010, the Liberal Democrats were still heavily reliant on temporary shifts in support and benefiting from rivals' difficulties. This, in turn, made them vulnerable if they ran into political problems. While recruiting Labour voters helped them hold and win seats against Labour in 2010, it also proved critical in contests against the Conservatives. Maintaining these coalitions of support was vital where support from 'soft Conservatives' had dried up. Despite the strength of the local campaign and efforts to build core support, the party relied on these somewhat transitory and fragile local voting alliances to win seats.

Likelihood of winning and tactical voting

In 2001, Charles Kennedy unveiled an election campaign poster showing a map of Britain with large parts shaded in yellow, adorned with the words, 'If you thought the Liberal Democrats could win in your area, this is how you'd vote'. Kennedy famously cited polling evidence that suggested 36 per cent of people would vote Liberal Democrat if they thought the party could win in their seat. The poster articulated the party's longstanding credibility problem. The electoral strategy under Rennard and later under Fox and Stephenson sought to tackle the credibility issue head on. The party tried to marry the goal of building wider support across the country with increasing the number of seats by ruthlessly targeting seats in which the party was perceived as being the credible alternative to the incumbent. Previous evidence suggests that, holding other predictors of Liberal Democrat support constant, where voters believed the party had a greater likelihood of winning the seat, they were more likely to vote for it (Russell and Fieldhouse, 2005). But is there any evidence that, as the party won more seats and increased its support, voters believed that it was a more credible option in their seat?

Both the 2005 and 2010 BES contained questions that asked individuals on an 11-point scale the likelihood of the three main parties (we exclude the other parties) winning in their constituencies. At the 2005 general election, the average score for the Liberal Democrats was 3.3, compared with 5.9 and 4.9 for Labour and the Conservatives respectively. On average, voters felt the Liberal Democrats had a lower chance of winning their seat than Labour and the Conservatives. Only 17 per cent of respondents gave the Liberal Democrats a score higher than five, compared with 56 per cent for Labour and 39 per cent for the Conservatives.

Five years later, the electoral context had changed. Despite previously securing 22 per cent of the national vote, the mean 'probability of winning' was 3.2 for the Liberal Democrats, compared with 4.7 for Labour and 5.5 for the Conservatives.

Only 19 per cent of respondents stated that the Liberal Democrats' probability of winning their seat was above 5, compared with 51 per cent for the Conservatives and 38 per cent for Labour. The number of respondents who said the Liberal Democrats were very unlikely to win in their seat increased by five percentage points, to 22 per cent. So, despite increases in third-party vote share to levels not seen since the height of the Alliance in the 1980s, Liberal Democrat credibility levels in large swathes of seats remain doggedly low. The party's attempts to diminish these credibility concerns on a national scale under both Kennedy and Clegg had not borne fruit.

Closer inspection of the data by incumbency, seat type and marginality reveal some positive signs, though the general pattern remained mixed. First, where the Liberal Democrats held the seat, respondents' mean 'probability of winning' score was much higher in 2010 than 2005. It was also notably higher in Liberal Democrat–Conservative battlegrounds than in those where Labour was in second place. The former often contained longstanding Liberal Democrat MPs with fairly substantial majorities who, in spite of the Conservative recovery post 2001, had not faced the prospect of losing their seats. Even in more marginal Liberal Democrat–Conservative seats, the expectation that the party was likely to win was higher in 2010 than in 2005. Second, the data suggest that the Liberal Democrats' likelihood of gaining further ground in 2005 had stalled, particularly against the Conservatives. Five years on, despite Labour's woes, Liberal Democrat credibility in Labour-held seats declined, with respondents' average scores actually higher for the Conservatives than for the Liberal Democrats despite the latter being in second place. The probability of the Conservatives holding on against a Liberal Democrat challenge even in the most marginal seats had grown. Overall, voters in 2010 felt that the Liberal Democrats were likely to hold on to what they had, but saw little prospect of growth against either rival. Where the Liberal Democrats had previously triumphed, the party's credibility was high, while elsewhere it remained well behind its competitors. Third, credibility improved during the 2010 campaign, perhaps reflecting 'Cleggmania' and the increased media attention on the party and/or the intensity of local campaigning. Yet, while respondents gave the Liberal Democrats slightly more chance of winning in their local seat, there was no quid pro quo decline in the prospect of either Labour or the Conservatives holding or winning back seats.

One of the consequences of credibility problems is that Liberal Democrat identifiers living in seats where the party has a low likelihood of winning switch to vote for the next best alternative. This can have a negative effect on the party's attempt to build long-term support in the constituency. In target seats where the Liberal Democrats are the main challenger and have a credible chance of winning, the party will use various tactics to persuade voters from other parties who want the incumbent defeated to vote for them. Given that the party enjoys fewer partisans than its rivals, it invariably relies on building a coalition of other party supporters and disillusioned incumbent voters to win. A sizeable proportion

Table 2.2 Tactical voting, by party, in the 2001, 2005 and 2010 general elections

Party	% tactical votes received			% party support from tactical votes			Preferred party of tactical voters		
	2001	2005	2010	2001	2005	2010	2001	2005	2010
Conservative	24	24	22	11	8	7	23	17	13
Labour	31	31	25	8	8	9	28	27	30
Liberal Democrats	38	36	40	24	17	19	30	39	24
Other	7	10	13	19	23	26	19	17	25
Don't know/did not answer	–	–	–	–	–	–	–	–	8
Total	12	11	11	12	11	11	100	100	100

2001, 2005 and 2010 BES post-election waves (all data weighted).

of its vote is therefore borrowed, as the party actively seeks to secure tactical votes. Nonetheless, the Liberal Democrats' electoral goal was to solidify its base and perhaps exploit growing volatility within the electorate by building an army of supporters who leaned towards the Liberal Democrat. Did the Liberal Democrats continue to be the main recipients of donated support in 2005 and 2010? And where did these tactical voters politically come from?

Table 2.2 presents the data from the 2001, 2005 and 2010 BES post-election cross-section surveys. Similar to 2001, tactical voters comprised around 11 per cent of the electorate in both 2005 and 2010.[3] First, at each of the three elections, the Liberal Democrats were recipients of the highest number of tactical votes. In 2010, 40 per cent of all tactical voters voted Liberal Democrat. Meanwhile, both the Conservatives and Labour saw a drop in tactical votes received in 2010. Second, while nearly a quarter of Liberal Democrat support in 2001 came from tactical votes, this dropped to 17 per cent in 2005. Interestingly, there was a slight increase in 2010, when 19 per cent of all Liberal Democrat votes were tactical. By comparison, only 7 and 9 per cent of Conservative and Labour votes in 2010 were tactical, respectively. Finally, the proportion of tactical voters who actually preferred the Liberal Democrats but voted for other parties dropped from 39 per cent in 2005 to 24 per cent in 2010. This could suggest that the party was starting to convince voters that it was more credible and that voting Liberal Democrat could make a difference. However, this seems unlikely given the rise in the proportion of Liberal Democrat votes that were tactical. It seems highly likely that in 2010 Labour voters were tactically supporting the Liberal Democrats in growing numbers and that the increase in Liberal Democrat support was soft.

Examining additional data from the 2010 BES post-election wave supports these conclusions (see Table 2.3). Here we focus on the extent of tactical voting in seats that the Liberal Democrats won in 2010, and compare this with the sub-sample where the party won the seat and the Conservatives were in second place.

Table 2.3 Tactical voting by party – Liberal Democrat seats won and Liberal Democrat seats won versus Conservatives: 2010 general election, England only

Party	% tactical votes received		% party support from tactical votes		Preferred party of tactical voters	
	LD win	LD–Con	LD win	LD–Con	LD win	LD–Con
Conservative	17	18	10	11	10	9
Labour	9	3	12	6	54	59
Lib Dem	70	76	30	33	9	11
Other	7	10	12	9	26	21
Total	20	22	20	22	100	100

2010 BES panel post-election wave (all data weighted).

We focus on England, given the more complex party system in Scotland and Wales. Unsurprisingly, of those who voted tactically, an overwhelming majority supported the Liberal Democrats: 70 per cent in all Liberal Democrat seats and 76 per cent where the party won the seat and the Conservatives were second. Two other points are striking. A third of the party's support in Liberal Democrat–Conservative seats came from tactical voters and nearly 60 per cent of these voters actually preferred Labour. Much of the Liberal Democrats' future success in these key seats was therefore reliant on keeping this borrowed Labour support on board, and if possible converting these voters into Liberal Democrat identifiers. Here, once again, the findings reveal a 'soft underbelly' of support. With few partisans, this left them vulnerable, particularly to the Conservatives if Labour supporters at future elections returned to their preferred party and the Conservatives remained electorally viable.

But how does this tactical voting group compare to those who switched to the party for non-tactical reasons? What was their socio-demographic or political make-up? Was tactical switching more prominent in certain types of seat or where campaigning had been more intensive? To address these questions, we run a multinomial model where those non-tactical switchers are the base category, compared against both loyal Liberal Democrat supporters and, crucially, those who tactically switched to vote Liberal Democrat (see Table 2.4). For brevity, we include and report those who did not vote Liberal Democrat, although this is not of huge interest here. Loyalists (in the second column of Table 2.4) were, as one would expect, strong partisans, but also more likely than non-tactical switchers to be younger, hold a degree, support EU membership and be mobilised by the local Liberal Democrat campaign.

Our focus is on the first column, which compares tactical switchers with non-tactical switchers. Here there is a clear difference. Those who tactically switched to the Liberal Democrats in 2010 were significantly more likely than non-tactical switchers to be younger, supportive of eco taxes and come from the left of the

Table 2.4 Multinomial regression comparing non-tactical Liberal Democrat switchers (base) against tactical Liberal Democrat switchers, Liberal Democrat loyal voters and non-Liberal Democrat voters: 2010 general election

Variables	Tactical LD switchers		LD loyal voters		Non-LD voters	
	β	SE	β	SE	β	SE
Constant	2.44*	0.62	−0.58	0.62	6.72*	0.48
Fairer taxes	−0.04	0.08	−0.15*	0.07	−0.26*	0.06
Eco taxes	0.18*	0.06	0.17*	0.05	0.10*	0.05
Trident renewal	−0.07	0.06	0.05	0.05	−0.28*	0.05
Closeness to Lib Dems tax–spend	−0.07	0.04	0.04	0.04	−0.14*	0.03
Approve of European Union	0.05	0.05	0.20*	0.06	−0.03	0.05
Education most important issue	−0.86	0.65	−0.59	0.47	0.29	0.43
University towns	0.01	0.06	0.07	0.06	−0.02	0.05
Student	−0.51	0.37	−1.87*	0.35	0.03	0.31
Socio-economic variables						
Male	−0.08	0.12	−0.02	0.11	−0.00	0.01
Age	−0.03*	0.00	−0.03*	0.00	−0.03*	0.00
Degree	−0.06	0.15	0.51*	0.14	−0.07	0.13
Professional/managerial class	0.05	0.14	−0.12	0.13	−0.06	0.11
Work in public sector	0.05	0.13	−0.14	0.12	−0.04	0.10
Non-white	0.34	0.27	0.48	0.29	−0.39	0.22
Economic prospects						
Personal economic expectations	−0.11	0.07	−0.18*	0.07	−0.06	0.06
Political						
Liberal Democrat partisanship	−0.43*	0.20	1.05*	0.15	−0.95*	0.15
Labour partisanship	1.04*	0.19	−1.08*	0.24	1.58*	0.15
Conservative partisanship	0.35	0.26	−1.29*	0.41	2.06*	0.18
Other partisanship	1.28*	0.31	−0.55	0.36	1.87*	0.26
Lib Dems Best on the economy	−1.01*	0.21	0.28*	0.12	−1.75*	0.20
Leadership						
Feelings towards Clegg	−0.24*	0.04	0.03	0.04	−0.46*	0.03
Feelings towards Brown	0.07*	0.03	−0.03	0.03	0.13*	0.02
Feelings towards Cameron	−0.00	0.03	−0.00	0.03	0.15*	0.02
Campaigning						
Labour contact	−0.13	0.16	−0.09	0.16	−0.73*	0.14
Conservative contact	−0.10	0.17	0.04	0.16	0.28*	0.14
Lib Dem contact	0.34*	0.17	0.41*	0.17	−0.78*	0.14
Seat Type (base = all other seats)						
Lib Dem – Conservative	1.24*	0.22	0.78*	0.20	−0.39	0.20
Conservative – Lib Dem	1.42*	0.17	0.40*	0.17	−0.21	0.14
Lib Dem – Labour	0.67	0.36	1.19*	0.32	0.01	0.29
Labour – Lib Dem	0.19	0.19	0.10	0.16	−0.19	0.14
Model fit						
Chi-square (P = <0.05)	2,543.23*		2,543.23*		2,543.23*	
Log likelihood	−5,656.89		−5,656.89		−5,656.89	
McFadden's R^2	0.40		0.40		0.40	
AIC	11,499.78		11,499.78		11,499.78	
N	10,466		10,466		10,466	

*Significant $p<0.05$. 2010 model includes validated voters only. BES Rolling Thunder Panel survey (post-election weight used).

political spectrum. Such switchers recorded positive feelings towards Gordon Brown and identified as Labour supporters. This group also contained other left-of-centre partisans, including Scottish and Welsh nationalists, but particularly Greens. Being contacted also mattered for these tactical switchers. Once again, place-based campaigning proved crucial for non-Liberal Democrat supporters to vote for them. Lastly, those who tactically switched were significantly more likely to do so in those close contests against the Conservatives –where the party was either defending or on the offensive. Aside from being older, non-tactical switchers to the Liberal Democrats were significantly more likely to possess partisan traits, were hugely supportive of Clegg and seemed to buy into the party's competence on the economy. Such switchers were more evenly spread across the country, not in key target contests, and significantly less likely than tactical switchers to have been influenced by local Liberal Democrat campaigning. Overall, there is some evidence that the Liberal Democrats were beginning to win over potential long-term supporters, notwithstanding the lingering issue of voter retention. However, it is also evident that tactical support was borrowed mainly from the progressive left, and in places where it mattered most in terms of winning seats. While such seats were also reliant on a strong loyal support, it is clear that success was dependent on this coalition with tactical switchers.

Converting latent support

Whether it was a low partisan base, continuing problems around retention and recruitment, credibility issues or the reliance on temporary tactical switching, the Liberal Democrats vote was soft. The party still relied on borrowed support and the unpopularity of its rivals, including where it mattered most. It would be unfair though to say that the political and electoral strategy had not made an impact. Our evidence does suggest that the party made progress in recruitment and particularly more concrete switching. This combined with growing support for the leader, and identity with the party and its policies, which can be distinguished from a rump of voters who supported the party out of political convenience.

One other established weakness was the Liberal Democrats' longstanding inability to convert sympathy for its policies into votes. Given the Liberal Democrats' traditionally fragile social base and a lack of core identifiers, the party has often turned to specific issues to persuade voters to support it. Such a strategy is often fraught with difficulty. Part of this comes with the territory of being a third party, where the so-called main parties benefit from the issue ownership perceptions of voters, which squeezes the opportunities for similar policies articulated by third parties to gain traction with voters. Earlier we noted how in both 2005 and 2010 the Liberal Democrats successfully carved out specific policy stances that allowed the party to distinguish itself from its rivals. Not only were these highly salient to particular voters, they by and large proved popular with the wider public. Yet closer inspection of 2010 BES data suggests that the Liberal Democrats' efforts

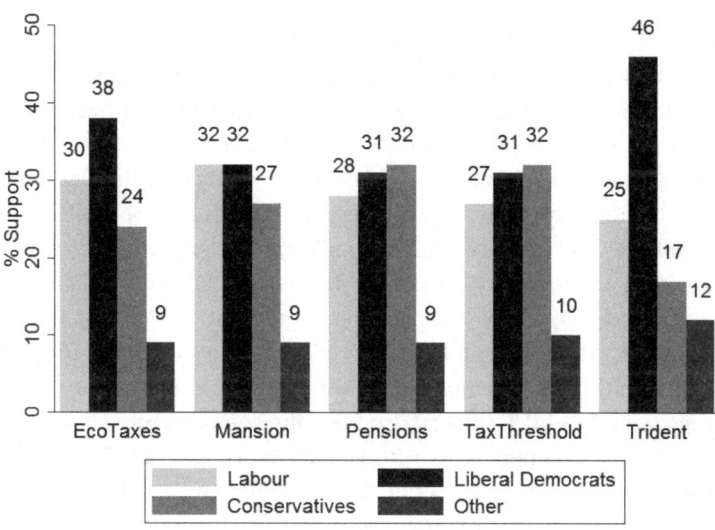

Figure 2.4 Party supporters' agreement with Liberal Democrat policy stances: 2010 general election (%). *Source*: 2010 British Election Study

to convert public agreement on these issues into votes were mixed (see Figure 2.4). Trident renewal proved popular in converting progressive left voters but put off Conservatives, while eco taxes appealed more to the party's identity on the environment and unsurprisingly won support across the spectrum but particularly on the left. There was also evidence that different policy positions allowed the party to 'look both ways', blurring its identity. The mansion tax appealed much more to Labour voters, while increasing the personal allowance, which largely benefited those on middle and upper incomes, appealed more to Conservatives. On both these issues the Liberal Democrats struggled to convert rival party sympathisers.

Of course there are other issues traditionally closer to the longstanding political identity of the Liberals/Liberal Democrats: approval of the UK's membership of the European Union and support for further European integration; individual rights, tolerance of others' and personal freedoms; and reform of the constitution and the electoral system. Yet examining respondent attitudes on the 2010 BES panel and cross-sectional post-election surveys reveals splits among Liberal Democrat voters on these issues. For instance, 53 per cent of all voters approved of EU membership, with around a third of these voters supporting the Liberal Democrats. Despite defining itself as a pro-European party (e.g. the 2010 manifesto pledge was to 'put Britain at the heart of Europe'), 20 per cent of all Liberal Democrat voters did not approve of EU membership. Of all those who agreed with closer EU cooperation, 43 per cent voted Liberal Democrat but two-fifths supported Labour; moreover, more than a third disagreed with further integration. Even on the flagship electoral reform policy, despite 36 per cent of those who agreed voting Liberal Democrat in

2010, more than a fifth of Liberal Democrat voters actually supported the current electoral system. Sizeable splits within the party's vote across issues relating to the tolerance of others and personal freedoms were also evident. In 2010, a number of these issues were not salient and did not make a fundamental difference to the Liberal Democrats' electoral performance. Nonetheless, the findings are illustrative of an underlying concern for the party, which the political and electoral strategy post 1997 had not resolved. From high-profile salient policy stances such as the mansion tax to policy areas that defined the Liberals' political identity, voters were largely supportive, but the party could not convert this into support at the ballot box. Moreover, on key policy platforms, a substantial proportion of Liberal Democrat voters were not aligned with party positions.

Post 1997, the Liberal Democrats successfully chipped away at New Labour's coalition of support. As popularity with Labour waned and the Liberal Democrats developed a distinctive agenda, 'softer' Labour voters saw the Liberal Democrats as a viable electoral alternative. Some of those switch voters were impressed by the leader and bought into the policy stances while others were only lending their vote tactically. Against the Conservatives, there was evidence that the party was not enjoying the same success of recruiting and retaining previously won support. Despite undoubted electoral success, the Liberal Democrat vote remained weak. Going into coalition, large swathes of the electorate were sympathetic to the Liberal Democrats but did not vote for them. Their vote was as high as it had been since the days of the Alliance, but support was still borrowed, lacked solidity and remained dependent on the failures of others. The chameleon nature of its policy position – with some policies appealing to the Conservatives and others attractive to Labour – allowed the party to tailor its message to the electoral contexts, and reap electoral benefits. However, it ultimately had a ceiling, as voters still struggled to define where the party stood.

The diminishing campaign advantage

Local campaigning remained an integral part of the Liberal Democrats' electoral strategy throughout the 1990s and 2000s. Yet by 2010 there was growing evidence that this advantage was diminishing. There are a number of reasons why this was the case:

- Rival parties had simply copied what worked best on the ground, and had started to do it either equally as well or better.
- Opponents (particularly the Conservatives) had become far more professional and effective at targeting their resources.
- Rival parties had begun to circumvent local spending rules by pouring money into marginal contests from the centre. As a consequence the increasing use of direct mail and national telephone banks advantaged the two main parties
- Rival parties, particularly the Conservatives, began to campaign more

intensively outside the conventional regulated election period. This represented a significant threat to the Liberal Democrats' 'all year round' campaigning strategy, as they simply did not have the resources to compete on a level playing field.

- Growing evidence suggests that local modes were becoming increasingly obsolete in the face of advances in technology, to the detriment of longstanding local community campaigning.
- There were mounting concerns that traditional Liberal Democrat campaigning strategies and methods were far less effective in defensive situations than when the party was on the front foot.

Like their rivals, while Liberal Democrat local parties continued to have discretion over local material – presenting the candidate and tailoring national policies to the local arena – the design, layout and messaging in key seats became largely nationally coordinated, based on templates. Outside of key marginal seats, including those it was defending (as these were often targets irrespective of the majority), local parties had much more freedom. In addition to the freepost election communication, the other major development over this 20-year time frame was the use of direct mail produced outside the constituency. By 2010, this had become a staple diet of the campaign. Alongside national telephone banks, there was a sense that the major parties were adapting to the realities of fewer members and activists on the ground, and the need to focus on vital swing voters. While the Liberal Democrats actively embraced these modern techniques, there is no doubt that such campaign developments were skewed against the labour-intensive traditional community-based activism, which had been the core of the party's ethos.

At the same time, technological advancement and the growth of the professionalised campaign led to a decline in the Liberal Democrats' local use of poster sites. Other materials, such as the traditional blue-ink target letters, looked less appealing than their opponents' more sophisticated approaches. These modes were not entirely on the way out, however. In 2010, the Conservatives extensively used billboard posters in target seats in the three months prior to the general election, although this was scaled back during the official campaign. In later elections direct mail target letters from leaders became highly personalised – see David Cameron's 'Prime Minister letters' in 2015. Online 'posters' now form a part of the campaign medium. While such changes are incremental, 2010 was a 'reordering' election in terms of campaigning techniques, which – if anything – moved away from the party's strengths. Moreover, with the direction of travel increasingly placing an emphasis on the centre to fund direct mail, national telephone banks, a voter identification database and leader visits, the financial 'arms race' was becoming more important than ever. In 2010, the Conservatives raised close to the £18.9 million expenditure limit, while Labour raised around only 60 per cent of the maximum allowed. The Liberal Democrats, meanwhile, spent only £5 million. While the party had always struggled to match its rivals financially, the changing character of professional campaigns meant that the advantage of Liberal Democrat tactics was diminishing.

Rival parties, noticeably the Conservatives, were also becoming far more effective, strategic and professional in the way they operationalised their campaign. While Labour under Blair had been widely lauded for its key seats campaign strategy in 1997 and tactical efficiency (albeit in 2001 its coordination had been a problem because Labour targeted too many seats), the Conservatives historically struggled to focus their campaign efforts. One of their major problems was the relative strength of campaigning in non-targets seats, especially those they were certain to hold. However, in 2010, campaign scholars noticed a considerable improvement for the Conservatives (Fisher *et al.*, 2011; Johnston *et al.*, 2012). Despite weaker overall levels of campaign intensity due to scarce resources, the Liberal Democrats traditionally concentrated efforts more intensely in target seats. However, using data from surveys of electoral agents, Fisher *et al.* (2011: 820–821) noted that the campaign intensity of both Liberal Democrat and Conservative campaigns in target seats were similar in 2010. Moreover, Fisher *et al.* (2011: 821) concluded that while campaign effort was higher in certainties than non-targets, for the Conservatives it was even higher in primary targets and least intense in 'long shots'. Labour was far more defensive, with campaign strength much higher in safer than in more vulnerable seats, while the intensity of the Liberal Democrat campaign was similar both where it was defending and seeking to take of seats from its opponents (as noted previously). While these observations reflect the electoral context and the political narrative that Labour was on the defensive and the Conservatives on the front foot, it is clear that 2010 was an election where Conservative targeting and tactics became as ruthless as those of its opponents. Further evidence from the 2010 BES suggests that the Conservatives contacted more voters than either Labour or the Liberal Democrats during the 2010 campaign period (see Figure 2.5). Moreover, they were more likely to use leafleting (albeit this was predominantly direct mail than personally delivered material) and doorstep canvassing as campaign tools than their two main rivals.

For a party that had historically been so reliant on the local campaign and emphasised the virtue of decentralisation and community politics, the increasing coordination and management from the centre was met with scepticism by some Liberal Democrats. Like its rivals, the party largely embraced the joined up national–local approach in terms of targeting, tactics, messaging, staffing and tools such as national telephone banks. However, the consequences of this shift were dramatic and detrimental to the Liberal Democrats. Later in the book, we will examine further how rival parties sought to 'buy' marginal seats by focusing national campaign funds on specific local contests. At first, this was through tools such as direct mail and telephone banks. In elections post 2010, however, the blurred lines between local and national spending led to an 'arms race' to produce targeted digital material with messages tailored explicitly to local contests. Parties

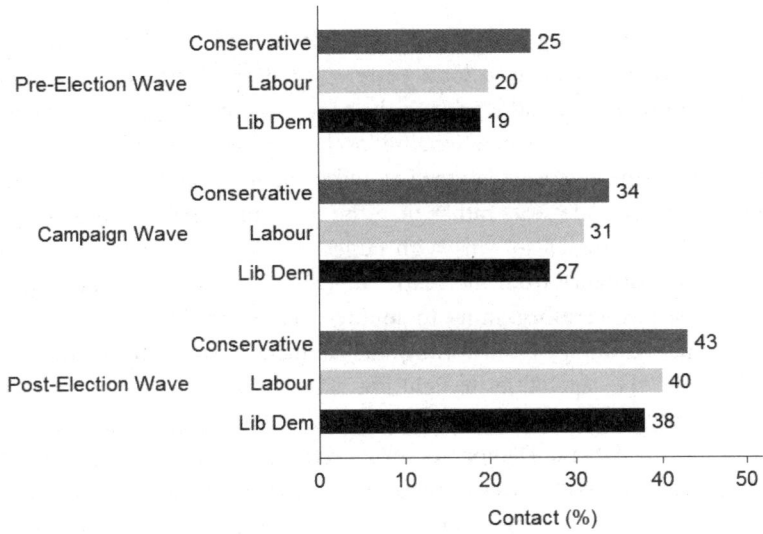

Figure 2.5 Party contact (%) in the 2010 general election. *Source*: 2010 BES panel survey (pre, campaign, post election)

could use digital media to gather data on individuals and target key voters in 'toss up' constituencies with local ads and carefully designed campaign messages. For an under-resourced party like the Liberal Democrats this was extremely difficult to combat.

Yet, there were warning signs before the 2010 general election that the national coordination of resources for key local contests was starting to influence constituency outcomes. Part of the long-term sell of the Liberal Democrats was their claim to 'work all year round and not just at election time'. Both the main parties were keen to devise strategies where central funds would assist local efforts, providing such activism was evident. A heavily resourced Conservative party went one step further. From 2007 onwards, a unit in the central party organisation, led by then Conservative Deputy Chairman, Lord Ashcroft, spent several million pounds outside of the election campaign period in an effort to win over voters in key battleground seats. In total, 144 Conservative constituency parties obtained grants from the target seat strategy over a three-year period: 76 received grants in one year only; 23 in two years; and 45 in all three (Cutts *et al.*, 2012). Evidence suggests that even after controlling for prior vote share and other variables, the value of the grants received during the non-election period had a significant and positive direct impact on the Conservatives' 2010 performance. The grants also had a small indirect effect on Conservative support through local campaign effort during the three-week campaign prior to polling day (Cutts *et al.*, 2012). The 'Ashcroft spending' effect not only made a difference to the Conservatives' electoral prospects, but it represented a direct challenge to the Liberal Democrats' ethos of continuous activism, which was reliant on local activists and volunteers.

Moreover, reflecting the growing professionalisation of the Conservatives, that party made grants available to local party associations (subject to a campaign plan) from around 30 months prior to the 2010 election. Associations could bid for agents to organise and operationalise local campaign activity and prepare for the election. Again, this was designed to offset the longstanding issue of agents being embedded in safe seats rather than the more marginal constituencies that the Conservatives needed to win. With target seats now being bombarded with resources and assistance from the centre, thereby sidestepping local expenditure rules, rival parties were beginning to counter the Liberal Democrats' perceived 'ground game' advantage by distorting the 'campaign playing field'. The Liberal Democrats had the capabilities to fight fire with fire, but the 2010 election reinforced the perception that the party lacked sufficient spending power to compete.

So, while the Liberal Democrats 'overstretched' their targeting strategy in 2010, both the Conservatives and Labour were far more efficient and increasingly professional. Despite its unpopularity, Labour showed the virtues of campaign management through the adoption of propensity modelling based on four criteria to target seats that the party had the best chance of defending. This sophisticated defensive strategy proved hugely effective in boosting support, scuppering the Conservatives' bid to achieve a majority, and denting any Liberal Democrat advance (Fisher *et al.*, 2011). The Conservatives with their new computer system (MERLIN) developed a voter identification database that could view local databases and exchange information between the centre and the local. Although it had teething problems and was not as advanced as Labour's Contact Creator database system, the ability to exchange campaign material between central and local databases meant that the Conservatives could respond to changing electoral scenarios and adapt campaign strategies quickly (Fisher, 2010). For the Liberal Democrats, there were also question marks over whether the longstanding EARS party software (later replaced by Connect) had begun to outlast its usefulness as competitors were beginning to adopt more sophisticated systems. This blunted the effectiveness of traditional tools and the ability of the party to respond to local threats, adding to a growing sense that the campaign pendulum on the ground was swinging away from the party.

Lastly, there was growing unease about the frailties of Liberal Democrat campaigning in defensive situations. Under Rennard, the party tailored its message to suit the electoral context. This proved to be effective when it was on the offensive, but it did come at a cost. By 2010, the Liberal Democrats were categorised as 'chameleon like', supporting particular policies in one seat and opposing the same policies in another. However, this approach left the Liberal Democrats vulnerable in defensive situations. Questions also remained about the effectiveness of the ground campaign where the Liberal Democrats were holding off better-resourced rivals. Post 2001, the Conservatives started to regain the electoral ground they lost in 1997, inevitably putting some Liberal Democrat seats in the firing line. Losses were kept to a minimum in 2005 (five seats: Devon West and Torridge,

Guilford, Ludlow, Newbury and Weston-super-Mare) but despite Cleggmania and an increased national vote share, a further 12 seats were lost in 2010.[4] Some of these coincided with the retirement of well-known local MPs, which represented the downside of a local vote that is more personal than party orientated. Overall, the Liberal Democrats ran highly organised, intensive local campaigns with help from the centre, but still lost out. Pounding the streets with literature and canvassers mattered, but they were increasingly unable to repel highly resourced, centrally funded targeted campaigns integrated with local effort. And whether these more sophisticated campaign strategies now choked the effectiveness of traditional methods seemed more up for debate at the end of the decade than at the start of the millennium.

Drifting away from social liberalism (and its voters)

Social liberalism has long been the cornerstone of Liberal Democrat thought. The philosophy emanated from T. H. Green's concept of positive liberty – individual opportunity for self-development with a positive, albeit limited, role of the state. It was not until the revisionist Edwardian liberal thinking of Hobhouse and Hobson, who both stressed the role of an interventionist state enhancing rather than under-mining individual liberty, that a more collectivist form of liberalism took hold. These forefathers of social liberalism influenced the legislation of the reforming pre-war Liberal governments. More importantly, social liberalism provided the Liberals (and later the Liberal Democrats) with an intellectual tradition that was non-socialist, but radical in its rebuke to the economic and social ills of capital-ism. Its intellectual impact transcended into Lloyd George's 1928 'Yellow Book', the theoretical work of Keynes, and the 'liberal radicalism' of Beveridge and the formation of the post-war British welfare state. Even under Grimond's leader-ship, which espoused decentralisation of power and community politics, there was a distinct centre-left positioning, where Grimond himself regarded individual liberty as best secured within a social context (Grayson, 2010).

This social liberal legacy remained an integral part of the newly formed Social Liberal Democrats (founded in 1988) which became the Liberal Democrats after a name change in 1989. Social liberalism stressed the values of community, decentralisation and active citizenship as an identity distinct from the more cen-tralist Labour and the free-market Conservatives. In addition, new leader Paddy Ashdown's notion of entitlements (in *Citizens' Britain*, 1989) also talked about citizens' rights to health, education and welfare, and the role of government to guarantee access to these to enhance the power of the individual (Ashdown, 1989). While Ashdown argued later for a more pro-market position, the party's 1992 manifesto ('Changing Britain for Good') talked about an enabling, regulatory state that prevented market failure to ensure the provision of public services. Policies that stressed more funds for health and hypothecated taxation to fund education ostensibly reinforced a centre-left party positioning.

The abandonment of equidistance in 1995 and Ashdown's plans to increase cooperation with Labour (known as the 'Project') reaffirmed a genuine desire for more progressive politics and a realignment of the left. While the size of Blair's 1997 majority blunted any prospect of Liberal Democrat representation in cabinet, it did lead to the implementation of the Joint Cabinet Committee to discuss constitutional affairs such as reforming the electoral system (Russell and Fieldhouse, 2005). Yet despite the appointment of Lord Jenkins to consult and produce a recommendation on proportional representation (AV plus) for changing the electoral system, Labour's political will to implement such changes had waned. Blair's dithering and evasion made it clear that the 'Project' was going nowhere. The failure to implement electoral reform gave the Liberal Democrats an opportunity to reignite the party's distinctive identity around constitutional affairs, which had become somewhat blurred by the consensus on devolution, House of Lords reform, and the incorporation of the European Convention on Human Rights into UK law. In hindsight, it is clear that Ashdown's personal relationship with Blair was central to the politics around possible cooperation. Others within the Labour and the Liberal Democrat parties (as Kennedy's limited support later suggests) were lukewarm at best about such a notion. Ashdown's ability to pull the party into a position where it was actively discussing formal cooperation, constitutional consultation and even cabinet posts illustrates his dominance over the party. Nonetheless, this points to something much deeper. The Liberal Democrats, despite its decentralising passion and its public portrayal as an open vehicle for discussion and disagreement, is essentially very top heavy. Liberal Democrats tend to be extremely loyal and obedient to the leader and, unlike their rivals, under-factionalised (Grayson, 2010). These characteristics enabled the revival of social liberal policies under Kennedy to be challenged, initially by a small group of influential figures, who rose to the top of the party and led the Liberal Democrats to part from its social liberal core.

The politics and internal ideological battles from the Kennedy era to the subsequent rise of Clegg have been the focus of much debate. Here we do not recount every twist and turn, but we can draw on the key themes that provide a narrative for similar struggles that the Liberal Democrats faced in the next decade. Under Kennedy, there was a clear attempt to embrace the Hobhouse traditions of social liberalism, which was relabelled 'New Liberalism' by some (Grayson, 2007). These included commitments to tackling social injustice through decentralising and democratising state control rather than reducing the overall role of the state (see 'Freedom in a Liberal Society', 2000). The party's platform included a strong environmental core, which meant the party could share common ground with Labour on goals but differ on the approach. However, ahead of the 2005 general election, the *Orange Book: Reclaiming Liberalism* was released; it provided a policy challenge to the ascendency of social liberal thought in the party. On one level, the caricature that the *Orange Book* reflected the social versus economic liberal schism within the party was overly simplistic. Nevertheless, a couple of the chapters did question the role of the state in the provision of public services and advocated more market-based solutions. For example, David Laws in his chapter stressed how the Liberal Democrats too readily accepted state interference (the so-called 'nanny state') and were deep rooted and resistant to change when it came to reforming public services such as the NHS and prison system (Laws and Marshall, 2004: 32–33). The book provoked a lively discussion in the party about the role of the state despite the limited support of most members. It drew a formal response in the form of *Reinventing the State: Social Liberalism for the 21st Century* (Brack et al., 2007), which sought to defend and elaborate on existing policies and even promote new policies through a social liberal lens of the state. However, while its authors sought to play down the existence of the social economic liberal divide in the party, there were already clear signals after Kennedy that social liberals were on the back foot. The 2007 party conference was noticeable for the abandonment of the 50p tax rate policy on incomes over £100,000 and the adoption of a 4p cut in the basic rate of income tax. Symbolically, the party vacated its long-held position to tax the rich more.

Yet it was not until the election of Clegg that modernisers from the economic liberal wing began to gain a decisive foothold. Two key shifts occurred almost immediately which were to have long-term consequences. The first was the adoption of the policy document 'Make It Happen', which advocated tax cuts for those on low to middle incomes. For opponents on the social liberal wing, going further on tax cuts came at the price of reducing spending on public services. By default, it was limiting the role of the state. The direction of travel on policy now seemed clear. The grip of the economic liberal wing was reinforced by the second key shift: growing professionalisation of the party's structures. Clegg set up the Bones Commission, which set out a series of recommendations for professionalising the party (Evans and Sanderson-Nash, 2011; Sanderson-Nash, 2012). Such changes to intra-party activity and internal structures strengthened the leader's hand (and arguably those in the parliamentary party). Conferences became little different from their rivals – largely stage-managed, designed to showcase support for the leader and present a united party to the public. These reforms sidelined deeper fractures to new forums away from the conference stage. For instance, as Grayson (2010) notes, the election of social liberals to the party's influential Federal Policy Committee became critical in retaining the party's policy to scrap tuition fees, despite leadership efforts to remove it. The final proposal at conference was ratified with little fuss, thereby insulating the leadership from any public showdown on the issue (Grayson, 2010). At the 2009 party conference, social liberals mobilised to block further efforts to abandon the policy on tuition fees, forcing Clegg to include a 'watered down' version in the 2010 manifesto. Despite these successes, the upshot of the reforms was a more modernised, professional party and a shift in political culture that was more in tune with the ambitions of the leadership team (Sanderson-Nash, 2012). The growing curbs on members' ability to influence policy outcomes only strengthened the control of Clegg and his team. By 2010, the economic liberal wing of the party held sway. Indeed the social composition and occupational background of the parliamentary party itself was more like the Conservatives than Labour, with nearly a third in 2010 coming from business (Sanderson-Nash, 2012).

While a sizeable and growing number of the parliamentary party seemingly leant towards economic liberalism, key parts of the 2010 manifesto – and large numbers of its voters – did not. Given the backdrop of the financial crisis, there was a consensus among the three main parties on using spending cuts rather than tax increases to repair the public finances. However, despite its growing economically liberal inclinations, it was the Conservatives that planned the largest spending squeeze over the first three years of the next administration, followed by Labour and then the Liberal Democrats. On the issue that was arguably at the forefront of the election, the Liberal Democrats' proposals were far closer to Labour than the Conservatives. Yet, given the leadership's direction of travel – watering down socially liberal policies such as public spending commitments and funding education through hypothecated taxation – key figures in the leadership were aligning closer to the Conservatives. Moreover, as Grayson (2010) pointed out, the under-factionalisation of the party strengthened the leadership's grip on the agenda and policy direction. Liberal Democrat MPs had little connection with competing ideological strands, as existing factions lacked coherence and the organisation necessary to put pressure on decision-making. All this proved pivotal when the Liberal Democrats were placed in the position of kingmakers in the aftermath of the 2010 general election. For Clegg and his close team, it ensured a rubber-stamping of the coalition agreement, with little fuss. Yet this embeddedness of economic liberalism ultimately left them hamstrung in subsequent elections, disconnected from competing views within the party and, crucially, the voters outside.

Summary

Any 2010 general election post-mortem was quickly put to one side as the Liberal Democrats entered national government (albeit as the junior partner in a coalition with the Conservatives) for the first time since the early 1920s. Nevertheless, beneath the surface it was abundantly clear that the Liberal Democrats were not as politically and electorally surefooted as they appeared. Even during the period of growth, the party had been unable to solve its voter loyalty problem, and volatile recruitment and retention remained causes for concern. The Liberal Democrat vote was temporary and worryingly soft. Despite high-profile policies, the party still struggled to convert sympathy for its policies into votes. While the Clegg-led Liberal Democrats sought to push back against Labour, there was mounting survey and polling evidence that the party was still ideologically closer to Labour than to the Conservatives (Kellner, 2011). Indeed, a TNS poll during the 2010 campaign showed that 29 per cent of Liberal Democrat voters placed Labour as their second party, compared with 22 per cent for the Conservatives (Cutts *et al.*, 2010). The gradual drift away from social liberalism and the electoral positioning in the aftermath of the 2010 election therefore seemed to be at odds with the centre-left axis to their vote. Moreover, Clegg's performance during the campaign diluted the impact of any internal dissent. This gave him (and his leadership team) the political space in the immediate post-election period to ensure economic liberal ideas held sway. Ultimately, though, structural barriers still hurt the Liberal Democrats badly. For many voters, the party could not pass the credibility test – either nationally or at the constituency level. Campaigning was a key tool in tackling the credibility problem, but there were worrying signs that the party was losing its competitive advantage. With the resource gap widening, rival parties had begun to copy Liberal Democrat campaigning tactics that worked, while simultaneously embracing technology and new tools. Increasingly centralised campaigns with a national, leader-centred focus may at first glance have favoured the Liberal Democrats. Cleggmania, for instance, gave an insight into how third parties could circumvent structural imbalances. Ultimately, however, it did not bear fruit electorally. It also accentuated the resource gap as bigger parties could challenge the Liberal Democrats through a national agenda and draw focus away from the local. A perfect storm was brewing for the Liberal Democrats. Financially powerful rivals could challenge the party's campaign advantage and scupper credibility efforts. Centralised campaign machines with a national focus underpinned by the leader increasingly became the primary vehicle for transmitting the core campaign message. For the Liberal Democrats, participation in the coalition offered an opportunity to tackle the credibility problem. The party wagered that being in government would give it legitimacy and embed it as the only viable challenger to the status quo. While the Liberal Democrats ultimately 'bet the house', the bet was fundamentally unsound. When the ill winds inevitably blew, it was unsurprising that the house fell down.

Part II. The coalition years: from government to obscurity

In Part II we examine the Liberal Democrats in government and the disastrous electoral fallout. Using coalition theory as a backdrop, Chapter 3 discusses whether the eventual outcome was inevitable. While acknowledging that the Liberal Democrats always faced an uphill task, we show how the party got the coalition wrong from the outset and at every turn amplified the problem through avoidable mistakes, strategic errors and miscalculations. Chapter 4 assesses where the Liberal Democrat vote went and why. Whereas the abandonment of the tuition fees pledge came to symbolise public toxicity towards the Liberal Democrats, we show that the electoral damage which ensued originated from simply going into coalition with the Conservatives. We detail how it exposed the feebleness of Liberal Democrat support and how voters' initial judgements were reinforced by the experience of coalition – signing up to the Conservatives' austerity package, breaking pre-election policies and so on – to the point that the party was neither blamed for failures nor credited for successes. Chapter 5 examines the damage to the party's local infrastructure and how it undermined its efforts to stave off electoral collapse. We also assess what happened to the Liberal Democrats' much vaunted grassroots campaign machine. Competing explanations are explored, including whether the party was outfought by better-resourced rivals who copied what the Liberal Democrats did but did it better, or whether the party experienced a drop-off in activism where it mattered most. We examine whether place-specific local operations built on and engaged in grassroots activism did ultimately matter, and whether such activism actually proved decisive in saving the Liberal Democrats from electoral extinction.

3

Getting the coalition wrong

The first formal, peacetime UK coalition government for nearly 80 years was a breakthrough opportunity for the Liberal Democrats. On 11 May 2010, they entered a coalition with the Conservatives, ending their post-war exile from national government. Their leader was made Deputy Prime Minister and several leading party figures became key players in the cabinet. They secured an agreement on holding a referendum on electoral reform that might have ensured their place at the core of British party politics for good. However, the party's promising position quickly turned to dust. Support for the Liberal Democrats fell dramatically. Far from securing a permanent place at the table, they lost their status as Britain's third party and their reputation was tarnished. The referendum on electoral reform was resoundingly defeated and by the time of the next general election, in 2015, the chance of a return to government seemed exceedingly thin. Furthermore, matters scarcely improved in the years that followed.

In this chapter, we examine whether that outcome was inevitable. Here we assess the Conservative–Liberal Democrat government through the lens of cross-national research on coalition-building. While coalition theory suggests that the Liberal Democrats as the junior partner were always going to find it tough, we show that many of the party's woes stemmed from their own misjudgements, errors and deficiencies. We discuss how the Liberal Democrats 'got the coalition wrong' from the outset, including the initial agreement and portfolios, through to presenting the coalition, messaging and misreading the politics. We also examine Clegg's misjudgements and campaign mistakes. The final section details the scale of the electoral catastrophe in 2015 and the legacy of coalition, which haunted the Liberal Democrats and scuppered any prospect of an imminent revival.

Was the outcome inevitable?

It was inevitable that the party would suffer, but the scale of it ultimately owed much to the Liberal Democrats' acts of 'self-harm' (Cutts and Russell, 2015) and to Conservative statecraft (Hayton, 2014; Heppell, 2019), which exploited the Liberal Democrats' institutional weaknesses and inexperience. Cross-national research on coalition formation provides some important insights here. The Conservative–Liberal Democrat government was a 'minimal winning coalition', in that it contained only those parties that were necessary to obtain a majority in the legislature (Gamson, 1961; Riker, 1962). This 'minimal winning coalition' contained the largest party and 'centripetal' actor in the negotiations (the Conservatives) and the 'pivotal' party (the Liberal Democrats), whose inclusion provided a resounding majority in the House of Commons (Bale, 2011). Minimising the number of coalition partners makes reaching an agreement easier (known as the 'size principle'), less costly and time-consuming (Leiserson, 1968; Martin and Stevenson, 2001). The presence of a 'pivotal' party (and fewer parties more generally) means that such 'minimal winning coalitions' last longer than coalitions that do not contain them. Durability and resilience are therefore intrinsic traits of 'minimal winning coalitions'. Cross-national research suggests that the chance of coalition break-up increases as time passes, and that unexpected events or crises can damage and divide parties (Strøm et al., 2008). Policy failures, particularly those pertaining to the economy, can be detrimental to coalition longevity, especially to Conservative parties (Debus et al., 2014).

Political culture and tradition also matter. Coalitions in parliamentary systems that are built on party discipline and traditions of executive collective responsibility (as in the case of the UK) are more likely to fall in times of flux (Bale, 2011, 2012). Unsurprisingly, resilience was the centrepiece of the negotiations between the Conservatives and the Liberal Democrats. The outcome proved to be simultaneously the first sign of Liberal Democrat 'self-harm' and the first indication of strategic leadership by the Conservatives under Cameron (Hayton, 2014).

To offset concerns about the coalition's durability, both parties agreed to introduce fixed-term parliaments. The term was fixed at five years, to set an expectation from the outset that the coalition would endure the full term. Both parties were thus seemingly 'locked in' for the duration of the coalition term, whatever the tensions, disagreements and political fallout. On the face of it, Cameron's willingness to give up the unilateral power of dissolution to ensure longevity during a period of economic uncertainty represented a notable constraint on the Prime Minister's power. It also put paid to any lingering doubts that the Conservatives were committed to the coalition agreement. For Cameron, this manoeuvre made strategic sense. Not only did it detract attention from the failure to win an outright majority, but it allowed Cameron to continue to modernise his party by reducing any prospect of him being held to ransom by the Conservative right (Cutts and Russell, 2015; Heppell and Seawright, 2012). The fixed term allowed Cameron to control events and use the Liberal Democrats as an ally in reforming internally where necessary. It also acted as a buffer for right-wing criticism. Cameron could successfully argue that his hands were tied by the coalition agreement and simultaneously stress the need to provide stability in uncertain times. Strategically, it proved to be a masterstroke.

For their part, the Liberal Democrats painted their decision to join the Conservatives in coalition as the responsible thing to do given the country's economic woes and 'talked up' the political consensus regarding the need for deficit reduction. The Liberal Democrats also felt that their participation would boost their own political credibility, as voters would be grateful to them for sacrificing their party goals for the national interest. Yet, cross-national evidence suggests voters seldom reward parties in government (known as a 'negative incumbency effect') for taking such stances (Strøm, 1990). If anything, in the 'minimal winning coalition' it is the party of the Prime Minister that tends to gain votes or 'ride out' any electoral damage, while the smaller party suffers (Hjermitslev, 2020; Strøm *et al.*, 2008). Evidence from Germany, where coalitions are common, suggests that it is the leader of the largest coalition partner who gains most from positive voter evaluations of economic outcomes (Debus *et al.*, 2014). Leaving aside that junior coalition partners are more likely to do worse in elections (Buelens and Hino, 2008), existing research also shows that smaller parties rarely get credit for things that go well, but often get the blame when anything goes wrong (Bale, 2012; Duch and Stevenson, 2008; Font, 2001). Although, others suggest this varies according to the institutional context (Hjermitslev, 2020). One persuasive explanation is that voters perceive parties in coalition to be more ideologically similar than they are in reality. As such, the policies advocated by the coalition partners remain attractive to an ever-decreasing section of the electorate over time (Fortunato and Stevenson, 2013). Inevitably, policy compromises result in voters perceiving that the coalition parties have reneged on their pre-coalition promises. Critically, this disproportionately impacts the junior partner, as voters perceive ideological convergence between smaller party coalition members and the Prime Minister. While voters attribute the Prime Minster's policies to the smaller partner, the opposite does not occur (Fortunato and Adams, 2015). This is a major headache for small parties. Negative incumbency effects are much harder for a smaller party to bear than for a larger, more established party. Given these perceptions of ideological convergence, it becomes much harder for voters to differentiate the smaller party from the larger party. Close collaboration with a larger party also makes it far more difficult for a junior partner to distinguish itself in office (Fortunato 2019; Fortunato and Adams, 2015; Hjermitslev, 2020). So, the smaller party is in a Catch-22 situation. Voters begin to perceive the largest party and/or the Prime Minister to be responsible for policy outcomes with the smaller party on the sidelines, unable to muster credit or escape blame.

For the Conservatives, tying the Liberal Democrats into a five-year coalition term was always going to be fruitful. By contrast, the Liberal Democrats were naïve. The party was stuck within the confines of a coalition, allowing Cameron's Conservatives to dictate the terms and left little wriggle room for the Liberal Democrats to distance themselves from unpopular policies. Just like many coalitions, the smaller party haemorrhaged public support, reinforced by events – in this case, Liberal Democrat voters' disgust with the party's capitulation over tuition fees. This combined to stir internal party rumblings about the need to make public disagreements with the Conservatives and restore the Liberal Democrats' identity (Russell, 2010). By January 2011, barely seven months after the signing of the coalition agreement, Clegg spoke of a 'new phase' for the coalition. He reassured colleagues and supporters that 'disagreement marks the starting point of most discussions with Cameron' and stressed the need to 'assert the party's distinctive identity' from the Conservatives (Watt, 2011). As time went on and anxiety grew, more phases came and went as Clegg and the party leadership struggled to restore a distinctive identity from within the coalition. A coup to oust Clegg was never realistic or practical, given loyalty to the leader and the dominance of the 'economic liberal' wing within the parliamentary party. This, however, left the Liberal Democrats in the final phase of the coalition 'belatedly trying to demonstrate "clear water", looking almost childishly petulant, undoing any advantage which serving in government might have done to our [the Liberal Democrats'] fortunes' (Harvey, 2015).

Notwithstanding coalition theory, a counter-argument often put forward by the Liberal Democrats is that the party had to sign up to the full term to make the coalition credible. Following the 2010 election, the electoral maths meant that the Liberal Democrats were the 'pivotal' party. One possible option for the Liberal Democrats was to join a rainbow coalition with Labour and the Nationalist parties although simple maths would have made it difficult to sustain this over the long term. Moreover, Labour's reluctance to cede to Liberal Democrat demands that Brown should step down before any deal could be done also proved a stumbling block (Wintour, 2010). Others point to Labour tribalism and senior figures in the party who favoured a period of opposition to coalition with the Liberal Democrats (Grayson, 2013). Alternatively, the Conservatives could have formed a minority government and stumbled on for 12 or 18 months before calling an inevitable election. Given the economic climate, the Liberal Democrats feared an electoral backlash if they had put selfish aims before that of the country. And once they had decided to join, a full term was vital for credibility and stability. Of course, the reality is that even in the worst-case scenario it is highly unlikely that the Liberal Democrats would have lost more seats than they eventually did if they had negotiated the 'short coalition' option. Moreover, it is conceivable that the party may have got some credit for standing up (albeit belatedly) against austerity policies. Instead, the party had become tarnished by them by 2015 and beyond. Put simply, the Liberal Democrats' willingness to agree a five-year coalition term proved to be a serious strategic error.

Traditional models of coalition formation also stress how politicians seek to minimise the costs of the bargaining process. As such, parties seek to form coalitions with parties where the different ideological positions in the policy space are small (Axelrod, 1970; de Swaan, 1973). For parties to reach stable coalition agreements, a trade-off between policy compromise and office considerations is necessary (Sened, 1996). Ideologically divided coalition executives do not survive as long as those that are more ideologically convergent and therefore possess a stronger capacity to compromise on policy (Warwick, 1994). During the coalition negotiations, Cameron's Conservatives and leading figures in the Liberal Democrats evidently shared a considerable amount of ideological common ground. For instance, an emerging consensus on the management of the economy and role of the state coincided with the economic ethos of self-reliance espoused by senior Liberal Democrats (Beech, 2011; Russell *et al.*, 2007). As we noted in Chapter 2, the electoral growth of the party in the early twenty-first century created a new power base for the Liberal Democrats – the parliamentary party – who came to exert a 'de facto veto' over much of the party's strategy and operation (Russell *et al.*, 2007). A cohort of new MPs – many of whom were potential party leaders and eager to make names for themselves – entered parliament from the private sector and wider corporate world. They brought with them a brand of economic liberalism that quickly gained prominence within the parliamentary party. The publication of *The Orange Book* in 2004 was an important totem to display the confidence of the new breed of Liberal Democrats. Following Clegg's narrow victory over Chris Huhne in the 2007 leadership election, the dominant economic ethos within the new Liberal Democrat parliamentary leadership eased the transition to Gladstonian self-reliance rather than the interventionism encapsulated by Liberal thinkers like Green, Hobhouse and Hobson. As such, *The Orange Book* was critical for lubricating the easy entry of the Liberal Democrats into coalition with the Conservatives – many of whom were surprised to find some common cause on issues of healthcare, pension reform and the environment. Of the ten contributors to *The Orange Book*, eight went on to be part of the coalition government.

Fractures did exist within the parliamentary party. A core group were loyal to the leadership, while a more socially liberal group – backed by a sizeable proportion of grassroots members – largely wore the scars of local battles with the Conservatives (Bale, 2010, 2011). Moreover, Clegg's professionalisation of the party and subsequent grip on internal party institutions meant that any discontent from MPs and grassroots activists did not irrevocably damage policy implementation or threaten the coalition's longevity. So, while leading Liberal Democrat figures shared some common ideological ground with Cameron's Conservatives, others in the party – not to mention a significant proportion of its borrowed, left-leaning vote – saw such ideological coherence as implausible and reasonless. When the reality hit, the political and electoral cost for the Liberal Democrats proved to be immediate and longstanding.

The Liberal Democrats' transition into government coincided with the apparent capture of the party by *The Orange Book* cohort. If David Laws is correct and Clegg's three predecessors as leader all advocated a coalition with Labour, it is hard to escape the conclusion that political agency played a significant role in the party's fortunes. The new cohort of Liberal Democrat parliamentarians and the elite level of the party management facilitated the coalition with the Tories and accepted the main plank of the Conservative economic critique of the New Labour years. A brand that had been built over a generation – the neither left nor right party; Ashdown's ending of equidistance and the cosy Ashdown–Blair 'Project', Kennedy's criticism of New Labour's authoritarianism at home and imperialism abroad; the hostility to student tuition fees that granted the party a key identifiable policy platform – was suddenly and irreversibly sacrificed by entry into government with the Conservatives. At a stroke, the Liberal Democrats became dependent on the success of the joint venture, and their enthusiastic adoption of it proved problematic. Structurally, the party might have had little option but to enter the coalition and make it work, but political agency was critical to the way that it played out although the party was slow to recognise this. British politics was very difficult in the aftermath of the 2008 financial crisis, but for the Liberal Democrats it quickly became impossible.

Getting the coalition wrong: the agreement

With neither main party able to get an overall majority in 2010, the resulting hung parliament seemingly placed the Liberal Democrats in a position of considerable bargaining strength. It was the 'kingmaker' – the only one of the three main parties that was in a position to negotiate a coalition agreement with either of the other two. Given its third-party status, this scenario had been discussed in excruciating detail by members and activists for decades. In a post-coalition interview, Clegg stressed that the Liberal Democrats had prepared well in advance – establishing a core group of negotiators (Alexander, Huhne, Laws and Stunell) – for the prospect of coalition and the wide range of scenarios (Thornton and Kidney-Bishop, 2018). Yet, remarking on the chain of events, others painted a different picture. As Harvey (2015: 36) notes, 'the Conservatives were so much better prepared for the hung parliament than we were ... the "big offer" was far from spontaneous: it had been well rehearsed and was carefully choreographed'. Negotiations took place at a rapid pace and in the early hours of 12 May, less than a week after the general election, the Liberal Democrats approved the coalition agreement. One group of scholars concluded that while both parties managed to shoehorn in their own priority policies, the agreement as a whole was closer to the Liberal Democrats' policy positions than to the Conservatives' (Quinn *et al.*, 2011). Nevertheless, given the leverage at their disposal, it quickly became clear that the Liberal Democrats had undersold their bargaining position. The party was outmanoeuvred and agreed to the Conservative narrative on the substantive issues that mattered.

Entry to the coalition represented a clear shift within the party. A place was found in the Treasury team for the co-editor of *The Orange Book,* David Laws, rather than for Liberal Democrat Treasury spokesman Vince Cable. More importantly, in order to form the coalition in the first place, the Liberal Democrat leadership had to undergo a dramatic change of heart over their instinctive approach to economic management. This precipitated the Liberal Democrats' rapid conversion to austerity politics. In common with Labour before the 2010 election, the Liberal Democrats had warned of the dangers of cutting too much too early from the deficit and thereby triggering a double-dip recession.

Within days of the election, however, the Liberal Democrats abandoned this position. The joint statement *Coalition Programme for Government* of 11 May 2010 made it clear that the Liberal Democrats' official view of the need for and timing of spending cuts had transformed dramatically. Apparently convinced by the Eurozone crisis and the desire to avoid a Greek-style economic collapse, the narrative of economic stability became the key theme of the coalition discussions. Putting forward a united front was deemed urgent to reassure the markets and prevent a run on sterling. In *The Coalition: Our Programme for Government* (HM Government 2010: 15) the two partner parties agreed a common line:

> The Parties agree that deficit reduction and continuing to ensure economic recovery is the most urgent issue facing Britain. We have therefore agreed that there will need to be: a *significantly accelerated reduction in the structural deficit* over the course of a parliament, with the main burden of deficit reduction borne by reduced spending rather than increased taxation; arrangements that will *protect those on low incomes from the effects of public sector pay constraint* and other spending constraints; and protection of jobs *by stopping Labour's proposed* jobs tax.

Both parties were in accord on the need to cut the budget deficit straightaway. Clegg even stressed that 'deficit reduction and political reform were to be the two main pillars of the coalition policy agenda' (Laws, 2016: 11). Austerity would be harder and faster than even the Conservatives had pledged before the election. It was not the last time that the Liberal Democrats would succumb to the Conservative view. The junior partner was now on board with one of the coalition government's core themes – austerity. As the government moved on, it became clear that the Liberal Democrats were enmeshed in the rhetoric of financial probity and spending cuts. David Laws' time at the Treasury was short-lived but his replacement, Danny Alexander, seemed equally committed to reigning in public spending. Critically, the Liberal Democrats failed to appreciate the damage that the optics of the early days of coalition was doing to the party brand in the country. Spending cut after spending cut was announced by the coalition, and in the brave new world of collective responsibility and cooperation, many were announced by Liberal Democrat ministers. Between them, Laws and Alexander in particular, but the Liberal Democrats in general, became the poster boys for austerity. Voters who instinctively agreed with these measures were unlikely to become Liberal Democrat converts because of their association with them but it was distinctly possible that those who were against would find it impossible to forgive the Liberal Democrats for their part in the programme of cuts.

The coalition agreement covered 11 major policy areas, including the spending review for the NHS and schools, tax measures, banking reform, immigration, political reform, pensions and welfare, education, the EU, civil liberties and the environment. Before the negotiations concluded, Cameron set out four 'red lines' – immediate action to reduce the budget deficit, maintaining a strong national defence (including maintaining the Trident nuclear deterrent system), not being 'soft' on immigration and no further transfer of powers to the EU. All were secured by the Conservatives in the final agreement. The Liberal Democrats prioritised fairer taxes, a greener economy, a pupil premium and political and electoral reform. Here the Liberal Democrats did secure some notable successes on capital gains tax (albeit this was watered down from the 2010 manifesto pledge), raising the tax allowance, pension reform and the pupil premium, although this was to be funded out of existing rather than new budgets as the Liberal Democrats had originally pledged. Other election proposals such as the mansion tax did not make it into the agreement, while abolishing identity cards was already very much in line with 'Cameron Conservative' thinking. Electoral reform proved a sticking point. The Conservatives initially proposed a committee of enquiry, but this was rejected out of hand by the Liberal Democrats. To puncture negotiations with Labour, the Conservatives then proposed a referendum on AV (the 'alternative vote' system) to replace the first-past-the-post electoral system. The Conservatives' u-turn reveals just how much influence the Liberal Democrats had (Quinn et al., 2011). Yet, the Liberal Democrats still managed to underplay their hand significantly, by accepting the concession and abandoning their manifesto preference for the proportional 'single transferable vote' system. This came back to embarrass the Liberal Democrats in the subsequent referendum when the 'No to AV' campaign quoted Nick Clegg describing the AV electoral system before the 2010 general election as a 'miserable little compromise' (Grice, 2010).

In order to secure the coalition agreement quickly, the two negotiating teams concocted pragmatic solutions to overcome policy areas where there were sincere differences. One thorny issue was tuition fees. Here the parties agreed to wait for the Browne review, which was due to report in October 2010. The agreement allowed Liberal Democrat MPs to abstain in any vote to increase tuition fees. This fell along way short of the Liberal Democrats' pre-election pledge to phase out tuition fees and vote against any increase. Other reviews were used on control orders for terror suspects and on stamp duty threshold to ensure the smooth and fast passage of the agreement. So while the Liberal Democrats did achieve some small victories, on the substantive issues of crime, defence and security the Conservatives gave up very little. Meanwhile, despite being in a pivotal position to 'call the shots', the Liberal Democrats conceded ground in a number of areas where they had cultivated a distinctive policy identity. By swallowing the hitherto Conservative-only narrative on the need for urgent spending cuts, the Liberal Democrats inadvertently tied themselves to the austerity label, and this was to haunt them for much of the decade.

Getting the coalition wrong: portfolios

The Liberal Democrats' status as the junior partner in the coalition was emphatically confirmed by the distribution of portfolios in the coalition government in 2010. Browne and Franklin (1973) developed the concept of the 'parity norm', whereby coalition partners should expect to receive the same percentage share of ministries as their share of the seats in parliament. Verzichelli (2008) provided many reasons not to expect such a proportional division of cabinet portfolios to junior partners in coalitions. Yet the Liberal Democrats were in fact slightly over-represented around the cabinet table. The Conservatives had 307 MPs, the Liberal Democrats 57 – 15.7 per cent of the seats in the House of Commons – but received a disproportionate presence in government with 17.2 per cent of the attendees at cabinet. In all, the Liberal Democrats held 23 of the posts in government – 17 ministers (one unpaid), three whips in the Commons and thee whips in the House of Lords (two of which were unpaid). In this respect at least the Liberal Democrats did well. Furthermore, as the two parties issued a common statement of policy intent, the Liberal Democrats managed to set a sizeable chunk of the administrative agenda for the new regime. Nevertheless, the prioritisation of deficit reduction trumped Liberal Democrat victories in lower-profile areas such as the pupil premium, which seemed insignificant compared with the abandonment of the party's opposition to student tuition fees.

The construction of a coalition government is rather like the assembly of an orchestra. In the playing of the symphony, attention will be paid to individual soloists, but the tone is set by the conductor's interpretation of the composer. The Liberal Democrats seemed to settle for a prominent place in all of the sections of the coalition orchestra but failed to secure a soloist. Nor did the party decide to concentrate its musicians into the string, woodwind, brass or percussion sections. Unlike the experience of junior partners in other coalitions, the Liberal Democrats were involved in the totality of government. This is in marked contrast to the well-known tactics of, for example, the German Free Democratic Party (FDP), whose leader, Hans-Deitrich Genscher, served as Federal Minister for Foreign Affairs from 1974 to 1992 in coalitions with both Christian Democrats and Social Democrats. Similarly, Sinn Fein had long identified the education portfolio of any power-sharing agreement in Northern Ireland (in the end, when Sinn Fein finally entered a power-sharing administration in Northern Ireland with the Democratic Unionist Party, it was given four portfolios to oversee, including education). This tactic in coalition-building sees the junior partner hope that it can create a distinctive set of policies in a specific arena without being engulfed in the detail of government machinery.

In contrast, the Liberal Democrats were placed in almost every department, but individual Liberal Democrat ministers were usually on their own. The Department of Business, Innovation and Skills (BIS) became the most Liberal Democrat ministry, as Vince Cable became Secretary for State and Ed Davey was made Under-Secretary. However, even in BIS, Liberal Democrats were outnumbered by five Conservative junior ministers. The advantage for the Liberal Democrats of being embedded in so many ministries was that they could apparently get early warning of Conservative plans. The acid test for this hypothesis came in 2013, when the Home Office, under the direction of Theresa May, began to embark on the 'hostile environment' for illegal immigrants. In a high-profile – and highly controversial – measure, the Home Office sent advertising vans around neighbourhoods with high rates of immigration to urge those who were in the UK illegally to 'go home or face arrest'. The Liberal Democrat minister in the Home Office, Jeremy

Browne, was sacked for his failure to block the vans. If the master plan was to keep an eye on the unpalatable plans of the coalition partner, the mechanism was either faulty in practice or ineffective in execution.

As much as the construction of the coalition gave the Liberal Democrats an impressive range of coverage in the government, there was a partisan disadvantage around the distribution of portfolios. The Conservatives mostly placed their big players in the departments they had shadowed in opposition – 14 of the Conservatives in or attending cabinet were given responsibility corresponding to their opposition role. On the other hand, all of the Liberal Democrats given a cabinet portfolio were assigned different briefs from those they had had responsibility for in the Liberal Democrat shadow cabinet. To continue the orchestra analogy, the Liberal Democrat ministers had to quickly learn a new instrument, and some who may have fancied themselves as virtuoso violinists were told to play the tuba.

One of the 'big wins' for the Liberal Democrats was the installing of Nick Clegg as Deputy Prime Minister (DPM). Clegg oversaw the political reform programme, but given that the coalition could not function unless both sides agreed, the DPM role had a much wider brief. Alongside the DPM veto – reading, processing and approving papers simultaneously with the Prime Minister (Thornton and Kidney-Bishop, 2018) – Clegg had to be fully consulted before any reallocation of posts and possessed the exclusive right to nominate Liberal Democrat MPs to fill cabinet positions. He was a core member of the 'Quad' – alongside Cameron, Alexander and Osborne – which informally met to resolve disputes and ensure the smooth running of the coalition. Clegg was also Chair of the Home Affairs Cabinet Committee and Vice Chair of the National Security Council. Yet he committed a major error by not bulking up his DPM operation from day one. Clegg's office was greatly under-resourced and under-staffed during the crucial first year of the coalition. As a consequence, Clegg 'lost precious time and political momentum' as he battled the Whitehall machinery (Thornton and Kidney-Bishop, 2018). While Clegg brought in advisers and staff as the coalition progressed, his obscurity in the early part of the coalition, when he was forced to be 'fighting fires' and immersed in policy, allowed the Conservatives to grab the initiative on dictating the politics of the coalition and presenting it to the wider public.

Meanwhile, Vince Cable – the party's strongest electoral asset (as its shadow Chancellor) – was made Secretary of State at Business, Innovation and Skills (BIS). David Laws – the party's Children, Schools and Families spokesperson – was made Chief Secretary to the Treasury, although an expenses scandal quickly forced him out of government, to be replaced by Danny Alexander. Chris Huhne was made Energy and Climate Change Secretary (his Liberal Democrat brief had been Home Affairs) and Danny Alexander was originally made Scottish Secretary – although his elevation to Chief Secretary to the Treasury opened up this post to Michael Moore, the party's International Development spokesperson. The Liberal Democrats did not get any of the big offices of state or full control of any ministries. Initially this was framed as a positive. Avoiding the 'hornets' nest' of the Home Office and high-profile roles (Secretary of State) in ministries such as Health, Education and Welfare meant that the Liberal Democrats did not have to implement the deep spending cuts directly. Ultimately, though, it backfired. First, it meant that the Liberal Democrats were unable to demonstrate delivery in an explicit manner to the electorate. Second, the premise of avoiding any control of these ministries assumes that voters could distinguish which party ran which ministry and as such would be more forgiving of the Liberal Democrats, given their 'bit part' role. The reality was different. Voters, particularly those on the centre-left who donated the Liberal Democrats their vote in the 2010 election, were unable to make that distinction and framed the Liberal Democrats as enablers of spending cuts.

The party leadership's decision to have the Liberal Democrat figures spread thinly in different portfolios across government was an error of judgement. It simply reduced their ability to showcase their governing ability and allow voters to distinguish between the parties on competence and delivery. Negotiating complete control of departments such as Education would have enhanced issue ownership and cemented party policy identity. It would have been possible to hold ministerial positions outside cabinet, thus enabling the Liberal Democrats to develop a distinctive policy platform and a track record that they could sell to voters, as well as a distinct voice from the Conservatives on policies that they had little or no influence over (Cutts and Russell, 2015; Russell, 2010). The party gambled that by prioritising deficit reduction and ensuring strong government it would be rewarded for the 'putting the nation first' and benefit from any economic recovery that followed. The strategy backfired, undermined by errors of judgement, inconsistent and disjointed presentation of the coalition, and a naivety in misreading the politics. All this diluted any prospect of the party gaining credit for policy successes and avoiding blame for failures.

Getting the coalition wrong: presentation and messaging

One of the consequences of the portfolio allocation was that the Conservatives controlled the 'big' offices of state. While the Liberal Democrats had to rubber-stamp policy decisions, the Conservatives dictated the agenda. However, the public image was somewhat different. Starting with Cameron and Clegg in the Rose Garden, the coalition was portrayed as an equal partnership. While Conservative MPs bemoaned the formation of the coalition and expressed their frustration at not achieving an overall majority, the Liberal Democrats talked up the positives and depicted an exuberance of being in government. As well as setting the tone for the next five years, the coalition agreement, as Clegg noted, came to be regarded more as a blueprint for Liberal Democrats to consult rather than a roadmap.

The party was also keen to stress how it had managed to get 75 per cent of its manifesto proposals into the coalition agreement (Huntbach, 2015; Laws, 2016;

Thornton and Kidney-Bishop, 2018), although scholarly evidence suggests the true figure was much lower (Quinn *et al.*, 2011). Selling the 'equal partnership' narrative early reflected the desire to exaggerate Liberal Democrat influence and gain credit for policy success. However, the leadership's complete 'buy-in' to the coalition framing and discourse backfired. The Liberal Democrats were instead inextricably tied to the coalition discourse and the policies, many of which, like deeper deficit reduction and public sector cuts, they had hitherto opposed. More importantly, the public did not buy the Liberal Democrats' presentation of the coalition. Eight months after it had taken office, a YouGov poll found that 61 per cent predicted it would be bad for the Liberal Democrats, and less than a quarter thought it would be positive. With the party haemorrhaging support, a similar YouGov poll found that 74 per cent of ex-Liberal Democrat supporters felt that the party had little or no influence on decisions taken in government (Pring, 2011). Rather than a blueprint for government, the reality was that Clegg and his fellow Liberal Democrat ministers were increasingly hamstrung by the coalition agreement. Exaggerating the 'equal partnership' undermined their attempt to walk the tightrope of being both an advocate and critic of coalition policies while occupying a distinctive policy space to the Conservatives. Perceived capitulation on manifesto commitments by a sizeable proportion of its 2010 voters meant that the Liberal Democrats 'wore the coalition badge'. As the coalition proceeded, Clegg and other senior Liberal Democrats began to distance themselves from unpopular policies and stress the party's policy successes. The success of that strategy, though belated, seems to be backed by some circumstantial polling evidence. In early 2013, 42 per cent of those asked in a Lord Ashcroft poll stated that they would more likely support the Liberal Democrats if they put forward policies that set them apart from the Conservatives (Ashcroft, 2013). Nonetheless, inconsistencies in tone, rhetoric and presentation of the coalition risked leaving the electorate confused and dismissive of the Liberal Democrats' role and influence.

Signs of tension first emerged when Vince Cable attacked Cameron's immigration remarks in April 2011, and then during the AV referendum campaign, which the Liberal Democrats comprehensively lost (the referendum result was 68 per cent against change and 32 per cent for AV). During that campaign, the Liberal Democrats – particularly Clegg himself – came under relentless attack from senior Conservatives involved in the 'No to AV' campaign. Former leader Paddy Ashdown accused Cameron and the Conservatives, who predominantly funded the 'No to AV' campaign, of reneging on a private agreement about the way in which the campaign would be conducted. Ashdown stated that this was not only a 'breach of faith' but also potentially damaging for the coalition (BBC News, 2011). Tensions became increasingly public as senior Liberal Democrats condemned the targeting of Clegg in 'No to AV' leaflets, and the exaggerated claims about the cost of implementing AV (Seawright, 2013). Huhne, for instance, at one stage threatened to sue Conservative cabinet members for peddling mistruths (Gibbon, 2011). Disputes then spilled over to House of Lords reform as Cameron dropped proposals to make it largely elected following a rebellion of Conservative MPs. The Liberal Democrats accused their coalition partner of 'not honouring their commitment … and breaking the coalition agreement' (Cutts and Russell, 2015) and withdrew their support for boundary changes – a Conservative manifesto pledge that was included in the coalition agreement. As Liberal Democrats' electoral prospects worsened, the rhetoric from senior party figures became more negative as they sought to distance themselves from the Conservatives. At the party conference in September 2013, Cable attacked the Conservatives' policies on immigration, the economy and Europe, accusing them of 'ugly and blinkered politics' and 'scapegoating the unions, benefit claimants and ethnic minorities to achieve their objectives' (BBC News, 2013). While Clegg's speech a few days later struck a more conciliatory tone, he talked up areas in which the Liberal Democrats had challenged the Conservatives, including cuts to inheritance tax for millionaires, profit-making in schools, firing workers without reason and ditching the Human Rights Act.

Sparring between the two parties became more heated as the 2015 general election loomed. The coalition fault line was most prominent on the economy. In early 2014, Chancellor George Osborne announced a five-point plan to mend the UK's budget deficit, which included £62 billion of public spending cuts over the next four years, with £25 billion of cuts in the first two years of the next parliament. Clegg openly attacked the plan as a 'monumental mistake' that was ideologically driven to cut back the state. Clegg stressed that the plan would place the burden on the 'narrowest shoulders' given that £12 billion of the £25 billion would be taken from those dependent on welfare. In a glimpse of the Liberal Democrats' 2015 election campaign strategy, Clegg bemoaned that 'You've got an agenda on the right which appears to believe in cuts for cuts' sake, and an agenda on the left which believes in spending for spending's sake' (Channel 4 News, 2014). As the rift on the economy grew bigger, other senior Liberal Democrats similarly attempted to dissociate the party from the Conservative plans. Part of the strategy was to label them as ideological and stress that their coalition partners had a policy of 'austerity forever'. The goal was to contrast this with the Liberal Democrats, who accepted deficit reduction only as a necessary evil that should not unduly impact the most vulnerable (Wintour, 2014). However, this increasingly proved difficult to sell. The party had supported the coalition's economic policies early on and now risked not acquiring the full credit for its role and influence, just when those policies were beginning to bear fruit (Cutts and Russell, 2015). This ultimately led to a parting of the ways on the economy just two months before polling day. While Osborne talked up the Liberal Democrats' involvement in the final coalition budget – increasing the personal tax allowance; tax-raising measures such as reducing the maximum size of pension pots and increasing the bank levy – the Liberal Democrats' Alexander unveiled a 'yellow budget' the following day, which stressed the party's differences with the Conservatives. While the Liberal Democrats signed up to the Conservative plan for 2015, the yellow budget put forward a different deficit-reduction strategy, one that favoured higher taxes for the wealthy over spending cuts. The event was ridiculed by the press and the opposition alike, who revelled in pointing out that the party had voted for the coalition budget and then delivered its own budget 24 hours later (Dathan, 2015).

The mixed messaging and incoherent presentation of the coalition and their role in it had broader consequences for the Liberal Democrats. Despite the narrative that the party was blamed for the coalition failures and not credited for the successes, evidence from the BES suggests that for most of the electorate the Liberal Democrats' role was largely immaterial. Moreover, following the u-turn on VAT, broken promises on tuition fees and support for tougher austerity measures, much of the electorate did not know what the party stood for. In October 2014, public relations firm Edelman found that only 25 per cent could correctly link the Liberal Democrats with its key policies (Bennett, 2014). Worryingly for the Liberal Democrats, less than one-fifth thought that the policy of increasing the tax threshold to £12,500 was a Liberal Democrat initiative, while more than third of voters thought it was a Conservative policy. Similarly, more than two-fifths of those asked thought that increasing tax on high-value properties was a Labour initiative, while less than a quarter correctly identified it as Liberal Democrat policy. Evidence from the BES found that Liberal Democrat priorities such as the pupil premium or raising the tax threshold enjoyed public support – but either lacked issue salience or were perceived by a sizeable number as being Conservative or Labour initiatives. The dire consequences of mixed messaging became increasingly apparent. The Liberal Democrats did not own any of the salient issues, struggled to hold on to their own priorities and generally lacked a policy direction that chimed with the electorate (Cutts and Russell, 2015).

Getting the coalition wrong: misreading the politics

Critically, while the coalition remained relatively popular among certain sections of the public, it was the Conservatives who reaped most of the rewards. The Liberal Democrats were far from unique in getting the rough end of the deal in electoral terms as junior partners. German Chancellor Angela Merkel famously (if inaccurately) said that the little party always suffers from coalition. Nevertheless, the extent to which the Conservatives got the credit for the successes of the coalition, and the Liberal Democrats the blame for its failures, was remarkable.

Some of this was structural. Having abandoned the anti-Conservative alliance that recruited many Labour identifiers to tactically vote Liberal Democrat, the party were bound to suffer a loss of support from contingent Labour supporters. Similarly, the anti-politics, 'none of the above' vote that the Liberal Democrats had benefited from in successive elections was suddenly gone. Political choices made by the party exacerbated its predicament. In other words, agency was crucial. Most obviously, the Liberal Democrats suffered from a loss of identity on entering the coalition, not just as an outsider party precluded from its fair share of news and power by a skewed electoral and political system, but also because of the compromises it had made in the policy arena.

The Browne review of funding for higher education (HE) recommended that university tuition fees needed to be increased sharply in order to sustain high rates of HE provision in England. The coalition government accepted the proposals and universities chose to triple student tuition fees, from £3,000 to £9,000, though the establishment of the Office for Students was designed to broaden access, to include students from traditionally disadvantaged backgrounds. This was a huge problem for the Liberal Democrats. Opposition to tuition fees had been a key part of their campaign in both the 2005 and the 2010 general elections – despite an attempt by the leadership to overturn the policy. In the weeks, months and years after the coalition permitted the tripling of tuition fees, dozens of photos of Liberal Democrat MPs standing next to placards proclaiming their opposition to fees were reproduced by opponents. The problem with the tuition fee u-turn was that it spoke to the special nature of Liberal Democrat support. It exposed the lack of genuine commitment to the cause. The Liberal Democrats were seemingly so bereft of a policy identity that losing control of one of the few policy arenas which the public largely viewed as distinctive and popular was unfortunate to say the least. The arguments about the pros and cons of the replacement scheme were insufficient to address the damage that the issue did to Liberal Democrat credibility. Suddenly the party that had placed so much emphasis on overcoming the 'no one knows what they stand for' obstacle was now accused of selling out on a key policy promise at the first opportunity.

Clegg even acknowledged the damage this had caused to the party's image. In 2012 he issued a fulsome apology for the u-turn (Wintour and Mulholland, 2012): 'We shouldn't have made a promise we weren't absolutely sure we could deliver'. The wording was telling: the apology was for the party having endorsed a policy that it was not really committed to, rather than apologising for the new policy (which, though unpopular, was still deemed to be an improvement). As a piece of damage limitation, the apology – and its viral variants on social media – was novel but ineffective. The public now associated the Liberal Democrats with something distinctive – the betrayal of their promises.

This routinised trope was even used by Conservative campaigners in the 2011 referendum on the voting system. Those opposing electoral reform used pictures of Cameron and Clegg outside Number 10. The message was that any system that tended to produce more coalitions would lead to more unscrupulous politicians. Clegg and the Liberal Democrats were now shorthand for the betrayal of trust. This portent of how the Conservatives would turn so effectively against their coalition partners was instructive – and apparently disgusted the Liberal Democrat hierarchy. In 2015, the Conservatives were able to turn this to their advantage by defeating many Liberal Democrats in order to win an unexpected majority.

Two of the strangest facets of the Liberal Democrat decline in the coalition years were its sheer magnitude and velocity. The party's decline developed a special characteristic all of its own – a kind of losers' momentum, founded in structure and agency. Structurally, the party was bound to find it difficult after 2010. Indeed, the 2010 election performance was already a sign that the party's electoral wave had passed its high point. A party that had surged in popularity during the time of an unpopular Conservative opposition to a Labour government that was alienating key swathes of its own support was always going to struggle under a Conservative revival led by the moderniser David Cameron. The Liberal Democrat vote was squeezed from Tory sympathisers who saw their party return with a prospect of power for the first time in 13 years, and from Labour loyalists who were susceptible to the party's plea that every vote mattered to prevent the return of a Tory government. This political stranglehold was significant but secondary to the structural problem of being marginalised in too many close contests. Being placed a distant second or third in too many seats meant the Liberal Democrats could never cash in on Clegg's apparent popularity. Furthermore, the party's local/national campaigning strategy had run its course in the early twenty-first century. The Liberal Democrats simply could not continue to function as a series of franchise units across Britain – eventually, the lack of consistent messaging would take its toll on Liberal Democrat candidates in all scenarios. This erosion of support was already evident in 2010 and the Liberal Democrats were losing votes to other parties. By 2015, the Liberal Democrat container ship was holed below the water line and the party seemed powerless to resist the forces working against it.

Perhaps the most surprising thing about the decline of the Liberal Democrats in the 2010s was how surprised they were about it. A party that had slowly grown out of community-based activism in the 1960s and then cashed in on drawing electoral support from unpopular parties in different local contexts was due an inevitable fall-back after entering coalition with one of those parties. Labour voters who had lent conditional, tactical support to the Liberal Democrats and those Labour supporters who voted Liberal Democrat in protest at Labour's neo-liberal, authoritarian policies were always going to be a difficult market for the Liberal Democrats once the party had governed with the Conservatives. All the Liberal Democrats could do with these voters was to wait it out and hope that the party's coalition record would be good enough to win some of them back. However, the party leadership must have known deep down that many of these voters would be lost – particularly when Labour's reaction to losing power (just as it had been in 1951 and 1979) was to veer to the left and back to those same voters. Meanwhile, those Conservatives who had lent support to the Liberal Democrats in the recognition that their brand of one-nation Toryism had been in abeyance during the Hague, Duncan Smith and Howard years saw a revival of their discourse under Cameron. The sheer scope of the Liberal Democrat success in levering so much of the party's manifesto into the coalition agreement may have even been counterproductive. If the Conservative-led administration was ready to cede so much ground on domestic policy and still rule with traditional Tory traits around economic competence, then the internal battle between the one-nation 'wets' and the economic right must have been settled. The coalition gave many of those looking for an excuse to return to the Conservatives a reason to repatriate and the Liberal Democrats seemed to miscalculate how many would be drawn back to the Tories by the *process* of coalition. The Liberal Democrats were forced into the political equivalent of being placed between a rock and a hard place: either the Conservatives were reasonable people who could be persuaded to govern responsibly with a little moderation (in which case, why did this moderation have to come from the Liberal Democrats?) or they remained an instinctively untrustworthy force saved only by the presence of the Liberal Democrats in coalition. The political dilemma for the Liberal Democrats was that the voters who believed the former now saw little reason not to vote for the Conservatives, while those who believed the latter were angry that the Liberal Democrats had put the Tories back into power in the first place.

Bleak though this analysis was for the Liberal Democrats, their problem was deeper still. A third group of voters – Conservative loyalists, the ideological neo-liberals, Thatcherites and Eurosceptics, many of whom were the driving force behind the organisation of the rank-and-file activist party – were angry at the coalition (and maybe even at the Tory leadership, who had failed to deliver a Conservative majority). For them, the Liberal Democrats were ruining the Conservative programme. The Liberal Democrats emphatically misread the room here. This group included many activists who had spent time campaigning for Conservative candidates who were defeated by Liberal Democrats in the 2010 election. It also included many winning Conservative MPs who, after years in opposition, suddenly saw their own career progression blocked by the arrival of Liberal Democrats in government. For both these groups, the Liberal Democrats were every bit the enemy, perhaps even more so than Labour in terms of the 'ground war' in local and national elections. Cameron complained that the Liberal Democrats were restraining his powers as Prime Minister, telling Tory activists that he was inclined to allow their pet projects (repeal of the Human Rights Act, an end to 'green crap' taxation, a definitive in–out referendum on EU membership) if it were not for their coalition partners. The Liberal Democrats tended to see Cameron's 'little black book' of Liberal Democrat obstacles as a badge of success, but it was also a rallying cry for Tory activists: *If you want a real Conservative government, with Conservative policies driven by Conservative ideals and values, put effort into defeating not just Labour but the Liberal Democrats at the next election.* Furthermore, the electoral geography of the Conservative–Liberal Democrat battleground meant that the Conservative electoral machine had an effective means of delivering victory. Liberal Democrat parliamentary growth from the 1990s to 2010 had been disproportionately at the expense of the Tories. Defending those gains was going to be harder if the Liberal Democrats were simply seen as Conservative spoilers or Tory enablers.

Getting the coalition wrong: 'Cleggfailure' and losers' momentum

From 'Cleggmania' to 'Cleggfailure', the sudden and dramatic fall from grace of the Liberal Democrat leader proved to be a huge political and electoral obstacle that, in the end, the party could not overcome. In the 2010 general election, Clegg took centre-stage as the Liberal Democrats capitalised on his exposure, generated from a highly successful performance in the first of the televised leadership debates. Clegg's personalisation of party policy enabled the Liberal Democrats to court a sizeable number of centre-left voters. Yet his personal standing and credit instantly receded following the decision to enter coalition with the Conservatives. Many of these centre-left tactical switchers who took Clegg at his word became immediately alienated. Rather than being the source of the problem, the tuition fees issue became a symbol of his personal failure (Cutts and Russell, 2015). His actions were seen as duplicitous. Having waxed lyrical about the 'broken promises' of his rivals, Clegg was seen as just as bad, if not worse.

Alongside the tuition fees debacle, Clegg made a series of other high-profile mistakes and gaffes, which damaged his standing with the public and weakened his popularity with some inside his party. For instance, his decision to hold a referendum on the voting system on the same day as local elections and devolved elections in Wales and Scotland to boost turnout badly backfired. As James Gurling, Chair of the Liberal Democrats' Campaigns and Communications Committee, noted in his internal review of the AV referendum, activists were overstretched and fighting on two fronts (Gurling, 2011). They simply could not dedicate enough time to the 'Yes to AV' campaign as they were tied up locally campaigning to save Liberal Democrat seats. Media airtime was predominantly focused on the referendum and the subsequent air war made it difficult for the Liberal Democrats to defend their territory. The Gurling review also noted that even those Conservative voters who were satisfied with the coalition were reluctant to lend support to the Liberal Democrats in marginal seats where they were primarily contesting with Labour, because of the heated nature of the AV debate. Some blamed Clegg outright for the 'failure to devise and lead an effective campaign ... and leaving it in the hands of nonentities with no campaigning experience' (Wilson, 2014).

Clegg's support for the NHS reorganisation bill also heightened public and internal party dissent. The bill was described by the Institute for Government and the King's Fund as 'one of the biggest-ever car crashes in politics and policy-making'; it was not even part of the coalition agreement (it had been devised by Letwin and Alexander in the days following). As Timmins (2012) describes, the emergence of a 'half horse–half donkey policy' as a compromise of different philosophies about the way the NHS should be run inevitably led to a revolt among Liberal Democrats at the party's 2012 spring conference, despite Clegg's insistence that the party had secured major concessions and that the bill should be passed. Critics argued that the reforms did not have a mandate and soundly defeated the Liberal Democrat leadership. It mattered little, as the bill was passed into law in 2012, although internal disputes raged on as activists and some senior MPs tried to force Clegg to repeal the legislation. Once again, the optics looked bad. While Clegg and the leadership team gained concessions and improved the bill, the party got little credit, was blamed by rivals for facilitating the reforms and was saddled with the unpopularity of the outcome.

From the get-go of the coalition, Clegg and the Liberal Democrats were unable to reverse a kind of 'losers' momentum'. After only six months of the coalition, the electorate had made up its mind. The party's poll rating hit 8 per cent in December 2010 and remained consistently low throughout the duration of the coalition government. Disastrous performances at local elections destroyed the Liberal Democrats' councillor and activist base. The party lost more than 1,300 seats in total over the course of the parliament. The Liberal Democrats also lost deposits in 11 of the 19 British by-elections where the party stood candidates and suffered major reversals in elections to the Senedd in Wales and the Scottish Parliament early in the electoral cycle. Even the 2013 by-election victory in Eastleigh revealed a worrying trend. The party polled only 32 per cent of the vote (down 14.4 points on 2010) and won only thanks to the Conservatives and UKIP splitting the opposition vote, despite putting the weight of its whole campaign machine into the seat.

Clegg's collapse in popularity mirrored the Liberal Democrats' electoral woes. In early 2011, a YouGov poll for the *Sunday Times* found that 80 per cent of 2010 Liberal Democrat voters did not trust Clegg to keep his promises (Pring, 2011). A Lord Ashcroft poll in early 2013 found that 20 per cent would be more likely to support the Liberal Democrats if they changed their leader. Crucially, 66 per cent said it would make no difference. Given the importance of the leader in 2010, such voter indifference to who led the Liberal Democrats was a further indication that the party was in serious electoral trouble (Ashcroft, 2013).

With public dismay and internal discontent mounting, Clegg used the 2014 European elections to engage directly with the public and stress his and the party's pro-European credentials to solidify its core support. The strategy backfired. Twice Clegg took on UKIP's Nigel Farage in fiery televised debates and came off second best, which further dented his wider appeal. Given growing public scepticism and restlessness on Europe, Clegg's inability to promote a more radical pro-European platform while simultaneously recognising the need for reform did little to appease voter concerns. The party went on to lose 10 of its 11 MEPs in the 2014 European elections, securing just 7 per cent of the vote. Combined with dire performance in the local elections on the same day, this prompted more than 300 activists to call for Clegg's resignation. Clegg thought about it but was persuaded to stay on (Wintour and Watt, 2015).

Given the factional nature of the parliamentary party, it remained questionable whether alternative candidates could have mustered similar levels of parliamentary support. In practical terms, it was difficult to see just how much difference a change of leader would have made. The Liberal Democrats were already boxed in to the coalition and most potential alternatives (aside from Farron) had government portfolios so were associated with it. The prospects of any renegotiation of the agreement and operation of the coalition would have almost certainly been resisted by Cameron and the Conservatives. Clegg had already begun to attack and distance himself from coalition policies, so simply replacing the leader only for the new incumbent to do the same was unlikely to catapult the Liberal Democrats out of the electoral mire that they found themselves in. Clegg remained, but his time as an electoral asset had passed.

Getting the coalition wrong: the campaign mistakes

So far we have outlined just how badly the Liberal Democrats got the coalition wrong. The collapse in support pre-dated the campaign period for the 2015 general election, but it is possible that a few more seats could have been saved if not for errors and mistakes made during that campaign. One major miscalculation during the coalition was the party reverting to an equidistance stance. Roughly six months out from the election, former Home Office minister Jeremy Browne warned that such a strategy risked putting the party in a 'political no-man's land'. As the campaign approached, 'Orange Bookers' warned about taking a deeply conservative approach while those on the social liberal wing stressed the need for bolder spending commitments. However, following the tuition fees debacle, Clegg appeared to be much restrained and reiterated the party's equidistance stance. Campaign slogans – for example, the Liberal Democrats will 'act as the heart of a Conservative-led government and the head of a Labour one' (Cutts and Russell, 2015) – seemed to confirm that the party's goal was to be a moderating force. Aside from having its vote squeezed, this equidistance stance jeopardised the party's policy uniqueness, as it was now inherently defined in terms of how others behaved (Cutts and Russell, 2015). As Ed Davey said, 'If you're in the middle of the road, you might get run over. We were in the middle of the road without any distinction – we had no visibility jacket on. No one could see us, so we really did get run over' (Wintour and Watt, 2015).

Another key problem with the Liberal Democrats' equidistance stance was that it handed the electoral initiative to the Conservatives. Given the surge of the Scottish National Party (SNP) in Scotland, the Conservatives were able to convincingly sell the possibility of a Labour–SNP administration at Westminster. The Liberal Democrats' adversarial stance towards the Conservatives during the final years of the coalition and their positioning as a moderating force enabled the Conservatives to stress that the Liberal Democrats could join this 'coalition of chaos'. The Conservative message was therefore a simple one: only through a majority Conservative government could voters get stability, decisive leadership and avoid the SNP being a 'backseat driver' in a Labour-led coalition. This countered the Liberal Democrats' strategy of targeting 'soft Tories', namely those who valued economic credibility and security but were worried about the scale of cuts for schools, social care, and law and order outlined in the Conservative manifesto. Winning over this group in seats that the Liberal Democrats were defending against the Conservatives was crucial. Unfortunately, warnings of a 'coalition of chaos' proved to be an effective wedge, splitting Labour and Liberal Democrat voters and spooking many of the 'soft Tory' voters they needed to win over. Alarmed at this turn of events, Clegg told the *Financial Times* that he would not join a coalition with Labour if it involved the SNP (Parker and Stacey, 2015) and then the Liberal Democrats decided to wheel out its own 'fear message', warning of a possible right-wing coalition which it termed BluKip.

This strategy also backfired. As UKIP struggled to win any seats, the likelihood of such a coalition was highly unlikely. It also cemented the Conservative narrative that the best way to obtain stable government and avoid coalitions, whether on the left or right, was to vote Conservative. Potential Conservative–Liberal Democrat waverers shifted over to the Conservatives to ensure a decisive outcome. Once again, the Liberal Democrats had misread the politics and failed to come up with a viable approach to deal with the political consequences of an SNP surge. This eventuality was not unforeseen, given the fallout from the 2014 Scottish independence referendum, yet the Liberal Democrats seemed unprepared for the Conservatives' targeted national messaging. One option was to rule out a coalition with the Conservatives, in the hope of winning back centre-left voters who had lent their support to the party in crucial Liberal Democrat–Conservative battle-grounds in 2010. However, this option seemed implausible given the level of distrust and anger with the Liberal Democrats among this cohort for entering a coalition with the Conservatives in the first place. A second, more realistic option was to rule out any coalition with Labour. At first glance, this seemed tactically astute. It would counter Conservative 'coalition of chaos' arguments and enable the Liberal Democrats to focus on their core message of 'economic credibility with a conscience', tailored to 'soft' Conservative voters. There were, however, three downsides to this. First, it would guarantee that any traction with centre-left voters that did exist would be fully extinguished. Second, it seemed a counterintuitive sell to the electorate, given that the Liberal Democrats had spent the final years of the coalition distancing themselves from (and in some cases publicly opposing) Conservative proposals. Third, it remained unclear how committing to a potential second coalition with the Conservatives would have been received by Liberal Democrat members. Put simply, such a strategy risked deepening existing divides along 'Orange Book' lines and sparking huge internal anger among loyal social liberal activists and members. The prospect of civil war in the party would have damaged the party's reputation and given ammunition to the Conservatives and Labour, allowing them to label the Liberal Democrats as unfit for public office. Placed in a 'no-win' situation, the Liberal Democrats chose to occupy the middle ground and subsequently got damaged on both sides.

Serious questions were raised about how the campaign had been run and conducted. As we allude to later in the book, the Liberal Democrats battled internal problems with their new Connect database and system of canvassing classification. Moreover, there were questions about how the use of key performance indicators to determine where resources were allocated actually worked out in practice. Perhaps a more significant contributory factor was the bungled restructuring of staff at party headquarters midway through the coalition. The proposed removal of geographically based staff was designed to place a greater emphasis on performance monitoring rather than on collaboration with seats. The proposals were watered down after internal protests but some key campaign activities – including responsibility for deriving/writing/artwork/branding literature for the region (and for key targets) – became the responsibility of the national campaign organisers rather than regional campaign directors. During the fallout, many experienced, dedicated and skilled organisers left the party, which undoubtedly had an impact on how campaigns in target seats were run and operationalised. More broadly, the electoral context exposed the deficiencies of the campaign strategy, tactics and messaging in defensive situations and reinforced the ever-decreasing campaign advantage that the party had over its opponents.

The electoral catastrophe of 2015

Obliteration, electoral meltdown, complete collapse were just some of the election-night headlines used to describe the Liberal Democrats' performance on 7 May 2015. Despite the travails of coalition government, few commentators, pundits, journalists or political science scholars predicted the scale of the collapse. In Chapter 8, we discuss the end of the Liberal Democrats' old electoral geography and examine why incumbency and personal standing failed to save party. However, it is worth briefly reflecting here on the scale of the collapse, given the long-term electoral damage it caused.

The final outcome made grim reading for the erstwhile third party in British politics. Across Britain, the Liberal Democrats polled 2.4 million votes, a drop of 4.4 million from 2010, and received just 8.1 per cent of the final poll, a fall of 15.5 percentage points. Nationally, the Liberal Democrats were pushed into fourth place by UKIP. Of the 57 parliamentary seats it held in 2010, the Liberal Democrats retained only eight in 2015. In England, the party held on to Carshalton and Wallington, Leeds North West, Norfolk North, Sheffield Hallam, Southport and Westmorland and Lonsdale. The party held onto one of its three seats in Wales – Ceredigion – and one of the 11 seats it held in Scotland – Orkney and Shetland. The collapse left the Liberal Democrats with eight MPs, its lowest number for 45 years. The Liberal Democrats had gone from the minor coalition partner in government to the joint fourth largest party in Westminster with the Democratic Unionists. The party failed to increase its vote in any of the 631 constituencies where it put up a candidate, and 341 candidates lost their deposits. To put this into context, no Liberal Democrat candidates lost their deposit in 2010, and the party had lost only 26 deposits since 1992.

In England, the Liberal Democrats saw their share of the vote decline from 24.2 per cent in 2010 to 8.2 per cent in 2015. Here the party only won six seats, 37 fewer than in 2010, as their vote collapsed everywhere. The Liberal Democrats' share of the vote fell most in England and least in Scotland. In the latter, their vote fell by 11.3 percentage points, but this did not prevent them from losing 10 of their 11 parliamentary seats. In Wales, the decline in vote share was less dramatic than in England, but mainly because of floor effects. Because the party's vote across Wales was concentrated in particular constituencies, in many others it was arithmetically not possible to fall by the national swing, hence the drop of 13.6 percentage points.

The brutal reality of the Liberal Democrats' electoral collapse is most starkly illustrated at the constituency level. Aside from retaining eight seats, it obtained second place in 63 seats, came third in a further 36 and fourth in 338 parliamentary constituencies. The party lost more support in seats where its vote prior to 2015 was strongest. To illustrate this, in the 155 seats where the Liberal Democrats polled less in 2010 than the national swing against them in 2015, it was mathematically impossible for them to lose any more support. In those seats where the Liberal Democrats polled 15.5 per cent or less in 2010, support dropped by 10.2 percentage points. In the 340 constituencies where the Liberal Democrats polled between 15.5 per cent and 30 per cent in 2010, the party saw a 15.8 percentage point drop in its vote. Where the Liberal Democrats polled best in 2010 (30 per cent or more, in 136 seats), the party's share of the vote declined by an average of 19.9 points. The Liberal Democrats were back to the levels of the 1970s, and were only around 25,000 votes from being completely wiped out.

Summary

Liberal Democrat electoral fortunes have always been dictated by the popularity of the party's rivals. During the early 2010s, it was also at the mercy of events: from the fallout from the financial crisis and the Scottish referendum to the broader 'hollowing out' of the centre ground in politics as parts of the electorate sought solace from the speed of social change and railed against perceived cultural threat. Going into coalition was an opportunity for the Liberal Democrats to take control of their own destiny. It was never without risk, but it provided a chance for the party to cement a distinct identity and reinvigorate its brand through the ownership of policy areas and keeping promises set out in the 2010 manifesto. In other words, it was an opportunity to fundamentally weaken the structural barriers that it had struggled against for more than 80 years. The truth is that the Liberal Democrats failed. Coalition with the Conservatives was always going to alienate those who supported the party on an anti-Conservative ticket. Through their own mistakes, the Liberal Democrats exacerbated the problem and cultivated widespread disaffection. By accepting the Conservatives' economic narrative, they became austerity enablers. By breaking promises, they became loathed and distrusted. By supporting Conservative policies, albeit as part of the agreed coalition compromise, they became assailants. Policy successes were overlooked and successful efforts at watering down Conservative proposals were ignored. For sizeable numbers of the electorate who felt misled by their coalescence with the Conservatives, they became 'Yellow Tories'. For others, they were neither loved nor loathed – just irrelevant. The 2015 electoral collapse left the party devoid of credibility and even after Clegg's political demise still beholden to a rump of economic liberal pro-coalition Westminster MPs. The old faces associated with the coalition still held sway, and this held back any repositioning of the party and consistently reminded weary voters of their coalition record. This legacy reduced the party to electoral rubble and proved a millstone round its neck in its attempts to recover. For elections to come it dominated the discourse on the Liberal Democrats, made worse by the party's haphazard (and in some cases reluctant) efforts to heal the wounds. The Liberal Democrats' innate capacity for self-harm did not recede.

4

Where did all the Liberal Democrat voters go?

It was on a Tuesday afternoon of 12 May 2010 when David Cameron and Nick Clegg entered the Downing Street rose garden for a press conference to announce the first UK peacetime coalition government since 1945. Despite the smiles, jokes and talk of a 'new politics', many of those who voted for the party five days earlier were less than impressed. Then after barely one month in coalition, Liberal Democrat support began to haemorrhage. By the end of 2010 it hit its electoral floor where it remained stuck until the 2015 general election, with inevitable disastrous consequences. Within 25,000 votes from electoral wipe-out, the Liberal Democrats were ruthlessly transported from power to political and electoral obscurity, fighting for their very existence.

In this chapter we explore the party in coalition and seek to explain the collapse in support. We focus on the symbiotic relationship between two broad explanations: what we term the Liberal Democrats' 'coalition legacy' and how this laid bare the underlying structural weaknesses in the party's support. Crucially we stress how going into coalition with the Conservatives betrayed a core group of those who voted for the Liberal Democrats in 2010. Furthermore, we argue that this effect was almost immediate. Twelve months after going into coalition, the Liberal Democrats were reduced to a core rump of longstanding partisans. The die was cast and they were never to recover. High-profile policy u-turns and support for austerity measures reinforced the sense of betrayal and deception. Any possibility of rebuilding the 2010 Liberal Democrats' voting alliance during the lifetime of the coalition government quickly became untenable. As the junior partner in the coalition, the Liberal Democrats struggled to get public recognition for policy successes as the decision to spread themselves across the government rather than solely occupying one or two departments came back to haunt them. Moreover, its longstanding inability to carve out a distinctive identity came to the fore as short-term quick fixes such as tuition fees were kicked to the side lines. Ultimately, a core of its 2010 vote distrusted and vehemently disliked the Liberal Democrats, rallying against it in 2015 with disastrous consequences for the party.

Alongside this, we also emphasise how going into coalition brutally exposed the underlying weaknesses of the Liberal Democrat vote and how the party was ill equipped to combat any electoral backlash from voters. Its small partisan core and reliance on tactical support always meant that any such alliance of Liberal

Democrat voters was likely to be volatile and unstable. Here we stress how the donated nature of its support proved to be its Achilles' heel in 2015 and remains a key explanation of why the party has struggled to fight back. Underpinning this weakness is the party's perennial 'credibility gap' problem. Any progress made under Ashdown, Kennedy and latterly Clegg (up to 2010) in chipping away at the credibility issue was completely undone during its five years in government. As a consequence, we show how voters across the political spectrum became less willing to lend the party their vote in 2015 and subsequently.

Becoming toxic: the first six months

We have consistently stressed how the Liberal Democrats are plagued by structural issues. The party struggles to retain voters due to low levels of loyalty and any partisanship is fragile. As a consequence, the Liberal Democrats always need to recruit voters, and much of this support tends to be tactical and borrowed. Even when the party polls strongly, as in 2010, the make-up of its vote appears brittle.

Of those who voted for the party both in 2005 and 2010 ('loyalists') 72 per cent identified with the Liberal Democrats but 30 per cent claimed they were not very strong identifiers. Of those who switched or were recruited by the Liberal Democrats in 2010, only 37 per cent identified with the party and 45 per cent 'not very strongly'. Reiterating the 'lent vote' narrative, 40 per cent of all tactical voters in 2010 voted Liberal Democrat. Worryingly for the party, 30 per cent of Liberal Democrat support in Liberal Democrat held seats were from tactical voting. This increased to a third in those party-held seats where the Liberal Democrats nearest challenger was the Conservatives, with 60 per cent of these tactical voters preferring Labour. In simple terms, the Liberal Democrats entered coalition with few loyal voters and a dependence on tactical support borrowed from other parties. Many of these voters were anti-Conservative in political make-up, with a significant proportion actually strongly identifying as Labour supporters. Without a strong partisan base, the Liberal Democrats seemed ill suited to withstand the anger and disgruntlement of voters over their coalition partnership with the Conservatives. There is plenty of evidence that the 'wheels began to fall off' immediately after the coalition agreement with the Conservatives had been signed – well before the experience of coalition government could be judged.

The Liberal Democrats' u-turn on tuition fees is often put forward as the catalyst for the party's collapse in the polls during the first year of the coalition. Having actively campaigned against fee increases in the run up to the 2010 general election, the party secured the right to abstain from any vote to increase them in the coalition agreement with the Conservatives. This 'compromise of sorts' did little to offset the anger and betrayal felt by many who voted for the Liberal Democrats in 2010. There is little doubt that the issue immediately became toxic and over time has become symbolic of voters' distrust and antipathy towards the party after the coalition. Nonetheless, there is plenty of evidence that the Liberal Democrats began to haemorrhage support before Lord Browne published his review of the funding of higher education in October. New government proposals following the review were announced in early November and the Westminster vote on increasing the maximum tuition fees occurred on 9 December. The 57 members of the Liberal Democrat parliamentary party were completely split on the issue, with 21 MPs voting against the proposal, eight abstaining and the remaining 28 voting for the proposal, including Deputy Prime Minister and Liberal Democrat leader, Nick Clegg. Using evidence from the Continuous Monitoring Survey (CMS), it is possible to track fluctuations in Liberal Democrat vote intention, likeability and feelings towards Clegg from June to December 2010.[1] The story is uniform across the different indicators. Vote intention mirrors polling data over this period. After one month in coalition, Liberal Democrat vote intention had dropped by more than seven percentage points. By July 2010 the decline was edging towards 10 percentage points. In December 2010 (at the time of the vote on tuition fees) Liberal Democrat vote intention was barely above 8 per cent. At the 2010 election, a third of electors strongly liked the Liberal Democrats. One month into the coalition this had fallen to a quarter and by the turn of the year only 13 per cent of respondents were positive towards the party. Most revealing though was the haemorrhaging of support for Nick Clegg. Support for Clegg dropped rapidly in the first six months of the coalition but in two stages. Going into coalition clearly damaged his likeability. By July 2010, Clegg's likeability had fallen from two-fifths of electors to around a quarter. The second major decline occurred after the Browne recommendations and the coalition's response was announced. By the end of 2010, less than 15 per cent of all electors strongly liked Clegg. The second drop in personal support is hardly surprising given Clegg's personal association with the tuition fees issue by signing the NUS pledge and his stress on the importance of trust.

Even at this early stage of the coalition, the collapse in Liberal Democrat support was primarily driven by the double whammy of serious retention problems and a lack of recruitment. According to the CMS, by July 2010 fewer than half of those who had voted Liberal Democrat that May stated they would support the party in an ensuing national election. Support ebbed away further in subsequent months; the second big shift occurred in October, when the figure dipped below 30 per cent. By December only 27 per cent of these voters pledged to support the party at the next election. This coincided with a drop in partisanship of 20 points or more and a decline of 33 percentage points in party likeability among 2010 Liberal Democrat voters. Once again, half of the drop in likeability occurred after the first month of being in coalition. More than 70 per cent of 2010 Liberal Democrat voters strongly liked Nick Clegg when polled in the 2010 general election. Just going into coalition shaved 11 percentage points off Clegg's likeability rating and after three months less than half of 2010 party supporters expressed positive feelings towards Clegg. This downward spiral continued throughout 2010 but there was a noticeable second surge in the last two months of the year. By December, less than a quarter of 2010 Liberal Democrat voters strongly liked Clegg.

These trends reveal that much of the damage originated from merely deciding to go into coalition with the Conservatives. The second stage of the drop off coincided with the publication of the Browne recommendations. This is noticeable in the vote intention of 2010 Liberal Democrat voters and among all respondents' and 2010 party supporters' feelings towards Clegg. This second smaller decline is then solidified by the time the tuition fees increase is approved by Parliament. It seems conceivable that the furore over the Liberal Democrats' voting stance on tuition fees and the general salience of the issue after October 2010 to the vote in December became the 'final straw' among those voters who had already espoused negative feelings towards the Liberal Democrats for going into coalition with the Conservatives. The honesty and trustworthiness of the government also appears to have been consistent concerns of voters. After the coalition formed around half of all electors felt that the government was honest and trustworthy. While the general trend was downwards from June to October 2010, the decline was relatively modest. By the end of the year, less than a third of all electors felt that the government was trustworthy. The decline though was much more apparent among those who voted Liberal Democrat in 2010. From June to December 2010, those who felt the coalition government was honest dropped by around 20 percentage points. The Liberal Democrats were in serious electoral trouble from the get-go. The weakness of their support base had been laid bare and the party seemed unable to bear the costs of coalition.

Losing its voters: 12 months on from the rose garden

To obtain a clearer insight we examine the electoral picture roughly one year into the coalition government. This was the first big electoral test for the Liberal Democrats since entering coalition with the Conservatives and it proved to be a chastening experience. Large-scale losses in English council elections and in elections to the Senedd and Scottish Parliament were overshadowed by a comprehensive defeat in the referendum on the Alternative Vote (AV) electoral system. By matching 2010 BES data to the AV post-referendum survey, it is possible even at this early stage of the coalition to determine the factors driving disgruntlement with the Liberal Democrats. Initially we focus on retention. Was the retention rate of 2010 Liberal Democrat voters as bad as what was alluded to above when analysing data from June to December 2010? The answer is yes. Twelve months on from going into coalition, only 42 per cent of 'loyal' Liberal Democrat voters (i.e. those who voted for the party in both 2005 and 2010) would vote for the party if there was a general election. Strikingly, only 14 per cent of Liberal Democrat switchers (those who transferred their vote from other parties or not voting to the Liberal Democrats in 2010) stated they would support the party. The Liberal Democrats had a small loyal core but were already haemorrhaging support from those who switched to the party in 2010. Using a logistic model of 2011 Liberal Democrat vote intention, it is possible to add further detail to these descriptive findings. Here we

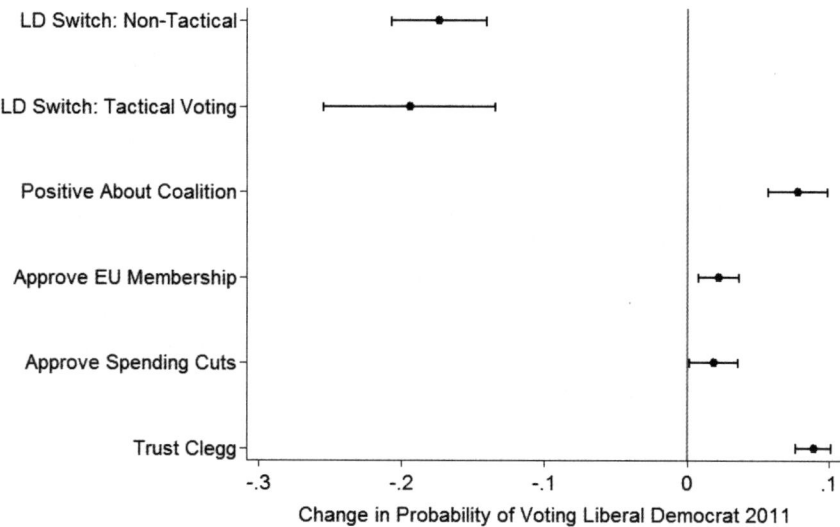

Figure 4.1 Significant drivers of the probability of intending to vote Liberal Democrat in 2011: AMEs (95 per cent CIs). *Source:* 2011 AV referendum and BES Cross-sectional Pre-Post election survey

model 2010 Liberal Democrat voters only and include those who switched to the party in 2010 for tactical and non-tactical reasons (support for the leader; party had the best policies) as predictor variables. We also add potential explanations for why some 2010 Liberal Democrats may have continued to support the party: approval of EU membership; support for coalition governments; approval of the increase in tuition fees; support for cuts in public expenditure; trust in Clegg. Moreover, we also control for socio-demographics such as gender, class, ethnicity, home ownership and age. The detailed results are reported in the Appendix (see Table A4.1) alongside the model fit statistics. For ease of interpretation we convert these logit coefficients into probabilities.

Figure 4.1 shows the average marginal effect (AME) of a one-unit change in terms of probability changes for each predictor for key predictors that are significant at the 95 per cent confidence level (p-value = <0.05). On average, strongly trusting Clegg increases the probability of voting Liberal Democrat by nine percentage points holding all other variables constant while approving of EU membership and public expenditure cuts increases the probability of these 2010 Liberal Democrat voters supporting the party by two percentage points respectively. Being positive about coalitions also increases the probability of voting Liberal Democrat by eight percentage points. These are the shared attitudes of a small but loyal group of supporters. Conversely, those who switched support to the Liberal Democrats in 2010 because they believed they had the best policies or the best leader were significantly less likely to support the party when compared with loyal voters. The AME is 18 per cent: on average, the probability non-tactical 2010 Liberal Democrat switchers supporting the party in 2011 is 18 percentage points lower than for loyal voters holding other variables constant. Being a tactical switcher decreases the probability of voting Liberal Democrat in 2011 by 17 percentage points.

So far we have found that tactical and non-tactical switchers had begun to abandon the Liberal Democrats almost immediately after they went into coalition with the Conservatives. Our evidence suggests that this was more than a tactical unwind and was driven for the most part by the desertion of voters that felt less attached to the party. Earlier we claimed that many of these leaned left on the political spectrum. But what about voters generally? One year on from the start of the coalition, were the Liberal Democrats largely unpopular among left-leaning voters? Did their appeal remain among those with traditional liberal values? Was the party able to recruit voters even if it had trouble retaining them? Here we exploit the 'feelings towards a party' variables on both the 2010 and 2011 datasets and calculate the change in feelings towards the Liberal Democrats between 2010 and 2011 for all respondents (see Fieldhouse et al., 2021).[2] As such, we are able to examine retention and recruitment. We run a linear model controlling for how respondents felt about the Liberal Democrats in 2010 and include other predictors that account for authoritarian–libertarian and economic left–right values, a redistribution measure based on Liberal Democrat policy positions in the 2010 general election and the party's 2010 policy positions on Trident renewal, tuition fees and feelings about EU membership. We also take account of the strength of Liberal Democrat partisanship in the 2010 election before the party entered coalition. The full results are provided in the appendix (see Table A4.2).

Figure 4.2 reveals significant effects for both economic left–right and authoritarian–libertarian values in the manner we might have expected. The 'feelings' scores for the Liberal Democrats dropped far more among those on the economic left than among those on the right. Whereas those respondents who espoused authoritarian values were increasingly unreceptive to the Liberal Democrats as the party maintained its support from those with traditional liberal leanings. It seems that it was voters with left-leaning values who had abandoned the party from the start of the coalition and that the Liberal Democrats had maintained support, predominantly from strongly attached partisans, among those who shared the traditional liberal values and 'Orange Book' economic liberal inclinations of the party leadership. Similarly, those who shared the redistribution goals of the Liberal Democrats' 2010 policy positions – the mansion tax, eco taxes, raising the personal tax allowance and so on – were increasingly much more hostile to the Liberal Democrats than those who did not. Unsurprisingly, Liberal Democrat popularity held up far better among those who approved of the increase in tuition fees and EU membership. The trajectory of prior partisanship also corroborated our earlier findings. On average, those who strongly identified with the Liberal Democrats in 2010 had similar feelings towards the party in 2011 as they

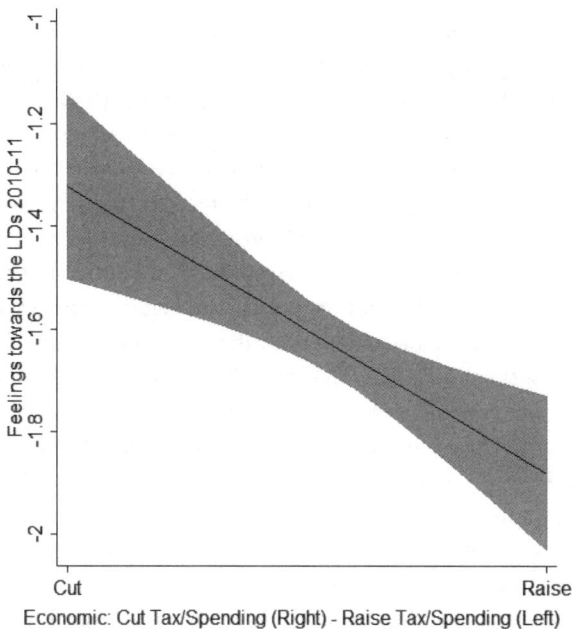

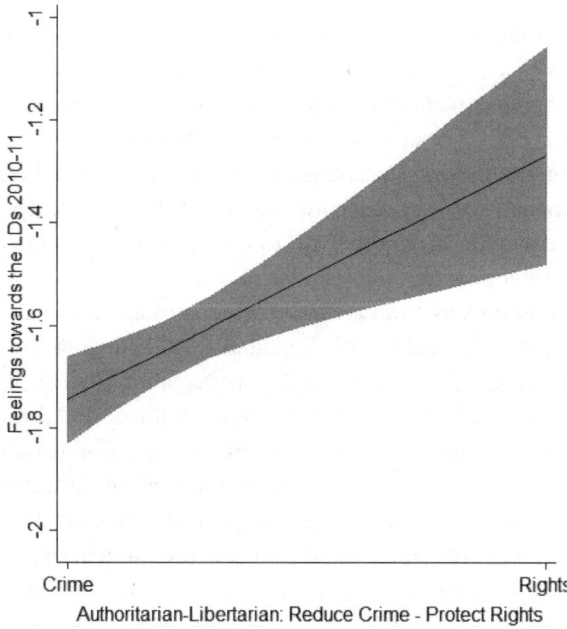

Figure 4.2 Change in feelings towards the Liberal Democrats 2010–2011 by authoritarian-libertarian (crime–rights) and economic left–right (tax–spend) values. *Source*: 2011 AV referendum and BES Pre–Post election survey

did in the general election, controlling for all other factors. Those who identified with other parties or no party saw the largest drop in Liberal Democrat popularity, although, as noted earlier in this chapter, those with weak levels of Liberal Democrat partisanship had also become considerably more hostile. From the early stages of the coalition, the fragility of its partisan base had been exposed. A larger base of core support seemingly would have shielded the party somewhat from the electoral disaster that was to follow (Fieldhouse *et al.*, 2021).

In order to overcome their weak partisan base, the Liberal Democrats knew that they would have to gain credit for policies in coalition and for these positive perceptions to override the discontent with their 'broken promises' and austerity policies. But were there any signs that the Liberal Democrats could be credited with any economic revival? Was there any evidence that a statesmanlike Nick Clegg could recruit voters or win back previous voters? Could they repel the 'tactical unwind' or win over Conservative voters? Here we pool the CMS data from January 2012 to December 2013 and run a multinomial regression on party vote intentions to examine such trends during this period. The key findings are presented in the Appendix (Table A4.3).

Our evidence suggests that by the mid-point of the coalition, the Liberal Democrats were simply not cutting through and were facing electoral turmoil. Here we focus on the contrast between the two coalition partners: the Conservatives and the Liberal Democrats. One of the notable differences between the two parties is that only the Conservatives' prospects are enhanced where the public perceives that the coalition government has handled the economic crisis well. Put simply, voters were significantly more likely to credit the Conservatives for any economic revival emanating from the coalition's economic policy to drive down debt than the Liberal Democrats. Any belief that the Liberal Democrats were likely to benefit from 'putting the country first' after accepting and then implementing a tougher economic plan to deal with the debt crisis was simply folly. The data do not contain public perceptions on other issues but, given that handling the economic crisis was central to the coalition's existence, it seems that if the Liberal Democrats could not be credited for this then they would struggle in other policy arenas. Alongside this, it was becoming increasingly clear that going into coalition with the Conservatives had nullified the Liberal Democrats, electoral effectiveness against their coalition partner. For instance, partisanship influences 'own party' vote intentions in the expected directions. Yet while Conservative partisanship harmed Liberal Democrat vote intention the reverse is not the case. Perhaps even more significant was the influence of Clegg. Positive feelings towards Nick Clegg improved Liberal Democrat vote intentions while a positive image of the Labour leader, Ed Miliband, and Cameron were more likely to have a negative impact. So while positive feelings towards Cameron affect Liberal Democrat vote intentions in the expected direction, our evidence suggests that Clegg had no significant influence on Conservative support. Increasingly, it was becoming apparent that any improvement in the popularity of Cameron or perceptions that the coalition had run the economy well were likely to benefit the Conservatives. The Liberal Democrats had been nullified and had few tools at their disposal to hurt Conservative support, which left them extremely vulnerable to their coalition partner.

The Liberal Democrats' 2015 story: drivers and explanations

In the first two sections of this chapter we have detailed how those who voted for the Liberal Democrats in 2010 turned their back on the party in their droves within six or seven months of its decision to enter into coalition with the Conservatives. With recruitment at a standstill, the Liberal Democrats were quickly reduced to having a small group of loyal supporters. Losing the AV referendum proved to be a bitter blow and confirmed that the Liberal Democrats were in the electoral mire. Of course, the eventual general election would not be for another four years after the referendum, and party insiders insisted this would be plenty of time for the public to make an informed assessment of the coalition and reward the Liberal Democrats for putting the country first in fragile economic times. This take proved to be way off the mark. By early 2011, the Liberal Democrats were bumping along the ground at 7 per cent in the polls, a figure that they duly recorded four years later. So far, our analysis of cross-sectional survey data confined to the first 12 months of the coalition has pinpointed the key drivers and provided clear insight into the emerging story of the Liberal Democrats' historic slump. Here we build on this analysis, taking in the coalition period as a whole and, crucially, the 2015 election itself. Who of their 2010 voters left the Liberal Democrats in 2015? Where did they go and why? What explains the historic collapse? And who remained loyal and why?

The triple whammy: partisanship, retention and recruitment

Within the context of a two-party system, partisanship (or primarily the lack of it) has proved to be a constant sore that the Liberal Democrats have been unable to heal, even when the party was riding high. As we have noted throughout, the Liberal Democrats have been dependent on a small loyal vote which they have topped up by borrowed votes from one election to the next. This is achieved through the construction of a strong local platform and intensive place-based grassroots campaigning. These work in synchrony with community politics designed to build a local liberal culture where local representatives are both guardians and continuously receptive to voters' interests and concerns. Retaining existing support but also recruiting new voters to the Liberal Democrat fold are therefore critical to ensure the sustainability and credibility of the party among the wider public. Winning makes the party look more viable and widens credibility. Attracting donated support can be fruitful and the easiest route to success in the short term. Turning that borrowed support into strong partisan identification is much harder. Sometimes a local incumbent can start the process but this has limitations when the support becomes conditional on the individual rather than the party. When a popular incumbent leaves, so can the vote. More widely, Liberal Democrat attempts to build partisan support and strengthen existing identification has been conducted in an era when partisan alignment has weakened and, unlike their rivals, the Liberal Democrats are starting from a low base. Alongside hardening existing partisanship, getting the balance right between retention and recruitment can be extremely difficult. With historic retention rates much lower for the Liberal Democrats than for their rivals, recruiting voters and gaining contingent support are vital. However, the party can be vulnerable to the electoral context and is reliant on others making mistakes before it can reap electoral rewards. This is why a small loyal core is problematic for the Liberal Democrats.

Voting theory suggests that partisanship acts as a perceptual screen that affects the acquisition and interpretation of political information. Through this filtering mechanism it exerts indirect effects on voting, by shaping individuals' attitudes towards parties and the issues they stand for, and their perceptions of the competence of party leaders and candidates in public office (Bartels, 2002; Campbell et al., 1960; Green et al., 2002). Partisans tend to engage in motivated reasoning and process material that preserves their existing partisanship (Lodge and Taber, 2013). Put simply, voters bring their observations in line with their prior opinions. Partisan voters are more likely to receive and take notice of favourable material about their party – literature, social media communications, personal interactions with activists. This reinforces partisan attachment. As a consequence, if your vote is predominantly donated or tactical – containing voters that lean favourably to an alternative party – then such voters will view the party's conduct, stance on issues etc. through these partisan filters, not from the party where the vote is borrowed. This scenario occurred in 2010 and played out in a brutal manner five years later. As we have noted, the 2010 Liberal Democrat vote was heavily borrowed from disgruntled Labour-leaners and a small but nonetheless sizeable number of Conservative sympathisers. When the Liberal Democrats went into coalition, these Labour-leaners processed the information through their partisan filters. The result was an almost immediate unravelling of the Liberal Democrat vote. By contrast, partisans are always more likely to give their party credit for positive changes and in a coalition scenario see that party as being more influential (Meyer and Strobhl, 2016). With fewer than 1 in 10 Liberal Democrat voters very strongly identifying with the Liberal Democrats in 2010, it is clear that the lack of partisan strength when compared with its rivals proved extremely costly. Its weak base meant it could not ride out any coalition storm, and the contingent characteristics of its prior vote only accelerated the party's downward spiral.

We can definitively gauge the individual shifts in support from 2010 to 2015 (known as flow of the vote) by using the BES, which tracks the same voters over time.[3] Figure 4.3 (graph 1) shows the 2010 votes of BES panel members by their 2015 vote. Here we include the two main parties (Labour and the Conservatives),

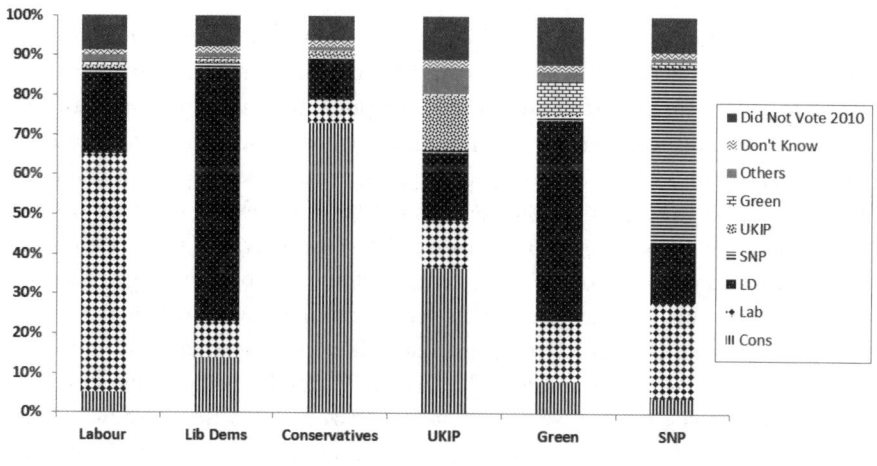

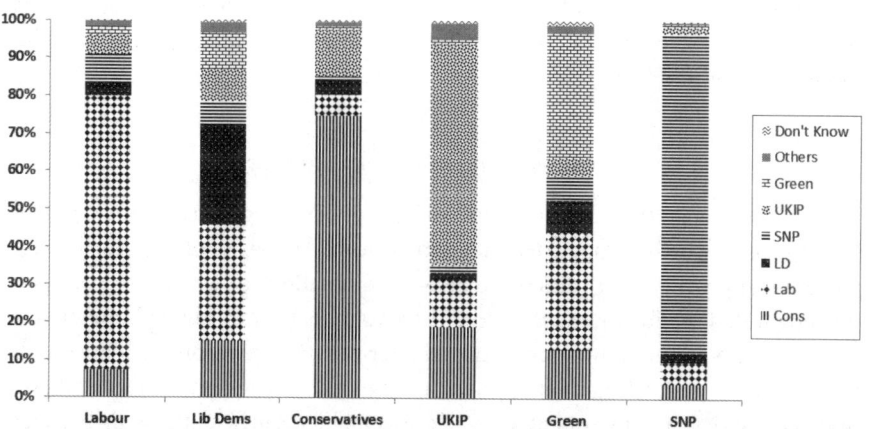

Figure 4.3 Voter identity and flow: 2010 vote of 2015 supporters (top) and 2015 support by 2010 vote (bottom)

the Liberal Democrats, the SNP, the Green party, UKIP and all other parties combined. Unsurprisingly, Labour and Conservative supporters in 2015 largely voted for these parties in 2010. Around 64 per cent of Liberal Democrat voters in 2015 had also voted for the party five years earlier. The Liberal Democrats did recruit some 2010 Conservative and Labour voters but, generally speaking, party recruitment was on a much smaller scale than in recent earlier elections. It was also overshadowed by the haemorrhaging of its 2010 voters to other parties. For instance, Labour obtained 21 per cent of its 2015 support from those who had voted Liberal Democrat in 2010, while for the Conservatives the figure was 10 per cent. The Greens had in excess of 50 per cent of their 2015 vote emanating from 2010 Liberal Democrat supporters. To put into context the scale of the Liberal Democrats' collapse, we can also examine 2015 support according to how individuals voted in 2010 (Figure 4.3, graph 2). It is immediately evident that both Labour and the Conservatives retained the loyalty of around 75 per cent of their 2010 voters. This is similar to previous elections. By contrast, Liberal Democrat loyalty fell markedly, to a low of 27 per cent, most of its support shifting to Labour, although a sizeable number (around 20 per cent of those who switched) went to the Conservatives. Both the Greens and the SNP picked up significant numbers of 2010 Liberal Democrat voters and even UKIP, despite being at the opposite end of the ideological spectrum, took a good-sized proportion (around 9 per cent overall, which equates to more than 11 per cent of all 2010 Liberal Democrat switchers). Hamstrung by longstanding weak partisanship, the Liberal Democrats saw retention levels reach a historic low. Such failings were then compounded by their inability to recruit voters in enough numbers from other parties to offset these retention problems.

The diminishing popularity of Clegg

Following the abandonment of the tuition fees policy, Clegg became toxic to left-leaning voters who had supported the party in 2010. At the end of May 2010, Clegg had a net approval rating (difference between evaluations of whether he was performing well or badly) of +44 per cent. Three months later this had plummeted to +6 per cent. A second downturn occurred after the Browne recommendations. By the end of the year, Clegg's net approval rating was -30 per cent. From April 2011 until February 2015, discontent with Clegg remained fairly static, with between two-thirds and three-quarters of voters stating that Clegg was doing badly. Indeed, in May 2014, it was closer to 80 per cent than three-quarters, with the Liberal Democrat leader recording net approval ratings of -60 per cent (YouGov, 2015). Unsurprisingly, trustworthiness seemed to be an Achilles' heel for Clegg. Looking at evidence from the 2011 AV referendum survey, more than 7 out of 10 respondents found Clegg to be untrustworthy, compared with 50 per cent for Miliband and around 55 per cent for Cameron.

Despite the dire polling ratings, there is some evidence that Clegg enjoyed a marginal uptick in approval as the 2015 election campaign drew nearer. Figure 4.4 compares the mean likeability scores of the three party leaders from 2010 to 2015 derived from BES data over this period. For much of the coalition period Clegg performed badly relative to his opponents. However, there were some minor increases in his likeability during the campaign and Clegg's post-election mean likeability score was higher than Miliband's. The shifts, though, are very much at the margins. Around 46 per cent of respondents disliked (scores on 0–3 scale) Clegg after the campaign, compared with 54 per cent before. Furthermore, 11 per

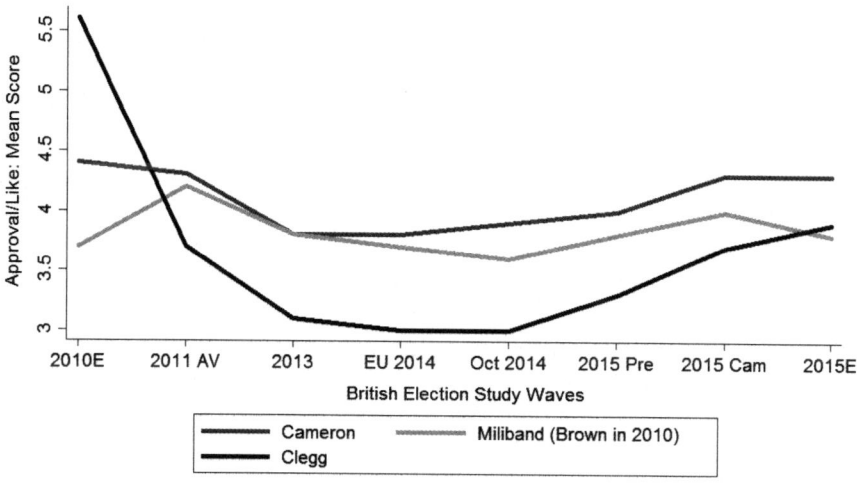

Figure 4.4 Party leader approval/like ratings (mean scores). *Source*: British Election Study 2010–2015

cent strongly liked the Liberal Democrat leader after the campaign, compared with 6 per cent at its start. Overall, there was no repeat of Clegg's first leadership debate performance and general 'campaign bounce'. Evidence from the BES suggests that only 3 per cent of respondents claimed that Clegg was the best leader during the campaign, while 13 per cent stated that he performed worst. On the latter measure he compared favourably to Miliband (30 per cent), Bennett (17 per cent) and Farage (14 per cent). In truth, the voting public was largely ambivalent about Clegg. Their mind was made up and as a figure he (and his party) had become an irrelevance.

As expected, Labour voters disliked Clegg far more than Conservative voters. Of those who voted Liberal Democrat in 2010 and voted Labour five years later, around 45 per cent strongly disliked the Liberal Democrat leader. The mean approval score they gave was better than the score of all Labour voters but was only equivalent to the overall mean. Interestingly, Clegg was far more popular among those 2010 Liberal Democrats who switched to the Conservatives (mean like/approval rating = 5.5) than among all 2015 Conservative voters.

These descriptive trends seem to be borne out by the findings from our OLS regression model. Table A4.4 in the Appendix examines the drivers of Clegg approval ratings in the 2015 general election of those voters who five years previously had supported the Liberal Democrats. Those who were significantly more likely to approve of Clegg included prior 2010 voters on the right of the political spectrum, who identified with the party, thought the Liberal Democrats were the best party on the most important issue, believed the economy was getting better while the party had been in coalition and supported EU membership. In other words, these were core supporters with an economic liberal stance. Those on the left, who tended to lean towards Labour, strongly opposed the tuition fees increase and believed that austerity cuts had gone too far, thought the economy had got worse under the coalition government, and believed that parties could not deliver on their promises when in coalition tended to strongly disapprove of the Liberal Democrat leader.

In summary, it seems likely that Clegg both directly and indirectly contributed to the tactical unwind of left-leaning voters to Labour, but his more hawkish economic approach on debt reduction and wider classical liberal leanings drew plaudits from some Conservatives, albeit not enough to keep them on the Liberal Democrat bandwagon. For this group, other factors than Clegg, such as Cameron's popularity (mean like/approval rating = 7.0), were probably decisive. Core Liberal Democrat identifiers remained loyal to Clegg but for other voters he was toxic, thereby nullifying a key party tool for retention and recruitment.

The experience of coalition. 1: Exposing the Liberal Democrats

The Liberal Democrats got the coalition wrong. Hamstrung by the coalition agreement, they sought to walk the tightrope as both defender and critic of coalition policies; work with the Conservatives as colleagues but remain bitter rivals; remain resolutely behind the goals of the coalition government while simultaneously seeking to carve a policy space to differentiate themselves; claim credit for coalition policies and recognition for blocking the excesses of their Conservative partner. This proved increasingly unsustainable over the long term. Previously, we discussed how the junior partner always struggles to get the credit for any coalition government successes owing to the Prime Minister's ability to control the agenda. As such, any credit or blame is commonly attributed to the larger coalition party. With the electoral consequences of the Liberal Democrats' decision to join the Conservatives in a coalition becoming ever starker, their presentation of the coalition became increasingly incoherent. Over time, the Liberal Democrats became less supportive and gradually more negative in tone. As the election neared, the party compounded mistakes seeking to distance itself from the Conservatives on the coalition's economic record amid criticisms over austerity policies just at the time when the economy was showing improvement. By trying to avoid blame, it risked disbarring itself from any credit. Yet the truth was that Liberal Democrats were neither blamed for the coalition failures nor credited for its successes.

Figure 4.5 shows that on six issues (ranging from immigration to the economy) between only 17 per cent and 21 per cent ascribed any credit or blame to the Liberal Democrats, while between 50 per cent and 73 per cent of respondents blamed the Conservatives for the coalition's failures or credited it for its successes. Even among those who voted Liberal Democrat in 2010 and switched to Labour in 2015 only between 16 per cent and 24 per cent attributed responsibility for policy changes to the Liberal Democrats. Others have taken this further and assessed

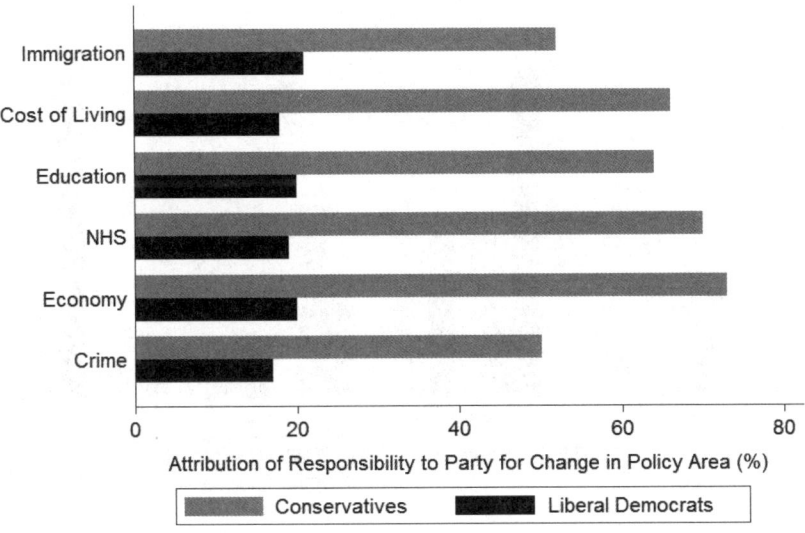

Figure 4.5 Respondents' attribution of responsibility to the Conservatives and Liberal Democrats for the change in immigration, the cost of living, education, the NHS, the economy and crime policies during the 2010–2015 coalition. *Source*: 2015 BES panel pre-election wave

whether Liberal Democrat identifiers gave credit to their own party for coalition successes (Fieldhouse *et al.*, 2021). The evidence is compelling. Generally speaking, respondents were less likely to attribute policy changes to the Liberal Democrats and, aside from education and the NHS, party loyalists were less likely to credit policy success to the Liberal Democrats than to their coalition partners (Fieldhouse *et al.*, 2021: 123–124). Rather than being held responsible or rewarded for coalition achievements, the Liberal Democrats succumbed to the fate of many other junior coalition partners: in simple terms, they were seen by voters as largely irrelevant.

In addition to being neither blamed nor credited for government actions, the coalition offered an opportunity for the Liberal Democrats to establish themselves among voters as a party which had clear 'home' issues and a policy focus. In the short term, this would have aided retention and, over the longer term, carving out a distinctive issue platform would have enabled the party to widen its appeal to other voters. Yet, misjudgements and mistakes from the outset and then throughout the coalition scuppered any prospect of solving this longstanding problem. As Figure 4.6 shows, a significant number of voters felt that the Liberal Democrats did not prioritise any of the key issues and lacked policy direction. From the economy to the NHS, only around a quarter of respondents agreed that these were Liberal Democrat priorities. Even on schools, where the Liberal Democrats had attempted to develop a distinctive policy agenda since as far back as the Ashdown years, the party did not enjoy an issue advantage in the minds of voters. When compared

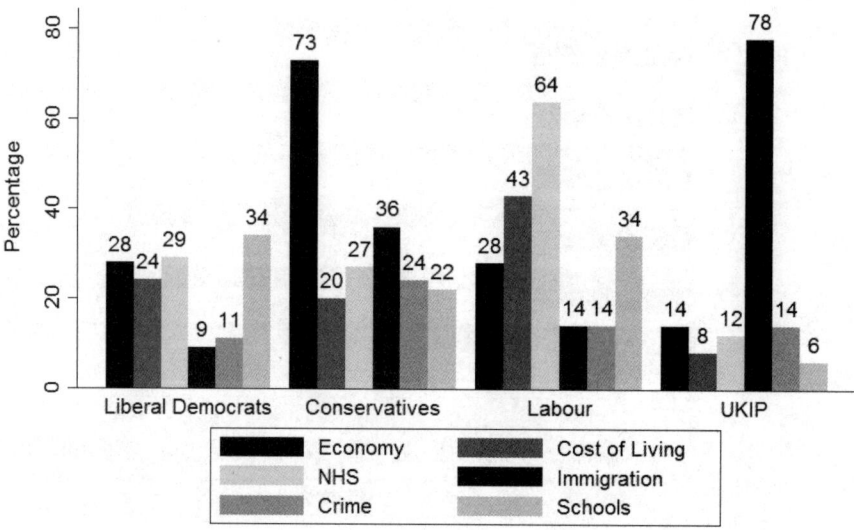

Figure 4.6 Voters assessment of party issue priorities at the 2015 general election

against its rivals, it is was clear that many of the issues that the Liberal Democrats pursued – from the pupil premium to raising the tax threshold – despite public support lacked salience for voters or were not recognised as Liberal Democrat priorities and as such were commonly incorrectly associated with the Conservatives. In 2015, only 3 per cent of voters thought the Liberal Democrats were the best party on the most important issue. So not only were they neither blamed nor rewarded for policies, or for holding back Conservative proposals, the Liberal Democrats failed to carve out a distinctive policy platform which voters could attach to the party. Worse still, many of their policies were mistakenly attributed to their rivals. For some voters, though, what did endure was the fallout from the years of austerity.

The experience of coalition. 2: The economy and the impact of austerity

So far we have highlighted how, within a year of the election, voters who had lent support to the Liberal Democrats in 2010 left in their droves, primarily in response to the party going into coalition with the Conservatives. Not only did the party backtrack on promises made at the election but Liberal Democrats signed up to an economic package designed to reduce the deficit at a pace so fast that it led to a period of austerity. The government's performance on the economy split public opinion. By the 2015 general election, only 28 per cent of respondents claimed that economy had got a little or a lot worse. Overall, 37 per cent stated the government had handled the economy fairly or very badly. Of those voters who supported the Liberal Democrats in 2010 but did not in 2015, only 45 per cent were negative about the government's economic performance. Yet a majority of respondents agreed that national cuts to public spending had been far too extensive. Around four-fifths of those 2010 Liberal Democrat voters who switched to Labour claimed that these cuts to national and local public services had gone too far. They were also critical of the government's handling of education, the cost of living and the NHS. Nine out of 10 switchers to Labour claimed that the government had handled the NHS fairly or very badly. Interestingly, the smaller group which switched from Liberal Democrat to the Conservatives in 2015 were more supportive of cuts to public spending. Just over 20 per cent stated they had gone too far, which was nearly 33 percentage points below the mean. A majority felt that NHS cuts were deeper than they felt necessary and 48 per cent were critical of increases in tuition fees. Yet both were significantly below the overall average. While these voters seemed supportive of the coalition's policies, the Liberal Democrats still failed to retain them.

As we noted above, the Liberal Democrats were neither credited nor blamed for the coalition's actions on the economy or other issues, such as education or health, mainly because many voters had made their mind up from the outset and knew what the party had signed up to. Tracing back those who switched to Labour using the BES, roughly 40 per cent had voted Labour and a similar proportion had voted Liberal Democrat in 2005. Many of these 2005 Liberal Democrat voters drifted to the party in opposition to the war in Iraq and in support of the more left leaning policies pursued by Kennedy in the election. These switchers were definitively on the left (mean score of 3.3 on the self-placement left right spectrum), with only 3 per cent of this cohort supporting the Conservatives in 2005. For them, joining a coalition with the Conservatives cemented the Liberal Democrats as 'Yellow Tories'. What they did in the coalition was an irrelevance. The party was seen as an 'austerity enabler' and was tarnished with a litany of broken promises.

To make matters worse, the Liberal Democrats was helpless to stop those who were satisfied with the government's performance on the wider economy, with the implementation of austerity measures in order to surface debt and the provision of public services from switching to the Conservatives. This group was not ostensibly right-wing (mean score of 6.1 on the self-placement left right spectrum) and although more than two-fifths had supported the Liberal Democrats in 2005, roughly one fifth had voted Labour and a similar number had voted Conservative in that election. Many of these voters attributed responsibility for the coalition's actions to Cameron and the Conservatives and, although not hostile to the Liberal Democrats, voted accordingly. The Liberal Democrats were left high and dry with little reward.

By modelling the data, we can provide further evidence of these trends. Here we use a multinomial logistic model of 2015 vote choice containing only voters in England given the complications of categorising nationalist and other support. The model estimates the likelihood of voters supporting the Conservatives, Labour, the Liberal Democrats, UKIP and Greens. One of these response categories (Labour) is the base. We calculate the log-odds for all the other categories relative to the base and then let the log-odds be a linear function of the predictors which in our case is voter evaluations of how well the economy is performing and attitudes to austerity (public spending cuts) in 2015. We then control for left right economic values, libertarian–authoritarian, attitudes to immigration, support for the EU, partisanship, subjective economic evaluations, whether voters believed Labour was to blame for the debt crisis, redistribution scale, and socio-demographic variables. For simplicity we focus on the Liberal Democrats and the two main parties.

Figure 4.7 shows the predicted probability of voting for the Conservatives, Labour and the Liberal Democrats in 2015 by voters' national economic evaluations. The evidence is pretty clear. The Conservatives did better and were thus rewarded if voters perceived that economy had improved and were damaged somewhat if the perception was that it had got worse. The opposite was true for Labour in 2015: it fared worse if voters perceived that the economy was improving and did better if the perception was that the economy was performing badly. The Liberal Democrats did badly across all categories in 2015. As the minor coalition partner, they got no reward for the economy doing better and, given the uptick in Labour performance among those who perceived the economy had got worse, suffered the inevitable consequences of losing votes to its rival. Figure 4.8 reveals a similar pattern for attitudes to austerity. Those who accepted the need for austerity were far more likely to support the Conservatives. The more anti-austerity the voter, the greater was the probability of voting Labour, even after controlling for political values and other significant predictors. For the Liberal Democrats, we find evidence of a 'pincer effect', with little support from either those who were against austerity measures or those who were in favour of them. The former turned to Labour if they believed public service cuts were not necessary and the latter if they held Labour responsible for the economic debt (relative log odds increase by 2.16) and were persuaded by the need to reduce the deficit through cutting spending. Whether it was support from the left or the centre-right, the story was the same.

Going into coalition exposed the weakness of the party's support and the damage was done almost before Clegg walked into the rose garden. The consequences of the decision to join a coalition – signing up to the Conservatives' economic programme, the legacy of austerity and the list of broken pre-election assurances – and then the experience of it not only rubber stamped voters' decisions to go elsewhere in 2015 but ultimately proved to be far more long lasting.

Losing electoral credibility

We have stressed in this and earlier chapters how electoral credibility is pivotal for the Liberal Democrats. Winning council seats and taking control of local councils had been primarily how the party had built a local platform from which it can target parliamentary seats. We illustrated how the Liberal Democrats collapsed in the polls and reached a plateau from which they were never to recover. Just as

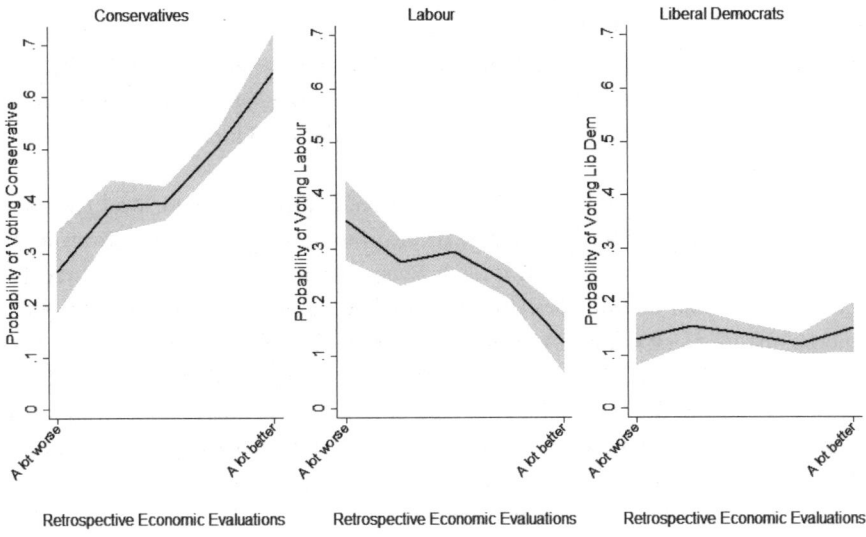

Figure 4.7 Predicted probability of party support in 2015 by 2015 national economic evaluations. *Source*: 2015 British Election Study

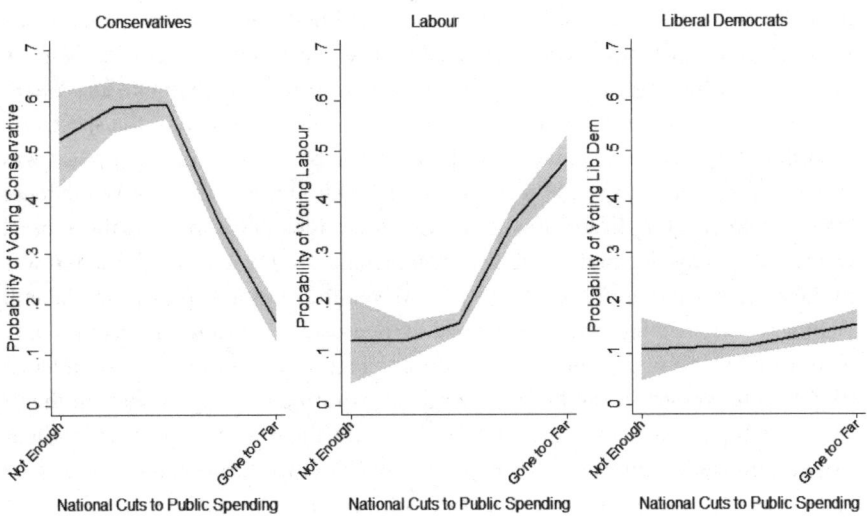

Figure 4.8 Predicted probabilities of party support in 2015 by 2015 voter attitudes to national cuts in public spending. *Source*: 2015 British Election Study

polls can reinforce credibility, they can on the downside undermine electors' faith in a party's electoral viability. When combined with losses at the local level year in year out, in European elections and in devolved elections, it is little surprise that, come the 2015 election, most voters simply believed the Liberal Democrats were not credible.

Yet what matters is the party's electoral credibility in certain local electoral contests. In many seats, the party is an also-ran so the expectation from local constituents of the party winning is likely to be extremely low. However, where the Liberal Democrats have historically polled well or maintain a strong local presence then constituent expectations of electoral success are likely to be much higher. Just how credible the Liberal Democrats are in these electoral races therefore determines whether the party is likely to gain or lose seats in an election. Given their reliance on borrowed support, if voters in these local contests feel that the Liberal Democrats are credible and have a chance of winning the seat then they are more likely to support them to stop their least preferred option from being successful. Alternatively, if the party is not seen as a viable option, then voters are less likely to waste their vote supporting a party who they perceive can't win.

Using the BES, it is possible to assess respondents' perceived likelihood of the Liberal Democrats winning in their constituencies before the election took place in both 2010 and 2015. We can determine just how much damage local election losses and the slump in the polls had on the Liberal Democrats' electoral credibility in 2015. Nationally, on a scale from 0 (very unlikely) to 10 (very likely), the mean likelihood of the Liberal Democrats winning a constituency declined from 3.07 in 2010 to 2.36 in 2015. Closer inspection of the figures reveals just how weak the Liberal Democrats' electoral credibility had become, as a result of being in coalition. In 2010, respondents' perceived likelihood of the Liberal Democrats winning in their constituencies was rated on average at 6 or above in 52 seats. By 2015, this was the case in only three seats – North Norfolk, Cheltenham and Yeovil – with the party holding on only to the former. At the other end of the spectrum, respondents' perceived likelihood of the Liberal Democrats winning the seat was below 2 (very unlikely) in 288 seats, compared with 147 seats in 2010. While these overall figures are entirely consistent with the wider perception of the Liberal Democrats losing electoral credibility from being coalition, a more critical test was in those seats where it polled well in 2010. Given the electoral context, the Liberal Democrats were on the defensive in 2015, so their primary goal was to save as many incumbent seats as possible in the election. Figure 4.9 compares respondents' perceived likelihood of the Liberal Democrats winning the constituency in the 57 seats won by the party in 2010 and defended as the incumbent in 2015. Incumbent seats are ranked according to their prior vote share, with notional previous vote used in 2010, to accommodate redistricting. The expectation is that smaller prior vote shares would by and large mean that voters would be more sceptical of the Liberal Democrats' electoral chances. The graphs in Figure 4.9 show a drop-off in 2015 when compared with 2010 across all incumbent seats, with the average score

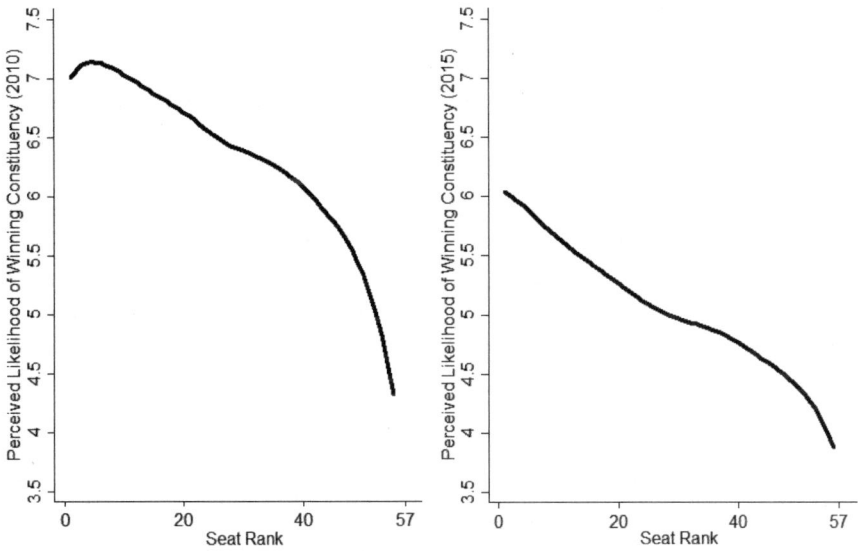

Figure 4.9 Comparing the perceived likelihood of Liberal Democrats winning the constituency in 2010 and 2015 in Liberal Democrat 2015 incumbent seats (ranked by prior vote share). *Source*: 2015 British Election Study (pre-election wave) and 2015 constituency data file

falling from 6.4 in 2010 to 5.1 in 2015. In 41 of the 57 seats, 2010 respondents on average rated the Liberal Democrats' chances of winning the seat as 60 per cent or more. In 2015, BES respondents in 23 of the 57 seats perceived that the Liberal Democrats had less than a 50 per cent chance of winning, while this had been the case in only seven seats five years earlier. Even in their safest seats, the Liberal Democrats' electoral credibility had been shaken so badly from being in coalition that voters living in these constituencies perceived that the party had only around a 50–50 chance of success. They were simply not a viable electoral option for many.

Modelling the Liberal Democrats' 2015 performance

So which of these drivers explains the Liberal Democrats' performance in 2015? Did austerity cuts drive the tactical unwind to Labour? Did the Liberal Democrats suffer from a pincer movement from both the left and right? To answer these questions, we first run a logistic regression model to estimate who voted for the Liberal Democrats in 2015. This is split into two parts, with model 1 accounting for respondents' partisanship, feelings towards leaders, issue perceptions, authoritarian–libertarian values, attitudes towards economic redistribution, left–right economic values, subjective economic evaluation, assessment of whether the economy has improved over the past five years and socio-demographic variables.

Model 2 includes all the indicators listed above but additionally a lagged Liberal Democrat vote intention measure. This is a major advantage of the panel design, because we can establish whether there were any changes in Liberal Democrat support during the campaign period and if so which variables were most influential. Lastly, we run a multinomial regression solely on those respondents who voted Liberal Democrat in 2010 to simultaneously assess the different factors that drove these voters to their rivals in 2015 and what mattered most.

The logistic regression estimates produced by two 2015 Liberal Democrat voting models (model 1 and model 2) are shown in Table A4.5 in the Appendix. For ease of interpretation we convert these logit coefficients into probabilities and these AMEs are shown in Figure 4.10. They show a familiar story. Of the socio-demographic variables, on average, having a degree increases the probability of voting by around two points compared with those without this qualification. Being a Liberal Democrat partisan mattered much more given that it increased the probability of voting Liberal Democrat by eight percentage points when compared with non-identifiers. Despite the small number of tactical switchers, being a lent voter still increased the likelihood of voting for the party in 2015. Issue perceptions were also vital. Those who believed the Liberal Democrats were the best party on the most important issue increased the probability of supporting the party by seven percentage points. The AMEs for those who were pro-European and liked Clegg were 2 and 1 per cent respectively: that is, on average, the probability of pro-European respondents voting Liberal Democrat was two points higher than it was for those with anti-European attitudes and one point greater for those who liked Clegg than for those who disliked the Liberal Democrat leader. Those who believed the Liberal Democrats had a positive impact on coalition policy and subjectively felt they were better off over the five years were also significantly more likely to support the party. Lastly, credibility mattered. Those who lived in a seat where respondents perceived the party had a greater chance of winning were 1.3 times more likely to support the party and on average the AME was nearly two points higher than in seats where likelihood of winning was believed to be small.

The second model adds the lagged Liberal Democrat vote variable and enables us to determine which variables influenced Liberal Democrat voting patterns during the election campaign. Aside from respondents' subjective economic evaluations, which are insignificant at the 5 per cent level (and so not shown in Figure 4.10), all the other important effects identified in model 1 still mattered, but they were generally weaker in terms of their impact. For instance, on average, being a partisan increased the probability of voting Liberal Democrat by four instead of eight percentage points once prior vote intention had been accounted for.

In summary, the models throw up few surprises, and reiterate the importance of partisanship, issue perceptions, winning over lent support and electoral credibility. The problem for the Liberal Democrats in 2015 was far more pronounced than in 2010 but nonetheless exhibited well-known themes. The party lacked partisans, seats where it was credible and the ability to garner donated support.

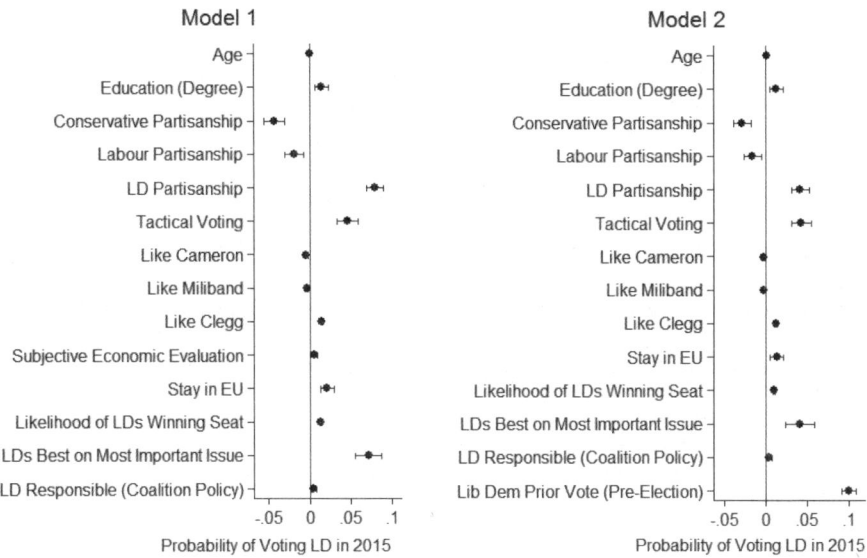

Figure 4.10 AMEs of voting Liberal Democrat in 2015: significant variables only.
Source: 2015 British Election Study

Too many voters did not know what they stood for and too few believed they had played any meaningful role in the coalition. They now struggled to capitalise on rival weaknesses as they had done previously. In 2015 when they were on the defensive and lacking a sizeable loyal following, it proved fatal.

In our discussion on the impact of austerity, we provided descriptive evidence of not only 2010 Liberal Democrat voters tactically unwinding to Labour but some voters who were positive about the coalition's management of the economy switching from the party to the Conservatives. However, when we control for possible influences on party switching, is there any evidence of this pincer movement against the Liberal Democrats? The results of a multinomial logistic regression of 2015 party choice of those who voted Liberal Democrat in 2010 suggests this is the case (see Table 4.1). Here we examine what drove these voters to switch to rival parties when compared against the reference category, which is those who voted Liberal Democrat in 2015. We use a similar set of variables as before, including partisanship, economic redistribution values, austerity measures, an authoritarian–libertarian factor, left–right values, subjective economic evaluations, perceptions of economic performance during the coalition and a number of socio-demographic variables. When compared against the reference category, being anti-European and a non-degree holder were key drivers for switching to either of the right-wing parties – UKIP and the Conservatives.

However, those who left the Liberal Democrats to support the Conservatives were seemingly persuaded by economic performance, even after

Table 4.1 Multinomial logistic model of 2015 vote choice: 2010 Liberal Democrat voters only

Variables	Conservative		Labour		UKIP		Green	
	β	SE	β	SE	β	SE	β	SE
Constant	1.86*	0.62	0.92	0.50	1.97*	0.72	0.50	0.73
Authoritarian–libertarian	0.01	0.09	0.10	0.08	−0.18	0.22	0.14	0.10
Redistribution (economic)	0.05	0.03	−0.08*	0.02	0.00	0.03	−0.10*	0.03
Stay in the EU	−0.52*	0.14	−0.03	0.13	−2.21*	0.24	0.14	0.19
Left–right economic values	−0.16	0.11	−0.12	0.08	−0.26	0.15	−0.22*	0.10
Tuition fees gone too far	0.13	0.08	0.17*	0.07	0.18	0.10	0.23*	0.10
National cuts gone too far	−0.60*	0.08	0.32*	0.07	−0.02	0.11	0.30*	0.10
Subjective economic evaluation	−0.19*	0.08	−0.15*	0.07	−0.19	0.09	−0.14	0.08
Change in economy	0.40*	0.09	−0.17*	0.07	−0.00	0.09	−0.33*	0.09
Immigration enriches culture	−0.12*	0.04	−0.01	0.04	−0.43*	0.05	0.10*	0.05
Partisanship: ref. = no party identification								
Conservative partisanship	1.64*	0.21	−0.65*	0.30	−0.61*	0.29	−1.61*	0.54
Labour partisanship	−0.78*	0.26	1.49*	0.15	−0.81*	0.23	−0.78*	0.20
Liberal Democrat partisanship	−1.19*	0.16	−1.24*	0.13	−2.16*	0.22	2.30*	0.19
Socio-demographic variables								
Male	−0.31*	0.14	−0.07	0.11	0.40*	0.16	0.05	0.14
Age	−0.01*	0.00	−0.03*	0.00	−0.00	0.01	−0.03*	0.00
Degree (or more)	−0.31*	0.15	−0.07	0.12	−0.53*	0.20	0.18	0.16
Non-white	0.29	0.34	−0.05	0.31	−0.15	0.60	−0.17	0.41
Model fit								
Wald chi-square <0.05	2,309.32*							
Log likelihood	−4,556.83							
R^2	0.26							
AIC	9,083.66							
BIC	9,609.77							
N	3,603							

* Significance $p<0.05$. Source: 2015 BEPS. Base category: Voted Liberal Democrat 2015.

accounting for other influences. The emphasis on deficit reduction was credited to the Conservatives and persuaded a number of 2010 Liberal Democrat voters to switch to their coalition rivals. The Liberal Democrats got little reward among those who felt the economy was improving.

Table 4.1 also suggests that the Liberal Democrats were caught in this left–right 'pincer movement'. Conservative voters were more supportive of harsh economic measures than Liberal Democrat 2015 voters and as such economic credibility lost the Liberal Democrat 2010 voters to their rival. Yet those who leaned left and vehemently opposed public service cuts were also significantly more likely to vote for Labour or the Greens in 2015. Here the tactical unwind to both Labour and to a lesser extent the Greens is clearly evident. Those who supported greater redistribution, felt that austerity public service cuts had gone too far, opposed the increase in tuition fees and believed the economy had got worse over the five years were significantly more likely to support Labour or the Greens than the Liberal Democrats. In addition, those on the left in terms of economic values and who believed immigration enriches cultural life favoured the Greens over the Liberal Democrats. The haemorrhaging of support to Labour and the Greens among younger voters who had supported the Liberal Democrats in 2010 is also noticeable, even after controlling for these other factors.

Summary

Going into coalition government with the Conservatives at Westminster proved to be a historic moment for the party. It had been nearly 100 years since Herbert Asquith had formed the last Liberal government – with support from the Irish nationalists – so the prospect of executive posts and the possibility of Liberal Democrat policy proposals becoming acts of parliament meant that the party could once again claim with some legitimacy that it was at the forefront of British politics. Ultimately, the Liberal Democrats' coalition years did prove historic, but for all the wrong reasons. On the morning of Friday 8 May 2015, the party was politically clinging on for dear life, reduced to electoral rubble and seemingly irreparably damaged. The longstanding structural weaknesses which had been camouflaged during the hysteria of Cleggmania were exposed and exploited by its rivals. It paid a heavy price for ill-thought-out decisions and agential flaws which, when blended with these enduring structural frailties, proved disastrous. Caught in a pincer movement, with little or no base to fall back on, the party was left on life support. The short- to medium-term prospects for the Liberal Democrats looked bleak. The party now had the millstone of the coalition legacy around its neck. It had always struggled to forge a political identity but now it had lost ownership and control of that identity. Negatively branded by different voters across the political spectrum, its capacity to be the home of the discontented was diminished. Fundamentally, though, the Liberal Democrats had lost national and local credibility. The latter was a longstanding challenge that the party had always struggled to overcome. It had always been a viable electoral choice for the disaffected and had a voice in the media, even if it was predominantly drowned out by the exposure given to the two main parties. Being untenable for many and an afterthought for others while simultaneously drifting out of the media spotlight into the wilderness brought with it new problems. Losing hard-won local credibility was bad enough. Losing both local and national credibility was seemingly impossible to square. So it proved post 2015.

5

Losing locally and being left behind

The 2015 general election was the litmus test for the Liberal Democrats' campaign machine and a pivotal moment for its grassroots model of activism.[1] A strong local operation over a sustained period bolstered by central support for a popular incumbent was hitherto impregnable to national circumstances and opposition activism. Yet there were warning signs that Liberal Democrat resources were overstretched and that traditional methods were being blunted by efficient and increasingly professional Conservative and Labour campaign machines (see Chapter 2). Cracks were emerging in the effectiveness of Liberal Democrat targeting strategies and messaging in defensive situations. Despite these frailties, the aura around the party's local base and campaign machine remained undiminished. So why did it fracture so badly, with disastrous consequences? The chapter is divided in two sections. First we examine whether the Liberal Democrat local collapse during the coalition was uniform or primarily concentrated in contests against its main party rivals, or in particular parts of the country, or both. We detail the damage to the party's local infrastructure and how that diminished its prospects in 2015. Of particular interest is whether the Liberal Democrats did better in 2015 where they had more local representation after controlling for other predictors of party support. We assess whether stronger local Liberal Democrat representation boosted party support directly and/or indirectly, through increased resources, thereby enhancing the local campaign, which in turn meant that the Liberal Democrats performed better in these places than elsewhere. Our evidence suggests that this was the case and probably helped save the Liberal Democrats from electoral annihilation. Yet despite this, we do not discount the possibility that there was a drop-off in Liberal Democrat activity compared with earlier elections. Were the Liberal Democrats simply out-fought by the Conservatives in the key battleground seats? Did Liberal Democrat campaigning have a significant impact or was it completely offset by intense Conservative activism? Had the Liberal Democrat campaign machine been left behind? The second part of the chapter examines these questions. While at first glance these are specific to 2015, they actually provide an important benchmark for much broader and longer-term questions about the role, operationalisation, technological advancement, competitiveness and effectiveness of Liberal Democrat campaigning. These questions are addressed later in the book.

The decline of the local base

There were plenty of warning signs that the Liberal Democrats were in electoral difficulty following a number of humiliating reversals throughout the coalition years. Of most concern though, given the party's ethos of community-based politics and emphasis on the 'local', was the steady demolition of its local councillor base. Not only did this damage electoral credibility but it severely hampered party attempts to maintain continuous grassroots campaign activity over the electoral cycle. The purpose of 'permanent campaigning', mainly through the use of local literature, was to offset the party's weak social and partisan base and prevent local Liberal Democrat core support from evaporating. Building up and maintaining its core vote over the electoral cycle meant that, as the general election grew closer, the party could begin to operationalise the more intensive phases of its local campaign strategy without having to start from a low base. Winning council seats and maintaining a local base were necessary to ensure this did not happen. However, the local decline set in almost immediately after the 2010 election.

In 2011, the Liberal Democrats lost around 40 per cent of the council seats it was defending, alongside control of nine councils. Many of the immediate losses occurred across the Midlands conurbation and northern metropolitan areas, where the party had incrementally built support during the Blair and Brown eras and replaced the Conservatives as the major challenger to Labour. In 2012, the party's national local councillor base dropped below 3,000 for the first time since the Liberal Democrats were formed, and one year later the party lost a further 124 seats in county council and unitary elections, at which it secured only 14 per cent of the national vote, its lowest ever poll in local elections. The Liberal Democrats achieved a new record low of 13 per cent in 2014, when it lost a further 310 council seats, 130 of which were in London. Going into the 2015 general election, the Liberal Democrats local councillor base stood at just over 2,200, a drop of more than 1,300 over the course of the parliament.[2] The party now had its lowest councillor base since 1982, the smallest number of councils it controlled (six) was the fewest since 1985. However, in reality the picture was far more mixed than the headline figures suggested.

Prior to entering the coalition, in those seats held by the Liberal Democrat where the main challenger was Labour, they held 30.5 per cent of the council seats. Four years later, after losing 186 councillors, their councillor base in these incumbent seats had declined by 16.8 percentage points to 13.7 per cent as the tactical unwind of left-leaning voters who had supported the Liberal Democrats pre-coalition gathered pace. Most of these Liberal Democrat losses were in England, with a decline in the local base of around 20 per cent, whereas in Scotland the party's councillor seat share fell by only 9 per cent, albeit the councillor base in Scotland was about 8 per cent lower to start with. However, in those 37 seats with a Liberal Democrat incumbent where the main challenger was the Conservatives, the party's local councillor base dropped by only 10.4 per cent.[3] Again, closer inspection of the data reveals a great deal of variation. In its battleground seats in the south-west of England, the Liberal Democrats' local base fell by 3.7 per cent and it went into the 2015 general election with half of its 14 seats in the region having in excess of 30 per cent representation on the local council.[4] Elsewhere the party suffered much heavier losses of councillors, particularly in those seats held by the Liberal Democrats around northern conurbations, such as Cheadle, Hazel Grove, Leeds North West and Southport. In those seats where the party was the incumbent, the main damage to the Liberal Democrats' local base was where Labour was the main challenger. While the party lost numerous council seats in the south of England where it was facing a strong Conservative challenge, generally speaking the erosion of its local base was nowhere near as severe.

Losing the local infrastructure

Losing councillors often leads to a drop-off in local activism, a reduction in experience, know-how, campaign skills and local knowledge. It also has additional knock-on effects for the local party organisation, making it more difficult to get existing members to renew their membership, to attract new members, to persuade both members and supporters to remain active, and to recruit campaign workers and volunteers at both non-election and election time. The accepted rule of thumb was that if core Liberal Democrat support in any of its incumbent seats had dropped below 25 per cent before it entered the final campaign phases, then it was always very difficult and often impossible to pull it back. Having a fully functioning active local organisation was therefore critical to ensure that local incumbents remained competitive outside of the election period and had a fighting chance come the election campaign.

Anecdotally, it seems that Liberal Democrat council losses during the coalition years severely weakened the party's local infrastructure. Using the 2010 and 2015 constituency election agent survey, we can directly compare local Liberal Democrat constituency campaign preparation and organisation at both elections.[5] Across the same constituencies, 22 per cent of Liberal Democrat local parties in both 2010 and 2015 started serious planning more than a year out from the election. Closer inspection of campaign preparation shows a drop-off in 2015, hinting that local losses had taken a toll. Tasks such as building a database, identifying supporters through canvassing, preparing the election address and electoral register are not only labour intensive but often undertaken during the non-election period, some in the years of the cycle between elections and others in the immediate run-up to the campaign itself. They provide a useful insight into the preparation of the Liberal Democrat campaign on the ground at the two elections.

As Figure 5.1 shows, local Liberal Democrat parties were far better prepared in 2010 than in 2015. Across the same set of constituencies, there was on average a 10-point drop between 2010 and 2015 in the proportion of local parties that had prepared the election address and the electoral register; further, while more than 60 per cent of local parties had built a database in 2010, five years later

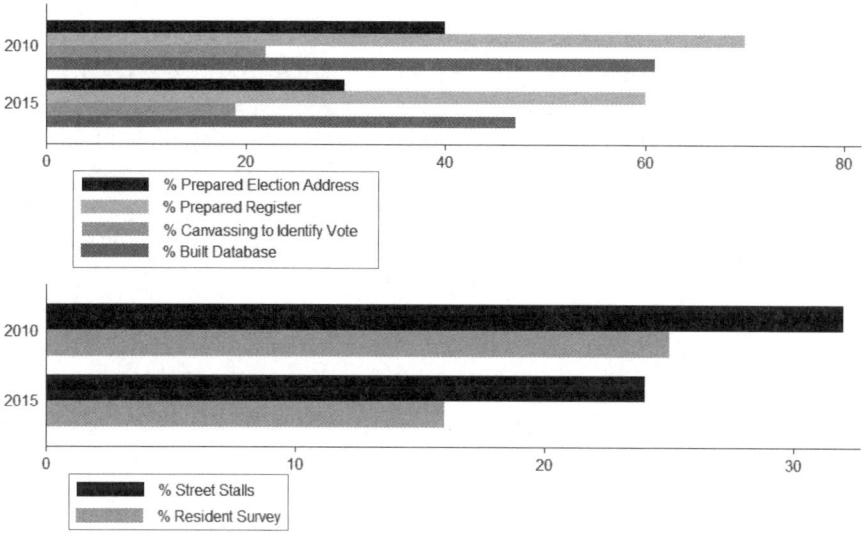

Figure 5.1 Comparing Liberal Democrat campaign preparation during the non-election period and pre-election activism in 2010 and 2015. *Source*: 2010 and 2015 British Election Study

only around 47 per cent had done so. Identifying supporters through canvassing requires experienced local activists. Given the challenging electoral climate, this activity was vital to keep the Liberal Democrat base together, so a concerted effort on the ground might be expected. On the other hand, the loss of councillors would be expected to have had a negative impact. Unsurprisingly we find a small decline. Around 22 per cent of local Liberal Democrat parties did this task before the 2010 election and this had dropped to 19 per cent by 2015.

An examination of other forms of pre-election activism – street stalls and surveys of residents – also suggests that local Liberal Democrat parties had been weakened by the loss of councillors during the coalition years. Street stalls are a staple of Liberal Democrat campaigns. They are primarily used to 'fly the flag' but also provide an opportunity for the candidate or incumbent and local activists to meet constituents, obtain casework and showcase party activity. Resident surveys are even more pivotal to the local Liberal Democrat campaign. Aside from designing the survey and strategically planning where to target them, the technique requires labour to deliver and collect from residents and know-how to get the right information to benefit the campaign (Cutts, 2006a). Again we find that Liberal Democrat local parties used both tools less in 2015 than in 2010. Across the same set of constituencies, close to a third of local parties ran street stalls in 2010 during the pre-election period but five years later this had fallen to less than a quarter. Similarly, more than 75 per cent of Liberal Democrat local parties used resident surveys prior to the campaign in 2010. In 2015, this had dropped across the same constituencies to less than 60 per cent. A quarter of Liberal Democrat local parties used resident surveys extensively in 2010 (see Figure 5.1). This fell to below 16 per cent in 2015. Even staple tools such as distributing leaflets dropped from 86 per cent to 75 per cent over the five-year period. There is some variation, though, by target status (based on marginality for held and non-held seats). Notwithstanding the caveat of a small sample size,[6] nearly 90 per cent of these seats in 2015 put a substantial effort into distributing leaflets, compared with around 75 per cent five years previously. In the safest and most competitive seats, the Liberal Democrats still had a large and active enough organisation to do the 'bread and butter' ground work outside of the election campaign period. However, fewer parties put substantial effort into using resident surveys in 2015 than five years earlier, mirroring previous evidence. Aside from the colossal number of councillors lost, our evidence suggests that the local Liberal Democrat infrastructure, campaign preparation and activism weakened over the five years.

Was the failing infrastructure evident during the 2015 election campaign? For the Liberal Democrats to remain competitive and embark on the intense place-based activism needed to win constituencies, local Liberal Democrat parties require an active local organisation over as much of the constituency as possible. It is also vital that they are able to recruit campaign workers and non-members to help out in the local campaign, and retain a strong local party membership so they can support the local effort. Once again, as in the non-election period, there was considerable circumstantial evidence that the local infrastructure had been badly weakened.

Figure 5.2 compares a number of these key indicators in 2010 and 2015 across the same set of constituencies. The proportion of the electorate in a constituency covered by an active local Liberal Democrat organisation is a useful proxy for volume and the 'health' and scale of the party's local infrastructure. In 2010, on average, 42 per cent of the electorate across the constituency sample were covered by an active local Liberal Democrat campaign organisation. Five years later, this figure had dropped to, on average, just over 25 per cent of the elector-ate. Anecdotally, it seems highly unlikely that the party had the local capacity to run constituency campaigns to the same intensity in 2015 as it did in 2010. This is backed up by further evidence. Across the same constituencies, 85 per cent of local Liberal Democrat parties recruited non-members in 2010 to help out in the campaign. Five years later this figure had fallen to 46 per cent. The mean number of campaign workers also declined dramatically, from 44 in 2010 to 13 in 2015. Even the mean number of party members fell, from 119 to 88, over the five-year period. The slump in membership mirrored the national picture, where it dropped to 42,000 in 2012 before recovering somewhat in 2015. However, national party membership was still lower in 2015 than in 2010.

Despite clear signs of wider weakening, there is some evidence that the local party infrastructure did hold up in Liberal Democrat target seats. For instance, on average, 64 per cent of the electorate in a constituency was covered by an active local Liberal Democrat organisation in 2015. This is only slightly lower than the 68 per cent in 2010 Liberal Democrat target seats but nonetheless is in the same ball

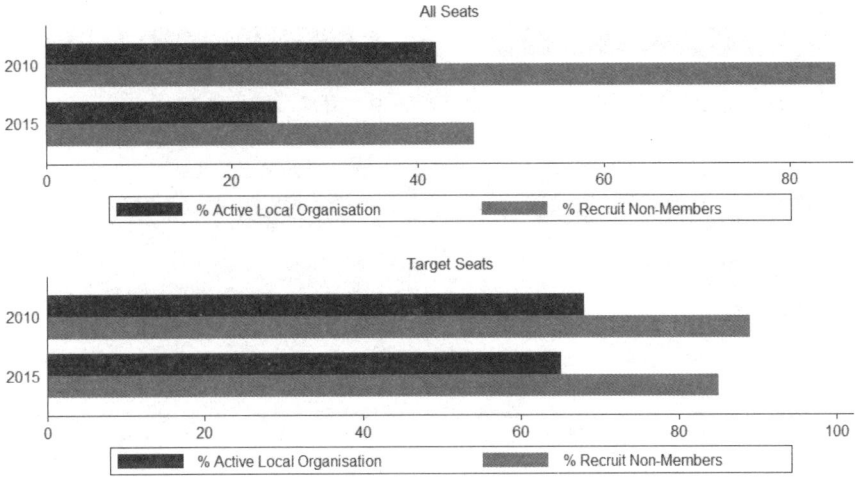

Figure 5.2 Comparing Liberal Democrat local campaign activities in all seats and target seats in the 2010 and 2015 general elections. *Source*: 2010 and 2015 British Election Study

park. Despite the losses, local ward organisations, particularly in incumbent seats, still remained intact. In 2010, 90 per cent of target seats recruited non-members to help out in the campaign. In 2015, this figure was only five points lower. There were however fewer members and campaign workers in 2015 target seats than in 2010.

While members are valued in campaigns for their loyalty, know-how and grassroots voice and are most likely to take on traditional campaigning roles, it is increasingly the case that supporter activity as a source of volunteer labour supplements member activism in generating stronger, more intensive campaigns (Fisher *et al.*, 2013). The downside for parties is that it is easier for supporters to withdraw their labour if for instance the election result is predictable or the party is suffering a downturn. Given that all parties, but especially grassroots-orientated third parties, are increasingly reliant on supporter activity during election campaigns, the drop-off in numbers of both members and recruited supporters is likely to have had a detrimental impact on Liberal Democrat activism during the three- to four-week campaign period in 2015.

Using the 2010 and 2015 surveys of electoral agents, we can compare Liberal Democrat members and supporters in those years across five traditional campaign activities: delivering leaflets, telephone canvassing, polling station number takers or tellers, doorstep canvassing and helping out at the campaign office. Our evidence shows that Liberal Democrat party members were not as active in 2015 as five years earlier: members in 86 per cent of local Liberal Democrat seats delivered leaflets in 2010 but this fell to less than 50 per cent in 2015. Those seats where Liberal Democrat members were undertaking doorstep canvassing dropped from

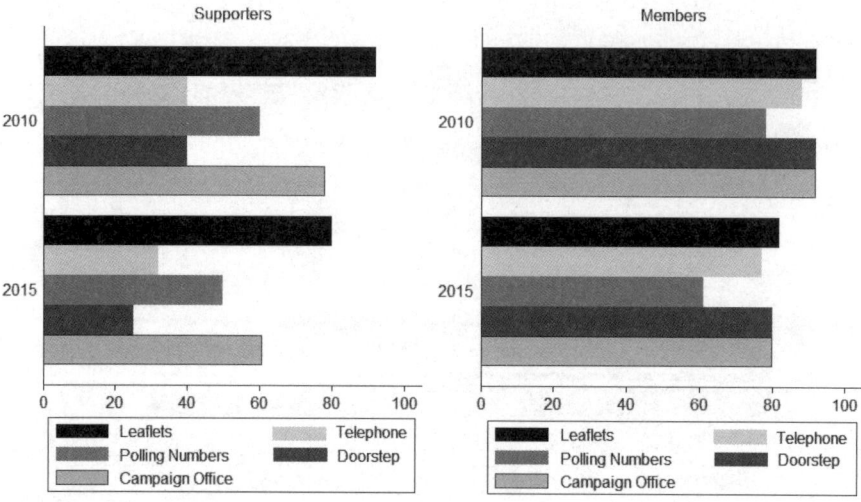

Figure 5.3 Activities of supporters and members – Liberal Democrats 2010 and 2015, target seats only. *Source*: 2010 and 2015 British Election Study

around 70 per cent in 2010 to just over a third five years later. This is an important finding given that local Liberal Democrat parties rely on party members to canvass due to the significance attached to collecting data. It also shields supporters from electors' policy questions and other queries or confrontations. There was a smaller drop off among those supporters recruited by the party. While there was a steep decline in the recruitment of non-member supporters after 2010, in those seats where they were recruited, supporter activity held up although there was a notable decline in those who took part in doorstep canvassing which mirrored the drop-off among members.

Figure 5.3 shows the activities of supporters and members in Liberal Democrat target seats at the 2015 election. While it is noticeable that supporter and member activism held up fairly well in these seats it is also apparent that across these five traditional campaign measures, activism was weaker than five years earlier. Moreover, as in other seats, fewer supporters were engaged in high-intensity voter contact (doorstep and telephone canvassing) in 2015 than members. Yet with some evidence that fewer members were engaged in these high-intensity campaign activities and others, such as delivering leaflets, it is seems clear that even in the best-resourced seats, cracks in the local infrastructure were visible.

Did the local base save the Liberal Democrats in 2015?

The chapter has so far shown that the Liberal Democrats haemorrhaged council seats during the coalition period and this had a damaging effect on the local infrastructure, membership and recruitment of supporters and activists which are so crucial to maintaining local permanent campaigns. Despite these losses, is there evidence that the Liberal Democrats' 2015 election performance was better in those seats where it had some semblance of a local council base? Did the local base save the party from electoral extinction?

In their predominantly Conservative-facing 'breakthrough' seats, the Liberal Democrats lost 10 councils and saw a drop in local representation of nine points. In 'heartland' seats, where alongside the Conservatives, Labour was more competitive, local Liberal Democrat representation fell by 12 percentage points. But the Liberal Democrats lost around 20 per cent of its local council representation in those 'new type' of seats gained in 2005, particularly where the main challenger was Labour. Seats where the party had won the constituency previously but then lost it at subsequent elections were particularly prone to collapses in their Liberal Democrat local base.

Turning to its 2015 performance, the Liberal Democrat vote collapsed by roughly 19 points in 'breakthrough' seats, around 15 points in heartland seats and 16 points across all seats won post 1997. Anecdotally, it seems that even where the Liberal Democrats held onto more of their local base over the five-year period, this could not save them from dramatic falls in party support at the 2015 general election. Yet the Liberal Democrats still recorded higher 2015 vote shares where it had a stronger local base. Where the party had no or only few council seats, the decline in vote share (−13.2 points) was much smaller reflecting floor effects. Its lack of a local base coincided with a low 2010 constituency vote meaning that party support could only drop, by in some cases, less than the average decline in Liberal Democrat vote change across all seats. More substantial declines in vote share between 2010 and 2015 were in constituencies where the Liberal Democrats had a significant local base or had control of the council. But in those constituencies where it either held the local council or had 40 per cent or more of the local councillors, its average 2015 vote share was just shy of 25 per cent.

But did the party do better in 2015 where it had a local presence after controlling for other influences? To address this, we use a 'Seemingly Unrelated Regression' (SUR) model, which takes into account the properties of multi-party vote share data by converting party vote shares into vote share ratios between parties using a logistic transformation. For the purpose of this analysis, we focus on the Conservatives, Labour and Liberal Democrats, which gives two variables, one for each party compared against the reference category (the Liberal Democrats). The model includes key determinants of Liberal Democrat support – historical factors, party incumbency, socio-demographic factors,[7] campaign intensity – and a measure of the local context in the form of the percentage of Liberal Democrat council seats held in the constituency prior to the 2015 general election. Including previous vote share alters the interpretation of the other parameters to reflect their impact on the change in vote share ratio from 2010 to 2015, rather than the absolute value.

Table 5.1 SUR model: Impact of local context on 2015 Liberal Democrat support against Conservatives and Labour

Variables	Con–LD		Lab–LD	
	Coef	SE	Coef	SE
Constant	+1.37*	0.09	+1.15*	0.11
Historical wins				
Liberal wins 1918–1935	−0.02	0.01	−0.03*	0.01
Labour wins 1918–1935	−0.00	0.01	+0.00	0.01
Local context				
% LD council seats 10–15	−0.01*	0.00	−0.01*	0.00
Socio-economic factors				
Affluent suburbs	−0.01	0.01	−0.16*	0.02
Urban deprived	+0.10*	0.02	+0.18*	0.02
University cities/towns	0.00	0.01	+0.07*	0.01
Campaign intensity				
Conservatives	+0.02*	0.00	+0.01*	0.00
Labour	+0.01*	0.00	+0.01*	0.00
Liberal Democrat	−0.03*	0.00	−0.03*	0.00
Incumbency				
Conservatives	+0.01	0.09	+0.25*	0.10
Labour	−0.02	0.09	+0.31	0.10
Liberal Democrat	−0.75*	0.10	−0.44*	0.12
2010 vote share of the electorate ratio				
Con–LD	+0.71*	0.02	–	
Lab–LD	–		+0.64*	0.02
Model fit				
R^2	0.91		0.94	
RMSE	0.27		0.30	
N	631		631	

*Significant $p<0.05$; Speaker's seat excluded. **Con–LD/Lab–LD:** Breusch–Pagan test of independence: chi2(1) = 348.10, Pr = 0.0000

The results are shown in Table 5.1. The R^2 for both equations show a high goodness fit and the Breusch–Pagan test, which is run to determine whether the errors are uncorrelated across equations, is highly significant. This indicates a violation of OLS assumptions and justifies our use of the SUR modelling technique. In terms of prior support, Conservative and the Liberal Democrats had a far more stable relative position over the 2010–2015 coalition era than Labour and the Liberal Democrats. The Liberal Democrats fared better against both its main opposition parties in those constituencies where it had strong local council representation even after controlling for prior vote, incumbency, party campaigning and socio-demographic factors.[8] Having councillors on the ground and a local presence meant that the party's vote held up more in these seats against Labour and the Conservatives than elsewhere.

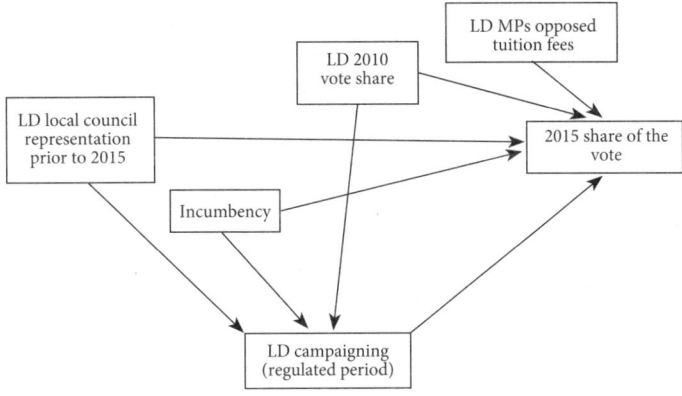

Figure 5.4 Mediator (within party) full model – direct, indirect and total effect of Liberal Democrat council representation on 2015 party support

Not only did the party perform better against both the Conservatives and Labour where it had stronger local council base but in those seats where Liberal Democrat campaigning was most intensive party support held up against both opposition parties. Aside from these direct effects on party support, as Cutts (2014) previously showed, a local presence not only enhances electoral credibility but boosts the local infrastructure and resources on the ground, which is so pivotal to grassroots campaigning. A strong local councillor base therefore can have an indirect effect via party campaigning on Liberal Democrat performance. By taking account of both the direct and indirect effect we can determine just how vital a strong local base was in propping up the Liberal Democrat vote. We address this question by using a mediator modelling design. Figure 5.4 shows a path diagram of the single mediator model where Liberal Democrat council representation from 2010 up until the 2015 general election (the independent variable) is related to the mediator variable (Liberal Democrat campaigning during the regulated period), which in turn is related to Liberal Democrat 2015 vote share (the dependent variable). The path from Liberal Democrat council success on Liberal Democrat vote share which does not go through Liberal Democrat campaigning is known as the direct effect. The indirect effect is where local Liberal Democrat council representation in the constituency is shown to affect 2015 Liberal Democrat performance through Liberal Democrat campaigning. The total effect is the sum of the direct and indirect effect (Cutts, 2014; Mackinnon, 2008). We include prior vote share and Liberal Democrat incumbency which is allowed to condition on party campaign effort and 2015 Liberal Democrat vote share (it has a direct effect and an indirect effect on party performance through Liberal Democrat campaigning). We also include other observed variables, such as seats where Liberal Democrat MPs voted against the rise in tuition fees and opposition campaign effort.

The results of the mediator model (both the unstandardised and standardised estimates (STYX)) are shown in Table 5.2. The base model (model 1) includes the three variables outlined above. The full model (model 2) includes prior vote share, which alters the parameters of the model to reflect the influence of the Liberal Democrat local base on the change in party vote share from 2010–2015. Other predictors previously highlighted are also included. Both models provide 'good' model fits according to established goodness-of-fit measures, while the final model explains 90 per cent of the variance in 2015 Liberal Democrat vote share. The standardised estimates from the base model clearly show that where the Liberal Democrats had a stronger local base they performed better. Such an effect was predominantly indirectly through the mediator Liberal Democrat campaign intensity, although the direct effect was also significant. These findings hold when other predictors of Liberal Democrat 2015 vote share are added to the model. After controlling for previous vote share, the Liberal Democrat vote held up more in seats where the party had a strong local base than where it did not. A local base boosted electoral credibility in the seat (the direct effect) but also had an influence on the party's parliamentary performance through Liberal Democrat campaign effort. Put simply, where a local base remained intact it was crucial to the operationalisation of the local campaign and led to the Liberal Democrats faring better in these seats than elsewhere.

Our analysis so far has only reaffirmed the positive direct and indirect influence of a strong local Liberal Democrat base on party support in 2015. What it has not done is address the question of change. However, calculating change is an issue. Even before entering coalition, Liberal Democrat local representation was far from evenly spread across the country. In a number of councils, the party had no councillors, or only one or two. If the party has no seats on the council in 2010 and continues to have no seats in 2015, there has been no change in the party's number of representatives, which, in a period where there has been change (most of which is negative), would not provide a clear picture about the party's low standing. Alongside floor effects is the thorny problem of varying council size, with metropolitan and unitary councils having many more council seats than those in English shires. Using an interval variable that measures just the change in council seat composition between 2010 and 2015 is therefore not appropriate. Although not an ideal solution, one option is to focus on those constituencies where the Liberal Democrats had 20 per cent or more of the council representation and lost a minimum of 20 per cent or more of their seats. Put simply, this differentiates between those seats which had a relatively strong local base but suffered a collapse over the five years, and all other seats. In accordance with earlier descriptive evidence, a simple OLS regression using this variable to measure change in the Liberal Democrat base suggests that 2015 party performance declined more in the seats where the party suffered severe local reversals compared with others, even after controlling for Liberal Democrat incumbency, campaigning and previous party vote share.[9]

Table 5.2 Path (mediator) model: direct, indirect and total effect of Liberal Democrat local representation on Liberal Democrat 2015 vote share

Dependent variable: 2015 Liberal Democrat vote share	Direct effect			Indirect effect			Total effect		
	β	SE	STYX	β	SE	STYX	β	SE	STYX
Base model									
LD local base 10–15	0.13**	0.02	0.20	0.26**	0.02	0.42	0.39**	0.02	0.62
LD local base 10–15 –> LD campaign intensity (regulated period)	0.63**	0.04	0.59	–			–		
LD campaign intensity (regulated period)	0.41**	0.02	0.71	–			0.41**	0.02	0.71
Full model									
LD local base 10–15	0.04**	0.01	0.07	0.02**	0.00	0.04	0.07**	0.01	0.11
LD local base 10–15 –> LD campaign intensity (regulated period)	0.13**	0.02	0.13	–			–		
LD campaign intensity (regulated period)	0.18**	0.02	0.30	–			0.18**	0.02	0.30

Notes: **Significant $p<0.05$. $N = 631$. Model 1 fit statistics: CFI 1.00, $R^2 = 0.72$. Model 2 fit statistics: CFI = 0.95, RMSEA = 0.12*, SRMR = 0.09, $R^2 = 0.91$.

Of particular interest though is whether the drop in local councillor representation harmed campaigning during the non-regulatory period. Continuous campaigning primarily ensures that local support is constantly 'topped up', so that when the election comes around the party can build on this solid foundation to mount successful constituency challenges. Anecdotal on-the-ground evidence suggests that a vicious circle developed: electoral reversals led to worsening morale and a drop-off in member activism, which resulted in local contact with the electorate becoming far more sporadic, which in turn led to further falls in support. While this decline was uneven and did not occur in all target seats, the drop-off in party activity in some did mean that the Liberal Democrats were left with the proverbial mountain to climb in winning back voters during the pre-election and election campaign periods. Using the mediation modelling approach outlined above, we can test whether there is any substance to this claim. Here we use a measure of Liberal Democrat local decline which reflects where the party suffered the most severe reversals in its local base, because it is in these 110 constituencies that we would expect any local decline to have detrimental effects on 2015 Liberal Democrat support.

The results are shown in Table 5.3, where the mediator is now Liberal Democrat campaigning during the non-regulatory period. We run the full model and include

Table 5.3 Mediator model: Party activism non-regulatory period; direct, indirect and total effect of Liberal Democrat local representation on Liberal Democrat 2015 vote share

Dependent variable: 2015 Liberal Democrat vote share	Direct effect			Indirect effect			Total effect		
	β	SE	STYX	β	SE	STYX	β	SE	STYX
Model 1									
LD local decline 10–15	−0.72**	0.31	0.03	0.14**	0.07	0.01	−0.58*	0.32	0.04
LD local decline 10–15 -> LD campaign intensity (non-regulated period)	0.43**	0.20	0.06	–			–		
LD campaign intensity (non-regulated period)	0.33**	0.06	0.11	–			0.33**	0.06	0.11

Notes: **Significant p<0.05; *<0.10. N = 631. Model 1 fit statistics (CFI = 0.95; RMSEA = 0.12*; SRMR = 0.06; R^2 = 0.89).

the equivalent observed variables used in Figure 5.4. Immediately it is evident that the decline in local council representation had a detrimental direct effect on party performance. Where the Liberal Democrats lost council seats, they did far worse than elsewhere. The total effect, where the mediator is the non-regulatory campaign, is also negative and significant. However, this is partially offset by the effects of local change in party performance through non-regulatory campaigning. Party activism remained strong in these seats which lost so much of their base, perhaps because it was ingrained locally among party representatives to continue to go out and be active and/or the local infrastructure was stronger in these seats, so campaigning still remained more intensive despite the losses here than in seats with weaker local organisations. In stark contrast to the anecdotal evidence presented above, those seats that suffered the most severe local Liberal Democrat losses were not only more active during the non-regulatory period but they offset even further falls in the party's general election vote through their local activity. There may be some truth in the idea that the Liberal Democrat campaign during the non-regulatory period was not as intensive as in the past, but this cannot be put down to the loss of its local base, as, in seats where it suffered most, Liberal Democrat campaigning was more intensive than in comparator seats. Of course, this raises pertinent questions about the effectiveness of place-based campaigning. Post 2010, why was local Liberal Democrat campaigning and the wider campaign strategy seemingly so ineffective where the party was trying to defend seats? Were the Liberal Democrats simply outfought and unable to combat rival activism? Was 2015 the moment when their main competitors not only caught up but passed them by?

Self-inflicted wounds

The trouble with successful blueprints is that they tend to get copied by others. Given the resources both Labour and the Conservatives had at their disposal, the risk of being out-gunned or surpassed by innovation was real. Also, Clegg was seen as toxic by many during the 2015 campaign and so any repeat of the 2010 result was highly unlikely. The party therefore needed to rely on its ground campaign to maintain an electoral presence. On the face of it, the Liberal Democrats seemed prepared for 2015. Following an internal review of its 2010 performance, the party adopted a number of organisational changes. First, it implemented a restructuring of campaign staff and their responsibilities. The goal was to shift the emphasis from geography to skills, with regionally based staff responsibilities being transferred to the centre. In 2010, there was a Liberal Democrat Director of Campaigns at the national level and four Deputy Directors of Campaigns, divided between the regions of the UK. Taking the south-west of England as an example, the Deputy Director was responsible for five campaign officers across the region. The Deputy Director oversaw the campaign literature in core target seats and wider campaigning in the region. Under the internal restructure, much of the collaboration with seats and responsibility for literature was now undertaken at national party headquarters. A national team of campaigners became responsible for artwork and key messages (in terms of branding and general content), which would be adapted for the local context. The remaining regional campaign organisers or campaign officers would focus on personal contact, monitor grassroots campaigning and wider local performance standards – oversee the campaign schedule and local plan – and support messaging, strategy, tactics and targeting in coordination with the local party. The goal was to run joined up campaigns in target seats, with party headquarters directing local campaign tactics, with the help of field campaign officers. Party headquarters was also responsible for providing grants and additional financial support outside of the regulation period to boost campaign activity.

Second, the Liberal Democrats replaced their longstanding EARS electoral database software with the same core database package – built for the party by NGP-Voter Activation Network – as the Obama campaign in the 2008 and 2012 US elections. This new web-based electoral database – Connect – provided improved security and data confidentiality but also facilitated remote campaigning, wherein activists could telephone canvass in a target constituency without having to go there. Alongside this, it introduced a new approach for selecting which voters to canvass and a new canvassing classification system, both designed to target messages and voters more effectively.

Third, the party revamped its internal process for the selection of target seats. Local parties had to overcome a series of hurdles to gain central funding. Party headquarters used a combination of key performance indicators (KPIs) based on party activity, performance in local elections, and extensive internal constituency polling. Candidates, agents and organisers also participated in training weekends and colleges where the national arm of the Liberal Democrat campaign machine would share information on which tactics and messages were working, latest internal polling, and advice on get-out-the vote strategies. Given all this, why did the party's ground campaign falter?

For a party that prided itself on place-based activism, local experience and an understanding of the local context, the internal reforms were painful. This was made doubly difficult by the party's poor handling of the restructuring. Widespread protests, personality differences and internal conflicts arose, leading to an exodus of highly skilled and experienced individuals. The remaining campaign organisers ended up having to cover a wide geographical area, which put further stress on local coordination and monitoring. To put this into context, one of our interviewees during this period was the Campaigns Officer for Western Counties, who, from October 2014 onwards, covered the constituencies of Bath, and Thornbury and Yate, but was also responsible for the Mid Dorset and North Poole constituency, some 60 miles away.

Ultimately, while the restructuring was done with the best intentions, given the available resources and evidence that opposition parties were closing the campaign gap, the timing and handling proved highly detrimental. Just when the Liberal Democrats needed stability, local know-how and continuity, the reforms resulted in chaos, disillusionment and anger. The long-term electoral consequences are incalculable but their short-term impact on intensity, tactics and continuous activism in the period up to the 2015 election must not be downplayed. Experienced activists in Bath, for example, complained about the lack of central control and regional input, particularly during the middle part of the electoral cycle. One example given was the quality of local campaign organisers from 2011 to 2013. In 2013, experienced local figures recognised that activism had dropped off considerably in parts of the constituency and they recruited an organiser to attempt to solve the problem. In the past, such appointments would have involved or been overseen by experienced regional organisers but during the internal changes the relationship between the centre, region and constituency was not a smooth one. According to experienced campaigners in Bath, it was not until the summer to early autumn of 2014 that the local party managed to get in place the right campaign organiser and regional support to facilitate intensive campaigning across the seat. In this case it is clear that the reforms, at least during the mid-part of the electoral cycle and likely beyond, were far from positive.

Aside from the negative impact of internal restructuring, a number of other factors also hurt the operationalisation and effectiveness of the campaign machine. Incumbency was seen as pivotal to any hope of the Liberal Democrats bucking the national trend. However, prior to the 2015 election, a number of party incumbents chose not to stand again. While some made their intentions clear early on, others did not. Sometimes this was for strategic reasons. In Bath, for instance, the incumbent Liberal Democrat MP, Don Foster, chose to stand down in spring 2014. Foster was worried a Conservative high-flyer would be selected to win back the seat, so he tried to negate this by delaying the announcement. However, this had unintended consequences, as Bath was one of the last Liberal Democrat key seats to be given a constituency poll, and campaign activity dropped as local activists campaigned for their nomination to replace Foster. When Steve Bradley was selected in early May 2014, the party had just 12 months to build his profile, get activists working (which occurred only after the appointment of a constituency organiser and an infrastructure builder in June 2014) and tailor the messages to suit the new context and candidate. The Bath example was not an outlier. Of the 57 Liberal Democrat incumbent seats, only 40 per cent by the start of 2014 had either re-selected the incumbent or replaced the retiring incumbent. Five of the eight seats that the party held in the 2015 election had re-selected their incumbent before early 2014.[10] By contrast, the Conservatives were working hard in Liberal Democrat incumbent seats, selecting early, building a profile and challenging Liberal Democrat messaging by stressing the significance of choosing a national government, not just a local MP. Over the same period, more than half of Conservative candidates had been selected in these top target seats. It was a strategy designed to blunt the Liberal Democrats' incumbent strength, but it was inadvertently aided by the Liberal Democrats dithering over re-selection in a number of key seats.

Much of the attention in the aftermath of the electoral defeat focused on the party's internal constituency polling. In particular, data from questions that named incumbent local Liberal Democrat MPs gave a misleading picture of the party's prospects. A failure to grasp the ensuing uniform collapse in support across party strongholds was somewhat amplified by teething problems analysing canvass returns from the ground. As noted above, the Liberal Democrats used the Connect database for the first time in 2015 and with it a new canvassing classification system. Connect represented a significant upgrade on the EARS system, as it allowed the centre to monitor local campaigns. Activists would enter information about local leafleting, doorstep canvassing, telephone canvassing, resident surveys and soft canvassing either after campaign sessions or in some cases through syncing with tablets and mobile phones while out campaigning. This added flexibility for both activists and campaign coordinators at the centre, meaning efforts could be targeted at certain times and adapted to changing circumstances. The canvassing classification in Connect was focused on four groups, known as the four 'S's (Safe; Switchers; Stay at Home; Squeeze). Post-election qualitative interviews with councillors and activists in key Liberal Democrat–Conservative target seats stressed the extent of party training on the new software and innovations. However, the interviewees accepted that, in practice, there were two negative consequences. First, there was increasing uncertainty among some activists, leading to voters being catalogued in the wrong group. This had a knock-on effect for target messaging and in some cases meant local resources were wasted. Second, the Liberal Democrats used a brand-new approach to select voters to canvass, which inevitably meant that the guidelines on interpreting the data were different from those at the last general election. Again, this caused confusion. Given that these data were framed around the new four 'S's canvass classification, it was inevitable that campaigns made errors in determining what the figures meant. In the heat of the ground battle, this confusion hindered the party's cause. There were also broader campaign issues, such as giving too much precedence to KPIs that emphasised intensity and the volume of campaign activism rather than honing down on key outcomes. Campaign tactics lacked innovation, with the party slow to test and implement successful pilots. This came to the fore in 2015 as opposition parties sought to close the campaign advantage still further.

Losing the campaign advantage?

So far we have shown that the Liberal Democrats' local infrastructure was badly damaged during the coalition years but that the party performed better where it had a stronger local presence. While the local base boosted credibility it also enhanced party performance through campaign effort. Liberal Democrat campaigning was far more intensive and effective in those places where the local base remained strongest and party support subsequently held up more in these seats. Despite the self-inflicted wounds, those seats which suffered the most severe local fracturing were still more active in the non-regulatory period than others and this local activity undoubtedly offset a more dramatic collapse in the Liberal Democrat vote. These findings do not diminish the local decline that took place but do reveal just how resilient the grassroots party had become, particularly in target seats. But while the Liberal Democrats on the ground struggled to keep their head above water did their rivals pounce and step up activism specifically in the seats that mattered most? Were the Liberal Democrats outgunned? According to evidence from the BEPS, this seems to be the case.

The Conservatives posed the biggest threat to the Liberal Democrats. In the 46 seats across England and Wales where the Liberal Democrats were the incumbent, the Conservatives were the primary competitor in 34. Of these, 22 were in the south of England, 14 of which were in the Liberal Democrats' traditional south-west heartland. Looking first at the non-regulatory period, there is clear evidence that both parties were evenly matched across the 34 key Liberal Democrat–Conservative battleground seats. Overall, the Liberal Democrats did record higher levels of reported contact, but after the 2014 European election there is a noticeable divergence, with reported contact rates higher for the Conservatives. The dip in Liberal Democrat activism may have been due to the party's poor performance in that election; however, closer inspection of reported contact rates in these key seats suggests this was not a one-off. In those highly competitive battleground seats in the south of England, overall Conservative activism during the non-regulation period was one percentage point higher than for the Liberal Democrats, while in the crucial south-west battlegrounds the Conservatives' reported contact was nearly five percentage points higher. If we break this down by types of campaign contact, in the south (including south-west) of England more voters stated they had received leaflets from the Conservatives than from the Liberal Democrats, which, given the centrality of leaflets to the continuous Liberal Democrat activism, is a startling finding. Of course, this may reflect a surge in the use of direct mail. Even so, this does not detract from the drop-off in Liberal Democrat intensity. It does suggest the Liberal Democrats' main rival had stepped up to challenging their campaign dominance. Moreover, across these 22 battlegrounds in the south of England the Liberal Democrats canvassed more people than the Conservatives but the reverse was true in the crucial south-west seats. Again, even accounting for the slightly lower contact rates from both parties in these seats than elsewhere, the evidence suggests that the Conservatives were at the very least matching and arguably outgunning the Liberal Democrats on the ground during the non-regulation period in the seats that mattered most.

But what about the regulatory – 'long' (pre-election) and the 'short' (election) – campaign periods? Historically, as polling day approaches the Liberal Democrats have profited from greater national media exposure of its leader and policies. Of course, in 2015, things were different, given that the party had just spent a bruising five years in coalition government. Here the story was more mixed but follows a similar pattern to the non-regulatory period. Across all of its 46 incumbent seats in England and Wales, the Liberal Democrats were in the ascendency with double-digit higher contact rates than the Conservatives. Even in the 34 Liberal Democrat–Conservative battleground seats, Liberal Democrat contact rates were eight percentage points higher in the 'pre-campaign' and 8.4 points in the three-week election campaign than the Conservatives' contact rates. Yet in the south of England battlegrounds the difference was just 3.7 percentage points and in the south-west frontline seats the two parties recorded virtually identical contact rates. As was the case in the non-regulatory period, in the vital Liberal Democrat–Conservative battlegrounds across the south of England, the Conservatives matched the Liberal Democrats' ground campaign effort in the run-up to polling day.

Yet, unlike in the non-regulation period, where no corresponding party campaign data exist prior to the 2010 general election, it is possible to examine data from 2015 to determine whether the reported party contact rates were similar or markedly different from those in 2010. One caveat is that these are two separate panels of respondents and not the same people being asked whether they were contacted in 2010 and 2015. Nonetheless, they provide some useful insight into the parties' campaign activities in these crucial battleground constituencies from one election to the other. Figure 5.5 shows the change in Liberal Democrat and Conservative reported contact rates between those two years across different seat types. Across all seats with a Liberal Democrat incumbent (and in England and Wales only) categorisations, average Liberal Democrat campaign contact rates were lower in 2015 than in 2010. The Conservatives also contacted fewer electors in battleground constituencies across England and Wales (and in the south of

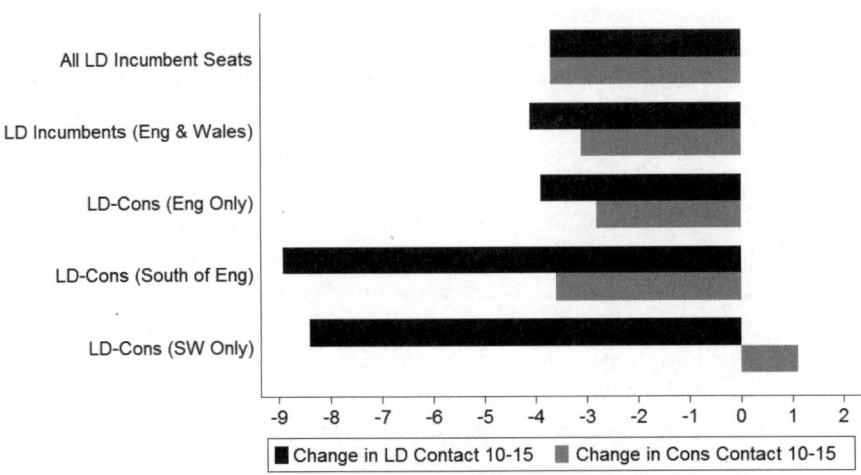

Figure 5.5 Changes in Liberal Democrat and Conservative reported contact rates between 2010 and 2015 across Liberal Democrat incumbent battlegrounds. *Source*: 2010 and 2015 British Election Study

England only). However, the decline in Liberal Democrat contact after 2010 was markedly more pronounced than the drop in Conservative contact. For instance, in the 22 battleground seats in the south of England, Liberal Democrat contact declined by, on average, 8.9 percentage points, compared with 3.6 points for the Conservatives, hence the evenly matched 2015 party contact rates identified above. Yet perhaps the most striking turnaround from 2010 was in the south-west of England. While Liberal Democrat campaign contact dropped by 8.4 points, Conservative campaign contact, on average, increased by 1.1 percentage points across these 14 seats. Generally speaking, it seems that in the seats that mattered, the Conservatives largely matched the levels of campaign contact of five years earlier, while the Liberal Democrats' famed ground campaign faltered considerably.

Was Liberal Democrat campaigning effective in the 2015 general election?

Above we presented evidence based on aggregate data that where Liberal Democrat campaigning remained intense and the party retained a strong local base, party support held up more than elsewhere. For the Liberal Democrats, the 2015 election was about defending what it had primarily against the Conservatives who posed the biggest threat. Our anecdotal evidence suggests that the Liberal Democrat campaign had faltered compared with five years earlier, while the Conservatives were on the up. Was the Liberal Democrat campaign – at different stages of the electoral cycle – still effective in these seats? Did activism during the 'short campaign' make a difference?

Our first set of binomial regression models examines the impact of party campaigning at different stages of the electoral cycle. We run separate logistic models

Table 5.4 Logistic regression of Liberal Democrat support in the 2015 general election: All seats (model 1) and Liberal Democrat–Conservative battlegrounds only (model 2)

Variables	Model 1 (all seats)		Model 2 (LD–Con=34)	
	β	SE	β	SE
Constant	−2.49*	0.36	−1.66	0.91
LD campaigning				
LD non-regulation	0.96*	0.21	0.16	0.67
LD regulation	1.75*	0.11	1.08*	0.32
LD non-regulation and regulation	2.56*	0.14	1.43*	0.34
Conservative campaigning				
Cons non-regulation	−0.13	0.19	−1.74*	0.59
Cons regulation	−0.58*	0.12	−1.29*	0.29
Cons non-regulation and regulation	−0.81*	0.15	−1.12*	0.33
Labour campaigning				
Lab non-regulation	−0.16	0.18	0.47	0.51
Lab regulation	−0.59*	0.11	0.02	0.26
Lab non-regulation and regulation	−1.11*	0.15	−0.18	0.36
UKIP campaigning				
UKIP non-regulation	−0.08	0.17	0.34	0.46
UKIP regulation	−0.48*	0.12	−0.53	0.27
UKIP non-regulation and regulation	−0.19	0.17	0.04	0.40
Party identification				
Liberal Democrat PID	1.80*	0.11	2.34*	0.32
Conservative PID	−0.95*	0.14	−1.02*	0.39
Labour PID	−0.66*	0.11	−1.25*	0.31
UKIP PID	−1.77*	0.40	−1.81*	0.90
Liking of party leader				
Clegg	0.34*	0.02	0.26*	0.05
Cameron	−0.04*	0.02	−0.05	0.05
Miliband	−0.09*	0.02	0.03	0.05
Farage	−0.10*	0.02	−0.18*	0.04
Political attitudes				
Left–right	−0.00	0.02	0.02	0.07
Coalition difficult to deliver	−0.00	0.04	−0.03	0.11
Immigration most important issue	−0.37*	0.14	−0.34	0.44
Prefer Conservative majority	−0.73*	0.13	−0.84*	0.32
National cuts gone too far	−0.16*	0.05	−0.10	0.14
Tuition fees gone too far	−0.06	0.05	−0.11	0.13
Stay in the EU	0.13	0.09	0.21	0.23
Tactical decision				
Tactical voting	0.74*	0.14	2.88*	0.31
Socio-economic				
Female	−0.18*	0.08	0.33	0.20
Age	0.00	0.00	0.02*	0.01
Degree	0.13	0.08	0.05	0.22
Non-white	−0.39*	0.19	−0.15	0.55
Model fit				
Chi square <0.05	2,561.31*		345.44*	
Log likelihood	−5,038.78		−535.87	
R^2	0.42		0.48	
AIC	10,143.56		1,137.74	
N	27,771		1,458	

*Significant p<0.05 Campaigning base category: no contact. Weighted: post-election wave weight (W6); voters only.

on the full data (respondents in all seats) and a subset of the BEPS – respondents in the 34 Liberal Democrat–Conservative battlegrounds (Table 5.4).[11] We capture a party's local campaign using direct effects of party contact at different points of the electoral cycle – those contacted during the non-regulated period only, regulated period only ('short' and 'long' campaign) and in both. All models also include established drivers of party support: party identification, leadership ratings, party–issue linkages (immigration; tuition fees; national cuts), left–right political placement, assessments of the coalition and standard socio-economic predictors of party support (Whiteley *et al.*, 2013).

Across all seats, after controlling for established influences on Liberal Democrat support (model 1), Liberal Democrat contact mattered at each stage of the electoral cycle. Those contacted only in the non-regulated and regulated period were 2.6 and 5.5 times more likely to support the party, respectively. Those individuals contacted in both campaign periods were 13.1 times more likely to vote Liberal Democrat than those who were not contacted. All the other predictors behave as expected, with party identification, liking of Clegg and tactical voting having a positive influence.

Model 2 shows the campaign effects in the sub-sample of 34 seats in England and Wales with a Liberal Democrat incumbent. To ease interpretation, we calculate AMEs. On average, being contacted by the Liberal Democrats only during the regulated period increased the probability of voting Liberal Democrat by 10 percentage points. Being contacted by the party during both the non-regulated and regulated periods increased the probability of voting Liberal Democrat by 15 percentage points. Crucially, those who were contacted by the Liberal Democrats only during the non-regulation period were not significantly more likely to support the party. This supports our earlier claim that Liberal Democrat activism during this period was haphazard. One suggestion is that large numbers of those contacted by the Liberal Democrats during the non-regulation period were hostile and so not contacted subsequently (the party only followed up those who were initially positive). This, though, would have required ruthless targeting and high levels of personal contact to determine voter attitudes. Our evidence suggests this is unlikely with more than 90 per cent of voters contacted by leaflet or direct mail during this period and only around 8 per cent through doorstep canvassing. However, decisions about whom to contact are also made through data analysis conducted outside the constituency, so it is plausible that these respondents were deemed unlikely to support the party based on previous behaviour/voting patterns, social group or in-house polling. Yet it is also probable that many voters were simply not followed up in the regulation period or that Liberal Democrat activism in the non-regulation period was scatter-gun and not sufficiently focused on maintaining and securing the party's core support.

Meanwhile, being contacted by the Conservatives in these battleground seats had a detrimental effect on the Liberal Democrat vote. On average, if an individual was contacted by the Conservatives in either the non-regulated or the regulated

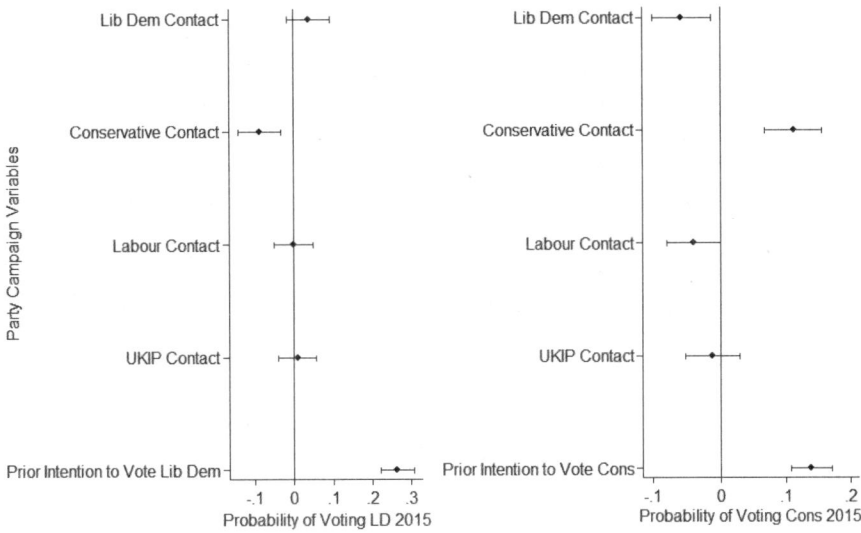

Figure 5.6 Party campaigning on the probability of voting Liberal Democrat and Conservative in the 'Short Campaign' (average marginal effects). *Source*: 2015 British Election Study (panel waves 4–6)

campaign period only, then they were less likely to vote Liberal Democrat by 16 and 14 points, respectively. Being contacted by the Conservatives during both the non-regulation and regulation periods, on average, reduced the probability of voting for the Liberal Democrats by 12 percentage points. Labour and UKIP campaigning had no statistically significant impact on voting Liberal Democrat, in these crucial battleground seats: Liberal Democrat activism was nullified by Conservative campaigning.

What about the final few weeks of the campaign? In previous elections, this is when the party's profile rose significantly. It was also when the ground campaign came into its own following months and years of hard work as the party sought to mobilise its core support. Here we include a lagged Liberal Democrat vote variable (BEPS wave 4 pre-campaign), which allows us to measure the impact of party campaigning and other predictors on Liberal Democrat performance during the regulation campaign period (see Table A5.1 in the Appendix). Most revealing is the impact of party campaigning in the 34 Liberal Democrat–Conservative battleground seats across England and Wales. Once again, net of other considerations, individuals exposed to Conservative mobilisation activities in these seats were less likely to vote Liberal Democrat by nine percentage points (see Figure 5.6). Supporting the anecdotal evidence reported above, Liberal Democrat campaigning proved ineffective at bolstering the party's vote in these Liberal Democrat–Conservative frontline seats.[12] But it did reduce the probability of voting Conservative in these key battleground seats. On average, Liberal Democrat campaigning reduced the probability of voting Conservative by five percentage points (see Figure 5.6). However, this was more than offset by the effect of Conservative activism on its own performance. On average, the probability of voting Conservative if electors were contacted by the Conservatives during the 'short' campaign was 11 percentage points higher than it was for those not contacted. Put simply, the Conservative campaign was far more effective at mobilising its own vote and reducing the Liberal Democrat vote than was its key opponent's campaign in these seats. Once again, where it mattered, the Liberal Democrats fell short.

Summary

Elections are a brutal business. Building up a core following and parliamentary representation can take decades and in one night of electoral mayhem it can all be undone. The Liberal Democrats' local base was meant to be bullet-proof, and the party's campaigning had a mythical aura of invincibility. Both unravelled. From a campaigning perspective, some of the problems seem to have been of the party's own making. Where it mattered most, the established party blueprint of continuous campaigning outside the election period broke down. This may be partly the result of losses in local elections but a combination of complacency, a lack of motivation, or just disillusionment given the electoral bruising the party had taken over the electoral cycle also played a role. Nonetheless, party support held up where the local base was strongest and undoubtedly saved the Liberal Democrats from oblivion. Yet the fracturing on the ground was still extensive and ultimately harmed the party. Questions must be asked about the lack of local leadership and just how effective party headquarters was in monitoring, overseeing and implementing strategies to combat the inactivity at local level. Did the loss of experienced campaign organisers on the ground following the party's re-structuring inadvertently affect the messaging, tactics and general local activism over the election cycle? Just how robust were the performance targets and why were the gaps in activity tolerated? Aside from intensity, there are also questions about the effectiveness of the party's campaign machine. Why was the internal polling so wrong and why did the wrong messages go to the wrong people? Did party headquarters focus too much on the volume of activity rather than the quality, thereby inadvertently missing the bigger picture? Party workers also experienced problems with the Connect software system and anecdotal evidence from observations on the ground suggest that the new classification system for canvassing may have led to incomplete or misleading data being collected. However, such problems were not unique to the Liberal Democrats.

The 2015 general election was when the aura of the Liberal Democrat campaign machine was banished. Rivals had seemingly copied what worked and were doing this better while simultaneously adding innovation, leaving the Liberal Democrats behind. The Conservatives overcame the Liberal Democrats' traditional campaign advantage by running a highly targeted, effective and efficient campaign which tailored modes of contact to personal preference. Their campaign was highly co-ordinated at the centre and operationalised from both Conservative headquarters and at ground level. It is no secret that the party poured previously unseen levels of resources into Liberal Democrat–Conservative battleground seats, which made constituency spending limits largely redundant. Our measures of reported contact capture a lot of this, because they are not reliant on the regulated spending limits or possible response biases from party agents' surveys; nevertheless, they are not fool-proof. For instance, some of the Conservatives activism outside constituencies is unlikely to have been picked up, such as the party's highly effective online campaigning through targeted advertising and videos on Facebook. Yet despite this, we show that Conservative campaigning in these key contests was extremely effective. This aside, it posed a huge long-term problem for the Liberal Democrats. The party was hamstrung by having considerably less in the way of resources and therefore was unable to counteract a rival that spent up to the legal limit in the constituency but then additionally spent huge amounts on it from outside, which was not subject to any legal restrictions. Without some tightening of these rules, it is evident that this electoral obstacle will be increasingly difficult for the Liberal Democrats to overcome eating away still further at any semblance of campaign advantage they have left.

Faltering activism, though, has major consequences, including the growing disconnect between party and the voter. During the non-election campaign, it is clear that there was a loss of personal contact with the voter, something which in its pomp the Liberal Democrat ground machine had been adept at. This then amplified as the election drew near. When those contacts were not made, it had a knock-on effect later in the campaign, undermining persuasion and mobilisation efforts. The large number of incumbent candidates standing down did not help maintain the personal touch and the lateness of some of these decisions was also clearly detrimental to campaign activity. Yet incumbency more broadly did not prove to be the safety net that the party thought it might be. Quite clearly, the 2015 election tells us that an incumbent's personal vote does not translate to party allegiance when a new candidate is selected. Moreover, the personal vote is not a panacea which can cut through and protect the incumbent from opposition advances. The failing of the personal vote in 2015 is likely to be correlated with the decline in grassroots activism which we highlighted in this chapter. However, the problem is far more deep-rooted and a conundrum for the Liberal Democrats. The whole community politics ethos relies on the local candidate building personal support from being active in the local area. It is their trump card at breaking the two-party stranglehold in constituency contests. If, on the one hand, this does not translate into longstanding allegiance and, on the other hand, cannot protect local incumbents from national political swings, then the Liberal Democrats are completely exposed to any shocks or events. Put simply, structural issues will always place a ceiling on seat expansion when times are good, while fighting for survival is the reality when things turn bad.

But was 2015 a one-off? Were the Liberal Democrats not doing enough of what worked? Or was this symptomatic of something much more fundamental? Why and how was the party's campaign changing? Campaigns and messages were increasingly nationally dominated for all parties, but to the detriment of the Liberal Democrats specifically, because they could not demand the media exposure of their main competitors. With the growth of the digital sphere, the ground campaign had become integrated and to some extent subsumed within these different facets of modern campaigning overseen by consultants, advisers and data analysts at the centre. Big questions now emerged about whether personal contact was sustainable or effective for the Liberal Democrats, given the resources at the disposal of their opponents. The frailties of relying on the personal vote for the local incumbent also undermined the very essence of grassroots community politics. Could boots on the ground ever overcome highly funded national campaigning targeted at competitive seats? Or could the advent of digital campaigning prove to be the vehicle which levelled up campaigning and, in synchronicity with traditional grassroots activity, reinstall opponents' fear of the Liberal Democrat campaign machine. In Part III of the book we address the bigger picture by looking beyond 2015.

Part III. The post-coalition story: fighting for survival

Part III examines the Liberal Democrats in the post-coalition era. Chapter 6 tells the story of the party's travails from Tim Farron to Ed Davey. From fighting for survival to some green shoots of hope, we examine how the legacy of coalition, embedded credibility concerns, agency failings and strategic blunders during a period of unprecedented events and shocks led to a series of false political dawns. Chapter 7 drills down on the Liberal Democrats' electoral performances post 2015 and evaluates why the party has been fighting for survival as opposed to seeing a revival. It assesses why the Liberal Democrats were ultimately observers rather than participants, unable to capitalise on rivals' woes or events, which would otherwise have offered the party both a lifeline and an electoral route back to relevance. Chapter 8 assesses how the Liberal Democrats' geography of support was dramatically reshaped after 2010 and why the legacy of coalition still influences it today. We also show how different shocks and events have accelerated deep-seated processes and why the party failed to capitalise on Brexit. The final part of the chapter strikes a more optimistic tone, noting the emergence of a group of 'Southern Crescent' seats which act as a platform for growth in the so-called 'Blue Wall'. We do, however, caution about relying on these new geographies as the route back to electoral health and show why uniting old and new is crucial. Chapter 9 returns to the thorny question of whether the Liberal Democrats' campaign machine has been left behind. Despite recent failings (some self-inflicted), we provide conclusive evidence that campaign intensity is on the up and that grassroots activism remains highly potent against rivals. Encouragingly, we examine how the party's digital campaign is punching above its weight and illustrate how it provides (together with traditional activism) a route to restoring its famed campaign advantage.

6

From life support to renewed hope

It may seem a truism that parties cannot survive without popular leaders or that popular leaders are an insufficient condition for electoral success. However, the context of the post-coalition Liberal Democrats meant that the party's fortunes were intrinsically linked to the leadership of the party. In reality, a mixture of structure and agency set the entire range of possibilities for the party. The ceiling for success was set by the structural conditions surrounding the party – previous results, the number of contestable seats, and the national mood for hearing the Liberal Democrat voice (all of which were harmed by the coalition years). Nevertheless, the course of action taken by party leaders had considerable influence on how well the party performed within these parameters. The structure provides the climatic conditions under which the leadership can adjust the thermostat but the range of control is already limited by the structural context in which the party finds itself.

It is our contention that after getting the politics of the coalition so wrong, the Liberal Democrats were destined to retreat to a comfort zone of pavement politics and super-localism. However, in the first section of this chapter we show how the leadership of Tim Farron shaped the party's retreat. From the Liberal Democrats' lack of a prominent role in the 2016 European referendum campaign to the disappointment of the 2017 general election, some blame can be attributed to mistakes made by the leadership. Structure set the boundaries of Liberal Democrat electoral performance, but agency determined the detail of relative success or failure within those boundaries. Farron's party underperformed during the 2015–2017 parliament and the 2017 election saw only a modest recovery from the party's 2015 nadir. The second section examines how Sir Vince Cable oversaw a party that veered between existential crisis (including the threat of being sidelined by a centrist Labour breakaway party) and the euphoric reaction to being the party most associated with resistance to Brexit and subsequent electoral success. Crucially, we detail how the Cable interregnum helped shape the environment in which the subsequent leader, Jo Swinson, had to operate. By 2019, the Liberal Democrats under Jo Swinson were a more vibrant party and looked set to be an impactful voice in the 2019 campaign. The third section details how the party remained constrained by the electoral mathematics inherited in 2017. It was simply not a credible force in enough seats to bring about the electoral shock that some felt possible. Even then, the agency of Swinson's leadership was important. The failures resulting from the dismal (though hubristic) Liberal Democrat campaign meant that the party underperformed significantly. The final section focuses on how Sir Ed Davey has steadied the ship and exploited his rivals' woes. Yet the jury remains out on whether this is another 'Liberal Democrat electoral moment' and whether it can maximise favourable political conditions given persistent structural obstacles.

Everything is broken: the party in retreat under Tim Farron

Farron's rise reflected his position as a community champion – the Liberal Democrat's Liberal Democrat. He successfully sold a vision to those who had stayed loyal to the party through the trauma of coalition and needed to feel good about themselves again. He led the party to believe that it could begin to recover only by retreating to a comfort zone of community politics and eschewing the tighter focus on the Westminster bubble after a bruising encounter with government. Farron had been defeated by Simon Hughes for the Deputy Leadership of the party in May 2010 but was elected as Party President the following September. This insider–outsider status gave him a critical edge when the Liberal Democrats began the search for a new leader to replace Nick Clegg in 2015. By December 2010, Farron had already defied the coalition line to vote against raising university tuition fees, and as President of the party from 2011 to 2015 he had been given – and took – leeway to criticise central planks of coalition strategy and policies. He acted as a useful rallying point for criticism of the Tories within the party, but he was no leader of a full-blown insurrection. In short, he was sufficiently the candidate of both continuity and change. While Farron had raised his profile as the friendly critic of coalition Liberal Democrats, his ascent to the leadership was assisted by the removal of several high-profile potential candidates in the 2015 general election. Cabinet ministers Sir Vince Cable, Sir Ed Davey and Jo Swinson had all lost their seats. All three would return to the Commons in 2017, but their absence in 2015 gave Farron a critical advantage.

Farron's populist courting of activists had been viewed with some suspicion by the inner circle of the coalition era. Unsurprisingly, a 'Stop Farron' candidate was found: Norman Lamb, Clegg's parliamentary private secretary from 2010 to 2012 and thereafter a minister in the Department for Business, Innovation and Skills for the remainder of the parliament. As Clegg's parliamentary private secretary, and with a reputation as an effective campaigner on well-being, health and social care, Lamb had orchestrated a Liberal Democrat revolt over aspects of the coalition's NHS reforms. In truth, he was always going to struggle to defeat a candidate portrayed as an outsider to the coalition inner circle, especially with a post-2015 surge in membership (16,500 new members after the 2015 election but before the leadership contest).

Just as Farron benefited from being a critic of the party's proximity to the Conservatives, he was also able to cash in another important cheque with the Liberal Democrat membership. He enjoyed a reputation as a winner, having taken his Lake District seat from Tory high-flyer Tim Collins in 2005 and turning it into a relatively safe parliamentary seat with a strong local base. The secret of his success was apparently local campaigning and 'get out the vote' strategies. This was music to the ears of Liberal Democrat activists, who, despite seeing an alarming drop in their numbers during the coalition years, were receptive to the message that the party could win again based on the secret to Liberal Democrat credibility – bottom-up knowledge of the local terrain. A new leader who apparently understood the contribution that the base made to overall party performance (rather than the directives from party headquarters) would be welcomed. Farron played a classic populist card with Liberal Democrat activists: the party had failed to listen to the popular will of the people (activists, supporters and voters) and the coalition effect had been disastrous for the activist lifeblood of the party. A reversion to community politics would be a way back for the party's integrity and public profile – not least because it had represented the party's playbook for so long. The coalition years, the Clegg leadership, the Westminster obsession – these had been the aberrant times and Farron offered the possibility of a return to Liberal Democrat politics as usual. He was also affable. His deep Christian faith gave him an ethical code of personability and humanity that was welcomed by some after the increasingly robotic final moments of the Clegg era. Unveiled as the new Liberal Democrat leader in July 2015 (defeating Lamb 56 per cent against 44 per cent), Farron enthusiastically set about leading a much heralded fightback. 'Lib Dem Fightback' became an attractive hashtag, but was in truth merely the start of a long march of 1,000 steps (and some of those were backwards).

Going AWOL: Farron and the EU referendum

Signs that the Liberal Democrats were failing to make significant progress under Farron's leadership became apparent during the 2016 referendum on the UK leaving the European Union. The party that had been most associated with enthusiasm for the European project since the UK's entry to the Common Market in the 1970s was strangely absent from the referendum discourse. Farron himself, despite leading the party that was most united on the wedge issue of European integration, was a very minor player in the Remain campaign. According to BES data, voters consistently identified the Liberal Democrats as the most Euro-friendly political party. This is not to say there had not been contradictions among those who voted for the Liberal Democrats and their predecessors. From the 1970s, the Liberals had built a bridgehead in some of the country's most Eurosceptic regions, especially in the south-west of England, where the agricultural and fisheries industries often sat uncomfortably with European Community policy. Nevertheless, it was remarkable that the party took such a backseat during the 2016 campaign. Some of this was outside the party's control. Being reduced to a mere eight seats at the 2015 election while the SNP had surged in Scotland meant that the Liberal Democrats had lost their third-party status in the Commons. They also lost their place in the media for the provision of a non-Conservative/non-Labour political perspective. Prior to the

2014 European elections, Clegg was pitched against the UKIP leader Nigel Farage in televised debates. These did not go well for Clegg, but they had at least presented a pro-European narrative in British politics around free European travel, work mobility and the benefits of migration – an agenda not addressed elsewhere. In 2016, the party might have stepped into the void left by Conservatives and Labour and appealed to those voters in England and Wales who might have been receptive to a more positive pro-European story.

However, Farron and the Liberal Democrats did not play – or were not asked to play – a significant role in the 2016 referendum campaign. That campaign included television debates and leading interviews with an array of high-profile politicians, but Farron did not feature. The only Liberal Democrats to play even a bit-part were from a bygone era (Ashdown briefly appeared alongside Kinnock in a rerun of 1992; Cable and Clegg made some interjections but received little coverage). Structural problems caused the Liberal Democrats to go missing in the campaign. A party with a reputation for grassroots campaign strength should have been the backbone of the Remain cause. Instead, the evisceration of the parliamentary party had a profound effect on the Liberal Democrats' ability to break through to the electorate. After the referendum, Farron announced a Liberal Democrat commitment to non-implementation of Brexit and claimed another surge of new members in the light of the result, but this failed to compensate for the party's invisibility during the campaign.

Farron's two years in charge of the Liberal Democrats were characterised by a sluggish – barely perceptible – recovery in the polls. Despite boosts in membership, the galvanisation of the party's active base never really took off. Excluding Richmond Park, the party performed poorly in by-elections. In the 2016 English local elections, the Liberal Democrats made only modest gains from a historically low base. The party retreated further in Wales in the Senedd elections and, despite winning two constituency seats in Scotland, did not increase its number of representatives in Holyrood.

The chaos within both rival parties in the aftermath of the Brexit vote provided an opportunity for Farron's Liberal Democrats to exploit and court the 48 per cent Remain vote. As new Prime Minister, Theresa May, repeated the mantra that 'Brexit means Brexit', Farron prepared to own the progressive opposition, arguing that 'if we trusted the people to vote for our departure then we must trust the people to vote for our destination' (Farron, 2016). From late October 2016, the Liberal Democrats began regularly to record double-digit poll ratings. The party also recorded more council by-election gains (31 in total and 28 net gains) in 2016 than before. Alongside this uptick in its local base, the party notched up a historic by-election win in the Richmond Park parliamentary constituency. The party had always maintained a strong local base and organisation, having held the seat from its creation in 1997 until 2010, and it also controlled the council. It was also a strong Remain constituency, with more than 70 per cent of residents voting to stay in the European Union. Liberal Democrat Sarah Olney took the seat, recording nearly 50 per cent of the overall share, an increase of more than 30 per cent from 2015, and with a swing of more than 21 per cent. Following Olney's victory, there was talk of a Brexit-based political realignment in British politics superseding traditional party cleavages. While there was scant evidence that the Liberal Democrats were hoovering up discontented Remain voters, Richmond Park did provide a welcome boost for the party's famed campaign machine that had misfired in 2015. However, there were doubts that heavily focused campaigns in target seats would be as successful in the heat of a general election, and it was still unclear that lessons had been learnt from the 2015 campaign.

No success like failure?

Whatever the contextual and structural difficulties facing the Liberal Democrats in 2017, it is hard to escape the conclusion that Farron's leadership compounded the party's underperformance. From the start, he stumbled over the compatibility of his Christian faith and being leader of a party built on tolerance and openness to others. His discomfort was clear when he declined to give a clear answer in an interview about whether homosexuality was sinful, and questions on Farron's views on the morality of homosexuality haunted the campaign. Farron's previous voting record – in particular his abstention on the third reading of the Marriage (Same Sex Couples) Bill in 2013 and voting against the Equality Act (Sexual Orientations) Regulations 2007 – was analysed. Although Farron subsequently spoke up for LGBTQ+ rights and supported equal marriage in Commons' votes, the focus was pulled away from the issues the Liberal Democrats wanted to highlight. Farron's personal stance seemed at odds with the very voters that the Liberal Democrats sought to win over: young, cosmopolitan, liberal Remainers who collectively celebrated sexual equality.

The issue dominated the first 24 hours and then dogged the latter parts of the 2017 general election campaign, just when the Liberal Democrats had an audience for their key election messages. In the past, media exposure during the 'short' campaign period had led to surges in Liberal Democrat support. However, debates about public policy and private faith wasted valuable time, drew negative publicity and distracted voters from the party's core message. As a result, Farron was unable to build a dialogue with the electorate. His approval ratings actually deteriorated during the campaign (see Chapter 7). By the final week, more than two-thirds of voters did not know if he was doing well or badly. Notwithstanding his personal apprehension about homosexuality, Farron had been dealt a bad hand, made worse by an ever-changing political context. With a Corbyn-led, populist left Labour party beginning to gain momentum and Conservative support solid, the Liberal Democrats simply seemed irrelevant to many. Moreover, given the extent of the collapse in 2015, there were simply not enough seats where the Liberal Democrats were credible enough to rebound immediately.

On the face of it, though, the snap 2017 general election gave cause for optimism. A shortened campaign period meant that the Conservatives were less well equipped to rerun 2015's decapitation strategy against the Liberal Democrats. Widespread dissatisfaction with Brexit also gave some in the party hope that it might bounce back to former glories. In reality, however, a significant Liberal Democrat resurgence was unlikely. While Remain-leaning seats offered the best opportunities for the Liberal Democrats to make significant gains, only a few seats were marginal enough for it to have a realistic chance of winning. More than half were held either by the pro-Remain SNP or by Labour. With gains likely to be more limited in these seats, many of the remaining viable seats had recorded Remain votes that were around or just under the national average, but where the Liberal Democrats were between 12–18 per cent behind the winning party in 2015. These were primarily Conservative-held, requiring a difficult, but not impossible, swing for the Liberal Democrats to win. To do so, they needed to be the undisputed party for Remain voters and still had to rely on some Leave voters either abstaining or voting for the Liberal Democrats based on non-Brexit issues. The party's manifesto – which included commitments to a penny in the pound increase in income tax to raise £6 billion for the NHS and social care, the reinstatement of university maintenance grants for the poorest students and the extension of free childcare to all two-year-olds – attempted to appeal to voters, particularly on the centre-left, who had abandoned the party during the coalition years. Yet such appeals were overshadowed by Labour's populist anti-austerity message, which partly singled out the Liberal Democrats as enablers during their coalition with the Conservatives. During the second half of the campaign, the Liberal Democrats did manage to get on the front foot against the Conservatives over the government's plans for elderly and social care – the 'dementia tax'. This gave the Liberal Democrats fresh hope of overturning Conservative majorities in a number of southern seats.

In reality, the electoral context had also changed dramatically from 2015, which undeniably made the Liberal Democrats' task tougher. UKIP had haemorrhaged both support and candidates, which benefited the Conservatives, especially in seats where the Liberal Democrats were the main challengers (Cutts and Goodwin, 2017; Evans and Mellon, 2016). The Conservatives' 'hard Brexit' message created a 'blue wall' of Conservative support in its strongholds and marginal seats that would be able resist Liberal Democrat challenges and even threaten a number of incumbent Liberal Democrat MPs (Cutts and Goodwin, 2017). Moreover, the Remain camp was increasingly fractured, with many believing that the government had a democratic obligation to deliver on the referendum result. While roughly a quarter supported the Liberal Democrats' policy of holding a second referendum, fewer than half of Remainers agreed with it. Meanwhile, more than three-quarters of Leavers opposed it. Evidence from the BES showed that few Conservative Remain voters were willing to abandon the Conservatives in favour of the Liberal Democrats. In 2017, the Liberal Democrats faced the twin problem of an impenetrable Leave vote that saw the Conservatives as the best vehicle to deliver Brexit, and a soft Remain vote that either accepted the outcome of the referendum or was unwilling to leave the Conservative fold. Moreover, this 'blue wall' in Liberal Democrat–Conservative seats posed a serious threat to Farron's party and made prospects bleak for a revival in old Liberal strongholds such as Cornwall, Devon and Somerset (Cutts and Goodwin, 2017).

The Liberal Democrats made very little progress in the 2017 general election. The party's vote share actually fell, although some successful targeting of resources allowed for the return of eight former seats to the Liberal Democrat fold. Four of these were won back by old incumbents – Eastbourne (Lloyd), East Dunbartonshire (Swinson), Kingston and Surbiton (Davey) and Twickenham (Cable) – bringing a welcome return of authority and experience to the parliamentary party. The party did, however, lose five seats: Richmond Park fell to the Conservatives after Sarah Olney's 2016 by-election win; in Southport the party fell to third place, behind Labour; Leeds North West went to Labour; in Ceredigion Mark Williams lost the Liberal Democrats' only Welsh seat to Plaid Cymru; and in Sheffield Hallam former leader Nick Clegg lost his seat to Labour after years of the constituency being a Conservative–Liberal Democrat battleground. Elsewhere, the Liberal Democrats' performance was seldom short of disastrous. In a dramatic symbol of the party's decline from government to the margins of British politics, the Liberal Democrats lost a massive 375 deposits across the 629 seats in which it stood. Farron's Liberal Democrats were, though, within 10 percentage points of the winning party in nine constituencies,[1] and within 10–20 percentage points behind the Conservatives in a further seven seats (Lewes, St Albans, Wells, Hazel Grove, North Cornwall, Winchester and Brecon and Radnorshire). The regional disparities in the Liberal Democrat vote share in 2017 demonstrated that the party's slump might be bottoming out but that the road back to recovery would be a long haul.

Farron was always less comfortable in the Commons than his predecessors. Under him, the party failed to appreciate the Westminster-heavy knock-on effects of the 2015 result. The profile of the Liberal Democrats sank from the minor coalition partner led by the Deputy Prime Minister to subterranean gang of eight with a largely anonymous leader. Farron himself only narrowly held on to his Westmorland and Lonsdale seat in 2017, which hitherto had been regarded as the template for Liberal Democrat revival after coalition. The inability of Farron's leadership to re-establish liberalism as a viable concern was his most marked failure. That the party chose 74-year-old veteran Vince Cable as his replacement in the summer of 2017 demonstrated a recognition that the party needed to re-establish itself as a parliamentary force again. The balance of top-down/bottom-up power in the party needed recalibration and Farron clearly was not the leader to do that.

Mr Mojo Risin'? The Vince Cable interregnum

Fresh from winning back his Twickenham seat in the 2017 election, Vince Cable was elected unopposed as the new leader in July 2017 with Jo Swinson as his Deputy. For Cable, this was literally a return to former glories. He was credited with an effective three-month spell as interim caretaker leader in 2007 before

Clegg was installed as Liberal Democrat leader. During that period, he had earned a reputation for being on top of his economic brief and as an effective performer in the Commons (famously referring to the demotion of Prime Minister Gordon Brown from 'Stalin to Mr Bean'). Nevertheless, the scenario in 2017 was less fruitful for the Liberal Democrats than in 2007. The party was in retreat and the bounce-back in electoral fortunes under Farron had been miserly at best.

Almost immediately, Cable sought to play the statesman. He made a virtue out of his time in public office, longevity in public life and wider political and business experiences. He recognised that the party (and the leader) needed to be far more proactive in courting media exposure in order to keep the Liberal Democrats at the forefront of public debate and to spur on party activists. Alongside this, Cable initially sought to provide clearer political messaging and policy positions, and stressed the need to address intergenerational inequality. Cable was keen to learn the lessons from the 2015 debacle by staying true to his social democratic leanings. He promised radical policies on second homes, tuition fees, taxing wealth and public investment in railways. On Brexit, despite previously stating that it would be politically counterproductive to have a second vote, Cable wasted little time in explicitly positioning the Liberal Democrats as the party of 'exit from Brexit'. He advocated a second referendum on whatever deal the government negotiated, or, if no deal was likely, with Remain on the ballot. While ruling out formal pacts with Labour and the SNP, Cable reached out to what he called 'sensible grown-ups' across the political spectrum who agreed with the Liberal Democrats' policy of keeping Britain in the single market and customs union.

Despite all the positive rhetoric, the first 18 months of Cable's leadership were largely lifeless. His proposal for a 'movement for moderates' – allowing people to join the party as supporters without paying fees; the ability to vote in leadership elections; transforming party campaigning online – was much more than an attempt to replicate the success of the Labour group Momentum. From a position of weakness, it was designed to remind those on the moderate left and right who were agitating for a new centrist force in British politics that one already existed, which adhered to the open, pragmatic, internationalist principles that they desired. Yet this had little impact on the polls. The Liberal Democrats remained stagnant, at 8 per cent. At the 2018 local elections, while a 16 per cent projected share of the vote was much higher than its poll ratings and three percentage points higher than in 2014, it was actually two percentage points lower than in 2017. It was in fact one of the worst local election performances by the Liberal Democrats since the party's formation. This provided the backdrop for renewed disagreements about the coalition legacy at the 2018 autumn conference. Former leader Clegg hailed its achievements and Swinson stressed the need for the Liberal Democrats to front up to their failures. Only Cable's description of Brexit as an 'erotic spasm' provided brief respite, though this seemed to reinforce the idea that Cable's time as leader was coming to an end.[2] Bedevilled by claims that he was merely a short-term caretaker, a year after becoming leader, Cable confirmed that he would stand down after Brexit was resolved or stopped and after he had transformed the party (Cutts and Russell, 2020). In truth, Cable struggled with the same structural factors that had constrained Farron's leadership. The party was no longer in the political spotlight and when it did have an opportunity to catch the eye of the public it still struggled to find an audience. However, dismissing Cable so easily proved rash and misguided.

During the first half of 2019, both the Conservatives and Labour were undergoing their own internal traumas and showed signs of rupturing as they faced increasing public disdain over Brexit. Prime Minister May's attempts to drive through her negotiated Brexit withdrawal agreement failed on three occasions. The last resulted in her demise as she was increasingly held hostage by her ultra-Leave European Reform Group of MPs and her partners, the Democratic Unionists. Corbyn was facing a backlash from a sizeable number of his MPs not only on his lack of clarity on Brexit, but also on his perceived failure to deal with antisemitism in the Labour party. His misguided responses to national security issues such as the on-going fallout from the Salisbury poisoning attack also rumbled on throughout the summer and into the autumn of 2018, severely denting Corbyn's popularity.

Eventually, the inevitable fracture took place as a group of MPs from both Labour and the Conservatives left to form the Independent Group. With 11 MPs, the same as the Liberal Democrats at the time, members of the new Independent Group put 'clear water' between themselves and the Liberal Democrats, stressing that the latter's brand was sullied by being in government with the Conservatives just a few years earlier. With the Independent Group seeking to capture many of the centrist, socially liberal, pro-Remain voters targeted by the Liberal Democrats, media speculation was rife that the party faced imminent danger. This speculation included possible financial hardship as donors and members departed to join the new group. Cable's response was typically thoughtful but resolute, stressing the Liberal Democrats' openness for electoral alliances around shared interests while noting the structural electoral barriers faced by two centrist parties seeking to court similar progressive voters. Crucially, Cable was quick to contrast the Liberal Democrats' underlying organisational strength, local base, campaign expertise and growing membership since 2016. It proved to be an accurate reflection of political and electoral reality. In mid-March, as the Brexit parliamentary process and media furore around the Independent Group both rumbled on, Cable announced his decision to step down to 'make way for a new generation' after the local elections (BBC News, 2019). Although the party framed the decision as an opportunity for renewal and a fresh start, the objective was clearly to diminish the novelty of its new centrist adversary. Around the same time, the Independent Group applied to the Electoral Commission to register for the 2019 European elections as 'Change UK – The Independent Group' in order to stand candidates. However, with Change UK not standing in the local elections and Brexit dominating the political agenda, an opening now emerged for the Liberal Democrats to take electoral advantage.

The electoral timetable favoured the Liberal Democrats, provided they could gain electoral impetus. The European elections were due to take place three weeks after the local elections. As a result, the party launched its European election campaign six days before people went to vote in those local elections. Cable was able to hammer home the Liberal Democrat message of a 'people's vote' on the issue of Europe and simultaneously stress that the party's desire to stand on a common 'stop Brexit' platform with Remain-supporting parties (particularly Change UK) had not been reciprocated. His denouncement of 'petty tribalism', with an expression of regret that such an arrangement had not been forthcoming, struck the right chord and cemented a growing public perception that the Liberal Democrats were the primary vehicle for pro-Remain voters. This perception became reality less than a week later when local elections results brought the Liberal Democrats much needed electoral momentum.

The party won 16 per cent of the seats up for election and 1,351 councillors (a net gain of 704). It now controlled 23 councils (after gaining 12), its highest number since 2010. Some internal concerns about the party's local capacity persisted, however, as the Liberal Democrats contested only 53 per cent of all seats – nearly 7 per cent lower than in 2011. The party's projected share of the vote was also a long way off the mid-20 per cent figures achieved in comparable electoral cycles since the early 1990s. However, these local election results gave the party much-needed public visibility. The party instantly built on this seven days later through the launch of its European election manifesto and campaign slogan 'Bollocks to Brexit'. The messaging provoked intense media headlines but achieved its aim of keeping the party and its Brexit message prominent throughout the campaign. It also meant that the Liberal Democrats could get across other manifesto proposals, on organised crime and a European-wide zero-carbon target, which, without its controversial anti-Brexit message, would have been largely ignored. As the Liberal Democrats flourished, its centrist competitor, Change UK, imploded. Some candidates withdrew after making controversial remarks, while others were openly critical of the leadership. One even defected and endorsed the Liberal Democrats. Splits within the Change UK leadership team about their failure to cooperate with the Liberal Democrats emerged as polling day in the European elections approached and the reality set in that voters saw the Liberal Democrats as the only viable choice to secure a second Brexit referendum.

As in the local elections three weeks earlier, it was the Liberal Democrats (and to a certain extent the Greens) that dominated the pro-Remain vote in the European elections. The Liberal Democrats won 16 seats, their best performance since 1979. The party won 3.4 million votes, 20 per cent of the national total, doubtless aided by topping the poll in London. It was the largest party in 44 local areas, 29 of which were in London itself and its hinterland in the south-east. The surge in support was smaller in Scotland and Wales, where the nationalist parties were more credible options for pro-Remain voters. Nonetheless, repeating a trend from the local elections, the Liberal Democrats had made significant headway in more affluent, pro-Remain areas where the Conservatives were traditionally strong (Cutts *et al.*, 2019). Against Labour, though, the evidence was inconclusive. There was little indication at the aggregate level that the Liberal Democrats capitalised on Labour's woes in places with younger electorates and where the party prospered before entering into coalition. Meanwhile, post-election polling suggested that it was 2017 Labour voters, especially newer 2017 Labour converts, that switched to the Liberal Democrats rather than Conservatives (Cutts *et al.*, 2019).

Cable was widely credited with giving the party its mojo back. However, the truth was that the 'Exit from Brexit' strategy was limited by structural factors like constituency context and Liberal Democrat credibility. Replicating this second-order electoral success in a general election was always going to be an uphill task. In reality, Cable's main achievements as leader of the party were similar to those from his period as interim leader. He had overseen the party in difficult times and ensured that it was handed over in a better state than he inherited it. Cable also successfully saw off Change UK rather than accommodating them. Change UK's failure to force a realignment at the centre of British politics was emblematic of the challenges and difficulties faced by the Liberal Democrats.

The arrival of Jo

For the first time since being routed in 2015, there was a sense that the party was gaining momentum. Local and European electoral success had positive consequences in the polls, for media profile and for party membership, which had increased to a record 120,000. After defeating Ed Davey in the leadership contest, hopes were high that Jo Swinson would provide a fresh alternative to the public and stir further impetus. Additionally, the Liberal Democrats were the main beneficiaries of splits within Change UK, when, 12 days after the European elections, six of the 11 MPs resigned from Change UK. A week or so later, Chuka Umunna became the first of them to join the Liberal Democrats. Defections provided publicity and a legitimacy boost for the Liberal Democrats and indeed Swinson herself, who was instrumental in persuading Luciana Berger and six other MPs to join the party. Three of these – Sam Gyimah, Philip Lee and Antoinette Sandbach – crossed the floor of the House of Commons and joined directly from the Conservatives. Success in the Brecon and Radnorshire by-election (a traditional Nonconformist area of Liberal strength) also suggested that the local and European election triumphs months earlier were not a flash in the pan and provided further evidence that the party was once again competitive in its pre-coalition strongholds.

Straightaway, Swinson sought to distinguish her leadership from the Cable era through an unequivocal commitment to 'Stop Brexit' and doubling down on equidistance. On Brexit, senior Liberal Democrat strategists and party figures around the Swinson team were keen to remove any ambiguity about the Liberal Democrats' Remain credentials. The goal was to exploit uncertainty around Labour's 'renegotiation' position (Cutts and Russell, 2020). However, there were also concerns that the Labour leadership, which was coming under increasing pressure from Remain Labour MPs and shadow cabinet members, would move closer to advocating a second referendum and muddy Liberal Democrat claims to be *the* Remain party. As a consequence, the Liberal Democrats sought to distinguish themselves from Labour and alternative Remain options by promising to stop Brexit altogether without a referendum if they won a majority at a general election. The core policy of supporting a second referendum with a Remain option still stood, but the party signalled to Remain voters that it would revoke Article 50 if it won power. This new direction mirrored the Change UK policy, which Cable had rejected less than six months before. Yet despite some dissent from delegates that cancelling Brexit without a referendum would turn off voters, the party's new 'revoke policy' got overwhelming approval from conference. It proved to be a key moment, but not necessarily in the manner that the Liberal Democrats had hoped.

The Liberal Democrats also espoused an explicit equidistance stance and ruled out supporting a Johnson- or Corbyn-led administration. Swinson was consistently vehement in her criticism of Boris Johnson, including over the proroguing of parliament, withdrawing the whip from pro-Remain Conservatives, and Johnson's insistence of keeping 'no deal' on the table in order to adhere to the deadline of 31 October 2019 for the completion of Brexit. Swinson also amplified the anti-Corbyn rhetoric from what it had been under Cable. Her resolve was tested early on when she rejected a proposal for the formation of a Corbyn-led caretaker government to avoid a no-deal Brexit in the event of a 'no confidence' vote in Johnson's Conservative government. Despite cross-party talks in late September 2019, Swinson remained adamant that she would not support Corbyn as an interim leader, instead suggesting alternative leading parliamentarians such as Ken Clarke, Harriet Harman and the widely respected Dame Margaret Beckett. Even in the face of indications from the SNP, Plaid Cymru and the Greens that they would back Corbyn as a caretaker Prime Minister, Swinson, alongside independent MPs, stood her ground. Both Swinson and other prominent Liberal Democrats simply questioned whether Corbyn could feasibly achieve a Commons majority. Part of the calculation reflected Corbyn's disinclination to support a second referendum himself. Increasingly, though, this assertion was also tied to accusations that Corbyn was personally unfit for the job. Part of this coincided with wider views over the Labour leadership's handling of antisemitism within the party, but the Liberal Democrats also began to use Conservative attack lines. Both Swinson and other senior Liberal Democrats, including ex-Labour MP Chuka Umunna, repeatedly framed Corbyn as a threat to national security through direct personal criticism of his response to the Salisbury poisoning incident. With an election looming, the personal nature of Swinson's equidistance stance hardened, with even a suggestion that some post-election cooperation could occur but only on the condition that Corbyn was not the leader (Kentish, 2019).

Swinson's 'revoke policy' and the Liberal Democrats' hardened equidistance stance put in danger party efforts to woo prospective Conservative and Labour switchers. Aside from risking message clarity, the ambiguity inherent to equidistance meant that their opponents could warn their respective voters that a vote for the Liberal Democrats could inadvertently let their rival into government. Given that the Liberal Democrats would need to syphon off particular types of voters, such as pro-Remain Conservative and Labour supporters, to win seats, it remained unclear how, for instance, a strong anti-Corbyn rhetoric would ease the fears among Remain-leaning Conservatives and persuade them to switch to the Liberal Democrats. Nonetheless, even accounting for the general volatility in the polls, the Liberal Democrats continued to poll well, vying with Labour to be the main Remain alternative to the Conservatives. Given this, it was unsurprising that Swinson, along with the SNP, pushed for an early general election. While it was largely driven by electoral considerations, there was also a sense that Remain-supporting parties were somewhat boxed in. There was a growing expectation that, through the support of some Labour MPs in Leave seats, Johnson now had the votes to get his Brexit deal through parliament. Some Liberal Democrats were also unsure whether the European Union would agree to another Brexit extension, which would risk a no-deal outcome. While some senior Liberal Democrats expressed concerns about falling into Johnson's 'electoral trap', Swinson took a far more positive view. This proved critical and left the Labour leadership little option but to accept a general election in December.

2019: Swinson's disastrous campaign

Swinson was projected by the party as the spokesperson for progressive Britain –a competent, pragmatic, moderate alternative to Boris Johnson and Jeremy Corbyn. Aside from internal party enthusiasm for Swinson, others saw her relative obscurity among the public as an advantage and a vehicle through which the party could attract support from those who were disillusioned with both main party leaders. As such, the party's campaign, branding and literature put Swinson centre stage. From the orange battle bus inscribed with her headshot photo and emblazoned with the phrase 'Jo Swinson's Liberal Democrats' to personalising high-profile policy announcements on free childcare for those aged two to four years and life-long learning, the campaign was all about 'Swinsonising' the message. The leader was at the heart of the party's hopes to break the two-party prism.

Yet, far from being an electoral asset, Swinson rapidly became a liability. At the party's formal election campaign launch, she asserted that she was campaigning to become Prime Minister. The claim haunted her throughout the campaign, with many considering it unrealistic and counterproductive. Despite this, in campaign speeches and media interviews Swinson continued to stress her prime ministerial credentials. This led to ridicule and claims that she was out of touch. Public support for her and the party began to tumble. As we show in Chapter

7, Swinson's popularity barely exceeded 25 per cent during her tenure. Initially, this was because the public did not really know enough about her to make a judgement. Yet the more the public saw of her, the less impressed they became. By the end of the campaign, Swinson had a net approval rating of –50 – worse than Corbyn's. The party gambled the house on Swinson as a fresh, credible alternative to Johnson and Corbyn in order to cut through the two-party stranglehold in England and Wales and the dominance of the SNP in Scotland. Placing so much hope on the leader reaffirmed the electoral bind the Liberal Democrats had found themselves in since the 2010 coalition.

Swinson also came with coalition baggage. As Business Minister, she had supported austerity measures, including the so-called 'bedroom tax', welfare cuts for people with illness or disability, private tendering for the NHS and cutting funding for young people seeking work, while simultaneously voting against increases in income tax for those earning over £150,000 and a tax on bankers' bonuses. This record was pointed out repeatedly by opponents in the national- and constituency-level campaign. Swinson faced online and in-person challenges about her voting record and she was forced on the BBC *Question Time* special to say 'sorry that we did not win more of those fights in coalition' (Merrick, 2019). While the apology for the austerity cuts became more heartfelt as the campaign proceeded, there was an attempt to defend the Liberal Democrats' role in the coalition, and that ended up diluting the message. For instance, at Sam Gyimah's campaign launch in Kensington, Swinson acknowledged Liberal Democrats' failings in coalition – using the bedroom tax as a prominent example – but pushed back against the narrative by stressing the party's role in raising the personal tax allowance and driving support for same-sex marriage. By early December, Swinson's tone had changed, and she openly apologised for voting for austerity cuts and admitted that they had gone too far. The wider message was that the party (and Swinson herself) had learnt from the experience. However, the need to repeat this throughout the election to offset mounting criticism had not been the original intention of the leader-focused campaign. Austerity remained a persistent political sore and repelled some of the voters that the party needed. Swinson's inability to distance herself – and the party – from the coalition record proved highly problematic and electorally damaging. As a reminder of the Liberal Democrat marginalisation since the coalition, Swinson was excluded from the first televised head-to-head election debate, despite the party's protests.

In policy terms, opposition to Brexit had become the core strategy of the party. Swinson began the campaign promising to revoke Article 50 if the Liberal Democrats won an outright majority. Not only did it prove to be a strategic error, it was also, according to Cable's description, a 'distraction', given that the party's prospects of winning a majority were slim. The policy not only lacked clarity and simplicity, but also proved insufficiently liberal or democratic. This was seized upon by rivals, who gleefully made hay at visible contradictions. A party that had been consistently vocal in its support for proportional representation as a response to winning parties forming governments on low national vote shares now proposed that winning a majority under the same voting system constituted an indisputable mandate for scrapping the EU referendum result. It seemed like an act of self-harm. During the final weeks of the campaign and with their national support dropping, the Liberal Democrats started to play down the revoke policy and instead talked up what senior party MPs called 'Plan A' – a second referendum (Cutts and Russell, 2020). It was as close to an admission of guilt as one could get that the policy had failed to attract the voters it needed.

The rationale for the Liberal Democrats' equidistance stance and the Swinson-centric campaign was borne out of the party's perception that both Johnson and Corbyn were intrinsically unpopular with the public. Pushing back against Corbyn also had the added benefit of exposing the Labour leader's lukewarm Remain credentials. Nonetheless, the party's equidistance stance predictably rebounded. The caustic rhetoric towards Corbyn, in particular, backfired. On the one hand, even though there was antipathy towards Labour under Corbyn from some Labour Remainers, the majority still saw Labour as best placed to stop Brexit. So Liberal Democrat efforts to parachute themselves above Labour in key target seats as the only credible Remain choice proved to be largely ineffective. Perhaps more importantly, the anti-Corbyn message cemented Conservative support, making it harder for the Liberal Democrats to gain momentum in Conservative–Liberal Democrat marginals. Persuading Remain-leaning Conservatives to switch was always going to be challenging but reinforcing the unsuitability of Labour under Corbyn only made it more difficult. Tactically, this proved not only to be a strategic mistake but electorally naïve.

Essentially, the Liberal Democrats gambled that the 2019 election was about – and only about – the UK's exit from the EU. The Liberal Democrat manifesto – which included plans to generate 80 per cent of electricity from renewables, tax frequent flyers, recruit 20,000 new teachers and provide free childcare for two- to four-year-olds – was secondary to the party's pledge to stop Brexit. The clear hope was that by designing a raft of policies around this single issue, the party could capitalise on Remainer support. However, the general election campaign failed to follow the preordained script, and the Liberal Democrats found it hard to reach the 48 per cent of voters who had chosen Remain. In the 2019 election, which Johnson had called to 'Get Brexit done', even fervent Remainers decided to cast their votes on other issues, or for parties other than the Liberal Democrats, which might stand a better chance of winning in their constituency.

In 2019, the Liberal Democrats remained a party of contradiction. Emphatically bottom-up in terms of party organisation, they continued to rely heavily on the appeal of the leader, and Swinson sat uncomfortably in the spotlight. Swinson's leadership was almost a perfect example of how structural constraints restrict the scope for third-party performance in British politics, but also how agency can affect that performance at the margins. Unfortunately for her, Swinson's effect on the 2019 campaign seemed to be almost wholly negative.

A small step in the right direction?

The election outcome was a mixed bag. The Liberal Democrats polled 1.3 million more votes than in 2017, and their national vote share was up 4.2 percentage points, to 11.5 per cent. Yet it was still only half that achieved in 2010 and lower than at any election between 1974 and 2010. At the regional level, Liberal Democrat support increased but the north–south divide grew wider (see Chapter 8). Two years on from Farron, the Liberal Democrats improved their performance in 574 of 611 constituencies.[3] Nevertheless, by gaining three seats – Fife North East, Richmond Park and St Albans – but losing four, the party managed a net loss of one MP. Leader Jo Swinson lost her East Dunbartonshire seat after an effective SNP squeeze on the local Labour vote. Aside from the personal humiliation, this seemed to be highly symbolic. The public had delivered their verdict on 'Jo Swinson's Liberal Democrats'. Other Liberal Democrat incumbents to be defeated included Stephen Lloyd in Eastbourne and Tom Brake in Carshalton and Wallington. The latter defeat was particularly unexpected and owed much to the party pouring resources into nearby Wimbledon in attempt to oust the sitting Conservative MP, thereby leaving Brake exposed. Norman Lamb's decision to retire in North Norfolk meant that seat fell easily to the Conservatives.

In 2017, the party polled more than 30 per cent of the vote in 28 constituencies but lost 375 deposits and came second in only 38 seats. In 2019, these figures were much improved. The Liberal Democrats topped 30 per cent in 51 seats, lost 138 deposits and came second in 91 seats, 80 of which were Conservative held. Of these 91 seats, the party was only 10 per cent behind the winning party in 15. Of these 15 seats, 10 were ultra-marginal (the Liberal Democrats were 5 per cent or less behind the incumbent), with eight of these held by the Conservatives. These facts reiterate that Swinson certainly left a party that was better equipped to challenge than the one she inherited. However, the Liberal Democrats also suffered from a pincer movement in the places they most needed to win. And here agency and party strategy hindered progress. Going into the 2019 election, 29 of the 38 seats where the party ended second were Conservative–Liberal Democrat battlegrounds. In most of these, support for the Liberal Democrats rose and in six constituencies they actually recorded double-digit increases in support. However, the party lost ground in five of these seats. Anecdotally, given the fall in Labour support in many of these contests, the Liberal Democrats had begun to regain some of the centre-left tactical switchers who had left it after 2010. Making inroads into the Conservative vote clearly proved hugely problematic as the spectre of a Corbyn-led Labour government seemed more realistic (or more frightening) to Conservative voters in 2019 than in 2017. The Liberal Democrats' hostility to Labour only exacerbated this. At the same time, it probably increased the determination of Labour and SNP activists to use Swinson's record in the Conservative-led coalition against her, not least in her own seat. This also undoubtedly played a role in the Liberal Democrats' failure both to capitalise in Cambridge and Sheffield Hallam (where the sitting Labour MP had been deselected following a series of misconduct allegations) and to make inroads into the Labour vote elsewhere.

As we show in Chapter 8, only one of the 11 seats that the Liberal Democrats won in 2019 – Caithness, Sutherland and Easter Ross – was a Leave–Remain 'toss-up' while in six of the others support for Remain in the referendum had exceeded 60 per cent. Liberal Democrat support was in excess of six percentage points higher in Remain than in Leave seats. However, beneath these headlines the picture is far patchier. The expected Liberal Democrat surge in 'hard Remain' (those with a Remain vote of 60 per cent or more) seats failed to materialise. Once again, structural forces were at play. First, the SNP electoral machine monopolised the Remain vote in Scotland. Second, outside of seats where the Liberal Democrats had enjoyed local and parliamentary success, most of the strong Remain seats were safe Labour ones. The lack of electoral credibility in these areas meant that any growth in Liberal Democrat support was always going to be constrained by this. Put simply, expecting these Labour bastions to fall by attacking Labour and adopting the 'revoke' position was at best misguided and at worse a bad electoral misjudgement.

The failure of Swinson to cut through to a wider audience in 2019 shows once again the importance of agency for the Liberal Democrats' electoral fortunes, but the underlying failings remained structural. A lack of credibility undermined the Liberal Democrats' ability to cash in on any hostility to Brexit. The party that Farron left to Cable and Cable handed over to Swinson was simply not in robust enough electoral health to make the leap forward, while the actions of the leadership did little to assist. Structural disadvantage may have set the tone for the Liberal Democrats' underperformance in 2019, but the specific cause of this was largely the badly judged high-profile personal campaign of the leadership.

Renewed hope or more heartache?

After 2019, the political outlook for the Liberal Democrats seemed gloomy. The battle to stop Brexit had been lost and the party was leaderless following Swinson's decision to step down. The Covid-19 pandemic delayed the leadership election until late August 2020, when Sir Ed Davey gained more than 63 per cent of members' votes and defeated Layla Moran. Davey was immediately faced by the same structural barriers that had beset his predecessors. In Westminster, the Liberal Democrats were the fourth largest party and so did not enjoy the privileges that would guarantee national attention. Davey himself was not well known among the public despite his stint in the coalition government, and the electorate continued to struggle with what the Liberal Democrats stood for. Yet, over a two-year period from August 2020, the Liberal Democrats began to re-emerge as a potent electoral threat.

The backdrop to this resurgence was the demise of the Johnson-led administration. British politics during Johnson's premiership was in state of perpetual turbulence. The government's handling of unprecedented shocks and events (even excluding the war in Ukraine, on which there was cross-party support) increasingly came under media and public scrutiny. A primary focus was Johnson himself. His character flaws seem to have been overlooked in the race to 'Get Brexit done', but these now became his Achilles' heel. Beset by a series of scandals – Covid contracts, 'Wallpapergate', but most prominently 'Partygate' – both his personal polling and that of the Conservative party began to fall. Johnson's handling of the case of Owen Paterson (a Conservative MP who broke lobbying rules) emboldened critics who claimed the party was mired in sleaze. Ultimately, it was Johnson's insistence he was unaware of accusations of inappropriate sexual conduct when promoting Chris Pincher to Deputy Chief Whip that proved to be the final straw. With the Conservatives lurching from one scandal to the next and the economy flat-lining as Britain became immersed in a 'cost of living crisis', it was only a matter of time before the parliamentary party acted.

Given the Conservatives' woes, the Liberal Democrats abandoned their equidistance stance and openly positioned themselves as anti-Conservative. Aside from a structural recognition that Liberal Democrat prospects were asymmetrical, the decision was also aided by Labour's rebranding and shift to the centre ground under Keir Starmer, which had a number of consequences for the Liberal Democrats. First, it made a Liberal Democrat vote less risky for Conservative Remainers. Starmer reframed Labour as pro-business and fiscally prudent, in a pitch for economic credibility. This meant that Conservative Remain voters, who previously prioritised economic competence, were now far more amenable to switching to the Liberal Democrats in crucial battleground seats against the Conservatives. Second, Starmer's retreat from Corbynite policies nullified the political discourse around the coalition legacy and helped detoxify the Liberal Democrat brand. For the Liberal Democrats, it meant that the legacy of coalition, which had beset the party and stunted its electoral recovery since 2015, had ebbed away. For Labour voters, this repositioning gave the green light to rebuild the tactical alliances of the past and lend their vote to the Liberal Democrats, united in the shared desire to get the Conservatives out. Once again, circumstances somewhat outside of the Liberal Democrats' control had played a part in them obtaining an electoral lifeline.

As we have noted throughout this book, when one of the main parties falters, the Liberal Democrats can prosper. Crucially, though, the Liberal Democrats have to be a viable proposition, make the right calls and be in position to take advantage. Agency is therefore vital. When these two things combine, Liberal Democrat growth ensues. As such, Sir Ed Davey has been a vital cog in the Liberal Democrats' revitalisation since 2019. It is not that Davey himself has wowed the electorate. With media attention elsewhere, he has remained largely under the radar. Nevertheless, as time has gone on, through his personal back story and major policy interventions in a series of on-going crises (the pandemic; health and social care; sewage crisis; policies to alleviate the cost-of-living crisis), his profile has grown. Davey's positioning has clear resonance with the Ashdown era (and Paddy himself). Since becoming leader, he has quietly begun to build 'the liberal alternative' and show his competence. At the time of writing, more than two years into his leadership, Davey has made very few wrong calls. His technocratic, steady though somewhat dull style contrasts markedly with the overtly presidential approach of Swinson. It also compares favourably with Johnson among progressives who can cope with dull if what comes with it is expertise, competence and a hardworking, professional approach to serious issues. So, this perceived weakness during Johnson's tenure was a considerable strength.

In some ways Davey has been riding a wave of good fortune that his predecessors did not enjoy. However, his low-key approach to leadership has been vindicated and reaped electoral rewards. At the local level, the Liberal Democrats made steady gains, especially in Conservative territory. In the 2021 local elections, despite a net gain of only eight councillors, the party made progress in key Remain-voting constituencies where they were second to the Conservatives (the 'Blue Wall' constituencies). On average, compared with the 2017 local elections, vote shares in wards contested in these Conservative-held constituencies were three percentage points higher for the Liberal Democrats, whereas Conservative support had dropped by nearly seven points. A year later, with the Johnson administration in mounting turmoil, the Liberal Democrats' projected national share of the vote was around 19 per cent. The party had made significant ground against the Conservatives in the south of England (in excess of four percentage points, while the Conservatives had dropped by around seven points). Across England, in Conservative-held wards where the Liberal Democrats were second (based on 2018 local election results), the Liberal Democrat vote went up by 8.6 points while the Conservative vote dropped by more than 10 percentage points (Ford, 2022).

Three spectacular by-election victories in safe Conservative seats – Chesham and Amersham, and North Shropshire in 2021, and Tiverton and Honiton in 2022 – further reinvigorated the Liberal Democrats. Winning by-elections is in the party's DNA, but even for the Liberal Democrats these were landmark victories. In Chesham and Amersham, a seat where the Conservatives had never once failed to win more than half of the vote, the 25 per cent swing from the Conservatives to the Liberal Democrats was just shy of the fabled Orpington by-election win in 1962, often described as the beginning of the Liberal revival. This, though, was mild compared with the 34 per cent swing from Conservative to Liberal Democrat in North Shropshire, topping even Christchurch in 1993. The defeat of the Conservatives in Tiverton and Honiton – where parts of the constituency had been continuously represented by the Conservatives since 1835 – on a 29.9 per cent swing from Conservative to Liberal Democrat – was also historic. While contest-specific factors played their part, the Liberal Democrats' success in all of these seats seemed to signal that something much deeper was afoot. Three observations stand out.

First, Chesham and Amersham typified the electoral problems for the Conservatives and the potential for the Liberal Democrats. The Conservatives had profited from the post-referendum Brexit realignment and demographic reconfiguring of the British electorate. Broadly speaking, keeping older, white, socially conservative non-graduates in the north and traditional Conservatives in Remain-leaning seats across the south happy was becoming problematic. The Conservatives' 'levelling up' plans in 'Red Wall' seats had led to resentment in constituencies in the Home Counties (like Chesham and Amersham) among long-standing supporters, who complained that their problems were being ignored. The Liberal Democrats tapped into this discontent. At the same time, many seats like Chesham and Amersham continued to experience rapid socio-demographic change as progressive, younger professional graduates relocated in large numbers from London (Cutts *et al.*, 2021). Although Chesham and Amersham was not entirely typical of the areas where the Liberal Democrats had made recent progress – because of higher numbers of over-65s and home-owners outright – it was a Remain-leaning seat in the south of England with a large graduate electorate and in the top 3 per cent of constituencies containing professionals. On paper, it had long-term potential, but its vulnerability, albeit in a one-off contest, revealed the Conservatives' growing susceptibility across parts of the south of England. The electoral winds were now blowing in the Liberal Democrats' favour.

Second, both North Shropshire and Tiverton and Honiton were archetypal Conservative strongholds and solid Leave constituencies, which shared relatively few of the so-called 'Blue Wall' attitudinal and socio-demographic drivers from which the Liberal Democrats had profited in 2019 and since. The scale of the Conservatives' collapse raised questions about the formidability of the Leave vote and its long-term alliance with the Tories. As Cutts and Russell (2021) stated, it seemed that, for many, getting Brexit done was a transaction. Davey's assurance that the Liberal Democrats had accepted the 2019 election result as an endorsement of leaving the European Union and that under his leadership the party would not apply to rejoin also diffused antipathy towards the party. More broadly, the scale of the swings was further proof that the Liberal Democrats had regained their ability to harness borrowed support from Labour voters to oust Conservative incumbents. Regaining the capacity to align disillusioned 'One Nation' Conservatives with Labour and Green identifiers was reminiscent of the party's heyday under Kennedy and pre-coalition Clegg – and reaffirmed that the Liberal Democrats were increasingly becoming a genuine electoral threat.

Third, these by-election victories were a much-needed boost for the Liberal Democrat campaign machine. The ability of the party to mobilise activists (both physically and online) in one-off contests remained unparalleled. It also provided a positive response to those who had criticised the party for investing so much of its resources into networks of field campaign staff. The party had prioritised this area and success was a clear indication that the investment was starting to bear fruit. Moreover, success was built on local gains made in the May 2021 local elections, giving further credence to the importance of establishing local credibility.

Summary

The travails of Liberal Democrats in the post-coalition era are a story that has been told many times. A party on the electoral brink has moments of hope but these inevitably end in political false-dawns. Agential attempts to jump embedded structural hurdles have a ceiling. Meanwhile, leadership errors, policy mistakes, strategic blunders, personal gaffes and the political millstone of the coalition legacy seemingly did for Farron and Swinson. What, how, when and why these influenced the geography and individual voting behaviour of the Liberal Democrats post 2010 is examined in the next two chapters. Yet, it is not all doom and gloom. The Davey era has offered fresh hope, not least because a rival seems politically wounded and the party has positioned itself to take advantage. The political winds are now blowing in the Liberal Democrats' favour. However, as we reveal in later chapters, caution needs to be maintained, as structure remains a seemingly immovable obstacle to any major electoral breakthrough.

7

Political shocks and the coalition legacy: austerity, Brexit and leadership woes

As the Liberal Democrats left government in 2015, dishevelled and stunned at the scale of their electoral losses, few observers would have predicted the political turbulence that followed. Over the next four years, a referendum on Britain's membership of the European Union would split the country, two Prime Ministers would come and go, and two general elections would take place, resulting, at least in the short term, in an electoral realignment in British politics. This period would witness the rise and demise of left-wing populism, the political entrenchment of independence in Holyrood, the proroguing of the Westminster parliament and the populist rebranding of the Conservative party under Johnson as the one to 'Get Brexit done'. Amidst this upheaval and turmoil, the Liberal Democrats sought to survive and then rebuild. In this chapter we explore this process. We assess whether the longstanding structural issues that had bedevilled the party since its formation ultimately limited meaningful electoral progress. We also examine the extent to which the coalition legacy and austerity undermined the Liberal Democrats' electoral recovery. The chapter also explores the salience of Brexit post 2016 and addresses why an electoral Remain lifeline for the party failed to materialise. We examine whether this was out of the party's control, or if the blame lay with strategic miscalculations and internal failings. Lastly, this chapter explores the thorny issue of leadership. Over the four-year period, three leaders came and went. We focus on the tenures of Farron and Swinson to assess whether the Liberal Democrats' continuing electoral travails lay at their respective doors. We contrast the bottom-up grassroots ethos with the presidential style, and evaluate just how costly perceived leadership frailties were in terms of recruiting new voters, winning back those who had left and retaining those who hitherto had stuck with the party. To address these questions, the first half of the chapter examines the Liberal Democrats' electoral performance in 2017, under Farron, while the second half evaluates the party's performance in 2019, under Swinson. The analysis addresses the core narrative of why the Liberal Democrats have struggled to rebuild and breakthrough since 2015, and why the party has remained somewhat in an electoral hiatus, vulnerable to changing political events and shocks.

The Farron years

After Nick Clegg resigned, Tim Farron became the newly elected leader. Farron pledged to return the party to its campaign tradition of bottom-up, pavement politics in order to rebuild local support and get the party's voice heard. He was seen by some within the party as an antidote to rivals' criticisms of the Liberal Democrats' coalition legacy, given his willingness to defy Clegg and the coalition government from the backbenches. Yet among some voters, the Liberal Democrats' coalition legacy ran deep, and the party struggled to reach double digits in the polls throughout 2015 and 2016. Somewhat sidelined in the EU referendum campaign, the party found it increasingly difficult to sell its anti-Brexit stance to Remain supporters. It remained on the fringes in Scotland and struggled to gain exposure as the Corbyn-led Labour party grew its support among the under-40s. Farron's perceived inability to reconcile his own religious beliefs with being leader of a party built on tolerance and openness to others also reared its head during campaign. In the face of persistent media questions, Farron's responses on the morality of homosexuality disrupted the Liberal Democrat campaign in the run-up to the 2017 general election. Nonetheless, the party did seem to gain traction towards the end of that campaign, tapping into concerns about the Conservatives' plans for the elderly and social care and the so-called 'dementia tax'. Ultimately, the Liberal Democrats made little ground: a net gain of four seats, while losing 0.5 percentage points on its 2015 vote share. To examine whether the party made any significant progress under Farron, we explore five key questions. Did the party suffer from a recruitment problem or did it simply fail to retain 2015 voters? Did the legacy of coalition and its austerity measures scupper any prospects of a Liberal Democrat recovery? To what extent did Corbyn's prominent opposition to austerity resonate with those Liberal Democrat voters who left in 2015? Why did the Liberal Democrats fail to capitalise on their Remain credentials? Was agency once again a problem for the Liberal Democrats?

Retention and recruitment: a familiar problem

At first glance, the 0.5 percentage point drop in vote share between 2015 and 2017 made the Liberal Democrat vote appear relatively stable. Yet, beneath the surface, there was significant churn. The party struggled to retain its prior vote, while simultaneously winning over rival voters in much greater numbers than two years previously. Figure 7.1 (Graph 1) shows how people voted in 2015, according to their 2017 vote, based on the BES and focusing only on Labour, Conservatives and the Liberal Democrats. As expected, the majority of 2017 Labour and Conservative voters had voted for these parties, respectively, in 2015. This was more the case for the Conservatives. Meanwhile, Labour attracted a larger proportion of those who did not vote in 2015. In contrast, only roughly two-fifths of Liberal Democrat voters in 2017 also voted for the party in 2015, suggesting the party recruited a much larger number of voters from its rivals than two years earlier. Interestingly,

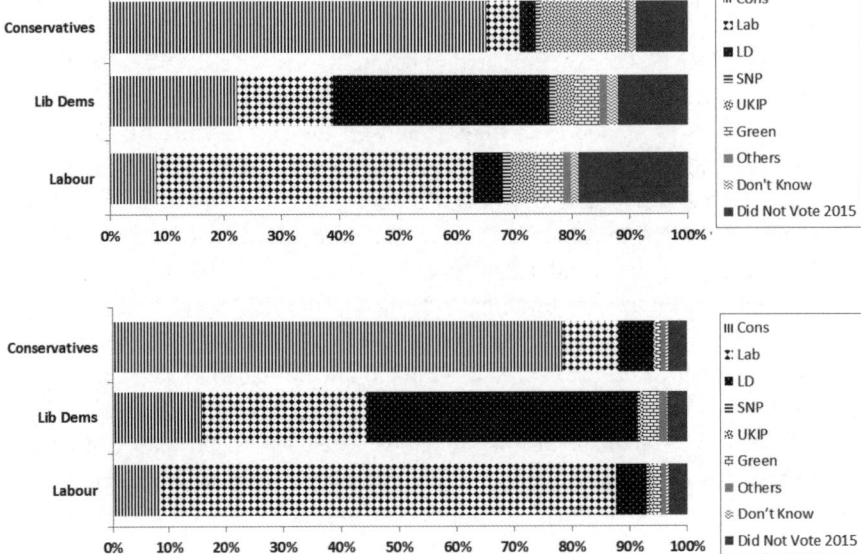

Figure 7.1 Voter identity and flow (Labour, Conservatives and Liberal Democrats only): 2015 vote of 2017 voters (top) and 2017 voters by 2015 vote (bottom). *Source*: 2017 British Election Study panel

there is some evidence that the Liberal Democrats recruited more voters from the Conservatives (22 per cent when non-voters are taken into account) than Labour (17 per cent). They also won over more than 4 per cent of prior Green supporters.

Figure 7.1 (Graph 2) shows how people voted in 2017, grouped according to how they had voted in 2015. While Labour and the Conservatives retained the loyalty of around 80 per cent of their 2015 voters, the Liberal Democrats only retained around 50 per cent of their 2015 voters. Given that the party was reduced to little more than its core vote in 2015, the fact it lost half of that in 2017 reiterates the underlying weakness in its vote.

As in the previous general election, the Liberal Democrats lost more of their 2015 support to Labour (29 per cent) than the Conservatives (16 per cent). While the party continued to haemorrhage support to its left, there were positive signs that it had started to win back Conservative voters. Nevertheless, the party was still a long way from its pre-coalition electoral standing. Of the Liberal Democrats' 2010 voters, just shy of 19 per cent supported them again in the 2017 general election. These 2010 Liberal Democrat voters accounted for around half of the party's vote in 2017. Of this group of voters who backed the party in both 2010 and 2017, around 30 per cent also voted for the Liberal Democrats in 2015. Meanwhile, around one-fifth returned to the fold in 2017 after switching from the party in 2015. To put this into context, these made up around one-tenth of those who had left the Liberal Democrats in 2015. It is also worth stressing that more than 40 per cent of

2010 Liberal Democrat voters supported Labour in 2017, compared with roughly 23 per cent who switched to the Conservatives. Overall, the electoral damage from the coalition persisted in 2017.

There were, however, some signs that the party's standing among voters recovered in 2017. The party's mean 'like' scores grew modestly, from 3.4 to 3.8. According to Fieldhouse *et al.* (2021: 131–133), three key patterns drove this improvement. First, economically left-leaning voters became slightly more positive towards the Liberal Democrats in 2017 than those on the economic right. That is, the recovery was uneven across the economic left–right dimension, with recovery on the left accentuating the peak in the centre and mean 'like' scores dropping at the two extremes (Fieldhouse *et al.*, 2021: 132). This is somewhat borne out by data from the 2015–2017 BES panel. For instance, voters positioned the Liberal Democrats slightly more to the left (4.2) in 2017 than in 2015 (4.8). It is therefore conceivable that the party enjoyed more positivity from those on the left. A simple bivariate linear regression between feelings towards the Liberal Democrats and voters' position on the left–right redistribution scale supports this. In 2015, there had been clear positive relationship between Liberal Democrat likeability and support for the government not intervening to reduce income inequality. Put simply, feelings towards the Liberal Democrats were much more positive on the right of the left–right redistribution scale. In contrast, in 2017, likeability towards the Liberal Democrats was higher among those on the left of the redistribution scale.[1]

The second key theme was the Liberal Democrats' strength among voters at the liberal end of the liberal–authoritarian values scale, suggesting a recovery among social liberals. Simultaneously, there was a clear drop-off in sentiment towards the Liberal Democrats among social conservatives in 2017 compared with 2015 (Fieldhouse *et al.*, 2021: 132). There is a similar trend according to voters' position on the national security–civil liberties scale. A simple bivariate linear regression shows no relationship between the Liberal Democrats' likeability and national security–civil liberties position in 2015, but a strong positive relationship in 2017.[2] Taken together, there was strong evidence that the party became more dependent on its traditional social liberal core in 2017.

Thirdly, in 2017, Liberal Democrat likeability increased most as Liberal Democrat partisanship got stronger. Given the party's weak base, its inability to win over those with no or other partisanship ultimately extinguished the possibility of any meaningful recovery (Fieldhouse *et al.*, 2021: 133).

But which voters did the Liberal Democrats actually recruit in 2017? We address this question using a multinomial logistic model. The dependent variable measures: those who switched from another party or non-voting to the Liberal Democrats in 2017; 'retainers' (those who voted Liberal Democrat in 2015 and 2017); and all other voters. Here we run two separate models: 'all other voters' is the reference category in model 1; and 'retainers' is the base in model 2. In short, this approach shows how 2017 Liberal Democrat recruits differed from all other voters – but also how they differed from those the party retained from 2015.

Table 7.1 Multinomial logistic model (combined) of Liberal Democrat recruitment in 2017

Variables	Model 1		Model 2	
	β	SE	β	SE
Constant	−5.95*	0.20	0.05	0.28
Authoritarian–libertarian	−0.06*	0.02	−0.03	0.03
Redistribution (economic)	0.04*	0.02	−0.00	0.03
Voted remain	1.11*	0.12	0.44*	0.18
Left–right political values	0.08*	0.02	0.08*	0.04
Like Farron	0.36*	0.02	0.10*	0.03
Tactical voter	1.44*	0.11	0.83*	0.16
Strength of LD partisanship: reference group = 'other' and no party identification				
Not very strong	1.03*	0.16	−1.68*	0.19
Fairly strong	1.29*	0.15	−2.05*	0.17
Very strong	2.44*	0.40	−2.75*	0.27
Model fit				
Log likelihood	−3,877.73			
R^2	0.27			
AIC	7,795.46			
BIC	−2,666.11			
N	21,730			

*= significant p<0.05. Model 1: base category = all other voters; Model 2: base category = voted Liberal Democrat in 2015 and 2017.

Table 7.1 shows the results from both models. Those with a stronger partisan loyalty to the Liberal Democrats were more likely to switch to the party than 'all other voters'. While around 70 per cent of 'fairly' and 'very strong' partisans voted Liberal Democrat in 2015 and 2017, as much as 20 per cent of these did not support the party in 2015 and subsequently switched back in 2017. As a consequence, the strength of Liberal Democrat partisanship works in the opposite direction when compared against those who remained loyal to the party across both elections.

According to model 1, 2017 recruits were more likely to lean towards the liberal end of the liberal–authoritarian scale, to like Farron and to have voted Remain. This is not entirely surprising when compared against all other non-Liberal Democrat voters. However, there are signs that those who switched to the Liberal Democrats were more on the right of the political and economic spectrum. Tentatively, this seems to back our descriptive evidence that the party made more headway among prior Conservative voters and those who leaned towards the right economically. Mirroring longstanding trends, those recruited by the Liberal Democrats were also significantly more likely to be voting tactically than were 'all other voters'. This implies that the 'softness' of the Liberal Democrat vote, which had hamstrung party recruitment before 2015, returned in 2017. Compared with those who stuck with the party in 2015 and 2017, those who switched back to the party in 2017 were more likely to be driven by tactical voting. Favouring the leader and being a Remain supporter also mattered more for Liberal Democrat 2017 recruits than retainers. Lastly, while there seems little difference economically, recruits were significantly more likely to be on the right of the political spectrum than retainers. Generally speaking, while the party haemorrhaged further support to Labour, it partially offset this by recruiting those who leaned more to the right.

The coalition legacy, austerity and battling Corbyn

The global financial crisis remained salient throughout the first part of the 2010s and had a telling impact on the 2015 general election. While Labour was the beneficiary of the tactical unwind of left-leaning 2010 Liberal Democrat voters and the party's role in austerity, other voters blamed Labour for the size of the national debt accrued under the party's watch. As a consequence, the Conservatives successfully managed to blame Labour for austerity measures and reassert issue ownership of economic management. They also uniquely benefited from the economic upturn in the final 12–18 months of the coalition government, while their Liberal Democrat partners sought to disassociate themselves from the tough economic measures taken. In the void that emerged, UKIP also benefited from perceptions of the earlier Labour government's economic mismanagement and dissatisfaction with its wider economic record. Nevertheless, by 2017 the saliency of the financial crisis had waned and Brexit became the key dividing line. With Corbyn's Labour owning the fight against austerity, the Conservatives watered down economic targets and became wary about fighting Labour on this territory. In 2015, the Liberal Democrats had paid a heavy price for throwing their lot in with the Conservatives. Nevertheless, with Brexit taking centre stage, to what extent did the legacy of coalition and austerity act as a brake on any Liberal Democrat recovery in 2017? Did Corbyn's anti-austerity pitch appeal to those Liberal Democrat voters who had left the party in 2015?

To address these questions, we examine those 2010 Liberal Democrat voters who voted Labour in 2017. Our expectation is that many of them continued to shun the Liberal Democrats in 2017 due to the party's role in coalition, its broken promises and its support for austerity measures. The second part of the analysis assesses those voters who supported the Liberal Democrats in 2015 but then moved to Labour two years later. Here our expectation is somewhat different. This subset of voters stuck with the Liberal Democrats in 2015 despite the party's travails, but abandoned them in 2017. We would therefore expect anti-austerity measures to be less potent and for those voters to be driven by other factors, such as Brexit and the popularity of Corbyn.

Table A7.1 in the Appendix shows the key drivers of those 2010 Liberal Democrat voters who switched to Labour in 2017. The first model includes an

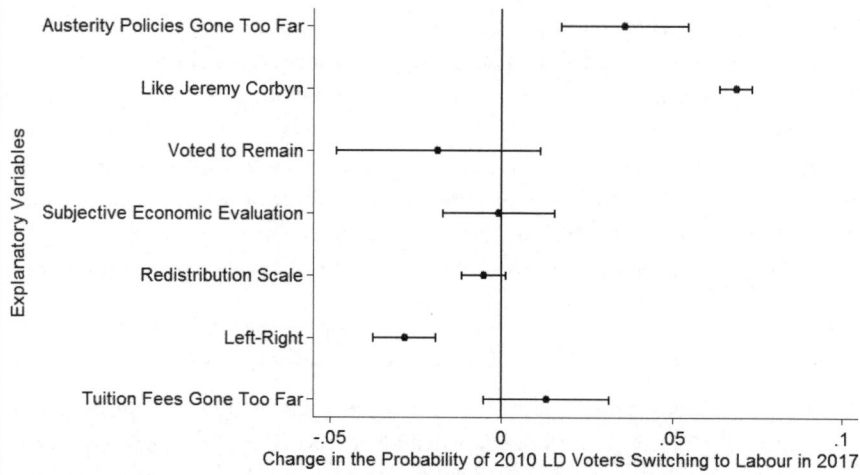

Figure 7.2 Effect of anti-austerity attitudes, Corbyn and other explanatory variables on the change in probability of 2010 Liberal Democrat voters supporting Labour in 2017 (average marginal effects): *Source*: British Election Study

austerity factor,[3] a variable measuring whether increases in tuition fees have gone too far and a number of control variables, including political left–right positioning, subjective economic evaluations and a measure of attitude to economic redistribution. As expected, those 2010 Liberal Democrat voters who felt that austerity measures had gone too far and opposed rises in tuition fees were more likely to switch to Labour. Predictably, those on the left of the political spectrum and those who felt that the government should intervene to reduce income inequality were also significantly more likely to support Labour. Do these drivers still hold when Brexit and liking of Corbyn are included in the model? On average, liking Corbyn increased the probability of 2010 Liberal Democrats voting Labour in 2017 by seven percentage points, holding all other variables constant (see Figure 7.2). Being on the left of the political spectrum also increased the probability of voting Labour in 2017, by three percentage points. Yet even accounting for these predictors, those 2010 Liberal Democrat voters who shared anti-austerity attitudes were still significantly more likely to support Labour in 2017. On average, being more anti-austerity increased the probability of voting Labour in 2017 by four percentage points. We know that the Liberal Democrats struggled to win back those who switched to Labour in 2015. If the party was going to recover some lost ground, it needed to make headway among this group of voters. Corbyn's prominent opposition to austerity meant that these voters were unable to forget the Liberal Democrats' coalition legacy. Moreover, anti-austerity attitudes remained a significant driver, ensuring that two years later the Liberal Democrats were still paying a heavy price for going into coalition with the Conservatives and signing up to that programme.

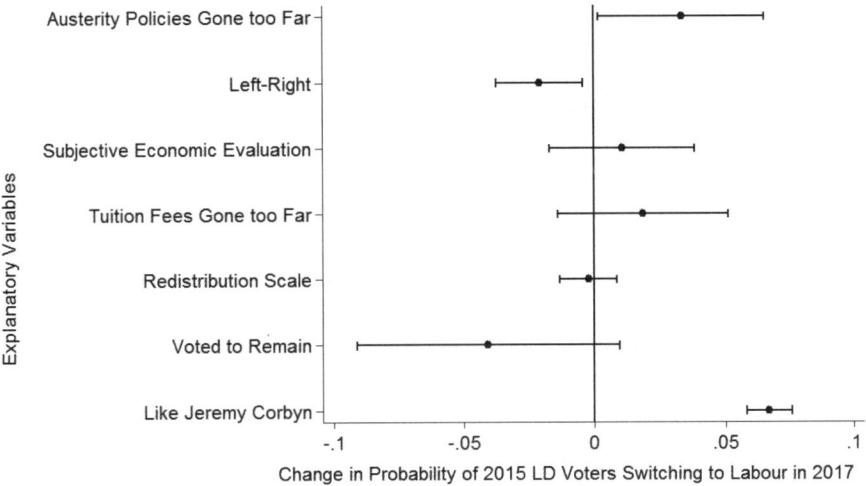

Figure 7.3 Effect of anti-austerity attitudes, Corbyn and other explanatory variables on the change in probability of 2015 Liberal Democrat voters supporting Labour in 2017 (average marginal effects). *Source*: British Election Study

There was also considerable churn in the Liberal Democrat vote between 2015 and 2017. Retaining 2015 Liberal Democrat supporters was vital, especially given the problems of winning back those centre-left voters who had voted for the party in 2010 but went to Labour in 2015. Given that these voters had stuck it out with the Liberal Democrats in 2015, one would anticipate that anti-austerity attitudes or dissatisfaction with the party's handling of tuition fees (and more generally association with the Conservatives) would have less of an impact on subsequent switchers to Labour. Yet, contrary to our expectations, this is not the case (see Table A7.2 in the Appendix and Figure 7.3). Corbyn clearly resonated with these voters. Liking Corbyn increased the probability of voting Labour by seven percentage points, holding all other variables constant. On average, holding strong anti-austerity attitudes increased the probability of voting Labour by three percentage points. Corbyn was undoubtedly a pull for these voters, and his persistent anti-austerity message boosted Labour support. It also reminded these voters of the Liberal Democrats' legacy. Combined with Labour attacks on the party's coalition record, the Liberal Democrats in 2017 struggled to hold on to any remaining left-leaning support. For the Liberal Democrats, it became a double whammy that ended any possibility of a meaningful recovery. It was always going to be an uphill task to persuade those who switched from Liberal Democrat in 2010 to Labour in 2015 to return to the fold in 2017. Retaining the fragile Liberal Democrat 2015 vote looked more plausible for the party. However, the coalition legacy remained a millstone around its neck that suppressed any prospect of recovery of the voters on its centre-left flank, at least in the short to medium term.

Brexit: a missed opportunity?

Twelve months after the 2016 referendum, there was clear evidence that Brexit had realigned voters and parties. Socio-cultural values and social divisions such as age and education cut across the traditional economic left–right value dimension (Clarke *et al.*, 2017; Evans and Menon, 2017). As British politics polarised, the Liberal Democrats – already reeling from the fallout from their coalition experience – became caught in the political crossfire, unable to garner public support. In the aftermath of the Brexit vote, the Conservatives moved quickly to back Brexit. As voters aligned opposition to immigration with the decision to leave the EU, the Conservatives' longstanding stance on the issue gained further credibility. They were deemed to be most competent to deliver these priorities and seamlessly occupied this political space.

The Remain vote, meanwhile, was up for grabs. Labour seemed split on the issue, with many openly pro-European Labour MPs favouring a second referendum. Corbyn and Labour's wider leadership team were more cautious, and adopted an election policy based around several tests that Brexit needed to meet. Crucially, Labour appeared united on ruling out a 'no deal' option, and while the policy sidestepped a second referendum, the party targeted tariff-free access to the EU single market, did not rule out remaining in the customs union and gave MPs the final say on any agreement. This compromise position was far more equivocal than the Liberal Democrats' pro-European message and support for a second referendum. So why did the Liberal Democrats struggle to win over Remain voters? Why was Brexit a missed opportunity?

To gain a deeper understanding, it is important to contextualise the relationship between Europe and support for the Liberal Democrats. One of the longstanding problems inflicting the party was voter ambiguity around the Liberal Democrats' stance on Europe. Like other policy areas, the party struggled to communicate its policy to the electorate. Even in the coalition period, around 31 per cent of voters in 2013 did not know the Liberal Democrats' position on the EU. This included 28 per cent of those who voted Liberal Democrat in 2010. Ambiguity still existed during the 2014 European election campaign, despite Clegg's notorious television debates with UKIP's Nigel Farage. Around 33 per cent of voters were still unsure about where the Liberal Democrats stood on Europe. Even 18 per cent of those who voted Liberal Democrat in that European election did not know or were not certain of the party's policy position. After the referendum, an increasing number of voters attributed a pro-European position to the party, according to BES data on EU integration scales. Nonetheless, close to a quarter remained uncertain – higher than was the case for either Labour or the Conservatives.

Even though the Liberal Democrats have historically been more pro-European than their rivals, party support has always contained a sizeable number of Eurosceptics. Indeed, notwithstanding ecological fallacy concerns, many of the party's traditional strongholds, particularly in the south-west region, and

Conservative-facing seats, were Eurosceptic. Within these seats, the party was adept at hoovering up pro-European support, albeit some tactically but it also relied on Eurosceptic voters who prioritised other issues in general elections. To put this into perspective, 36 per cent of 2010 Liberal Democrat voters voted Leave in 2016. Around 15 per cent of those who voted Leave in 2016 had supported the Liberal Democrats in 2010. This declined to 5 per cent in the 2015 general election and to 3 per cent two years later. Despite the Liberal Democrat collapse in 2015, around a third of those who supported the party in the election voted Leave a year later. This figure dropped to 20 per cent in 2017, perhaps reflecting the salience of the issue and the Liberal Democrats' unapologetic pro-European stance. It is therefore a myth that the Liberal Democrat vote has always been overwhelmingly pro-European. Unsurprisingly, one of the consequences of the party's anti-Brexit policy was greater disconnection with its Leave voters, even among those who stuck with the party in 2015.

The Liberal Democrats have historically used their pro-European stance to distinguish itself from its main rivals. Yet, this did not materialise at the ballot box. In 2010, the pro-European vote was split fairly evenly. Of those who voted Remain in 2016, 30 per cent had voted Liberal Democrat in 2010, 33 per cent Labour and 27 per cent Conservative. For the Liberal Democrats, this figure had dropped to 11 per cent in 2015 and increased slightly, to 14 per cent, two years later. The haemorrhaging of its Leave vote meant that those who supported the Liberal Democrats were increasingly pro-European Remain supporters, up from 64 per cent in 2015 to 80 per cent in 2017. However, this hides a great deal of churn in 2017. The simple truth is that the Liberal Democrats did not recruit many more Remain supporters than they actually lost. Of the party's new recruits in 2017, 80 per cent had voted Remain. A sizeable number were from the Conservatives, but this was largely offset by losses to Labour. Corbyn's Labour became a magnet for Remain voters in 2017, winning significant numbers from the Conservatives, Greens and nearly a quarter from the Liberal Democrats. The party haemorrhaged voters who backed them in 2015 and voted Leave in 2016, primarily to the Conservatives.

So why did the Liberal Democrats fail to recruit more Remain voters in 2017? The simple answer is political and electoral viability (or lack of it). Notwithstanding the millstone of the Liberal Democrats' coalition legacy, Labour's left-wing populist appeal under Corbyn reached out to certain demographic groups (younger, more educated) who held more cosmopolitan attitudes and largely backed Remain. Labour's relentless anti-austerity message resonated with many, particularly those who did not own capital, were too young to benefit from universal provision, were straddled with debt and faced uncertain economic opportunities. Moreover, Labour consistently framed the Liberal Democrats as aiders and abettors in this inequality, thereby hindering that party's efforts to move on from the coalition. As a consequence, many Remain voters (such as Green supporters) switched to Labour long before the 2017 campaign, driven by Corbyn's environmental credentials and other policy stances.

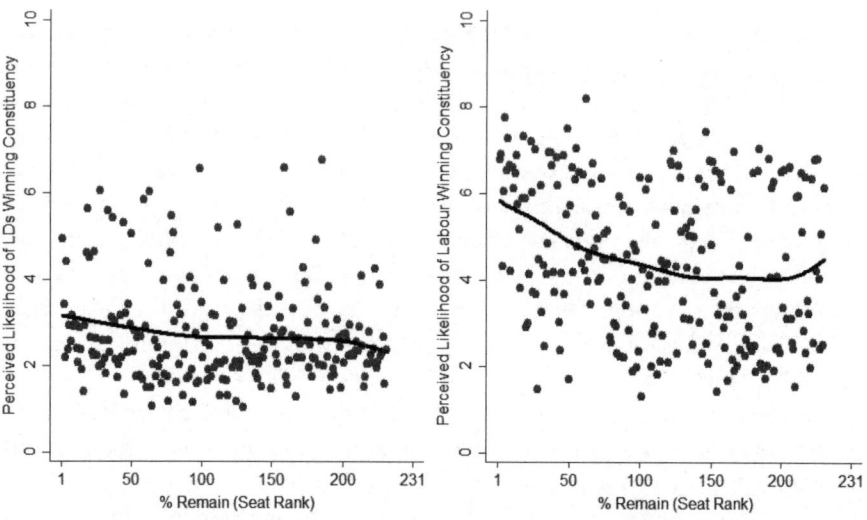

Figure 7.4 Comparing the perceived likelihood of Liberal Democrats and Labour winning a respondent's seat in 2017 general election by % Remain seat rank of prior Liberal Democrat and Labour vote share (2015). *Source*: 2017 British Election Study

Electoral credibility also continued to undermine the Liberal Democrats' ability to win over Remain voters. When BES respondents were asked the likelihood of the party winning in their constituency (its 'credibility') on a scale from 0 (very unlikely) to 10 (very likely), the party's mean score increased slightly from 2.36 in 2015 to 2.49 in 2017. Two major patterns stand out here (see also Fieldhouse *et al.*, 2021). While the party's electoral credibility grew among voters overall, it actually fell from 5.15 in 2015 to 4.65 in 2017 in the 50 constituencies where the Liberal Democrats had the best chance of winning (based on previous election performance). The party's perceived likelihood of winning grew in the seats that the Liberal Democrats had no real chance of winning. In reality, the Liberal Democrats were worse off because its perceived credibility fell in precisely the seats that it needed to win (and on paper had the best chance of winning) to mount a recovery. Of these 50 constituencies in which, overall, there was a drop in credibility, 28 were majority Remain-voting seats.

Across all Remain-voting constituencies, the mean perceived likelihood of the Liberal Democrats winning was 2.72 – only slightly above the 2.49 figure for all seats. To put this into some perspective, we can compare voters' expectations of the Liberal Democrats winning in Remain seats with the perceived likelihood of Labour winning. As Figure 7.4 shows, the mean perceived likelihood of Labour winning (4.43) was much higher. Of the 231 Remain seats, voters' expectations for the Liberal Democrats were higher than Labour's in only 51 constituencies. In many of these 51 seats, the difference was marginal. In only 14 seats did the

Liberal Democrats enjoy a sizeable perceived likelihood advantage over Labour. Of course, Labour did enjoy an incumbency advantage in a number of Remain seats, including many that had voted heavily for Remain. This naturally made it extremely difficult for the Liberal Democrats to build electoral credibility.[4] Hypothetically, even if Remain voters preferred the Liberal Democrats' second-referendum policy (notwithstanding other drivers for supporting their rivals), the party was simply not seen as a viable option. Overall, the party remained hamstrung by its failure to solve the credibility problem. Two years on from the party's 2015 collapse, when a pathway to recovery opened up amidst the Brexit fallout, the credibility problem once again nullified any prospect of progress.

Farron's failings: an after-thought or simply unpopular?

From the outset, Farron faced an uphill battle. A few months after the 2015 election, nearly two-thirds of voters were not clear about what the Liberal Democrats stood for. Three-fifths thought the party was untrustworthy. Nearly half believed the party would not be a force in British politics at all in 10 years (Dahlgreen, 2015). With only a handful of seats at Westminster, Farron found it difficult to garner media attention. His net approval leadership rating remained in negative territory throughout his tenure as leader and consistently sizeable parts of the electorate did not know who he was. In September 2016, nearly two-thirds of voters did not know if Farron was doing well or badly, including roughly a third of current Liberal Democrat supporters. Shortly before the 2017 general election, 52 per cent of those asked could not name the Liberal Democrat leader (*Telegraph*, 2017). This figure dropped during the election campaign. Nevertheless, even by the final week, 35 per cent of those polled did not know if Farron was doing well or badly as leader, compared with 11 per cent for May and 13 per cent for Corbyn. Even after the election, nearly a quarter of BES respondents stated that they did not know whether they liked or disliked him, compared with around 5 per cent who were unsure about May or Corbyn.[5]

Using evidence from the BEPS, Farron's mean likeability ratings remained fairly stable – between 3.8 and 3.4 – throughout the two-year period of his tenure. Until the start of the 2017 general election campaign, Farron's likeability was not that dissimilar to Corbyn's. However, this dramatically changed during that campaign as Corbyn's likeability soared, while May's fell. Farron's difficulty in squaring his own evangelical Christian beliefs with party policy did not seem to dramatically affect his leadership ratings, however. There was no significant decline in Farron's likeability over the four-week campaign period.[6] His competency rating (3.4) trailed significantly behind those of May (4.1) and Corbyn (5.0). While Labour voters rated Farron slightly higher than the mean in terms of competence and likeability, his scores were much lower among Conservatives. Crushed by the events of 2015, for large sections of the electorate the Liberal Democrats and its leader remained somewhat of an irrelevance.

To put these ratings into historical context, Farron's leadership rating in 2017 was actually worse (3.4) than Clegg's (3.8) in 2015. Farron's rating compares unfavourably to every other Liberal Democrat leader going into a general election since 1992. Similar questions were not asked about Ashdown in 1992, but 60 per cent stated that he was a strong and capable leader, and roughly 80 per cent rated him as caring and responsive. In 2017 the party was on the electoral brink, weighed down by the legacy of coalition and snookered by the rise of left populism under Corbyn and a dominant SNP. It was also, seemingly, hamstrung by one of its most unpopular leaders since its formation.

The Farron era: a reflection

In retrospect, it is harsh to label the Farron era an abject failure. The Liberal Democrats were at a historic low point and struggling to survive. The spectre of the coalition resonated strongly with traditional Labour supporters and those who had lent support to the Liberal Democrats in 2010. The rise of Corbyn, and Labour's relentless anti-austerity rhetoric, ensured that voters were constantly reminded of the Liberal Democrats' 'betrayal'. Among left-leaning voters, the coalition legacy was real, raw and – given the short two-year interval between general elections – remained unforgiveable. Given this impossible task, keeping the Liberal Democrats above the waterline was perhaps an achievement in itself. Yet the election starkly exposed the deep structural problems that now stymied the party. Brexit appeared to offer a lifeline, but the reality of the traditional Liberal Democrat vote was out of step with the party's longstanding outward appearance as a united pro-European party. While it was expected to benefit, its voice had been reduced to a whisper. The party simply did not have the political viability and electoral credibility to embrace this opportunity. The 2015 election had badly damaged the party's local credibility, many were unwilling to lend support due to the coalition, while others were sceptical that voting Liberal Democrat would see their desired Brexit outcome materialise. As a result, voters went elsewhere.

In the past, the Liberal Democrats would lean on agency to paper over any credibility gaps. It was never foolproof, but in tight contests it gave the party a fighting chance. In 2017 that option was unavailable – and part of this does lie at Farron's door. Up until the election campaign, Farron found it difficult to cut through as he and the party were banished to the sidelines. With sky-high scepticism surrounding Corbyn, the campaign provided an opportunity for Farron to sell himself and position the party as a vehicle for moderation. Any hope quickly vanished after his prevaricating response to Cathy Newman's question of whether gay sex is a sin. It exposed the apparent contradiction between Farron's evangelical personal beliefs and his party's pro-LGBTQ+ stance. Unsurprisingly, Farron's indecisiveness and hesitancy on the issue stirred up discontent within the party, resulting in the resignation of Lord Paddick as its home affairs spokesperson. This trumped efforts to promote the party's policies during a crucial part of the campaign and for many confirmed that Farron was not leader material. As we show, Farron's handling of the subject had no undue effect on his popularity, which was already bumping along the ground. However, this was effectively Farron's job interview. Most voters were ambivalent about him, because the Liberal Democrats were simply not seen as viable. Those who were willing to watch were largely sceptical. For these voters, Farron failed the job interview and remained an also-ran. Henceforth, any lingering possibility of the party making some kind of electoral ground disappeared.

Understanding the 2019 general election: 'Jo Swinson's Liberal Democrats'

Jo Swinson became the new leader of the Liberal Democrats in July 2019, during a period of unprecedented success for the party. Just over four months later, Swinson had lost her seat and resigned as leader. From polling in the high teens and low twenties throughout October, in the December 2019 general election the Liberal Democrats had lost seats at Westminster, seeing their national vote slump to less than 12 per cent. So what explains this dramatic downturn? Did the long-standing credibility and structural problems kill off any Liberal Democrat revival? Were Swinson and the party's presidential strategy to blame for the failure to match expectations? How influential was the Liberal Democrats' 'revoke' policy on 2019 performance? Did the party manage to shrug off the legacy of coalition or was it still an important driver? In the following sections we explore these questions.

Loyalty and partisanship: a small step forward?

In the aftermath of the 2019 general election, media pundits and commentators alike were quick to characterise the Liberal Democrats' performance as yet another abject failure. Yet there was some progress. Alongside the increase of four percentage points in support from 2017, the party retained more of its previous support and recruited more voters from rival parties than it had in 2017. Around 63 per cent of 2017 Liberal Democrats voters voted for the Liberal Democrats again in 2019. By comparison, the Conservatives retained the loyalty of nearly 87 per cent of their 2017 voters, while Labour saw its retention rate drop to around 70 per cent. The Liberal Democrats did see 16 per cent of their 2017 support switch to Labour, 13 per cent to the Conservatives and 4 per cent to the Greens. So despite signs that the Liberal Democrats were beginning to win over Labour voters, this was partially offset by their 2017 voters switching – principally to Labour and the Greens. Yet the Liberal Democrats still struggled to win back many of those 2010 voters that had left the party en masse in 2015. Around a quarter, slightly higher than in 2017, voted for the party again. This represented 50 per cent of the party's total vote in 2019. Around 37 per cent of 2010 Liberal Democrat voters supported Labour in 2019, while around 27 per cent backed the Conservatives. Of those 2010 Liberal Democrat voters who switched to Labour in 2015, only 16 per cent supported the Liberal Democrats in 2019. Evidently, a sizeable section of these left-leaning, potentially tactical, voters remained reluctant to support the Liberal Democrats. This continued to place a ceiling on the party's ability to make electoral progress. Partisanship also remained a weakness. In 2019, less than 7 per cent of voters identified as Liberal Democrat partisans, and of these, only 7 per cent identified very strongly. As in 2017, the party's weak base hindered its recovery (Fieldhouse *et al.*, 2021). Popularity remained fragile among the voters most needed in order to kick-start a meaningful recovery. As such, it is unsurprising that the Liberal Democrats ultimately failed to make the electoral ground that they expected.

Recruitment: positive signs?

According to BES data, the Liberal Democrats in 2019 recruited a similar number of voters from the Conservatives as they did in 2017 (21 per cent in 2019 compared with 22 per cent in 2017). But they recruited more than a quarter from Labour (around 27 per cent), which was considerably more than in 2017. Using separate multinomial logistic models, we can compare these new recruits with voters the Liberal Democrats retained from 2017 in terms of socio-demographic make-up and underlying values (Table 7.2 below). From this, we can gauge if and how the Liberal Democrats expanded their voter base. Model 1 reports estimates only for those who switched from Conservative to Liberal Democrat in 2019. The base category is voters who supported the Conservatives in both 2017 and 2019. Model 2 uses the same format for Labour.

Recruits from the Conservatives tended to lean more to the left politically than voters who supported the Conservatives in both 2017 and 2019. They also tended to be in favour of greater redistribution, and were more likely to share libertarian attitudes. Aside from age, when these values are taken into account there are no influential socio-demographic drivers. As a group, these recruits exhibited many of the value traits of One-Nation Conservatives, sitting closer to the centre-ground than Conservative loyalist voters but leaning right compared with Liberal Democrat loyalists. Meanwhile, recruits from Labour were more right wing than loyal Labour voters, albeit clearly on the centre-left and more in favour of redistribution, where they sat to the left of the national average. This suggests that Liberal Democrats were more successful at peeling off soft-left voters than longstanding left-wing supporters.

Controlling for other factors, those switching from the Conservatives to the Liberal Democrats were no more motivated by tactical voting than were Conservative loyalists. Yet the probability of Liberal Democrat recruitment from Labour is on average two percentage points higher for individuals voting tactically than for those not among those with the same socio-demographics and political attitudes. There are both positives and negatives to take from this. On the one hand, it is possible that Conservative switchers turned to the Liberal Democrats for more ideological political reasons, rather than just lending their vote tactically.

Table 7.2 Multinomial logistic models of Liberal Democrat recruitment from the Conservatives and Labour in 2019

Variables	Model 1: Cons to LD		Model 2: Lab to LD	
	β	SE	β	SE
Constant	−0.66	0.56	−3.55*	0.64
Male	0.08	0.17	−0.12	0.18
Age	−0.01*	0.00	−0.00	0.00
Degree	0.28	0.20	0.20	0.22
Social grade	0.09	0.06	0.05	0.06
Own home	0.52	0.27	0.21	0.24
Values				
Redistribution (economic)	−0.06*	0.03	0.10*	0.04
Left–right political values	−0.16*	0.05	0.22*	0.05
Libertarian–authoritarian	−0.17*	0.05	−0.01	0.05
Economic growth–environment	0.06	0.04	0.02	0.04
Credibility				
Liberal Democrats' likelihood of winning seat	0.20*	0.04	0.21*	0.03
Tactical voter	0.48	0.39	0.68*	0.21
Wasted vote	−0.32*	0.08	−0.46*	0.10
Model fit				
Wald chi-square <0.05	1,412.07*		1,196.32*	
Log likelihood	−3,909.46		−4,612.35	
R^2	0.28		0.20	
AIC (used by Stata)	8,285.38		9,328.70	
BIC (used by Stata)	7,922.92		9,691.16	
N	7,867		7,867	

*Significant $p<0.05$.

The party had an opportunity to nurture this vote. Relying on borrowed, tactical support is a necessary evil for a third party to gain electoral ground and enhance its political credibility. However, this support can be flimsy. Cementing this support and turning these voters into long-term Liberal Democrat leaners or identifiers remained a critical problem. Unsurprisingly, Labour and Conservative voters who were less likely to think that voting for a third party was a wasted vote were more likely to switch to the Liberal Democrats.

But electoral credibility was pivotal to party recruitment in 2019. The perception that the Liberal Democrats could win in the voter's own constituency was a significant driver of switching to the party, holding other predictors constant. For ease of interpretation, we can calculate predicted probabilities for the perceived likelihood of the Liberal Democrats winning the seat in increments from 0 to 10. The values are the average predicted probabilities using the mean values of other predictors (see Figure 7.5). As expected, for the reference category – Conservative and Labour loyalists – the fitted line decreases from left to right as

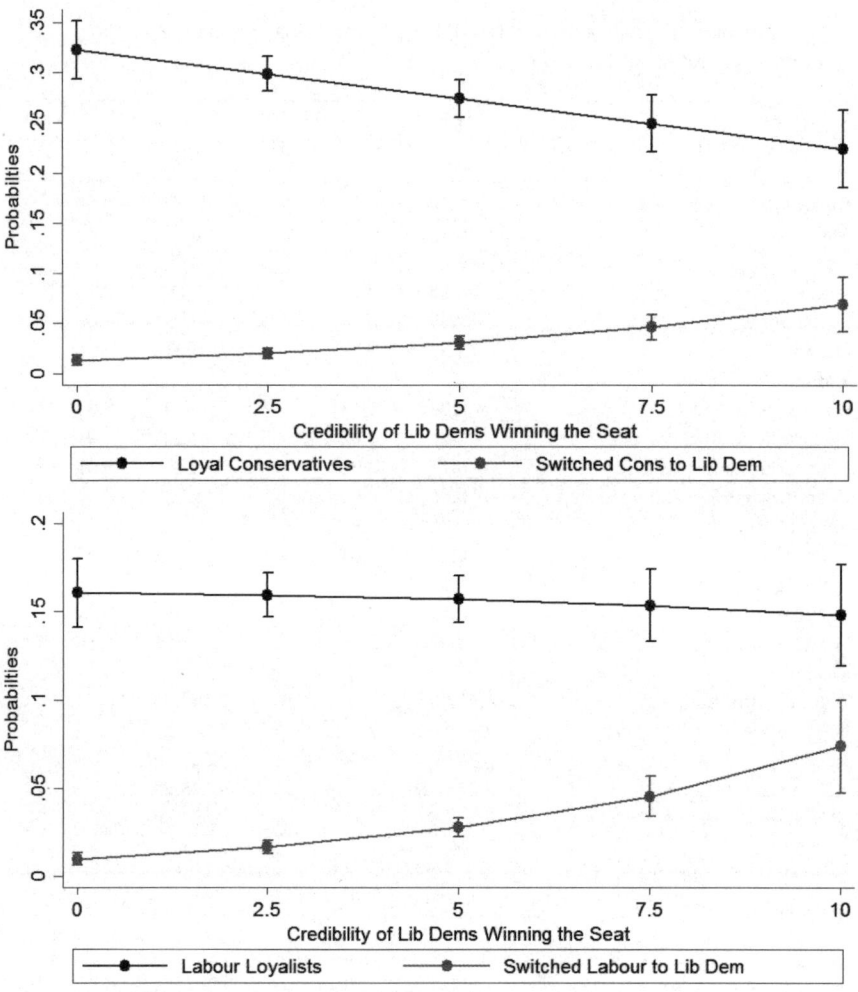

Figure 7.5 Average predicted probabilities of 2019 switching from Conservatives (top plot) and Labour (bottom plot) to Liberal Democrats based on perceptions of credibility.
Source: 2019 British Election Study

Liberal Democrat credibility increases and for those who switched it increases as perceptions that the Liberal Democrats could win the seat rise.

Where did Liberal Democrat credibility come from in 2019?

According to BEPS data, the Liberal Democrats were more credible in 2019 than at any time since 2010. On the scale from 0 (very unlikely) to 10 (very likely), the Liberal Democrats' score for perceived likelihood of winning in a constituency increased from 2.49 in 2017 to 3.55 in 2019. At the upper end, there were 44 seats where average perceptions that Liberal Democrats could win the seat were 50 per cent or more. Mean perceptions of the party's chances of winning locally remained high in former 2010 Liberal Democrat seats – for example, Eastleigh, and Thornbury and Yate – despite requiring swings of 12 per cent or more to recapture the seat, as it did also in very marginal contests. Part of the explanation could be tactical voting websites: Best for Britain, Remain United and The People's Vote, in particular, received large numbers of site visits as well as column inches in the press during the 2019 election campaign. Remain United, for instance, led by the pro-Remain businesswomen Gina Miller, backed 50 Liberal Democrat candidates in an attempt to unite Remain voters to defeat the Conservatives. This tactic, of course, did not prevent a Conservative majority in 2019, but according to BEPS data, around 12 per cent of 2019 Liberal Democrat voters used tactical voting websites, compared with 6 per cent of all voters.

But what influenced individuals' perceptions of a party's chances of winning in their seat or not? Data from the 2019 BEPS go a long way to explain why cred-ibility is so intrinsically linked to the Liberal Democrats' electoral success. It also details why tactical voting websites were always likely to come up short. Of those sampled – regardless of the party they voted for in 2019 – 31 per cent based their assessment of a party's likelihood of winning in their seat on the past election result or local results, while 15 per cent relied on talking to local people, and 10–14 per cent used national or local newspapers, television and radio, and the internet. Campaigning in the form of leaflets influenced around 5 per cent of respondents before the election and 7 per cent during the campaign.

By contrast, 44 per cent of 2019 Liberal Democrat voters based their assessment of who would win in their constituency on the 2017 result, while 42 per cent based their assessment on local election results. For those who switched to the Liberal Democrats in 2019, these figures were 42 per cent and 40 per cent, respectively. Local activism also mattered for 2019 Liberal Democrat voters: 12 per cent of them based their opinion of party credibility on receiving local Liberal Democrat leaflets. Online tactical websites did not feature heavily in voters' assessment of different parties' credibility. In sum, Liberal Democrat credibility was and is built on winning elections, building a local base, and remaining active in the area. Expectations that the Liberal Democrats were going to surge back to the top of British politics were always going to be wide of the mark. Electoral repair was always likely to be a slow and incremental process.

All about Jo or 'revoke', or both?

Going into the 2019 election, the Liberal Democrats made two distinct pitches. First, the party adopted an equidistance stance, which placed Swinson front and centre of a presidential-style campaign. The goal was to contrast the bold, fresh leadership of Jo Swinson with the marmite and perceived extremism of Johnson and Corbyn. Strategically, despite mistakes post coalition, as a third party it can partially subvert, although not fully overcome, structural barriers. Second, the Liberal Democrats adopted a distinctive policy on Brexit. In order to position themselves as the unequivocal voice of Remain, they promised to revoke article 50 without a referendum on the proviso they won a parliamentary majority. Both of these pitches appeared to backfire. The presidential-style campaign fell flat as public opinion towards Swinson deteriorated over the four-week campaign period. As we saw in Chapter 6, the 'revoke' policy also caused turmoil within the party. Some openly questioned the policy, and the party began backtracking publicly as its polling position declined. When the votes were counted, it became clear that the Liberal Democrats had lost a considerable amount of support during the election campaign. But to what extent was this driven by Swinson's popularity or the revoke policy? Were other factors to blame? To answer these questions, we examine two groups of voters: 2017 Liberal Democrat voters who switched to other parties in 2019; and those voters who intended to vote Liberal Democrat before the campaign but then switched to others during the campaign.

Swinson's declining popularity

Figure 7.6 shows Swinson's leadership approval ratings from her taking office in July 2019 to polling day on 12 December that year. Her net approval rating (the difference between approval and disapproval) remained negative throughout her leadership. It declined steadily after she took office, before levelling out a little at the end of October. It then fell more rapidly from late November to polling day. In YouGov's post-election poll, only 19 per cent of the public approved of Swinson, with 63 per cent disapproving, representing a net approval rate of −44 per cent.

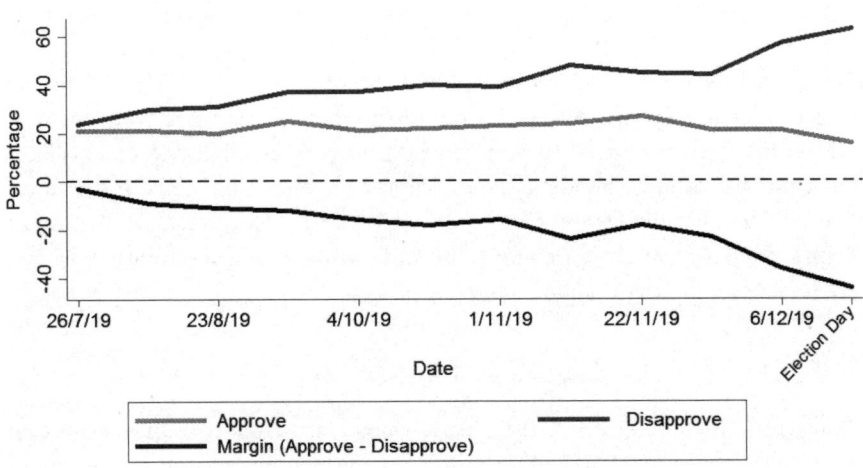

Figure 7.6 Swinson's leadership approval ratings from taking office to 2019 general election. *Source*: YouGov and Opinium leadership polls

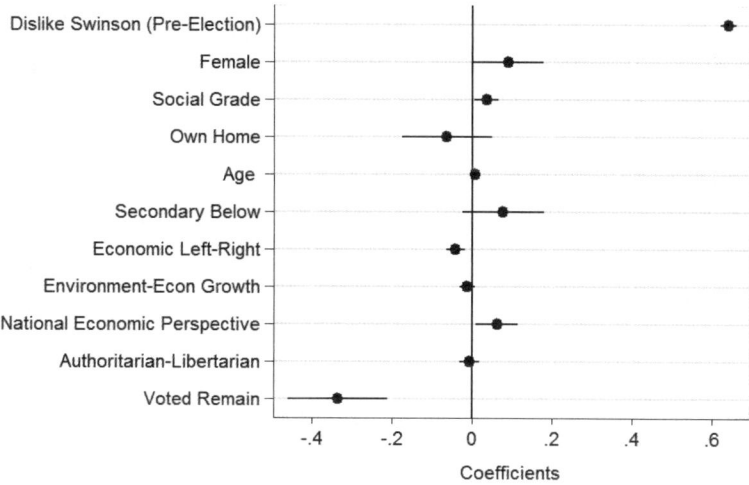

Figure 7.7 Linear model of dislike towards Swinson during the 2019 general election campaign: *Source*: 2019 British Election Study campaign panel

This compared with a net approval rating of –50 per cent for Corbyn (still higher than Swinson's) and –11 per cent for Johnson.

BEPS data paint a similar picture. Swinson's likeability fell from 3.3 at the beginning of the campaign to 2.9 four weeks later. This was only marginally higher than Corbyn's, whose mean likeability rating dropped from 2.8 to 2.7. Johnson's, by contrast, remained fairly stable, at 4.2 compared with 4.1 before the campaign began.[7] At the end of the campaign, 49 per cent of voters gave Swinson a score of 2 or below. By comparison, 59 per cent of voters gave Corbyn scores 2 or below, while 42 per cent gave such a score for Johnson. Of the three leaders, Corbyn and Johnson's scores remained remarkably static while Swinson's likeability dropped, particularly in the final weeks of the campaign. Just to reiterate how ill-advised the presidential-style campaign proved, Swinson's likeability rating was so bad it trumped Farron's dire scores from just two years earlier.

Who became more hostile to Swinson? Figure 7.7 shows a coefficient plot from a linear regression that models Swinson's likeability during the campaign based on socio-demographic and value-scale drivers. We reverse the likeability scale so that 10 is strongly dislike. To focus on who became hostile towards Swinson during the campaign, we control for her likeability in the pre-campaign wave. The linear model is weighted using the panel wave 17–wave 19 weight.

Based on the BEPS data, women became significantly more hostile to Swinson during the campaign than men.[8] It should, though, be noted that we do not have definitive data examining why this was the case. Swinson's popularity also fell during the campaign among older people, and those among the professional and managerial classes. Voters who felt optimistic about the country's economic situation were also more likely to turn against Swinson. This could explain why Remain-voting Conservatives were so difficult to win over in key target seats, despite the Liberal Democrats' pro-Remain credentials. There is also evidence that economically left-leaning voters were more likely to turn against Swinson than those on the right. Meanwhile, Remain voters warmed to Swinson as the campaign proceeded. In this regard, the revoke Brexit policy and Swinson's unapologetically pro-European stance did garner personal support.

More broadly, there was a positive correlation between liking the Liberal Democrats and liking Swinson ($R = 0.74^*$). Nonetheless, Swinson underperformed her party's likeability scores among voters of all parties, including Liberal Democrats and opposition supporters who supported Remain. Crucially, while likeability for Swinson and the Liberal Democrats declined during the election campaign, the drop was far more sizeable for the former than the latter. Among Labour voters, for example, feelings towards the Liberal Democrats remained fairly static over the campaign (dropping from 4.5 to 4.2), whereas Swinson became far more disliked (falling from 4.1 to 3.3). Meanwhile, Conservative voters were far more hostile to the Liberal Democrats and Swinson than other voters. This was evident before the campaign had begun. Yet while feelings towards the party barely changed (on average they fell from 2.2 to 2.1) antagonism towards Swinson deepened still further over the four weeks (mean likeability dropped from 2.2 to 1.8). Again, this suggests a strategic miscalculation in how the presidential-style campaign was operationalised. Not only was Swinson unpopular but the equidistance stance was unlikely to appeal to Conservative voters and likely to turn off Labour voters, who were more amenable to Liberal Democrat messaging and switching than their Conservative counterparts.

Was 'revoke' unpopular?

The revoke policy was intrinsically tied to Swinson. Throughout the campaign (and even after it) Swinson defended the policy as an honest reflection of the party's pro-European ethos and argued that it was popular with the public. The latter point has been the source of much debate in Liberal Democrat circles. On the one hand, polling evidence suggests that the policy was seen as legitimate by and was popular among Remain voters, whom the party was aiming to win over. Shortly after the revoke policy was agreed at the party's September 2019 conference, a poll found that 41 per cent of voters felt that remaining in the EU without a referendum would be legitimate (YouGov, 2019a). However, 70 per cent of Remain voters – and 58 per cent of Labour voters – thought the policy was legitimate. At the end of October 2019, 56 per cent of Remain voters were more likely to vote for the Liberal Democrats because of their revoke policy (Survation, 2019). Interestingly, 43 per cent of 2017 Labour voters also seemed supportive of the policy. In late November, another YouGov poll asked whether the Liberal Democrats were right or wrong to propose revoking article 50. While overall only 28 per cent said they

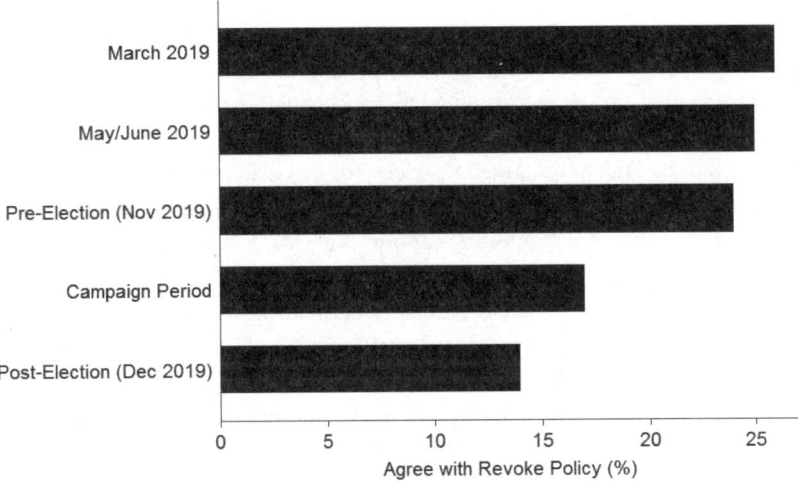

Figure 7.8 Support for 'revoke policy' from March 2019 through to the 2019 general election: *Source*: British Election Study (waves 15–19)

were right, the figure was 42 per cent for 2017 Labour voters and 50 per cent for those who had supported Remain in the EU referendum (YouGov, 2019b). Even in the final days of the campaign, 30 per cent of voters felt that cancelling Brexit best described their stance towards the issue. Again, cancelling Brexit was more popular among Labour voters (40 per cent) and those who had voted Remain in the 2016 referendum (49 per cent). These polls show that there was a lack of consistency among pollsters about how the question was asked. It is also the case that regarding a policy as acceptable or legitimate is different to actually supporting it over alternatives. Being supportive of a policy does not necessarily translate into votes. Opinium's final election poll, for instance, accurately predicted the Liberal Democrat vote share and showed relatively strong support for 'revoke' among 2017 Labour supporters and 2016 Remain voters (Opinium, 2019).

From March 2019 onwards, the BEPS asked respondents about cancelling Brexit without a referendum ('the revoke policy'), alongside other options, such as having a referendum on a deal, leaving the EU with a deal and no referendum, and leave with no deal. BEPS respondents were also asked whether each option was acceptable or unacceptable. From the data, we can examine support for 'revoke', differentiate between support and whether it was seen as acceptable, and assess how these trends affected voting. Moreover, we can identify who these voters were.

Figure 7.8 shows that support for cancelling Brexit without a referendum fell markedly from March 2019 to election day. Support was relatively stable until the campaign, when it fell from 24 to 14 per cent.[9] Comparing support for 'revoke' over this time period reveals a number of key findings. First, support fell among Remain voters. In June 2019, 45 per cent of Remain voters agreed with the policy. By December, this figure had fallen to 24 per cent. Second, support for the policy also declined among Liberal Democrat voters. Of Liberal Democrat supporters in June 2019, 54 per cent supported 'revoke', while 46 per cent did not. Come the general election, this had dropped to 30 per cent. Labour was the main beneficiaries of voters moving away from the Liberal Democrats from June to December. In June 2019, of Remain voters who were supportive of revoke, 36 per cent intended to vote Liberal Democrat, and 24 per cent of this group intended to vote Labour. By polling day, Liberal Democrat support among pro-revoke Remainers was 28 per cent, while 52 per cent supported Labour. Ninety per cent of those who switched from Liberal Democrat to Labour during this period voted Remain, and 31 per cent agreed with cancelling Brexit without a referendum.

During the campaign period, support for cancelling Brexit without a referendum dropped from 19 to 14 per cent.[10] Of the 19 per cent who supported 'revoke' before the campaign, 90 per cent were Remain voters. It seems, therefore, that Remain voters turned their back on the policy. Notwithstanding some churn (some voters did move from other options to the revoke policy even though it declined overall), only 56 per cent of those who supported the policy before the election opted for it come polling day. Just over a quarter had shifted to the 'referendum on a deal' option, which was closest to Labour's policy. By the end of the 2019 campaign, not only had support for revoke declined, but half of supporters of the policy voted Labour. Meanwhile, more than 60 per cent of those whose preference was a second referendum on a deal also backed Labour.

In 2019, the Liberal Democrats suffered from a triple whammy. 'Revoke' became more unpopular as the campaign went on, and those who did prefer it mostly voted Labour. Fundamentally, though, the 'revoke' policy also did not sit well with many Remain voters. As the campaign proceeded, their support for it waned, while the proportion who felt that it was acceptable barely changed (39 to 41 per cent). Those who supported the Liberal Democrats in June overwhelmingly supported Remain. These drifted to Labour slowly at first as Labour's Brexit stance shifted. Among Remain voters, support for revoke and a referendum on a deal were fairly even at the start of the campaign. By the end of the campaign, nearly 40 per cent of Remain voters preferred Labour's policy position, more than a fifth favoured Johnson's option and less than a quarter preferred revoke. As Remain voters drifted to Labour and Conservative voters hardened their support for 'getting Brexit done', the Liberal Democrats suffered. Despite the churn, support for 'revoke' was much higher among Liberal Democrat voters than among Labour voters. Indeed, those who remained loyal to the Liberal Democrats from 2017 to 2019 were the most supportive.

But did the party's 'revoke' policy influence 2017 Liberal Democrat voters to switch to Labour and the Conservatives in 2019? To answer this, we run a multinomial regression model comparing switchers with those who stuck with the Liberal Democrats in 2017 and 2019. The results are shown in Table A7.3 in the Appendix. Once again, Swinson's unpopularity stands out. It was a key driver for Liberal Democrat switchers to both parties, holding other variables constant. For those who switched to Labour, credibility also mattered. Those who gave the

Liberal Democrats less chance of electoral success were significantly more likely to switch to Labour. Those who switched to Labour were far more likely to find the 'revoke' policy unacceptable. There was no equivalent effect for those who switched to the Conservatives. In summary, the 'revoke' policy appeared to trigger a steady drift of voters away from the Liberal Democrats from the autumn of 2019 onwards. During the campaign, Labour began to benefit from predominantly Remain voters turning their back on the policy. Combined with Swinson's popularity and the party's electoral credibility, 'revoke' was a pivotal driver of prior Liberal Democrat voters switching to Labour in 2019.

But is the evidence as clear-cut for those Remain voters who stayed loyal to the Conservatives? This was a crucial target group for the Liberal Democrats in target seats. We use a logistic regression to examine what drove Remain voters to vote Conservative in 2019. The model includes variables used throughout the chapter – left–right political values, the redistribution value scale and core socio-demographics – alongside party leadership, best party on the most important issue, partisanship, Liberal Democrats' electoral credibility and the party's 'revoke' policy. Figure 7.9 shows the logistic regression coefficients from the model (see also Table A7.4 in the Appendix).

So what drove Remain voters to support the Conservatives in 2019? 'Remainers' who politically and economically placed themselves on the right, whose partisan orientation was Conservative and who thought that party was the best on the most important issue were all significantly more likely to vote Conservative than for other parties. Remain voters who supported the Liberal Democrats' 'revoke' policy were significantly less likely to vote Conservative. On average, support for

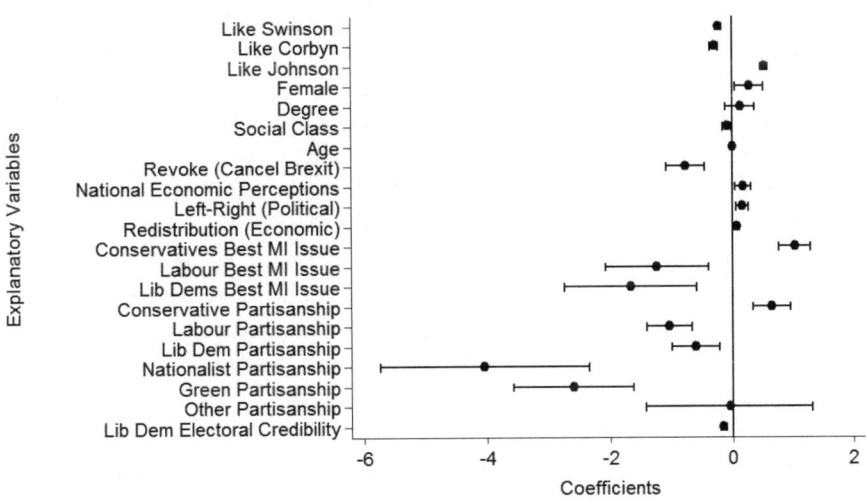

Figure 7.9 Logistic regression of voting Conservative in 2019: coefficient plot (2016 Remain voters only). *Source*: 2019 British Election Study

the policy decreased the probability of voting Conservative by three percentage points, holding other variables constant. Standing on the 'cancelling Brexit' ticket therefore damaged the party's electoral fortunes among those Remainers who leaned right. Leadership also mattered. For a one-unit change in likeability of Boris Johnson, the odds of voting Conservative increase by a factor of 1.71; that is, for every additional point on the 0–10 (dislike to like) Johnson likeability scale, the odds increase by 70.6 per cent holding other variables constant. Johnson is therefore a considerable driver. Like Corbyn, Swinson proved unpopular with Remainers voting Conservative. For a one-unit increase in liking Swinson, the odds of voting Conservative decrease by a factor of 0.79: that is for every additional point moving from dislike to like, the odds of voting Conservative decreases by more than 20 per cent holding other variables constant. With more than 60 per cent of Conservative Remainers recording a likeability rating for Swinson between 0 and 3 (a mean of 2.96), it is evident that Swinson proved ineffective at persuading right-leaning voters to turn their backs on the Conservatives. Lastly, the Liberal Democrats' structural problems remained an issue for these Conservative voters. Even after controlling for other variables, the less credible the Liberal Democrats were in the constituency contest the more likely it was these Remain voters supported the Conservatives.

Austerity and the legacy of coalition: did they still matter?

Any possibility of a Liberal Democrat 'bounce-back' depended on the party's ability to recruit voters. Strategically, those who had voted for the Liberal Democrats previously were likely to be the most receptive to party messaging and aware of the party's chances locally. In the latter part of the book, we have looked at the party's 2010 support and the voters who left the party after it went into coalition with the Conservatives. If the Liberal Democrats were to make a comeback, it was these voters who offered the most viable route. Yet, earlier in the chapter, we showed how anti-austerity sentiments and the legacy of coalition thwarted Farron's attempts to win back those who voted Liberal Democrat in 2010 but subsequently shifted to Labour in 2015. In 2017, the austerity legacy was reinforced by Corbyn's anti-austerity credentials and messaging. As Chapter 6 shows, Swinson was unable to distance the Liberal Democrats or herself from the coalition given her ministerial portfolio in that administration. This legacy remained salient for the crucial group of voters on the centre-left who supported the party in 2010 but switched to Labour and other left-wing parties subsequently. To assess whether austerity mattered, we select a subset of the BEPS data – only those who voted for the Liberal Democrats in 2010. Then, using a multinomial model – placing those who voted Liberal Democrat in 2010 and again in 2019 as the base category – we can determine whether anti-austerity sentiments[11] still underpinned support for Labour or whether negative feelings towards Swinson or the party's 'revoke' position damaged Liberal Democrat attempts to win over these voters. We also

Table 7.3 Multinomial logistic regression of 2019 party choice (2010 Liberal Democrat voters only)

Variables	Cons19		Lab19		Green/Nat19		BP/UKIP19	
	β	SE	β	SE	β	SE	β	SE
Constant	0.36	0.80	3.24*	0.64	3.07*	0.76	3.21*	1.03
Austerity (gone too far)	−0.47*	0.19	0.35*	0.16	0.15	0.16	−0.25	0.26
Left–right political values	−0.01	0.11	−0.25*	0.08	−0.31*	0.12	−0.28	0.15
Redistribution (economic)	−0.04	0.07	−0.03	0.06	−0.02	0.06	−0.12	0.08
Like Swinson	−0.18*	0.08	−0.36*	0.05	−0.39*	0.07	−0.63*	0.09
Like Johnson	0.68*	0.07	−0.03	0.06	0.07	0.08	0.36*	0.08
Like Corbyn	−0.08	0.07	0.37*	0.05	0.14*	0.05	−0.02	0.09
Revoke unacceptable	−1.44*	0.58	−0.31	0.23	−0.15	0.35	0.82	0.60
Liberal Democrats' likelihood of winning seat	−0.27*	0.06	−0.35*	0.05	−0.36*	0.06	−0.35*	0.07
Female	0.68*	0.29	−0.09	0.21	0.78*	0.30	0.04	0.38
Age (30 and under)	0.90	0.67	−0.18	0.57	−0.18	0.57	−13.6*	0.55
Degree	−0.32	0.33	−0.32	0.22	−0.32	0.22	0.06	0.39
Social grade (class)	0.01	0.10	−0.01	0.07	−0.01	0.07	−0.12	0.12
Model fit								
Log likelihood	−763.58							
R^2	0.44							
AIC	1,631.15							
BIC	−7,283.06							
N	1,283							

*Significant p<0.05. Base category – voted Liberal Democrat in 2010 and 2019.

examine why these voters supported the Conservatives and whether voting for other parties (Greens and nationalist parties) also had its roots in the 'austerity enabler' legacy from the coalition. The findings are presented in Table 7.3.

Four key points stand out from the results. First, when compared against those who voted Liberal Democrat in 2010 and 2019, irrespective of which party was supported in 2019, Swinson was universally unpopular. Second, perceived electoral credibility also mattered regardless of the party supported. Those who did not support the Liberal Democrats simply did not regard the party as electorally viable in their local constituency contest. Third, the Liberal Democrats' 'revoke' policy did influence those who voted Conservative, but did not drive support for other parties when compared against those who supported the Liberal Democrats. Other factors acted as expected, with those on the left significantly more likely to support Labour or progressive parties such as the Scottish or Welsh nationalists and the Greens. Predictably, Johnson was popular among right-leaning voters while those on the left were far more supportive of Corbyn. Lastly, austerity mattered for those who supported the Conservatives and Labour. As regards the former, those 2010 Liberal Democrat voters who felt that national, local and NHS cuts had not gone too far were more likely to support the Conservatives. However, given the sizeable number of 2010 Liberal Democrat voters who supported Labour in 2019, opposition to austerity cuts remained a key driver just as it had done two years previously. For these Labour voters, the Liberal Democrats' historic role and legacy as 'austerity enablers' still carried weight. These were the voters who left the Liberal Democrats in their droves during the coalition period and had not returned. Interestingly, when we ran exactly the same model either on the whole BEPS sample or non-Liberal Democrat 2010 voters, austerity concerns did not have a significant effect on voting Labour in 2019.[12] Such findings come with a health warning. Nonetheless, they do provide anecdotal evidence that it was precisely this group of Labour voters, who in theory should have been more receptive to the Liberal Democrats, who were in fact the most conscious of the party's coalition legacy which as a consequence contributed to their reluctance to vote Liberal Democrat in 2019.

Summary

The post-coalition era proved to be a period of survival than revival for the Liberal Democrats. During this four-year period of political instability, the Liberal Democrats were largely by-standers, unable to influence or capitalise on the travails of their rivals. In 2017, the Liberal Democrats made very little electoral headway, but instead doubled down on retaining their traditional core vote and remaining partisans. If anything, the party recruited those from the right politically and economically, but any advancement was largely offset by switchers. Two years later, there were small steps on the road to recovery. Nevertheless, these were drowned out by the 'big picture' narrative of the Liberal Democrats losing support over the extended campaign period. Broadly speaking, the party retained more voters in 2019 than in either 2017 or 2015, but the party's weak base continued to hinder recovery, as retention was offset by switchers to Labour, Conservatives and the Greens. The party, though, did begin to recruit moderate Conservatives and centre-ground Labour voters, though the latter were driven more by tactical concerns. Electoral credibility underpinned recruitment and retention, and remained fundamental to the Liberal Democrats' electoral chances. With the party hamstrung locally following its collapse in 2015, building momentum proved difficult as voters looked for more viable alternatives. Overcoming this vicious circle takes time and cannot be achieved through tactical voting websites but requires old-fashioned hard graft of winning council seats and councils.

Notwithstanding the continuing structural frailties that have long bedevilled the Liberal Democrats, three other core themes explain why they struggled. First, they continued to pay a heavy price for going into coalition with the Conservatives. In both 2017 and 2019, Labour supporters who donated their vote to the Liberal Democrats in 2010 only to tactically unwind and return to Labour in 2015 persisted in their resentment towards the Liberal Democrats. The party struggled to shrug off this millstone round its neck, and Labour in particular was keen to exploit this weakness. The 'austerity enabler' messages resonated and curbed any prospect of recovery among sections of the electorate that hitherto were instrumental in the Liberal Democrats' pre-2015 success. Second, the Brexit lifeline proved misplaced. In 2017, the party failed demonstrably to recruit Remain voters, due to a lack of political and electoral viability. Younger, more educated voters who shared cosmopolitan attitudes and had overwhelmingly voted Remain also bought into Labour's anti-austerity message. The under-40s bore the brunt of debt, inequality and insecurity. This group, who, as Remain voters, would otherwise be a prime target for the Liberal Democrats, instead saw the party as accomplices in perpetuating these growing political and economic divides. Third, any hope that Farron could cut through quickly diminished. Farron was unpopular, thwarted by electoral realities and personal miscalculations. He was also by-passed and ignored by the media and voters alike.

Two years later, the Liberal Democrats initially appeared to be on the crest of an electoral wave. Having struggled to get a foothold in the Brexit debate at the 2017 general election, and with a leader unable to cut through, the Liberal Democrats pressed the nuclear button. Buoyed by growing discontent with both Corbyn and Johnson, the party put Swinson front and centre. The Liberal Democrats also unequivocally sought clear blue water between themselves and Labour over Brexit through their 'revoke' policy. The strategy backfired. Swinson was less popular than the party and this gap grew as the campaign proceeded. Those who switched to rival parties were driven by negative perceptions of Swinson. The Liberal Democrat leader also hampered efforts to recruit Conservative Remain voters, and was perceived negatively among left-leaning Labour supporters who had voted Liberal Democrat in 2010. Both of these groups had initially appeared vulnerable to Liberal Democrat overtures, but Swinson was a key reason why conversion to the Liberal Democrats remained limited. The Liberal Democrats' 'cancel Brexit' policy also cost the party support. The party's surge in local and European elections as well as in national polling was driven overwhelmingly by Remain supporters, but their support for the party's 'revoke' policy began to wane early on and tumbled during the election campaign. Many of the voters who flirted with the Liberal Democrats in the summer of 2019 drifted back to Labour, while Conservative-leaning Remain voters toughened their support for getting Brexit finalised. Notwithstanding this, 'revoke' also led prior Liberal Democrat voters to switch support to Labour in 2019. Far from uniting Remain voters, the policy undermined the Liberal Democrats' anti-Brexit message and the party's popularity suffered as a result. As a consequence, the Liberal Democrats emerged from the 2019 election still a spectator rather than an influencer in British politics.

The changing geography of the Liberal Democrat vote

Geography matters for the Liberal Democrats. From the late 1920s, the Liberals had a distinctive electoral geography, based on regional and religious identity. While the Nonconformist 'Celtic fringe' shielded the party from Labour's class-based clutches for more than 60 years, the party struggled beyond these strongholds. The electoral breakthrough finally came in the late 1990s. This also proved to be a stepping stone for further success throughout the 2000s as the Liberal Democrats became more adept at converting votes into seats. The party was built on solid dual foundations, with its credibility ostensibly assured in traditional Liberal-voting areas and rapid advancement in new areas. In the latter, the growth came in the form of increasing local council representation and by-election success, underpinned by ruthlessly targeted 'all year round' campaigning. Despite the party's loss of five seats in 2010, the geography of Liberal Democrat support had become established and embedded. Ten years and three general elections later, the electoral picture was very different.

Previous chapters have shown, at the individual level, what happened to the Liberal Democrat vote and why since 2010. Now we turn to the big picture – the changing geography of Liberal Democrat support. The first half of this chapter details the emergence of a new Liberal Democrat geography of support. It describes the party's growing north–south divide and how the Liberal Democrats have increasingly become a 'south of England' party. It also discusses how the 2015 and 2017 general elections ripped up the post-1997 electoral geography and exposed the party's support in traditional Liberal territory. Prior to the 2015 election, many assumed that the party's traditional strongholds in the Celtic fringe would act as some kind of buffer against any significant collapse in support. The reality proved different, suggesting that the longstanding culture of Liberal support in these areas had waned considerably. The sheer scale of this erosion in support is why in 2019 there were few signs of any resurgence in these areas despite a modest recovery elsewhere. Simply put, the Liberal Democrats had become a party without heartlands of support, and a minor player outside the south of England.

The second half of the chapter examines how political events drove the party's post-2010 collapse in support. After exploring the changing socio-demographic composition of the Liberal Democrat vote, we assess the impact of two key political shocks on the geography of Liberal Democrat support in Britain. The unionist–nationalist divide in Scotland after the 2014 referendum on Scottish independence and the seismic influence of Brexit both laid bare underlying structural weaknesses in the party's support. Amid these shocks, we stress how the enduring coalition legacy and the party's association with austerity scuppered any major electoral fightback. Nonetheless, based on the nature of the party's modest revival in 2019, we point to green shoots of recovery in particular types of Remain-leaning seats and areas where a local platform is beginning to become established. We then extend this to classify and examine the so-called 'Blue Wall'. We assess just how competitive the Liberal Democrats are in these seats (including under the new boundaries), whether they alone provide the gateway to electoral recovery, or whether the party needs to unite old geographies of support with these new areas of growth in order to have a sustainable electoral future.

The growing north–south divide: a south-of-England party?

The current geography of Liberal Democrat support is unrecognisable from that in 2010. Over the course of the three general elections between 2010 and 2019, the Liberal Democrat political map transformed. In 2015, the party saw its vote collapse across the UK by, on average, 15 percentage points. However, this collapse was not evenly spread. The Liberal Democrats suffered larger declines in areas where the party was previously strongest.

As Figure 8.1 shows, these include its traditional strongholds in the South West region of England, the South East, East Anglia and Greater Manchester.

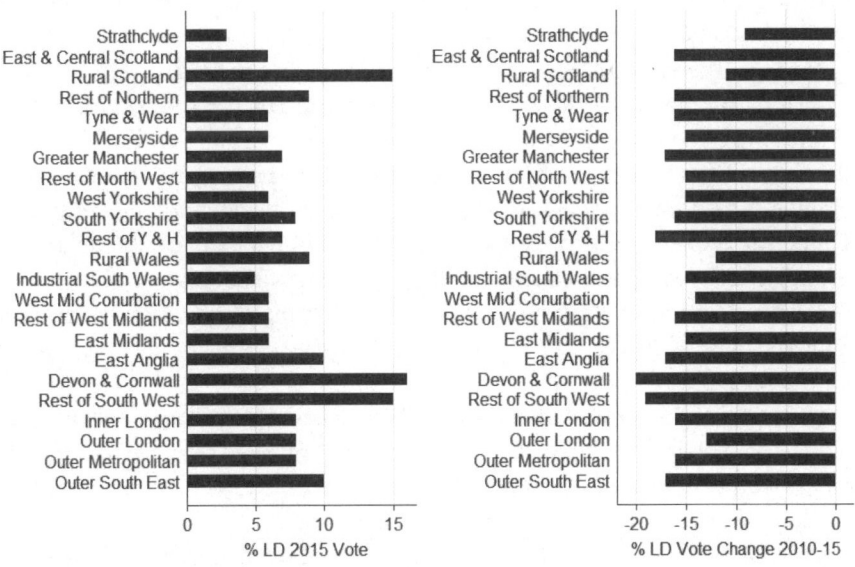

Figure 8.1 Percentage Liberal Democrat vote and vote change by region: 2015 general election

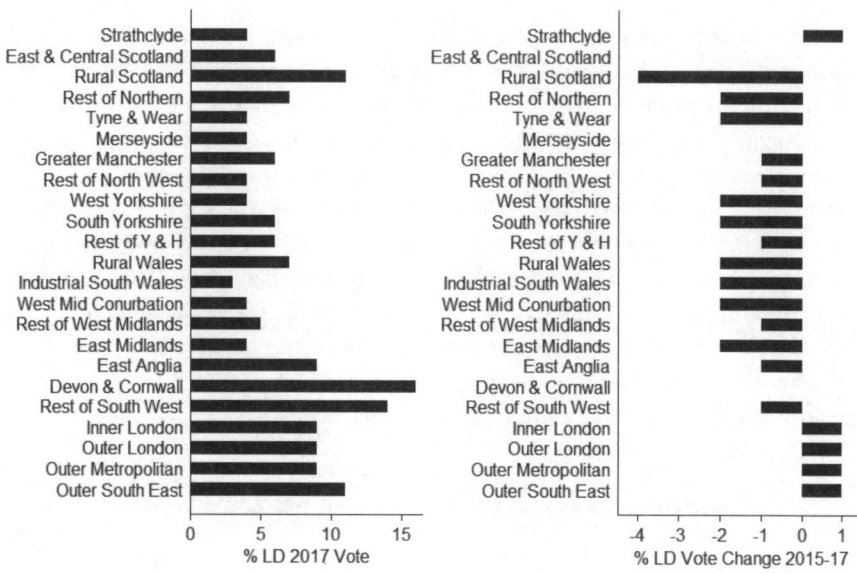

Figure 8.2 Percentage Liberal Democrat vote and vote change by region: 2017 general election

In the East Midlands, West Midlands and Merseyside, the party's vote declined, but the Liberal Democrats had long struggled in these areas. In 2017, amid a further drop in national vote share, there was a little more variation in the party's performance. Outside the far South West, London and the South East of England, Liberal Democrat support eroded further. The downward trend also continued in Wales and Rural Scotland (see Figure 8.2).

In 2019, the Liberal Democrats recovered somewhat nationally, with support increasing by more than four percentage points, to 11.5 per cent (12.4 per cent in England). The party gained ground across all regions, and raised the floor of its vote – in the Midlands – by around 3.5 points and parts of Yorkshire and the Humber by close to five percentage points. However, the largest growth came in London and the Outer Metropolitan areas surrounding the capital and the rest of the South East region (see Figure 8.3). The Liberal Democrats also started to make some headway in the old Wessex region incorporating Dorset, Gloucestershire, Somerset and Wiltshire, but continued to struggle in Devon and their prior strongholds in Cornwall.

Yet, despite the recovery in 2019, the Liberal Democrats still won only half the national vote share that they had in 2010. There are clear signs that the recovery was far from even. In London and the surrounding Outer Metropolitan constituencies, the Liberal Democrats were less than 10 points behind the regional vote shares achieved in 2010. Across the rest of the South East region of England, the party had narrowed the gap on 2010 performance levels to 11 percentage points. In the South West region, particularly Devon and Cornwall, the picture was gloomier. In 2019,

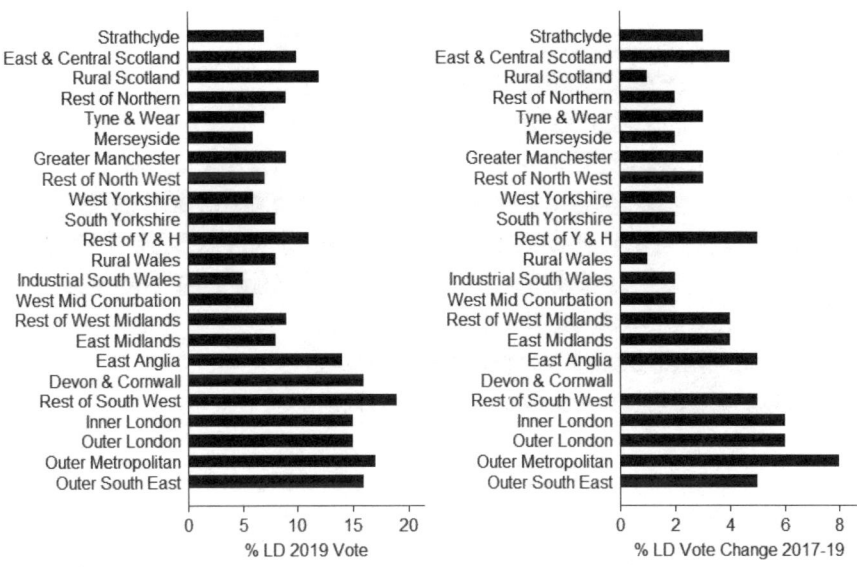

Figure 8.3 Percentage Liberal Democrat vote and vote change by region: 2019 general election

the party polled as much as 20 percentage points below what it achieved nine years earlier. While the Liberal Democrats still enjoyed stronger support in the South West than in other regions, it was far below the levels recorded in 2005 and 2010, and there were few signs of recovery. Elsewhere, the decline was between 13 and 15 percentage points from 2010.

One of the electoral consequences of the collapse in Liberal Democrat vote share since 2010 has been the emergence of a visible 'north–south' divide in its support. Figure 8.4 (graph 1) shows how the north–south divide in the vote Liberal Democrats and their predecessors has fluctuated in England since 1983. Graph 2 shows the north–south divide in seats over the same period. Generally speaking, the Liberal Democrats consistently polled higher in the south than elsewhere in England. During the 1980s, more than half of the Alliance's national vote share came from the 264 constituencies across the south of England. A more targeted approach in 1992, and the abandonment of equidistance between 1992 and 1997, increased this divide as the party drew more than 60 per cent of its vote from the south of England. The electoral breakthrough in 1997, for instance, was largely made at the expense of the Conservatives' strongholds in the south of England. Of the 34 English seats won by the Liberal Democrats in 1997, 28 were in the south.

Prior to this, the distribution of Liberal Democrat seats was relatively even, though in 1992 seven of the 10 seats won in England were in the south, with five of these in the South West region. After the 1997 election, the party started to gain more support in the north of England, reflecting the party's target to become the main competitor in Labour strongholds. In both 2005 and 2010, the party still

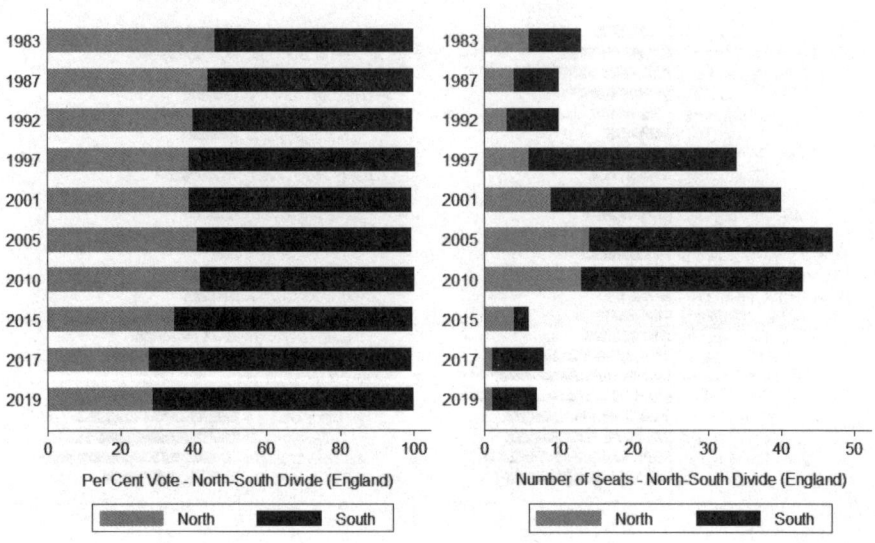

Figure 8.4 North–south divide in votes and seats 1983–2019: England only

polled higher in the south, but the gap had started to diminish and had fallen below the 1992 figure. The party was also winning more seats in the north – 14 in 2005 and 13 in 2010 were historical highs – while simultaneously struggling to make further inroads in Conservative seats in the south.

After 2010, there was a marked geographical shift in Liberal Democrat support. One of the noticeable consequences of the 2015 electoral collapse was the increase in the party's north–south divide. In 2015, while four of the six seats won were in the north, nearly 65 per cent of the Liberal Democrat vote in England was concentrated in the south. This partly reflected the ruthlessness of the Conservatives' electoral strategy. The majority of their head-to-head contests with the Liberal Democrats were in southern seats, primarily in Outer London and the South West region, while in the north the Liberal Democrats were far more successful at holding off Labour in seats such as Leeds North West and Sheffield Hallam.

In 2017, the party held steady in the South West region and East Anglia and even made ground in London and other parts of the South East region of England. Conversely, across the Midlands, North East, and South and West Yorkshire the Liberal Democrats declined still further. Liberal Democrat support across Merseyside and the rest of the North West region outside Greater Manchester struggled to reach 4 per cent. Consequently, more than 70 per cent of the party's 2017 vote came from the south of England.[1] As we will see, the further drop in 2017 partly reflected the saliency of Brexit as the Liberal Democrats suffered in Leave-voting constituencies in the north, while doing better in Remain-voting southern seats in and around London. However, this did not represent the whole story.

Liberal Democrat support held steady in the predominantly Leave-voting South West, East Anglia and large parts of the South East region. Labour's 2017 resurgence under Jeremy Corbyn also contributed to the collapse in Liberal Democrat support across the Midlands and northern England. In such seats, Labour won back supporters who had previously backed the Liberal Democrats. Indeed, part of this process of unwind took place in 2015, which probably accounts for the growth in the north–south gap. In many of these seats, Labour also represented the best chance to avoid a 'hard' or 'no deal' Brexit, which signified the best of a bad hand for many pro-Europeans given that the Liberal Democrats had little prospect of winning. The recognition that many of these contests were two-party battles between Labour and the Conservatives also led to further switching away from the Liberal Democrats as British politics polarised. Despite these factors, though, the geographical shift in Liberal Democrat support away from the north started before Brexit and the rise of Corbyn.

The north–south gap remained fairly stable in 2019. The Liberal Democrats made headway in the south of England, including sizeable increases in vote share in Outer London and its commuter belt. Nevertheless, these were partially offset by increases in the floor of the Liberal Democrat vote across the northern regions of England. With Corbyn now unpopular with many and Labour's Brexit stance ambiguous at best, Labour struggled to squeeze the Liberal Democrat vote in these northern constituencies as it had done two years earlier. Elsewhere, the Liberal Democrats continued to progress in Remain-voting southern seats, but failed to make any advance in Leave-voting Devon and Cornwall. The north–south gap in seats became increasingly evident with the party winning only one seat – Westmorland and Lonsdale – in the north of England at both the 2017 and the 2019 elections. If the Liberal Democrat party (and its predecessors) was not a southern-leaning party before 2010, it was by 2019. In 2017 and 2019, around 64 per cent of the Liberal Democrats' national vote share came from the south of England.

Losing its traditional heartlands

For 12 of the 14 general elections from 1945 to 1992, more than 50 per cent of Liberal Democrat (and its predecessors) representation came from strongholds in the Celtic Fringe (see Figure 8.5). After 1992, the party began to rely less on this traditional base as it benefited from aggressive targeting and coalitions of support against both Conservative and Labour incumbents in places where the party had built electoral credibility. By 2010, only 30 per cent of seats held by the Liberal Democrats were in the Celtic fringe, although the party still won more seats where it was traditionally strong. At the party's high-water mark in 2005, for example, it won 31 per cent of its seats in the Celtic fringe – its largest seat share during the 1945–2017 period. The Liberal Democrats also regularly picked up 25 per cent or more of its seats in the Celtic fringe between 1997 and 2010. However, the upward trend was not uniform. In Scotland, established electoral credibility led to

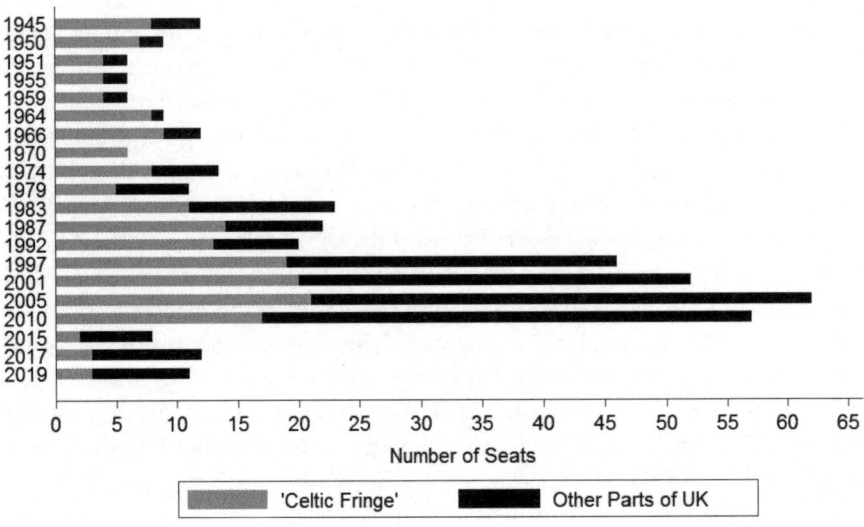

Figure 8.5 Seats won by the Liberal Democrats (and their predecessors) in the Celtic fringe and in all other parts of the UK, 1945–2019

'contagion', where the party built outwards on longstanding success particularly in the Highlands and in parts of Aberdeenshire.

In Cornwall and Devon, contagion through intensive campaigning fused with enduring credibility allowed the party to advance in parts of Cornwall outside its hotspots of Truro and North Cornwall, and in Devon around the English riviera in Torbay and Newton Abbot. Yet in rural Wales decline had set in in the early part of the post-war period. Even during its high points in the 2000s, outside of traditional strongholds – Ceredigion, Montgomeryshire and Brecon and Radnorshire – the Liberal Democrats failed to make further electoral ground. Crucially, though, there was an expectation that a core group of Celtic fringe seats would always provide a base from which the Liberal Democrats would maintain parliamentary presence whatever the electoral circumstances. Even accounting for redistricting, over the general elections between 1945 and 2019, certain seats within the Celtic fringe – Orkney and Shetland; Caithness and Sutherland; Inverness; Gordon; Ross; Skye and Lochaber; Fife North East in Scotland; the old Cardigan area (now Ceredigion) and Montgomeryshire in Wales; Cornwall North; Devon North, Truro in England – had all at various times kept the Liberal flag flying in Westminster.

The Liberal collapse in the Celtic fringe: a party with no heartlands?

The Liberal Democrats started to gain more ground outside their traditional heart-lands during the 2000s as they sought to capitalise initially on anti-Conservative feeling, and latterly on discontent with New Labour. With only 17 of the 57 seats won in 2010 within the Celtic fringe, there were already warning signs that the Liberal Democrats' traditional strongholds were under long-term threat. However, it was the party's catastrophic collapse in 2015 that accelerated this process. Liberal Democrat support declined in 2015 to the same degree in the Celtic fringe as it did nationally, while in 2017 it receded at a rate which was slightly higher. More worryingly for the Liberal Democrats, its recovery in 2019 was minimal. While party support increased by more than four points outside of the Celtic fringe, it barely grew at all within its previous heartlands and failed to regain any seats. In the Celtic fringe, Liberal Democrat support dropped by 15 percentage points between 2010 and 2019, compared with 12 points elsewhere.

But the party's performance varied significantly within the Celtic fringe across the 2015, 2017 and 2019 elections. In 2015, the Liberal Democrat vote fell most in England where it had been historically strong. While support tailed off dramatically in Somerset, Gloucestershire and the old Avon area (including Bristol and Bath), in Devon and Cornwall the party's vote collapsed by an unprecedented 20 percentage points. While it did not lose any further ground across Devon and Cornwall in 2017, the Liberal Democrats failed to take back any of the five seats it lost two years before. There was, however, a huge amount of unevenness. Across the six seats in Cornwall, party support dropped from 43 per cent in 2010 to 22 per cent in 2015, and marginally recovered to 23 per cent in 2017, when popular former incumbents stood again. However, despite a recovery elsewhere, the Liberal Democrat vote across Cornwall fell below 20 per cent in 2019. The long-term prospects in Devon also looked gloomy. Aside from the longstanding flagship seat of North Devon and the local party machine under the astute stewardship of Adrian Sanders in Torbay, the Liberal Democrats had struggled since 2005 to assert electoral dominance across Devon. Both North Devon and Torbay were lost in 2015 and, despite something of a recovery in North Devon with former incumbent Nick Harvey standing again, the party lost further ground in 2017. Two years later there were few signs of any long-term recovery. Worryingly for the Liberal Democrats, the scale of the collapse in its traditional South West regional heartland after 2010 was arguably masked by the popularity of certain MPs. Some of these former incumbents have now gone, and with them their personal following, which has left the Liberal Democrats' ability to cultivate or even just hold on to the longstanding Liberal voting culture in the South West region of England under real threat.

Across rural Wales, the Liberal Democrats' plight is even more desperate. The apparent floor effects in Nonconformist South West region of England in 2017 was not evident in rural Wales. While Liberal Democrat support fell by only 14 percentage points between the 2015 and 2017 general elections, the party's vote had started to crumble before then. In 2010, it narrowly lost Montgomeryshire, one of the most historic Liberal seats in Britain. Before that, the Liberals had only lost Montgomeryshire once – in 1979 – since 1874. Neighbouring Brecon and

Radnorshire fell during the party's collapse in 2015, while Ceredigion, another historic Liberal seat, was narrowly lost in 2017 (to Plaid Cymru). While the Liberal Democrats were given a lifeline in Brecon and Radnorshire through a by-election victory in the summer of 2019, the Conservatives easily regained the seat at the general election a few months later. As in 2017, the party did not win any seats in Wales and made little progress in these Celtic fringe seats in 2019. The long-standing local culture of voting Liberal in much of the old Nonconformist fringe seemed to be waning.

The story in rural Scotland is a little more complicated than the party's collapse in rural Wales and the far south-west of England. Outside of Cornwall, rural Scotland has been a longstanding source of Liberal support and representation. However, it was not immune from the 2015 Liberal Democrat collapse, as only Orkney and Shetland was held. On the face of it, Liberal Democrat support in rural Scotland fell less than in the rest of the UK, although seats with larger numbers of Nonconformists saw a bigger decline in the Liberal Democrat vote ($R = -0.29^*$) as the party did worse where it was previously strong. In 2017, the Liberal Democrats won back a longstanding stronghold, Caithness and Sutherland, and only narrowly failed to win Fife North East. Conversely, Liberal Democrat support in rural Scotland fell by a further four percentage points. Performance, however, varied, with some historical strongholds experiencing a decline in Liberal Democrat support across both 2015 and 2017. Like elsewhere in the Celtic fringe, personal incumbency seemed to stem the tide somewhat in 2015, although this was short-lived.[2] When previous Liberal Democrat incumbents or new local candidates who performed well in 2015 decided not to stand in 2017, Liberal Democrat support collapsed.[3] In both the two success stories – Caithness and Sutherland and Fife North East – the Liberal Democrat vote barely increased but was helped by a Conservative resurgence and a drop in SNP support. In 2019, the party regained the marginal Fife North East seat from the SNP and saw an increase in support outside of rural Scotland. Yet, like the rest of the Celtic fringe across the UK, the Liberal Democrat vote hardly changed in rural Scotland, suggesting that the party's problems in these former strongholds were deep-seated. In these traditional heartlands, the party could no longer rely on a dwindling Nonconformist electorate to bail it out.

In the Celtic fringe, as elsewhere, the Liberal Democrats' woes pre-dated the party's 2015 collapse – though this certainly accelerated the process. Despite the crumbling of its longstanding bedrock of support, the Liberal Democrats maintained a healthy presence but were struggling to recover, rebuild credibility and convert others to their cause. The Liberal Democrats in Scotland were victims of a pincer movement between the long-term decline of Nonconformism as the foundation of their support, and the fallout from Scottish independence referendum result and growing nationalist–unionist divide. These both had profound effects on the party's ability to recover the losses that it endured when in coalition at Westminster.

A changing geography by seat types: legacy, incumbency and party battles

Another meaningful way to probe the changing geography of the Liberal Democrat vote is through grouping seat types into four categories. We compare Liberal Democrat performance in: the party's historical 'legacy' seats – the 14 seats won in February 1974 which from 1945 to 1983 represented its best haul in Westminster elections; the 'heartland' seats won in 1992, 13 of which were Celtic fringe constituencies; 'breakthrough' seats, namely those won following the party's abandonment of equidistance in 1997; and finally the 57 seats won in 2010 under Nick Clegg, which enabled the party to enter the coalition (Figure 8.6). Immediately noticeable is how Liberal Democrat support collapsed most in its legacy and heartland seats. The 2015 collapse in the latter was above the national average (–18.5 per cent), but also continued to fall in the two subsequent elections. In 2019, Liberal Democrat support across its legacy seats fell below 20 per cent for the first time. Elsewhere, the Liberal Democrat vote fell by around the national average in the seats won under Clegg, and declined further in 2017 as personal incumbency effects subsided. Over the course of the three elections, mean support across the 57 'Clegg' seats declined by more than 18 percentage points.

Meanwhile, the party experienced a revival in its breakthrough seats. In 2015, the Liberal Democrats lost, on average, more than 19 percentage points in these seats. However, in subsequent elections, the party reversed the trend with increases of two and four percentage points in 2017 and 2019, respectively. All of these breakthrough seats were Conservative–Liberal Democrat battlegrounds,

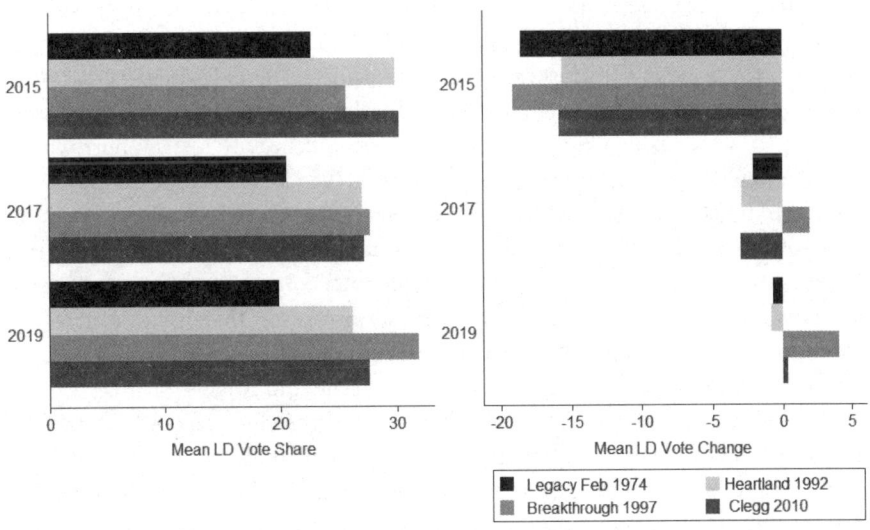

Figure 8.6 Changing geography of the Liberal Democrat vote 2010–2019: legacy, heartland, breakthrough and pre-coalition seats. *Source*: 2010–2019 British Constituency database

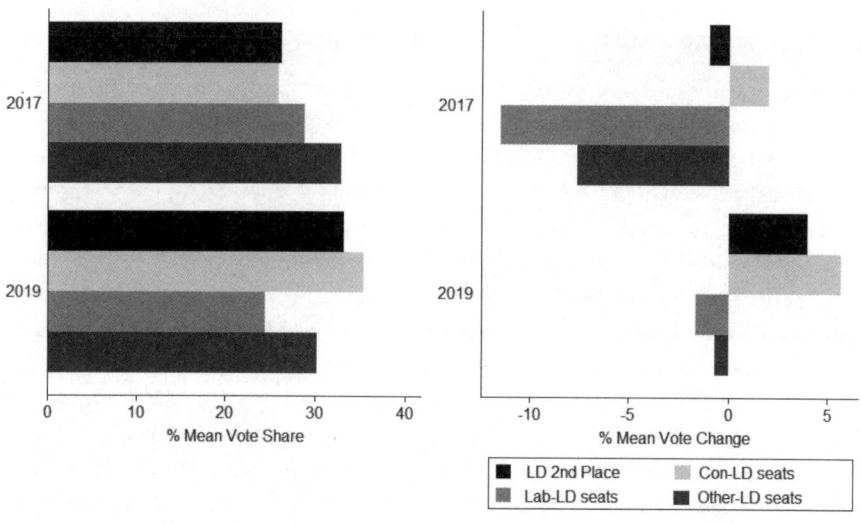

Figure 8.7 Changing geography of the Liberal Democrat vote 2010–2019: seat types and battlegrounds. *Source*: 2010–2019 British Constituency database

where the party had enjoyed success in 1997 under Ashdown explicitly standing on an anti-Conservative platform. Again, though, there is a great deal of unevenness. In seven of these seats – including three in the South West region (St Ives, South East Cornwall and Torbay) the Liberal Democrats actually lost ground in 2019. In nearly half of these seats, though, the Liberal Democrats recorded vote-share increases above the national average. In two breakthrough seats – Harrogate and Knaresborough, and Winchester – the party achieved double-digit increases in support. More generally, though, the Liberal Democrats gained ground after 2015 where they were challenging the Conservatives, and heavily lost support where they were fighting Labour (see Figure 8.7). In 2019, the Liberal Democrats increased their vote by an average of four points across all seats in which they started off in second place. However, in the 29 seats where the party was challenging the Conservatives, the increase was just shy of six points. The Liberal Democrats also saw larger increases in their vote in safer Conservative seats than in more marginal contests ($R = 0.38^*$). This applies to many 'breakthrough' seats and possibly reflects why impressive increases in support did not translate into seats.

Incumbency also drove the party's gains in breakthrough seats. All five Liberal Democrat incumbents standing in these seats saw their 2019 vote increase, although this was not enough to save Tom Brake in Carshalton and Wallington. To circumvent the problems of credibility and the difficulty of translating votes into seats, the party placed a great deal of emphasis on the local and the personal attributes of Liberal Democrat candidates and incumbents. Many in-cumbents built strong personal votes through intensive activism and work in the

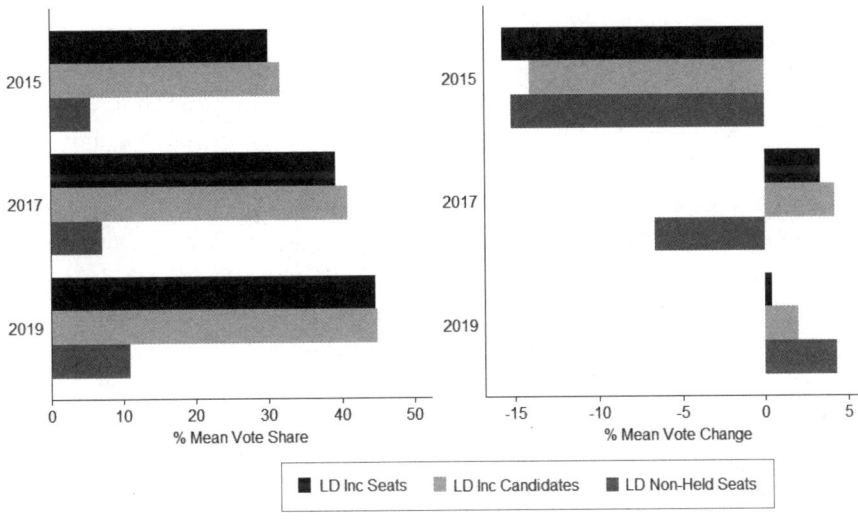

Figure 8.8 Changing geography of the Liberal Democrat vote 2010–2019: incumbency.
Source: 2010–2019 British Constituency database

constituency, which were designed to maximise support in the good times and act as a buffer when the party was experiencing a downturn. Nevertheless, personal incumbency did not save the Liberal Democrats in 2015 (see Figure 8.8). Across the 57 incumbent seats, Liberal Democrat support fell by 15.7 points. In the 33 seats where the Conservatives were the main challengers, the Liberal Democrat vote fell, on average, by 17 percentage points.

In the South West region of England, where the Conservatives ran a highly successful 'decapitation strategy' – in the form of an unprecedented focus of resources and the spending of considerable amounts of money over a sustained period of time – the Liberal Democrat vote declined by more than 18 percentage points. Against Labour, Liberal Democrat incumbents did not perform much better, losing more than 16 percentage points. Where an incumbent Liberal Democrat stood for re-election, their vote share, on average, fell by 14.1 points, compared with 21.7 percentage points in those seats where the sitting Liberal Democrat MP had retired. So, the Liberal Democrats did better in those incumbent seats where sitting MPs were seeking re-election than where they were not.

The 'myth of incumbency' is not entirely borne out when comparing Liberal Democrat performance in the 2015 general election with support in local elections that took place on the same day. This is far from an exact science, and carries some caveats as a number of interrelated factors explain split-ticket voting.[4] Nonetheless, split-ticket voting can provide an indication of personal support for the parliamentary candidate. Only 40 per cent of Liberal Democrat 'party loyalists' reported voting for the party at both local and national levels, compared with 65 per cent in 2010. Ticket-splitting seemed much more prevalent among Liberal Democrats in 2015 than in preceding elections. Of the 29 parliamentary constituencies where there were comparable local elections, the Liberal Democrat incumbents exceeded their local election performance in 16. In six of these constituencies, the difference was greater than 5 per cent, including two seats that the Liberal Democrats held (Leeds North West and Norfolk North) and one (Cambridge) where the party narrowly failed to hold on against Labour. From this limited data, it seems that the personal standing of Liberal Democrat incumbents certainly boosted the party's performance in 2015.

Personal votes also aided Liberal Democrat incumbents in 2017 and 2019. In 2017, despite the party losing five of its nine seats, Liberal Democrat support rose by 3.3 percentage points in the seats won in 2015. Incumbency did not save four Liberal Democrat MPs, but once again those Liberal Democrat incumbents seeking re-election did fare better. Where a Liberal Democrat incumbent stood again, party support increased by 4.2 points, while the national vote fell. And the 10 incumbents who stood in 2019 recorded, on average, nearly 45 per cent of the vote, an increase of two percentage points from 2017. Yet, as the loss of leader Jo Swinson suggests, relying on local personal support is far from fool-proof. While Liberal Democrat incumbents often enjoy a personal vote, the past few elections have shown that this in itself cannot stem 2015-sized electoral tsunamis or sustained opposition targeting as Farron and Swinson experienced in 2017 and 2019, respectively.

Any evidence of a Liberal Democrat recovery as there was after 2015 came at the expense of the Conservatives, rather than Labour or the SNP. However, much of it came in seats where the Conservatives already enjoyed a hefty advantage. This partly stemmed from 2015 when the Conservatives were the primary beneficiaries of the collapse in Liberal Democrat support. Going into the 2019 election, only five of the 29 Conservative–Liberal Democrat contests were genuine marginals. While the Liberal Democrats saw significant increases in support in seats where it was a long way behind the Conservative incumbent, in these closer marginals it was far less efficient failing to win three – Cheadle, Cheltenham and St Ives – of these five seats. So the changing Liberal Democrat geography in 2019 was partly about recovering ground lost to the Conservatives, particularly in the 'breakthrough' seats won in the late 1990s, without overly threatening to win the seats (bar the odd exception).

The changing socio-demographic profile of the Liberal Democrat vote, 2010–2019

Prior to its collapse in support, there was growing evidence that Liberal Democrats' support – while not as concentrated as for the main two parties – had begun to develop a distinctive socio-demographic profile. Historically, the party performed better in seats with more educated, middle-class populations, in constituencies with higher numbers of public sector professionals (particularly in education), and in seats with a strong Nonconformist tradition (Russell and Fieldhouse, 2005). The party also started to gain support in new types of seats, such as those we have termed 'university' seats and constituencies with higher numbers of Muslims, driven by opposition to the Iraq war. While support in constituencies with larger Muslim populations had already started to wane by 2010, the Liberal Democrats' policy on tuition fees meant that they continued to be a natural home for students and performed strongly in a number of university seats. But how did the socio-demographic profile of Liberal Democrat support change after 2010?

Education

Education has traditionally been an important determinant of Liberal Democrat support. In the four general elections from 2010 to 2019, the Liberal Democrats performed better in seats containing larger numbers of degree-holders. The correlation was weaker in 2015 ($R = 0.23^*$ in 2015; 0.25^* in 2010) before recovering somewhat in 2017 and strengthening in 2019 ($R = 0.45^*$). As a result, seats with a large proportion of degree-holders were increasingly a prerequisite for strong Liberal Democrat support. Figure 8.9 adds weight to these findings. The Liberal Democrats lost support in seats with more highly educated populations in 2015 ($R = -0.12^*$ – though significant, the negative correlation is weak), before improving their vote in such constituencies in both 2017 and 2019 ($R = 0.21^*$; 0.38^*).

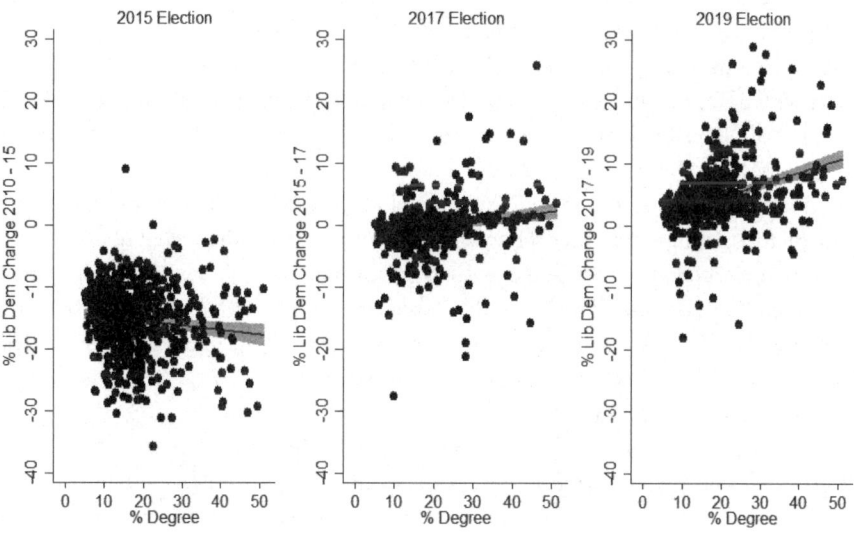

Figure 8.9 Change in Liberal Democrat vote by percentage of the constituency population holding a degree, 2010–2019 general elections. *Source*: 2010–2019 British Constituency database

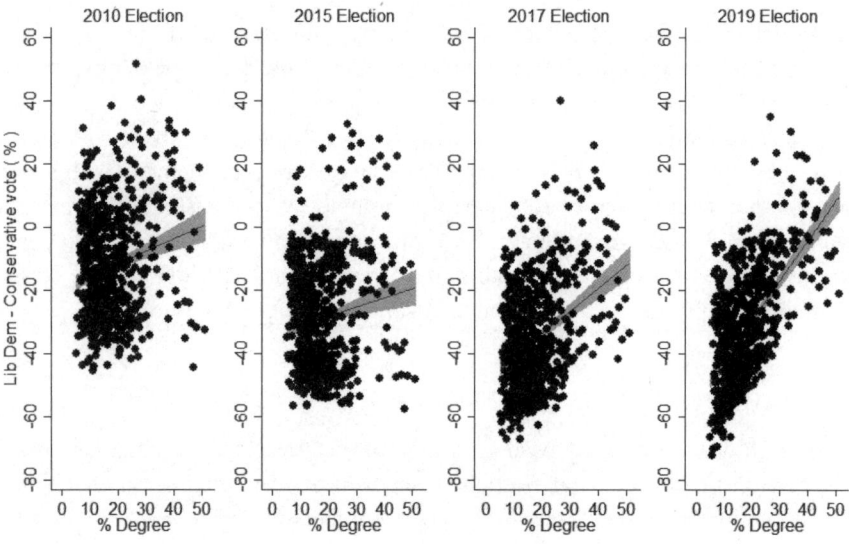

Figure 8.10 The difference between Liberal Democrat and Conservative vote share by percentage of the constituency population holding a degree, 2010–2019 general elections. *Source*: 2010–2019 British Constituency database

Education once again seems to be integral to both Liberal Democrat support and its rehabilitation after the coalition and Brexit.

There is some evidence that any recovery in these seats was at the expense of the Conservatives. Figure 8.10 presents the electoral margin of the Liberal Democrats over the Conservatives for each UK constituency, by the percentage of the population with a degree. Across the four elections, but especially after 2015, the Liberal Democrats enjoyed a greater margin over the Conservatives in seats with more degree-holders. It is noticeable that the line of best fit becomes steeper in 2017 and even more pronounced in 2019. The cone-shaped distribution in 2019 reflects the 'big picture' realignment that took place (the signs were evident even in 2017).

Broadly speaking, the Conservatives performed well in seats with less well educated populations, mainly at the expense of Labour, and by cannibalising previous UKIP support. In many of these seats, the Liberal Democrats struggled to make an impact. While the floor of their vote rose in 2019, the Conservative vote increased, hence the gap remained similar to that in 2017 or grew slightly. In a number of Conservative–Liberal Democrat battlegrounds the party closed the gap on the Conservatives, winning support from both the main parties but without taking the seat. Again, this was more pronounced in seats with a larger proportion of degree-holders. These seats may present the best electoral opportunities for the Liberal Democrats over the long term.

While the Liberal Democrats have started to regain ground in seats with more degree-holders, recovery has been limited in constituencies containing

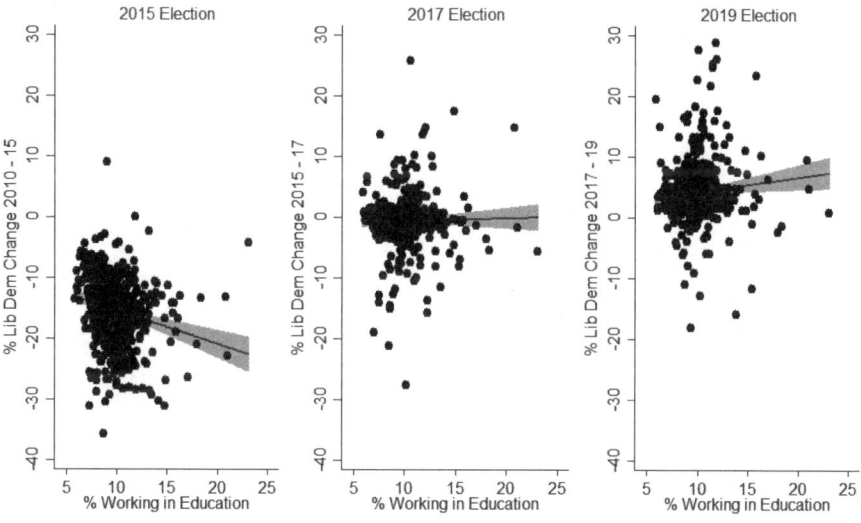

Figure 8.11 Change in Liberal Democrat vote by percentage of the constituency population working in education, 2015–2019 general elections. *Source*: 2015–2019 British Constituency database

larger numbers of people employed in education. Another notable change in the party's geography of support post 2010 has been the decline in university seats – those with large concentrations of full-time students.[5] In 2010, 12 of the 57 seats won by the party were university seats (containing 15 per cent or more full-time students). Five of these also had more than 15 per cent of the population working in education. Indeed, 24 of the 57 Liberal Democrat seats had above-average numbers of people employed in education. Unsurprisingly, both recorded a positive correlation ($R = 0.32^*$ – working in education; $R = 0.14^*$) with 2010 Liberal Democrat support. While the positive correlation between Liberal Democrat vote and the proportion of people employed in education remained in subsequent elections ($R = 0.26^*$ in 2015; 0.26^* in 2017; 0.29^* in 2019), the party lost support in these seats in 2015 (Figure 8.11) before recovering very modestly four years later ($R = 0.10^*$).

Yet there is little evidence of any revival in university seats. Part of the new Liberal Democrat geography of support during the 2000s, these hard-won gains under Kennedy and Clegg unravelled after the Liberal Democrats entered coalition government. In the 2015, 2017 and 2019 general elections there was no discernible relationship between the percentage of full-time students in a seat and Liberal Democrat support. Support collapsed in university seats ($R = -0.19^*$) in 2015 compared with five years earlier, and while it flat-lined in 2017, it dropped again two years later ($R = -0.10^*$). Unsurprisingly, Labour was the main beneficiary. After capturing many of these university seats from the Liberal Democrats in

2015, Labour's grip on them tightened in 2017 and 2019. These previously Liberal Democrat seats now appeared largely beyond the reach of the party.

Analysing the socio-demographic make-up of the
Liberal Democrat vote, 2010-2019

So what socio-demographic factors have driven the changing electoral geography of Liberal Democrat vote since 2010? Here we run three separate linear regression models on Liberal Democrat support in 2010 and 2019 alongside 'change in the vote' models for 2010–2019. The first two models provide a baseline that allows us to determine whether similar or different socio-demographics mattered in 2010, when the party was a potent electoral force, and 2019, when it polled half of what it did three elections previously and won few seats in comparison. The change model provides an insight into what socio-demographic variables buttressed the Liberal Democrat vote between 2010 and 2019. The Liberal Democrats gained support in only 25 seats between 2010 and 2019. As such, the change model will tell us in which types of places the party lost the least ground. We include seven socio-demographic predictor variables, all of which had an impact on Liberal Democrat support prior to 2010 (Cutts, 2006b; Fieldhouse *et al.*, 2006). These include two traditional drivers – the percentage of the local population who were degree-holders and the percentage working in education – and two socio-demographic variables that influenced the changing geography of Liberal Democrat support in the 2000s – the percentage of full-time students and the percentage of Muslim voters.

Traditionally, the Liberal Democrats have also tended to do better in affluent areas, so we use the percentage of the constituency population with two cars or more as a reliable proxy. Lastly, we add a rural–urban measure, where the percentage employed in agriculture and the percentage working in manufacturing are used as respective surrogates. Historically, the Liberal Democrats have secured more support in rural areas. Nevertheless, during the 2000s, the party made some headway against Labour in a number of urban centres. Unfortunately, we could not include Nonconformism due to the lack of UK-wide coverage.

Figure 8.12 shows the average marginal effects (AMEs), which in a linear model can be interpreted as the regression coefficients. The seven socio-demographic variables explained 21 per cent of the variance (R^2 = 0.21) in 2010 support compared with 41 per cent in 2019 (R^2 = 0.41). The socio-demographic make-up of a seat was, therefore, increasingly integral to explaining Liberal Democrat support. In the change model (model 3), 22 per cent of the variance is explained (R^2 = 0.22). In 2010, the Liberal Democrats did better in more educated, affluent, rural seats. Reflecting the impetus among student voters and those employed in education, the party also performed well in university seats. The party did not perform as well in more urban, deprived constituencies. There is no visible effect in seats containing a larger Muslim population, possibly reflecting the short-term saliency of the Iraq war and the personal stance of former leader Charles Kennedy.

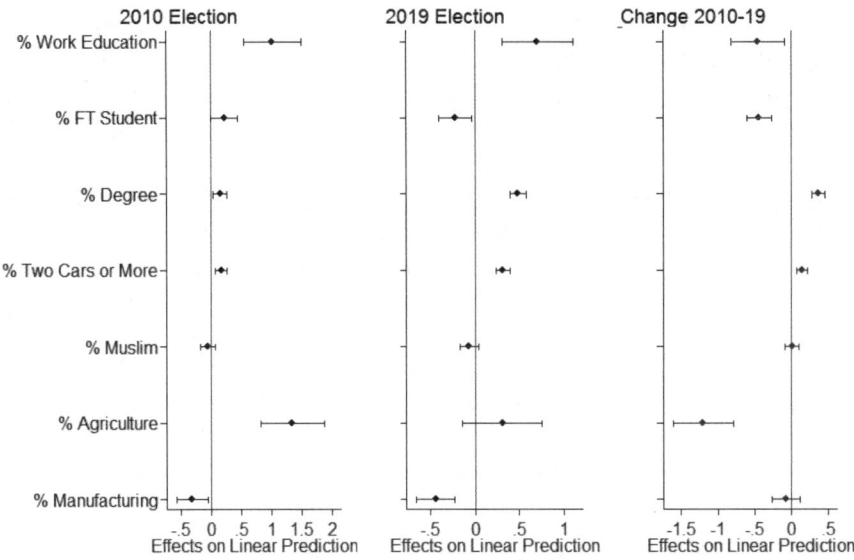

Figure 8.12 Linear regression model of socio-demographic variables on Liberal Democrat support in 2010 and 2019 and change in vote 2010–2019: AMEs. *Source*: 2010–2019 British Constituency database

In 2019, party support was driven by three factors. As expected, the Liberal Democrats did better in seats containing larger numbers of degree-holders. The more affluent the seat, the larger was the Liberal Democrat vote, while the party also performed better in seats with larger numbers working in education. Yet there are differences, with the party losing ground in University seats and urban areas more generally. In 2019, the Liberal Democrats' minor recovery was driven by longstanding demographic factors. Reiterating the reliance on traditional socio-demographic influences, the change model shows that the Liberal Democrat vote held up best in the better-educated, affluent areas and haemorrhaged votes between 2010 and 2019 in rural constituencies, university seats and constituencies with larger numbers of people employed in education. Put simply, there has been an unwind of the geographies of support that newly emerged post 2001. Party survival and subsequent improvement occurred predominantly in the types of seats mirroring the demographics that had historically driven Liberal support.

The changing geography of Liberal Democrat support shaped by political events

Between 2010 and 2019, political discourse in UK politics was shaped by dramatic events. The fallout from the global financial crisis of 2008 led to the era of austerity implemented by the Conservative–Liberal Democrat coalition. Amid the hardship of austerity, two political events had a dramatic effect on wider UK politics and the geography of Liberal Democrat support – the 2014 referendum on Scottish independence and the 2016 referendum on the UK's membership of the EU. In this section, we focus on how the growing unionist–nationalist schism explains the party's struggles in Scotland. We also examine how Brexit simultaneously stalled any post-coalition recovery and reinforced entrenched socio-demographic drivers, thereby offering opportunities in certain favourable areas. Ultimately, though, structure matters, as these opportunities were dependent on being both the most credible option and the likeliest to win in any particular seat.

The fallout from the 2014 Scottish referendum

For the Liberal Democrats, Nonconformism and support for Scottish independence were inextricably linked: the higher the level of Nonconformism in the seat the greater was the support for independence ($R = 0.31^*$). While the influence of Nonconformism on Liberal Democrat support was waning before 2014, it is highly possible that the subsequent union–independence split accelerated the process. By entering into coalition government with the Conservatives, the Liberal Democrats had already paid a high political price in Scotland. In the 2011 devolved election, the party lost more than 8 per cent of its vote and 12 seats. That election marked a critical moment in Scottish politics. For the first time, the SNP secured a landslide victory and won enough seats to run a majority government in Holyrood and secure a mandate to hold an independence referendum. Following an agreement between the devolved Scottish government and the UK government, the referendum took place in September 2014. The 'No' side (voting against independence) won the vote by 55.3 to 44.7 per cent. Despite the result, the deep union–independence fault lines spilled over to the 2015 UK general election nine months later, when with the SNP won 56 of the 59 Scottish parliamentary constituencies.

The transformation in the geography of the Liberal Democrat vote was dramatic. While it is difficult to unpick whether the union–independence divide harmed the Liberal Democrats in 2015, or whether the haemorrhaging of pro-union votes to its rivals and pro-independence votes to the SNP was reflective of its involvement in the coalition, the data suggest that both mattered. Across Scotland, the Liberal Democrat vote fell by more than 11 percentage points. However, the losses were unevenly spread: the Liberal Democrats lacked any real presence in many Scottish seats, so did not have much vote to lose. In seven seats, six of which were pro-union, the Liberal Democrat vote fell by more than 20 percentage points. These included Orkney and Shetland (which the party held), and Berwickshire, Roxburgh and Selkirk (where incumbent Michael Moore was relegated to third place). Many of these seats were constituencies where the Liberal Democrats had challenged Labour throughout the 2000s but after the independence referendum had experienced an SNP surge.

Using the 2015 BES, we can detail the scale of the pincer effect on 2015 Liberal Democrat support. Around 58 per cent of 2010 Liberal Democrat voters voted 'No', while just over 42 per cent voted for independence. Of those 2010 Liberal Democrat voters who voted for independence, only 7.8 per cent supported the party again in 2015. More than 85 per cent stopped supporting the Liberal Democrats and directly went to the SNP. By contrast, the unionist vote split. The Liberal Democrats held on to some, but in many cases it haemorrhaged votes to better-placed unionist parties. Around 30 per cent of 2010 Liberal Democrat voters who voted to remain part of the UK supported the party again in 2015. However, 40 per cent switched to Labour and 11 per cent went to the Conservatives. Even the SNP picked up more than 10 per cent of these voters. As a consequence, the Liberal Democrats were often demoted to fourth place. This mattered in subsequent elections, as pro-union voters in a number of seats coalesced around the most credible challenger to the SNP. Being consigned to 'also ran' status meant that outside of held seats and a few areas of traditional support, the Liberal Democrats had little prospect of recovery. They also suffered in pro-union seats where a 2010 Liberal Democrat incumbent had been defeated in 2015 and decided not to stand again two years later. Again, voters turned to other pro-union parties in order to challenge the SNP.

Figure 8.13 illustrates these trends in 2015, 2017 and 2019. Compared to 2015, the line of best fit becomes much flatter. This is because for the majority of Scottish constituencies, the Liberal Democrat vote had reached its floor. In 2017, given the slight drop in the national vote there was always unlikely to be a significant shift in either direction. However, the graph does suggest that the Liberal Democrats fared better in some seats – Orkney and Shetland, and East Dunbartonshire – through local strength, campaign effort and/or popularity of the candidate. This enabled the party to be the main beneficiaries of the unionist vote. Yet, the line of best fit is dragged down by a Liberal Democrat collapse in specific pro-union seats. These are predominantly where the defeated Liberal Democrat incumbent in 2015 did not stand again, and in one case where the incumbent did stand (Alan Reid in Argyll and Bute). One of the key trends in 2017 was the general shift of the unionist vote to the Conservatives. For instance, in the 11 seats won by the Liberal Democrats in Scotland in 2010, the Liberal Democrat vote went down by seven percentage points between 2015 and 2017, while the Conservative vote increased by more than 15 percentage points. This was two points higher than across all 59 Scottish constituencies, suggesting that the Conservatives were the main beneficiaries of the anti-independence vote and benefited from the absence of well-known and credible Liberal candidates. The drift of 2015 Liberal Democrat pro-union voters to the Conservatives is borne out by individual data. According to the 2017 BEPS, 44 per cent of 2015 Liberal Democrat pro-union voters remained loyal to the party in 2017. Around 38 per cent switched to the Conservatives and 17 per cent to Labour. In 2019, the Liberal Democrats increased their vote by, on average, 2.8 percentage points. Aside from the major setback in East Dunbartonshire, there is evidence of pro-unionist tactical voting benefiting the Liberal Democrats – in Fife North East, for instance. There were also seats in which party support was squeezed still further as pro-unionist supporters chose a more credible option.

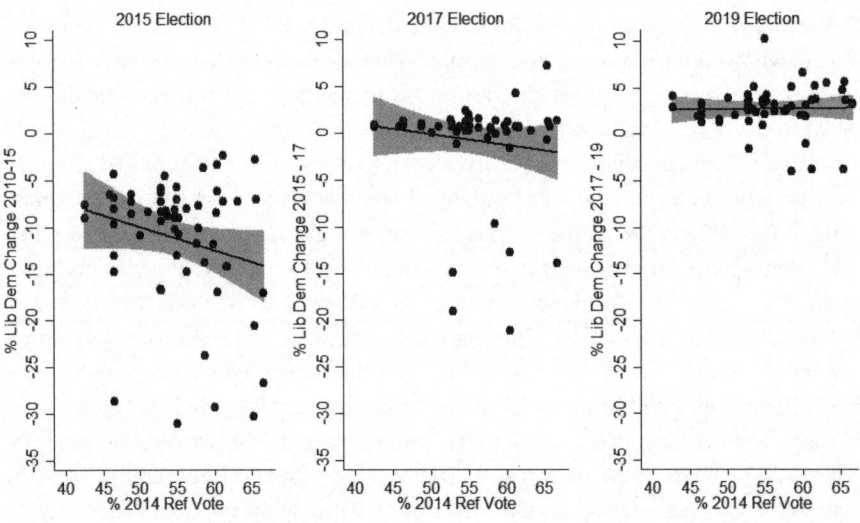

Figure 8.13 Change in Liberal Democrat vote by percentage 2014 Scottish referendum pro-union vote, 2015–2019 general elections. *Source*: 2010–2019 British Constituency database

Scottish politics has undergone a rapid transformation since 2010. The rise of the SNP and the independence referendum realigned politics north of the border. Scotland's overwhelming vote to remain in the EU further deepened the divide between Edinburgh and London. In the 2017 general election, the SNP was unable to persuade pro-union Remain voters to switch allegiances in large numbers and suffered somewhat from a unionist backlash. In 2019, the increasing salience of a second independence referendum in light of Johnson's pledge to 'Get Brexit done' and rising disenchantment with the Conservative government at Westminster led to the SNP strengthening its electoral grip across Scotland.

For the Liberal Democrats, the coalition legacy and the political fallout from the independence referendum hit the party hard in Scotland. It currently faces a major electoral and political dilemma. If the nationalist–unionist divide persists, it faces a battle to oust the SNP in a number of previous strongholds. However, where it is the main challenger, it will be the sole beneficiary of the pro-unionist vote. Where the party lacks longstanding electoral credibility, this looks an insurmountable problem in the short to medium term. Even where it was formerly strong, the loss of popular candidates means that without an effective rebuilding process the party faces the risk of being gazumped by its rival unionist parties. In the short to medium term, pro-union voters will simply view the party as an unviable proposition. There is evidence that this is already happening. The worry for the Liberal Democrats, given the decline of Nonconformism, is that, bar a handful of seats, the party could retreat permanently to the margins of Scottish politics.

Brexit and the Liberal Democrats

In the midst of the post-coalition doom and gloom, the Liberal Democrats were given a somewhat unexpected lifeline. Cameron's decision to hold a referendum on whether to remain in or leave the European Union gave the party an opportunity to divert attention away from the legacy of coalition, raise the new leader's profile and campaign on a distinctly pro-European platform that had historically been central to the party's identity. In theory, Brexit polarisation offered the Liberal Democrats, as a strongly pro-Remain party, an opportunity to court large numbers of the 48 per cent of voters who endorsed Remain and recover some of its 2015 losses. However, this did not happen. In the two preceding chapters we noted how the Liberal Democrats 'misread the room'. Both their 'second referendum' policy in the 2017 general election and their 'revoke' policy in 2019 failed to resonate, which meant they could not exploit Labour splits and general ambiguity on the issue. While the politics of the referendum and policy errors played a vital role, the 2015 result had fundamentally changed the Liberal Democrats' electoral geography and exposed serious credibility issues. We argue that such structural barriers were insurmountable in the short term and prevented the party from capitalising on Brexit. Nevertheless, as the process of realignment continues to play out, the long-term potential, notwithstanding credibility concerns, does offer hope.

Figure 8.14 shows the relationship between Liberal Democrat vote change 2015–2017 and 2017–2019 and the percentage 'Remain' vote for all UK constituencies. In 2017, there was a positive correlation ($R = 0.15^*$) between the change in Liberal Democrat support and the Remain vote, albeit the line is relatively flat. In

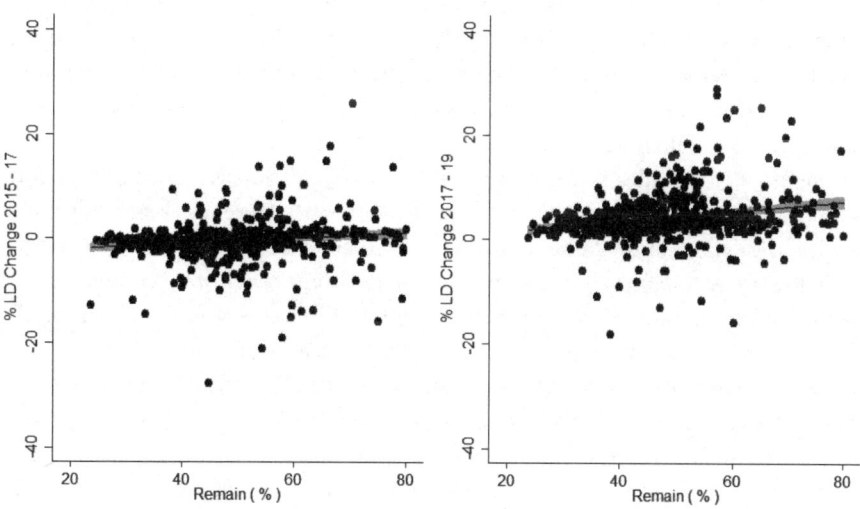

Figure 8.14 Liberal Democrat vote change 2015–2017 and 2017–2019 by percentage Remain vote. *Source*: 2015–2019 British Constituency database

2019, the relationship is slightly stronger ($R = 0.24^*$), as indicated by the somewhat steeper best-fit line. This seems to be driven by a stronger performance in soft Remain seats in 2019.

Over the past three elections, the gap in Liberal Democrat support between Leave and Remain seats has widened, albeit at a slow pace. Using 2015 as a benchmark, the Liberal Democrats lost more support in their incumbent seats, 33 of which voted Remain in the referendum a year later. In 2015, Liberal Democrat support was higher in Remain areas by 2.8 percentage points. Two years later, the gap increased to four points, although this was predominantly down to the party losing further ground in Leave seats. However, the real story was the lack of growth in all Remain seats between 2015 and 2017. What is noticeable is that the Liberal Democrat vote in 'hard' Brexit areas (with a 60 per cent or more Leave vote) was 3.3 points lower than in 'soft' Brexit' seats (where Leave achieved 50–59.9 per cent of the vote). This was not dissimilar to two years earlier. Liberal Democrat support was fractionally higher in 'hard' Remain seats (those with 60 per cent or more) but the difference was minimal and little changed from 2015. The gap widened in 2019: Liberal Democrat support was higher by more than six points in Remain than in Leave seats, and around four points higher than the party's national vote share. Importantly, the Liberal Democrats actually increased their support by more than three points in 'soft' Leave seats versus 'hard' Leave seats.

Overall, party vote share was 4.5 points higher in soft Brexit than in hard Brexit seats. Leaving aside potential ecological fallacy issues, it seems probable that Labour was the beneficiary of some Liberal Democrat switching across Leave seats in 2017, as the Liberal Democrat support hit the floor. However, two years on, while Remain voters did not abandon Labour for the Liberal Democrats in droves, the latter party's ability to lift the floor of its vote in a number of these Leave areas undoubtedly harmed Labour's chances of fending off the Conservatives. The Liberal Democrats improved their vote share, on average, by 5.6 points across Remain constituencies but the growth was nearly one percentage point stronger in soft than in hard Remain seats.

Figure 8.15 provides further insight into how Brexit shaped Liberal Democrat support in 2017 and 2019 against the party's main rivals. Here we classify constituencies in England and Wales according to whether they backed Remain (hollow triangle, where support for Leave was less than 45 per cent); were comparatively evenly balanced (hollow square, where support for Leave was 45–55 per cent); or whether they strongly backed Leave (black circle, where support for Leave was over 55 per cent). Across both elections, Liberal Democrat support haemorrhaged more where their rivals made electoral headway. In 2015, there were a few strong Remain seats where the Liberal Democrats made some vote gains, but these were largely at the expense of the Conservatives. Notwithstanding this, there were some strong Remain seats where the Liberal Democrats did lose some support and Labour gained in excess of a 10-point increase in their vote. In Leave seats, the Liberal Democrats lost support to both of their rivals, although such losses

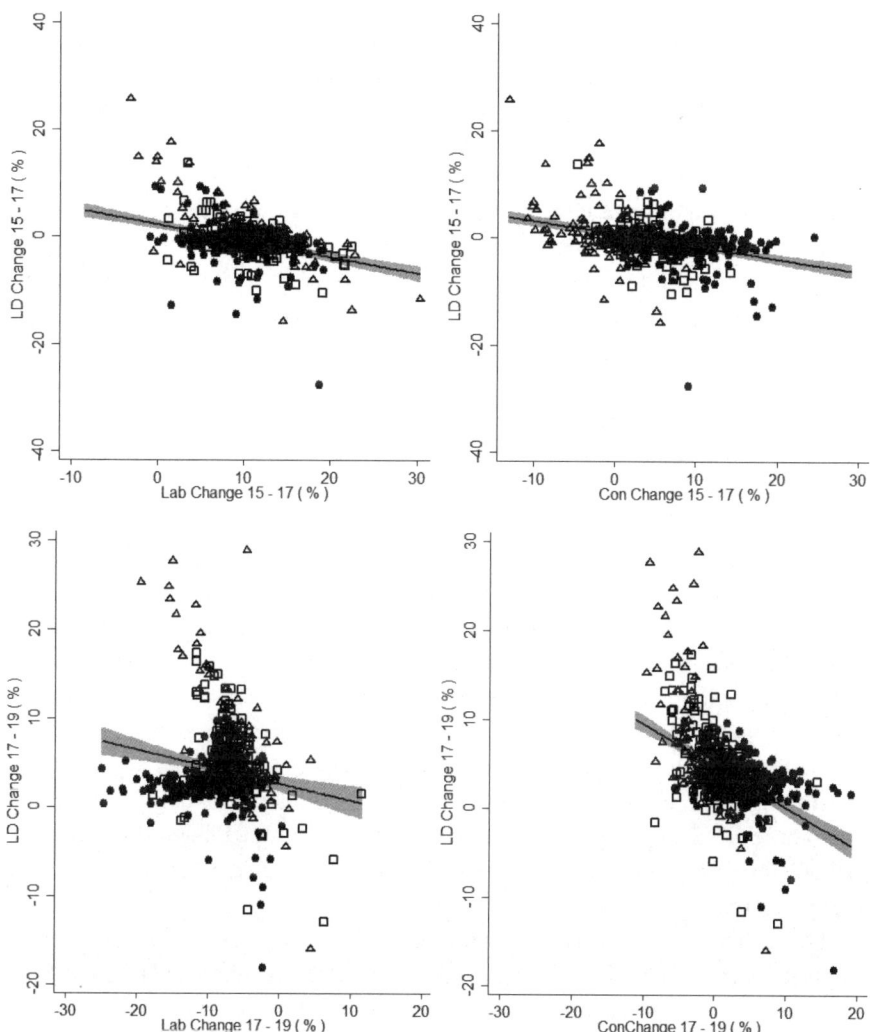

Figure 8.15 Liberal Democrat vote change and rival vote change, 2015–2017 and 2017–2019, by Brexit support in the 2016 referendum (hollow triangle, where support for Leave < 45 per cent; hollow square, support for Leave 45–55 per cent; black circle, support for Leave > 55 per cent). *Source*: 2015–2019 British Constituency database

were relatively modest, because the party was already close to its voting floor. In 2019, the electoral picture changed somewhat. The Liberal Democrats made modest gains in Leave and largely working-class seats from a low base, principally where Labour collapsed. In Remain and largely middle-class constituencies, the Liberal Democrats saw their vote rise substantially – predominantly, but not exclusively, at the expense of Labour. However, there was also a sizeable number of strong Remain seats where the Labour vote held up and the Liberal Democrats were unable to make any significant gains. Against the Conservatives, the Liberal Democrats made modest progress in evenly balanced Brexit areas and in strong Remain seats. This did not translate into seat gains in 2019, but it does reiterate the southern emphasis of Liberal Democrat support wherein Conservative, middle-class, Remain areas have become more vulnerable to the Liberal Democrats.

So, what explains the Liberal Democrats' failure to capitalise on the salience of the European issue? Of course, the party was at a low ebb after its 2015 electoral collapse. The local infrastructure was threadbare after sustained losses during the coalition period. Crucially, local credibility had taken an enormous hit. Being a credible, second-placed challenger is critical for the party to court tactical votes and build a coalition of support. However, the combined effect of the coalition legacy and weakening credibility badly damaged the party. When the geography of Brexit is also considered, it becomes fairly evident why the Liberal Democrats found it so difficult to exploit the Brexit fallout.

Of the 62 seats in 2015 where the Liberal Democrats were second-placed, 27 voted Leave in the 2016 EU referendum, while 23 could be classed as 'soft' Remain and 12 as 'hard' Remain (same criteria as above). Things got decidedly worse for the party in 2017. While the Liberal Democrats polled more than 30 per cent of the vote in 28 constituencies in 2017, the party lost 375 deposits – 40 more than in 2015. Going into the 2019 election, the Liberal Democrats were placed second in 38 seats, of which 14 were Leave seats. The seven Labour seats were hard Remain, pre-dominantly university seats where the tuition fees debacle negated any prospect of winning back substantial support. Meanwhile, both the SNP and Plaid Cymru stood on a pro-European platform, making it harder for the Liberal Democrats to rely solely on anti-Brexit voters in these seats. Evidently, there was a low ceiling on the number of winnable seats.

Post 2015, it is immediately obvious that the Liberal Democrats had fewer opportunities to make electoral ground as the number of winnable marginal seats declined steadily over time. Going into the 2017 general election, there were three seat clusters illustrating the difficulties facing the Liberal Democrats. First, there was a cluster of 13 of the 16 most marginal seats where the Liberal Democrats were less than 10 per cent behind the incumbent, eight of which were strongly Remain and seemingly provided the best opportunities for gains. Eight of these 13 seats were held by the Conservatives and two by Labour. The remaining three seats were held by the pro-EU SNP. A second cluster, of 16 seats, was where the Remain vote was 50 per cent or more and the Liberal Democrats were up to 25 per cent behind the winning party. Again, even a Brexit realignment would have limited Liberal Democrat electoral opportunities – only seven of these 16 seats were Conservative-held; three were Labour and the other six SNP. The final cluster included a mix of extremely marginal and less marginal seats, the majority of which were around or just under the national average Remain vote, although seven were hard Leave areas. These were principally Conservative-held seats and posed an electoral problem for the Liberal Democrats. For the party to win these seats, they needed to cannibalise the Remain vote but still persuade some Leave voters, to support them.

But the party faced the dual problem of an impenetrable Conservative Leave vote, reinforced by ex-UKIP supporters who regarded the Conservatives as the only viable party to deliver Brexit, and a soft Remain vote, a majority of whom accepted the referendum result and were unwilling to leave the Conservative fold (Cutts and Russell, 2018). Moreover, despite the ambiguity of Labour's Brexit position, Corbyn's left-populist appeal to the under-40s, many of whom had voted Remain and who lived in Remain areas, nullified the Liberal Democrats' pro-European message. For many of these voters, the Liberal Democrats' coalition legacy also loomed large. Overall, despite winning some marginal seats back from the Conservatives – Twickenham, Kingston and Surbiton, Bath – and the SNP – East Dunbartonshire and Edinburgh West – the Liberal Democrats faced a pincer movement and fell further back in both Remain and Leave constituencies.

In 2017, across these 50 marginal seats, the Liberal Democrat vote fell by 3.4 percentage points. The decline was larger in soft Remain areas (–5.7 points) and soft Leave seats (–3.1 points). Going into the 2017 election, of the 50 most marginal non-held Liberal Democrat seats, the party was less than 20 per cent behind in 42. Two years later, the Liberal Democrats were 20 per cent or less behind the incumbent in 18 seats. The margin was below 10 per cent in only nine constituencies. Of these 50 marginal seats, 38 were held by the Conservatives. While there was a fairly even split between Leave (24) and Remain (26) seats in 2017, 29 of the 50 marginal non-incumbent Liberal Democrat seats had voted Remain by 2019. Again, we can identify three clusters. Aside from the predominantly soft Remain most marginal seats, the remaining two clusters break down along Remain–Leave lines. Of the 32 seats where the Liberal Democrats were more than 20 per cent behind the incumbent, 25 were held by the Conservatives, and 14 of these were in Leave areas. Fading local credibility was also a factor: 21 of these 32 seats were held by the Liberal Democrats in 2010 and a number of others five years before that. Once defeated, many of these previous Liberal Democrat incumbents did not stand again and hence the personal vote ebbed away. A severely weakened local infrastructure put pay to any activist-led fightback, diminishing still further any Liberal Democrat claims of being a credible alternative to the incumbent. Unsurprisingly, 10 of the 14 Leave seats where the party was more than 20 per cent behind the incumbent prior to the 2019 election had a Liberal Democrat MP in 2010. Similar patterns occur in a number of soft Remain seats, where a weakened local base damaged credibility and made selling a new candidate and courting Remain Conservatives virtually impossible.

Figure 8.16 demonstrates how this loss of local credibility and Brexit combined to shape Liberal Democrat support in 2019 in these 50 most marginal non-incumbent Liberal Democrat contests. Again, we breakdown the Brexit effect according to the degree to which constituencies voted to Remain (see above and figure captions). In the hard Leave seats – a number of which had a Liberal

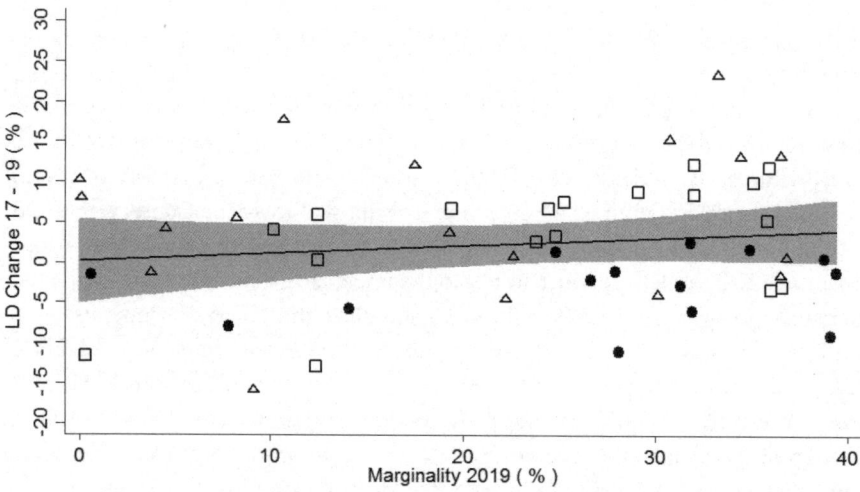

Figure 8.16 Liberal Democrat vote change between 2017 and 2019 and 2019 marginality of seat, by Brexit vote in the 2016 referendum (hollow triangle, where support for Leave < 45 per cent; hollow square, support for Leave 45–55 per cent; black circle, support for Leave > 55 per cent). *Source*: 2017–2019 British Constituency database

Democrat MP in 2010 – Liberal Democrat support dropped in 2019 by an average of 3.1 percentage points despite the party's vote nationwide increasing by more than four points. Irrespective of marginality, the general trend was against the party. The picture is slightly more nuanced, though, in 'soft Leave' seats such as Taunton Deane and Sutton and Cheam, which recorded a steady growth in Liberal Democrat support. Alongside this is the emergence of a new geography of Remain constituencies partly made up of old 'breakthrough' seats – Guilford, Harrogate and Knaresborough, Hazel Grove, and Winchester – and others where the Liberal Democrats were more credible and gaining strength – St Albans, South Cambridgeshire, Witney and Woking. In many of these seats (and others that were not among the top 50 marginal Liberal Democrat contests going into the 2019 election), primarily where the Conservatives were the incumbents, the Liberal Democrats were viable contenders.

The Blue Wall: towards a new electoral geography?

Out of the ruins of the 2019 election emerged a small group of what we term 'southern crescent' seats in the commuter belt around London. These traditionally Conservative strongholds have over time become small but significant hotbeds of Liberal Democrat support. Increasingly, seats contiguous to these have themselves become vulnerable to a Liberal Democrat insurgency as the party used these hotbeds as the catalyst for reshaping the Liberal Democrats' geography of support. Broadly speaking, these commuter-belt seats take in the home counties of Surrey, Hertfordshire, and Buckinghamshire, and even stretch into Oxfordshire and Cambridgeshire. They have been subject to significant socio-demographic change and, in the wake of Brexit, are drifting from the Conservatives and towards Labour and the Liberal Democrats. Consequently, academics, pollsters and media pundits have claimed that this traditional 'Blue Wall' of Conservative seats is under threat.

Unlike the 'Red Wall', coined to describe numerous Labour strongholds in the north of England and the Midlands that fell to the Conservatives in 2019 (Kanagasooriam, 2019), there is no universal definition of the 'Blue Wall', or agreement about which seats do and do not fall into the category. Alongside a couple of key papers (Curtice, 2021; Wager *et al.*, 2021), a number of definitions have emerged.

Pollster and analyst Steve Akehurst uses three criteria to define the 'Blue Wall': seats with a Conservative incumbent since 2010 (at least); where the Conservative majority in 2019 was under 10,000 votes; and where either Labour or the Liberal Democrats did better than the national swing versus the Conservatives in both 2017 and 2019 (Akehurst, 2021). Akehurst identified 41 'Blue Wall' seats that meet these criteria, with 38 of these in England. Polling company YouGov has also specified the 'Blue Wall' according to three criteria: seats in the south of England, which voted Remain and which have more than 25 per cent of the constituency population with a degree (English, 2021). Under YouGov's criteria, there are 53 'Blue Wall' seats. Centre-right think-tank Onward has questioned both definitions and even the existence of a 'Blue Wall'. Part of its criticism, which we would agree with, is that a sizeable number of 'Blue Wall' seats are not actually Conservative strongholds, given that they have been won by either Labour or the Liberal Democrats in recent times. Onward also questions why the existing definitions focus on education at the expense of other socio-demographic factors, such as age, occupation and housing. Applying the same methodology that defined the 'Red Wall' prior to the 2019 general election, Onward concluded that if an equivalent 'Blue Wall' exists, it is situated in the West Midlands and Cheshire and not the London commuter belt (Blagden and Tanner, 2022). Put simply, there is no 'Blue Wall' comparable to the 'Red Wall', but rather a 'Blue Drift' away from the Conservatives in the south of England over recent elections – and, in Cambridgeshire and East Sussex, over three decades or more (Blagden and Tanner, 2022).

Taking on board the various definitions, we classify 'Blue Wall' seats from the perspective of the Liberal Democrats using the following criteria: (1) seats not held by the Liberal Democrats since its formation; (2) seats that voted Remain in the EU referendum; and (3) seats in the top 20 per cent or 80th percentile in the percentage of the population holding a degree and percentage employed in a professional occupation. Electoral credibility is a vital ingredient for Liberal Democrat success, so being the main opposition to the incumbent is a crucial first step. Based on our criteria, there were 33 'Blue Wall' seats where the Liberal Democrats came second in 2019. Of these 33 seats, 26 have not been held by the party since their formation. We consider these to be Liberal Democrat 'Blue Wall' seats.[6]

Of the 91 seats in the 2019 general election where the Liberal Democrats came second, the overwhelming majority were located in the South East or South West regions of England or London. In 61 of these 91, the party was more than 20 percentage points behind the incumbent.[7] Only 14 of these seats were marginal (where the party was less than 10 points behind the winner), of which 10 were ultra-marginal (the party was less than five points behind the incumbent). Twelve of these 14 seats were held by the Conservatives in 2019. Among those seats that were fairly safe (between 10 and 19.99 points behind the incumbent), only Cambridge was held by Labour, while the remaining 14 seats were held by the Conservatives. Here we use the 20 per cent boundary as a cut-off point. It is rare in British general elections for parties to overturn previous electoral majorities of 20 per cent or more but not unprecedented[8] or impossible given increasing voter volatility and the vote-share increases made by the Liberal Democrats in these seats in 2019. Using this classification, there are 29 seats in total, 11 of which are in the 'Blue Wall' (the other 18 therefore termed 'non-Blue Wall' seats).[9] Of these 11 'Blue Wall' seats, only four are either ultra-marginal or marginal. While the 'Blue Wall' has been much discussed, for the Liberal Democrats at least, they are unlikely to yield the number of seats gains required to return the party back to 2010 levels. Indeed, both Cities of London and Westminster, and Finchley and Golders Green had ex-Labour MPs standing for the Liberal Democrats with high-profile names in 2019. Both are traditionally Conservative–Labour battle-grounds wherein the Liberal Democrats could fall back into third place at the next election. The number of electorally viable 'Blue Wall' seats may, in reality, be less than the 11 stated. Nonetheless, there is little doubt that these and other seats with similar changing demographics provide the Liberal Democrats with an opportunity to establish new strongholds of support. However, this is a long-term project. To make electoral headway in the short term, they need to win in places where they have done well before.

The 'non-Blue Wall' seats

The 18 'non-Blue Wall' seats where the Liberal Democrats are most competitive have a history of Liberal Democrat support. All 18 have been held by the Liberal Democrats since the party's formation. Fifteen of them were last won in 2010. Based on our earlier classifications, only Cheltenham can be considered a 'traditional' stronghold. By contrast, 10 of the 18 'non-Blue Wall' seats can be classified as 'breakthrough' seats. If there has been a Liberal Democrat recovery in previously held seats, it is in these types of places where the party first made an advance in 1997. Of the remaining seven 'non-Blue Wall' seats, five were won under the leadership of Kennedy either in 2001 or 2005 while the other two were

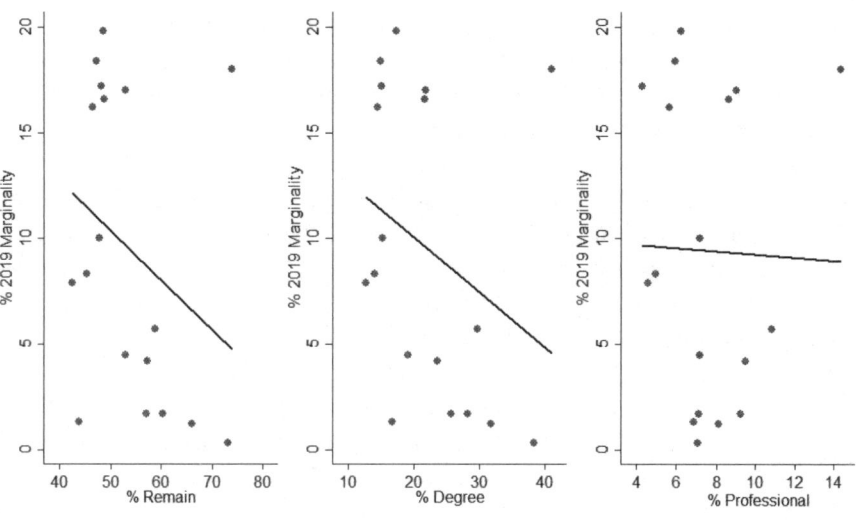

Figure 8.17 Examining 'non-Blue Wall' seats by 'Blue Wall' criteria and 2019 marginality

first captured in 2010.[10] So, in terms of the Liberal Democrat recovery after 2015, it is a bit of a mixed bag. The party has regained support in some of the places where it was previously strong but in other previously Liberal Democrat seats it has remained uncompetitive.

Do these 'non-Blue Wall' seats have populations with similar socio-demographic profiles to 'Blue Wall' seats and also lean towards Remain? Our evidence seems to suggest that while the 'non-Blue Wall' constituencies do not uniformly share the same criteria as 'Blue Wall' seats, some do have similar socio-demographic profiles (see Figure 8.17). While these seats are evenly split between Remain and Leave, of the seven ultra-marginal seats, six voted Remain in the EU referendum, including four – Cambridge, East Dunbartonshire, Sheffield Hallam and Winchester – where local Remain support was in excess of 60 per cent. This is shown by the line of best fit, which is pulled downwards, reflecting larger Remain support in more marginal seats. A similar pattern can be identified with university degrees: seven of the 18 seats are in the top 20 per cent or 80th percentile of populations with a degree and six of these are marginal. The relationship is less clear with professional occupation, with only two seats in the 90th percentile – Cambridge and Guildford – and seven seats ranked in the top 20 per cent or 80th percentile, although these include both marginal and less marginal seats.

Other seats share comparable characteristics. East Dunbartonshire and Sheffield Hallam, for instance, are in the top 10th percentile for owner occupation, university degrees, working in education and those from a professional and mana-gerial class. Seats such as Cheadle share parallel traits but are slightly different, being in the top 10 per cent or 90th percentile for owner occupation, being an area with no deprivation indicators and large numbers of people who are from the professional and managerial class. Winchester has slightly fewer owner occupiers but has more people working in education than Cheadle; otherwise, they are similar in profile. Yet aside from Cambridge and to some extent Hazel Grove, and Harrogate and Knaresborough, which do share some of these characteristics, many of the remaining 'non-Blue Wall' seats have less predictable socio-demographic profiles. This cuts across both fairly safe and marginal seats where the Liberal Democrats are challenging. For instance, two marginal seats which are Leave constituencies – Carshalton and Wallington, and St Ives – do not register any of these socio-demographic indicators in the top 20 per cent or 80th percentile, and the same is true of the traditional Nonconformist seat Brecon and Radnorshire. In these seats, other factors, such as having a Liberal heritage and a high-profile local candidate and previous incumbent running in a recent election, may partly explain the party's performance. While winning back these 'heritage' seats remains viable, the Liberal Democrats' electoral prospects look more favourable in marginal 'Blue Wall' and 'non-Blue Wall' seats that share a socio-demographic profile and where the party has credibility. In reality, this is unlikely to yield a surge in Liberal Democrat representation. Our evidence suggests a moderate rise in the number of Westminster seats is more likely, assuming the party's recovery is sustained against the Conservatives.

Will the new boundaries make a difference?

Proposals for new electoral boundaries England, Wales and Scotland were put forward in November 2022. These recommendations were due to be agreed (or otherwise) on 1 June 2023 (after the time of writing). The proposal was to keep the number of seats in Westminster at 650, with England allocated 543 (up 10), Scotland 57 (down 2), Wales 32 (down 8), and Northern Ireland 18 (unchanged). This is likely to remain the case. Based on these November 2022 revisions, there are three 2019 incumbent seats – Caithness, Sutherland and Easter Ross, Fife North East, and Westmorland and Lonsdale – where current seat projections suggest that the party would not hold a notional 2019 majority. Excluding Fife North East, where the seat remains extremely tight, both Caithness, Sutherland and Easter Ross, and Westmorland and Lonsdale have experienced significant redistricting and as such will require a strong rear-guard action from the party to retain them.

Making estimates of notional majorities from proposals that, at the time of writing, had yet to be finalised carries numerous caveats. Nonetheless, at first glance they reiterate the structural barriers facing the Liberal Democrats and reinforce our reticence about the saliency of the 'Blue Wall' to the party's electoral fortunes in the short term. In certain 'Blue Wall' seats – Esher and Walton, South Cambridgeshire, and Wimbledon and Coombe – the Liberal Democrats remain highly competitive. Moreover, the proposed new Godalming and Ash seat ('Blue Wall') – which includes a sizeable part of the old Surrey South West seat and smaller parts of the previous Guilford, Mole Valley and Surrey Heath constituencies – could also be a viable target. Long-term targets such as the new Hitchin seat and Wokingham, though, remain more challenging, as do perennial Conservative–Liberal Democrat battlegrounds such as Guilford and Winchester. The boundary proposals also harm the Liberal Democrats' prospects in Chippenham and the proposed new Wells and Mendip seat. Meanwhile, in Wales, the enlargement of Brecon and Radnorshire to encompass parts of the old Neath constituency could result in Labour rather than the Liberal Democrats challenging the Conservatives. Establishing a foothold in Ceredigion Preseli also looks difficult, leaving only the proposed new Montgomeryshire and Glyndwr seat as a constituency with recent Liberal heritage, but the inclusion of wards from the old Clwyd South constituency again favours Labour. In Scotland, the proposed new Bearsden and Campsie Fells seat contains nearly 80 per cent of the old East Dunbartonshire constituency but the inclusion of parts of the recently more SNP-friendly Coatbridge, Chryston and Bellshill, and Cumbernauld, Kilsyth and Kirkintilloch East constituencies makes a comeback win at the next election far more difficult for the Liberal Democrats. On the positive side, among the 'non-Blue Wall' seats, Hazel Grove looks to be more favourable to the Liberal Democrats, while the boundary proposals for Carshalton and Wallington, Cheltenham, Eastbourne, Harrogate and Knaresborough, Lewes, and Sutton and Cheam do not excessively harm the party's prospects.

Outside of these seats, there is a cluster of predominantly new 'Blue Wall' leaning Conservative–Liberal Democrat battleground seats in the south-east of England which notionally are hovering just above 20 per cent support for the Liberal Democrats. These are long-term targets but it is conceivable, given socio-demographic change and voters' difficulty in assessing the different parties' likelihoods of winning in a new seat, that the Liberal Democrats could build credibility and momentum in some of these places if discontent with the Conservatives is maintained. The take-home message, though, remains clear. Under the proposed new boundaries, as with the old ones, any short-term recovery will be through winning in places the Liberal Democrats have won before. The door is ajar in these 'Blue Wall' seats, so it is possible that advances could be made, but focusing purely on these places is not going to deliver to the party its 2010 levels of representation, at least not in the short term.

Summary

Since 2010, there has been a seismic shift in the geography of the Liberal Democrat vote. In 2015, the party paid a heavy price for its part in the coalition government, and that continues to shape its geography today. When the dust settled from this electoral fallout, it became clear that the Liberal Democrats no longer had any heartlands. The old Liberal Democrat adage that 'there's no such thing as a safe Liberal Democrat seat' has never been more true. The party retreated to southern England, became a bit-part player in much of the north of England

and the Midlands, was largely left behind in Scotland in favour of more viable unionist alternatives, and was virtually wiped out in Wales. The legacy of coalition changed the socio-demographic make-up of the Liberal Democrat vote, though it still remained strongest in professional, middle-class, graduate areas. The catastrophic breakdown in the party's representation in local government during the coalition undermined the local electoral credibility that had been so vital to the party's success for decades. Subsequent political shocks accelerated the process. In Scotland, the Liberal Democrats remain on the fringe of the union–independence debate and were deemed competitive in only a handful of seats. They also failed to capitalise on the fallout from Brexit. Nonetheless, there are causes for optimism. A group of 'southern crescent' seats could act as the catalyst for reshaping the Liberal Democrats' geography of support. If discontent with the Conservatives deepens, Liberal Democrat prospects in the 'Blue Wall' will improve, although structural barriers and exposure to any political shocks or volatile shifts in support place a ceiling on the likely scale of any advances. Any longstanding rebuild therefore requires the party to unite emerging and prior geographies.

Liberal Democrat campaigning at a crossroads: the big picture

It would be easy to dismiss the inability of the Liberal Democrat campaign machine to stem the Conservative electoral tide in 2015 as a one-off event. A combination of self-inflicted wounds, internal campaign malfunctions and a drop-off in activism across the electoral cycle blunted the effect of the Liberal Democrat campaign machine in the face of a Conservative onslaught. Yet for all the destruction of the local infrastructure and limitations of the ground campaign, what was left of that infrastructure and the campaign such as it was undoubtedly saved the party from total annihilation. Of far greater importance is whether the 2015 collapse was symptomatic of longer-term trends, reinforced latterly by the party's relative electoral standstill in 2017 and 2019. Such concerns strike at the heart of the Liberal Democrats' community-based ethos of personalised place-based activism. Had the Liberal Democrats simply stopped doing what worked? Or, in light of a well-resourced opposition national campaign with messaging targeted at competitive seats, had the Liberal Democrat 'personal contact' mode of electioneering actually become less effective? In the first part of the chapter we address these big-picture questions using survey and experimental evidence from elections throughout the 2010s.

The rest of the chapter examines two underlying questions. First, with developments in the digital field after 2010 – evident in the Conservatives' targeted efforts through Facebook and Labour's growing organic reach across multiple social media platforms – had the Liberal Democrats been left behind? We also assess whether the Liberal Democrats had simply been the victims of embedded online political inequities that reinforce the imbalances in offline resources. Here we use interviews with key figures in the party's digital campaigning team during the 2019 general election campaign. This provides a unique insight into the party's digital campaigning strategy and puts into perspective the extent to which the digital sphere can level out underlying campaign imbalances. Second, using the Liberal Democrats' 2019 campaign strategy and tactics as a yardstick, we critically evaluate whether the party's campaigning was still at a crossroads or whether it was showing signs of winning back their comparative advantage.

Personal campaign contact: underused, outfought or ineffective?

Traditionally, the Liberal Democrats have relied heavily on the power of personal, door-to-door campaigning, locally delivered leaflets and a ground-driven polling-day operation to mobilise or turn out voters. In the ground game, this has given the Liberal Democrats a considerable advantage. However, as shown in Chapter 5, the Conservatives enacted an offensive strategy against Liberal Democrat incumbents in 2015 that challenged their superiority. Intensive Conservative activism was combined with messaging that stressed the importance of choosing a national government, not just a local MP, directly challenging Liberal Democrat incumbents' personal appeal. The resources used in this 'decapitation strategy' of Liberal Democrat incumbents in its south-west heartlands were unprecedented. This remained embedded in Conservative electoral strategy after 2015, when fighting Labour, and in predominantly defensive situations holding off the Liberal Democrats. Leaving aside the Conservatives' resource advantage and how other parties have adopted similar strategies, these developments in campaign tactics and strategy raise fundamental questions about the ability of the Liberal Democrats to fight off this electoral threat. Were the Liberal Democrats being outgunned on the 'ground' in battleground seats (the 2015 experience), or were the party becoming less reliant on face-face activism and traditional, personal contact methods? Or is it simply the case that these methods were now becoming less effective?

To address these questions, we use post-2010 data from the survey of constituency electoral agents to compile indexes in order to measure different aspects of the campaign (Fisher and Denver, 2008). As our focus is on traditional campaign methods and personal contact, we use the well-established Traditionalism index and the newer Face to Face index.[1] The key difference between the two is that the Face to Face index includes campaign activism during the pre-election period – street stalls, resident surveys and doorstep canvassing – in addition to indicators of campaign effort during the campaign period itself, whereas the Traditionalism index focuses on the campaign period and is a well-rounded measure, incorporating leafleting, canvassing and aspects of the polling-day operation. Given that mobilisation is an integral part of the ground campaign, we also use an index to capture the polling-day activities; this Polling Day index includes a number of indicators that are not included in the other two.[2] Scores on all three indexes are calculated as the (standardised) scores for each constituency on the basis of a factor analysis. For ease of presentation, the scores have been adjusted to give a mean of 100 and a standard deviation of 33.3. For example, campaigns with scores greater than 100 have higher Face to Face and Traditional contact while scores lower than 100 indicate lower than average Face to Face contact and use of Traditional campaign methods.[3] Together, these indexes provide a unique insight into the extent of personalised contact and use of traditional methods in the constituency ground campaign over the four general elections considered in this volume (2010, 2015, 2017, 2019).

Table 9.1 Traditionalism, Face to Face and Polling Day activism mean scores by party, 2010–2019 general elections

	2010	2015	2017	2019
Traditionalism				
Conservative	117	111	111	103
Labour	95	102	114	110
Liberal Democrat	93	88	84	87
Face to Face				
Conservative	118	113	111	103
Labour	99	118	117	115
Liberal Democrat	87	85	83	83
Polling Day				
Conservative	113	114	109	103
Labour	97	112	114	112
Liberal Democrat	94	88	84	85

Table 9.1 shows the Traditional, Face to Face and Polling Day mean scores for the three main parties across the four general elections. The scores illustrate the 'big picture' trajectory. Since 2010, the Conservatives have become less reliant on traditional and face-to-face methods. Polling-day activity has also dropped off since 2015. Meanwhile, despite a small decline in 2019, Labour's use of traditional methods, face-to-face contact and polling-day activism was on average higher in 2019 than in 2010. By comparison, the Liberal Democrats' mean campaign scores are lower than those of Labour and the Conservatives due to their comparatively limited resources. However, these figures are still useful in determining the general trend. On every metric, the Liberal Democrats saw a decline after 2010. There are signs of a slight pick-up in the use of traditional contact methods in 2019 but the mean score is still lower than in the 2010 and 2015 general elections.

The growing professionalisation of campaigning has led parties of all colours to target resources in those seats where they can make the greatest impact. Depending on the electoral context, these are usually marginal seats either to defend or capture from their opponents. Increasingly, however, seats that look less vulnerable on paper can be exposed to significant shifts in political opinion. This is driven by political shocks and growing electoral volatility, combined with steady changes in seat demographics. The upshot is significant changes in the geography of intensive party campaigning as parties seek to exploit these events. Since 2010, the Liberal Democrats have largely been on the wrong side of these shocks: losing support in Scotland following the referendum to leave the UK; and after being in coalition government with the Conservatives. The post-Brexit fallout also contributed to the changing geography of the Liberal Democrat vote. The electoral context is therefore extremely salient when reviewing the Liberal Democrats' campaigning prowess over the four elections. In 2010, it was on the

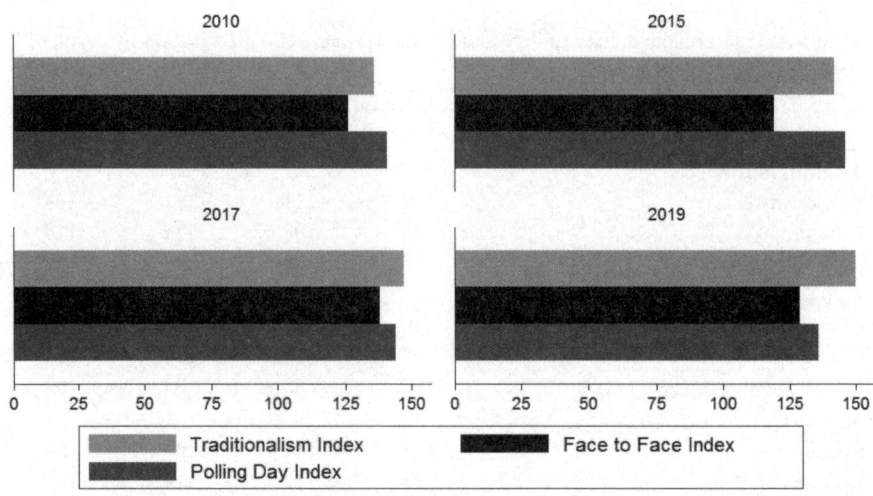

Figure 9.1 Liberal Democrat target seats 2010–2019: Traditionalism index, Face to Face index and Polling Day index mean scores. *Source*: 2010–2019 Survey of Electoral Agents

offensive, while five years later it was desperately defending the 57 seats it held. In 2017 and 2019 it was back on the offensive – but only because it was starting with so few seats. In both elections, the party poured resources into incumbent seats as well as those it felt it could win from its opponents.

Figure 9.1 shows the mean scores for the three indexes in those seats targeted by the Liberal Democrats. Interestingly, when we look at target seats only, Traditionalism scores grew between 2010 and 2019. Unsurprisingly given the emphasis on personalised methods during Farron's tenure as leader, the Face to Face score in target seats was highest in 2017 and was still slightly higher in the 2019 general election than in 2010. Polling Day activism was more prominent in 2015 and 2017 in Liberal Democrat target seats than in the 2010 general election – with a slight drop-off in 2019 largely due to a decline in the number of campaign workers and a subsequent drop in the proportion of the Liberal Democrat target seats covered by polling-day activism to get out the vote. Despite this, our evidence suggests that Liberal Democrat ground campaigns in target seats still strongly embraced traditional techniques and personalised methods and, if anything, intensity increased after 2010.

We can delve a little deeper into the personalised tools that form these indexes. Doorstep canvassing – the flagship of personalised campaign methods – in Liberal Democrat target seats grew in intensity. Two trends stand out. First, fewer target seats had less than 10 per cent of the electorate canvassed by the Liberal Democrats in the three more recent elections than in 2010, which suggests that doorstep canvassing remains integral to the Liberal Democrat ground campaign. Second, the proportion of target seats where the party canvassed 40 per cent or more of the electorate grew in every election from 2010 onwards. In 2019, in more than one-fifth of Liberal Democrat target seats 40 per cent or more of the electors were contacted through this highly personalised mode.

The evidence is more mixed for leafleting – especially in the pre-election period. For instance, more than four-fifths of Liberal Democrat target seats in 2010 engaged in a 'substantial' or 'very substantial' amount of leafleting. In 2019, this dropped to just over half. The use of resident surveys has also declined considerably. These surveys are not only ostensibly personal in nature, but historically have helped local Liberal Democrats pick up local casework and gather data which can then be used for targeting purposes. In 2010, in nearly two-thirds of Liberal Democrat target seats a substantial amount of effort was put into running resident surveys during the pre-election period. This figure dropped to just a quarter of target seats in 2019. Yet during the campaign itself, there is no evidence that leafleting in target seats diminished over the four elections. It remained integral to a highly targeted and intensive Liberal Democrat ground campaign. The only major change was the growing dominance of nationally produced as opposed to locally produced leaflets. In 2010, nearly three-quarters of target seats locally produced 100,000 or more leaflets. This had dropped to two-fifths by 2019. By comparison, in 2010, only 16 per cent of Liberal Democrat target seats distributed in excess of 100,000 nationally produced leaflets. This figure increased to 36 per cent in 2019, reflecting the increasing role of the national party in local 'ground' campaigns during election time. On the whole, despite the political shocks and setbacks, our evidence suggests that over these four general elections, traditional modes and personalised contact remained embedded and pivotal to the Liberal Democrat ground campaign in the party's key target seats. Given this, why did the Liberal Democrats' campaign machine struggle so badly to hold off opponents and win back seats? Rather than focusing solely on the Liberal Democrats' campaign activism, one possible explanation (as alluded to in Chapter 5) is that opponents had upped their game. Put simply, the Liberal Democrats were outfought in the seats that matter most.

Despite the changing political and electoral context, the key battles for the Liberal Democrats over the four elections were chiefly against the Conservatives. As such, it is worth comparing the use of traditional methods and personalised contact in these key seats between those two parties. Table 9.2 shows the results. It is worth pointing out that these are Liberal Democrat target seats where the Conservatives either hold the seat or are the main challengers. The seats vary by election in accordance to changes in the Liberal Democrats' targeting strategy. Some seats are included in all four elections while others are not.

Our results counter assumptions that the intensity and personalised nature of the Liberal Democrat ground campaign trumped that of its opponents. In 2010, the Liberal Democrats enjoyed a comparative campaign advantage on two of the three indexes. However, even in 2010 the Conservatives used more face-to-face forms of contact in the battleground seats with the Liberal Democrats. Indeed,

Table 9.2 Traditionalism, Face to Face and Polling Day activism mean scores in Conservative–Liberal Democrat battlegrounds, 2010–2019 general elections

	2010	2015	2017	2019
Traditionalism				
Liberal Democrat	148	145	133	154
Conservatives	133	151	163	139
Face to Face				
Liberal Democrat	130	118	129	136
Conservatives	139	132	151	137
Polling Day				
Liberal Democrat	151	144	133	140
Conservatives	132	134	143	144

Source: 2010–2019 Survey of Electoral Agents.

this is the case across all four elections (albeit in 2019 the mean scores are similar). Moreover, in 2015, it was the Conservatives who ran more intensive ground campaigns in these battleground seats using traditional forms of voter contact (see Chapter 5). This trend continued in 2017, when the Conservatives had a campaign advantage on all three indexes. There is also evidence that Conservatives ran more intensive local polling-day operations after 2015 in these most competitive Conservative–Liberal Democrat seats. Nonetheless, the data do suggest a spike in the use of personalised methods and traditional contact modes by the Liberal Democrats in these target seats after 2017, with mean scores higher in 2019 than in 2010, 2015 and 2017.

We can demonstrate further evidence of a pick-up in Liberal Democrat activism in 2019 by focusing on two tight Conservative–Liberal Democrat battleground seats in that and the preceding general elections (Table 9.3). For confidentiality reasons, we cannot disclose the two seats but both were previously held by the Liberal Democrats and were subsequently won by the Conservatives. The story mirrors the general trends across Conservative–Liberal Democrat battle-grounds. In 2017, the Liberal Democrats were simply outfought on every campaign measure in both constituencies. There were clear signs of a turnaround two years later. In Constituency A, the Conservatives' use of traditional techniques such as local leafleting and doorstep canvassing dropped off, while Liberal Democrats' use of personal forms of contact during the ground campaign increased. The relatively close scores for the polling-day operations does, though, suggest that the Conservatives were far more focused on mobilising their vote rather than seeking to contact and persuade voters during the campaign period. A similar pattern is visible in Constituency B. Indeed, in 2019, there is evidence that the Conservatives relied heavily on traditional forms of campaigning, even outgunning the Liberal Democrats in this regard. Nonetheless, overall, the Liberal Democrats ran a far more intensive campaign in the constituency than the Conservatives.

Table 9.3 Traditionalism, Face to Face, Campaign intensity and Polling Day activism mean scores in two Conservative–Liberal Democrat battlegrounds (Constituency A and B), 2017–2019 general elections

Constituency A	2017	2019	Constituency B	2017	2019
Traditionalism			**Traditionalism**		
Liberal Democrat	145	195	Liberal Democrat	192	189
Conservatives	157	125	Conservatives	250	199
Face to Face			**Face to Face**		
Liberal Democrat	151	187	Liberal Democrat	156	167
Conservatives	173	147	Conservatives	202	142
Polling Day			**Polling Day**		
Liberal Democrat	129	162	Liberal Democrat	163	193
Conservatives	133	157	Conservatives	235	176
Campaign intensity			**Campaign intensity**		
Liberal Democrat	161	182	Liberal Democrat	162	179
Conservatives	168	156	Conservatives	202	154

In both constituencies, the Liberal Democrats failed to win back the seat, although it came close in Constituency B, where it increased its vote by more than 10 percentage points. By contrast, in Constituency A, despite the intensive use of personal contact methods and outgunning the Conservatives on virtually every campaign index metric, both parties saw their vote share increase by a small margin, leaving the outcome virtually unchanged from 2017. Overall, it seems that Liberal Democrat ground campaign in Constituency A was largely ineffective. The party suffered an electoral horror show in 2015 and was unable to breakthrough offensively in 2017 and 2019. One possibility, therefore, despite evidence of a pick-up in face-to-face personalised campaigning in 2019, is that these traditional methods are not the electoral weapons they once were.

In Chapter 5, we questioned the validity of this argument. Leaving aside our evidence that the party had lost its campaign advantage, local Liberal Democrat activism through mobilisation efforts in the 2015 general election undoubtedly saved the party from total annihilation. Mobilising identifiers and possible supporters are where these traditional tools in the ground campaign come into their own and, as such, they make the difference for the Liberal Democrats in tight contests. Yet, so far, our evidence of their continued effectiveness is based on survey data. To address this weakness, we apply evidence from a field study experiment which for the first time addresses the influence and effectiveness of Liberal Democrat traditional campaign methods.

Are Liberal Democrat traditional 'get out the vote' methods still effective?

In this section we explore the impact of traditional and personal Liberal Democrat campaign modes using an experimental study conducted with the party during the

English local elections in 2017. We examine whether Liberal Democrat traditional ground campaign methods impacted mobilisation by assessing the effect of party leaflets versus the additive impact of canvass visits, and whether the effects differ between higher-propensity and lower-propensity voters. Most field experiments that test the impact of different campaign methods have been conducted outside Britain. Those that have explored the effect of British political parties' campaigning activities typically focus on the Conservatives and Labour. To our knowledge, this represents the only experiment to date testing the impact of Liberal Democrat personalised campaigning.

Field experiments allow researchers to tease out causal effects of campaigning on individuals' behaviour. Participants are randomly assigned to either a treatment group (the one that is exposed to campaigning in some form) or a control group (which is not exposed to any campaigning). By randomly assigning to groups, each individual then has an equal chance of being exposed to treatment thereby ensuring that those who are exposed to the stimulus/treatment share broadly similar characteristics with those who are not exposed. As such, these other factors that may be increasing turnout for certain individuals are 'controlled for'. While 'treatment' in surveys could be skewed towards people who are likely to vote anyway, in field experiments there is no such selection bias. Field experiments also have the advantage of allowing the researcher to control, or at least know, when exactly subjects are exposed to treatment. This allows their effects to be more accurately measured. Altogether, field experiments' main advantage over observational approaches is their ability to convincingly identify causation through randomised treatment of subjects (Gerber and Green, 2000; 2012).

Research design

Are personalised methods still effective for the Liberal Democrats, a party in 2017 at its lowest electoral ebb, with its longstanding campaign advantage diminished, yet reliant on *Focus* leaflets and doorstep canvass visits to attract and crucially mobilise voters? To address this question, we conducted a randomised field experiment with the Liberal Democrats at the English local elections in 2017.[4] The experimental population comprised registered postal voters and non-postal voters in a county council ward in England. As the household was the unit of randomisation and contact, voters in the ward were first clustered into their households. In order to compare the effect of the 'treatment' between postal voters and non-postal voters, the former needed to be separated from the latter. As postal voters do not all live in the same household as other postal voters, it was first necessary to separate households on whether or not they contained postal voters. Households containing at least one postal voter (i.e. households comprised entirely of postal voters or a mix of postal voters and non-postal voters) were placed into the 'postal voter' component of the experiment. Most participants (76 per cent) in this half of the experiment were postal voters. These 'postal voter households' were then

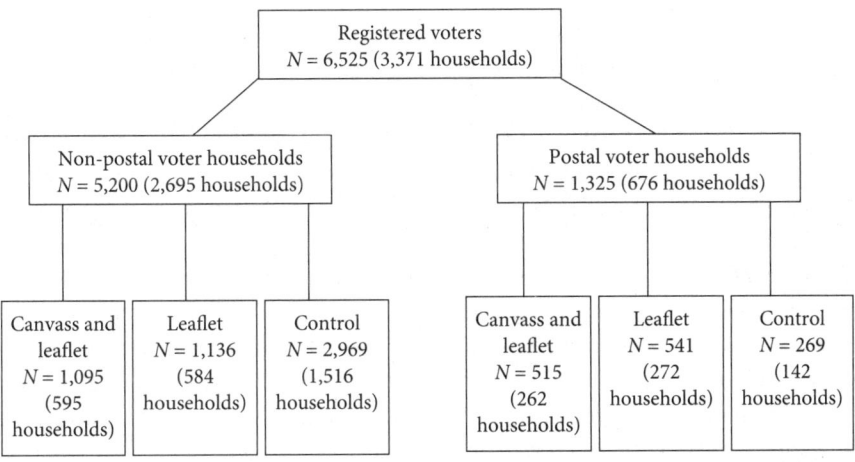

Figure 9.2 Research design for 2017 Liberal Democrat campaign experiment

randomly assigned to either a control group or one of two treatment groups. Meanwhile, the remaining households (those containing only non-postal voters) were placed into the 'non-postal voter household' component of the experiment, and randomly assigned to separate control or treatment groups.[5] This design ensured that no individuals lived in a household with an individual assigned to another treatment or control group – postal voter or non-postal voter. Likewise, no households contained individual(s) in the postal voter experiment and individual(s) in the non-postal voter experiment.

The result was six randomly assigned groups: a control and two treatment groups in the postal voter household experiment, and a control and two treatment groups for the 'non-postal voter household' experiment. This process is summarised in Figure 9.2.[6] The experimental design estimates effects at the household level. It cannot test the turnout effect of direct exposure to the treatments. Rather, any effects could also be due to downstream effects within the household (Cutts and Fieldhouse, 2009; Fieldhouse and Cutts, 2018; Nickerson, 2008) caused by an individual being taken to the polls by their partner (known as 'voting together') after speaking to a canvasser or activist. Moreover, while all non-postal voter households contain entirely non-postal voters, some of the postal voter households contain non-postal voters (24 per cent of subjects in the postal voter household experiment were not registered postal voters). Given this, the comparison between the two can reveal only how voters in households containing postal voters react to a 'treatment' compared with non-postal voters. To reiterate, while there are leaflet-only and leaflet + canvass treatment groups, the design does not include a canvass-only treatment group. The limitation of this decision is that the experiment cannot test for potential synergy effects, for example whether the effect of the canvass + leaflet combination is or is not larger than the combined effects of the leaflet-only and canvass-only effects.

The timing of the treatments was also an issue, given that postal voters receive their ballots in the post around two weeks before non-postal voters cast their ballots on election day. If the treatments were carried out during the period leading up to the in-person polling day, it is likely that some, if not many, postal voters would have already voted. The decision was made to contact all voters in the two-week period prior to their being able to cast their respective ballots. This meant contacting postal voters during the two-week period prior to their ballots being sent out, and contacting non-postal voters during the two-week period prior to polling stations opening on election day. All treatments were partisan in nature and carried out by the researcher or a volunteer. Treatments were as authentic as possible (i.e. as close to what the local campaign would do anyway). The first treatment was a Liberal Democrat party leaflet. It was printed in full colour A3 and contained the legally required party imprint, as well as Liberal Democrat party branding. The leaflet was locally produced and delivered in person. It contained numerous local policy issues and manifesto commitments covering issues that were under the remit of the council for which the election was being held, including libraries, transport, and schools. The aim was to test the impact of typical, standalone leaflets that contain more information on the upcoming election. Party literature usually contains information about local issues and the candidate. Published evidence suggests that voters respond positively to photographs and personal attributes of the candidates (Mattes and Milazzo, 2014). As such, the leaflet emphasised the local and the personal, and included photographs of and information about the candidate and attention-grabbing information about salient issues at the election. One treatment group was assigned to receive a Liberal Democrat leaflet, while the other group received the same leaflet at the same time, followed by a canvass visit from a volunteer. In all cases, the canvass visit preceded the leaflet delivery by fewer than three days. The control group was not directly exposed to any Liberal Democrat campaign treatment. Canvass scripts were partisan in nature to replicate personal visits carried out by campaigns at local elections. Canvassers were instructed to deliver the script, but not to stick rigidly to it, and to be as friendly as they liked. In sum, a random sample of households received either a) a leaflet, or b) a leaflet followed by a doorstep visit from a party activist. As this second treatment group received the same party leaflet, in essence, the study was designed to examine what, if any, additional effect a canvass visit has on turnout on top of a party leaflet.

To compare the effects among postal voter households and non-postal voter households, both received the same treatments. This presented difficulties in terms of timing, as postal voters are sent their ballots a few weeks prior to election day in order to allow enough time to vote. Meanwhile, non-postal voters vote on election day itself. To take this into account, the same treatments were applied to both,

Table 9.4 Sample sizes and contact rates by treatment group in the 2017 Liberal Democrat campaign experiment

	Registered voters	Leaflet contact rate	Canvass contacts achieved	Canvass contact rate
Postal voter households				
Canvas + leaflet	515	100%	143	28%
Letter only	541	100%	–	–
Control	269	–	–	–
Non-postal voter households				
Canvass + leaflet	1,095	100%	302	28%
Leaflet only	1,136	100%	–	–
Control	2,969	–	–	–
N	6,525			

but at different times. Postal voter households were treated within the two-week period prior to their postal votes being sent out by the local authority (on 17 April, 2017). Leaflets were delivered between 4 and 14 April 2017, while those assigned to the canvass group were canvassed between 10 and 16 April 2017. All contacts were therefore made just before postal voters received their ballots. Non-postal voter households began receiving their treatments a week later, all within the two-week period leading up to polling day. It is possible that the differential timing of the treatment could mean that turnout-inducing events might affect one type of household and not the other, thereby confounding the treatment method and time. However, given that both the postal voter and the non-postal voter components of the experiment had their own control groups, the experiment was designed to measure the difference in turnout between the treatment groups and their respective control groups, to allow effect comparisons. For robustness, when producing the estimates for the treatment effects, we include a dummy variable that distinguishes between the postal voter and non-postal voter experiments to account for the confounding factor resulting from the differential timings of the treatments. The final sample sizes and contact rates are shown in Table 9.4. All leaflets in the postal voter household experiment, and the non-postal voter experiment were successfully delivered; that is, the leaflet contact rate was 100 per cent. In total, 534 postal voter households, and 1,179 non-postal voter households, received a leaflet. However, like most experiments involving canvass visits, one-sided noncompliance was an issue among those living in households assigned to receive a canvass visit in addition to the leaflet. Among this group, compliance is defined as the voter living in a household in which at least one person opened the door and interacted with the canvasser. In total, 262 postal voter households (containing 515 registered voters) and 595 non-postal voter households (containing

1,095 registered voters) were assigned to receive a canvass visit in addition to a leaflet. The successful canvass contact rate was 28 per cent. This is towards the lower end of the range found in other European canvassing experiments, although not dissimilar to Bhatti *et al.* (2016) who had a contact rate of 22 per cent in their Labour Market Union.

Experiment findings

Turnout data at the 2017 local election were obtained from the local council's official records released after the election and matched to the experimental records. To estimate the effects, we used the Intent-To-Treat (ITT) – a standard way to measure treatment effects in experimental research. The ITT is calculated by comparing the turnout rate (%) between those assigned to the control and treatment groups. The ITT therefore shows the effect of being assigned to a treatment group compared to a control group, and avoids the spuriousness associated with a turnout comparison of those successfully contacted and those not contacted (because those who were not successfully contacted are more likely to be deceased or have moved house). The results for the full sample and for the postal voter and non-postal voter experiments separately are presented in Table 9.5. The three models show the estimated ITT effects of (1) any campaign contact, (2) a leaflet only, and (3) a leaflet + canvass visit combination. The models are estimated using linear regression with standard errors clustered at household level. Covariates covering the factors described above – sex, party support, ward, postal voter registration, previous turnout and age group – are included in the model. Adjusting for covariates has the advantage of correcting for any minor imbalances in the assignment process and thereby increases the precision of the estimates while still producing unbiased effect estimates (Gerber and Green, 2012: 109). In order to illustrate the effects visually, we also present the predicted marginal effects of the treatments in Figure 9.3.

All effect sizes that are statistically significant at the 95 per cent confidence level are highlighted in bold for ease of interpretation. Looking first at model 1, subjects who were exposed to the Liberal Democrat campaign – in any form – were 3.6 percentage points more likely to vote, significant at the 95% level. This effect is stronger among the non-postal voter households, for whom the campaign increased turnout by 4.6 percentage points. Models 2 and 3 present the effects of the two treatments. Model 2 shows the effect of the leaflet, which increased turnout by 2.8 percentage points across all voters, though this is statistically insignificant at conventional levels. Again, this effect is stronger among non-postal voting households, at 4.3 percentage points. Model 3 shows the effect of the canvass visit and leaflet combination, which boosted turnout by 4.5 percentage points, which is significant at the 95 per cent level. This appears to suggest that while leaflets alone are ineffective, the leaflet and canvass visit combination has strong effects on voter turnout. However, this is only the case among the full sample. Among subjects in

Table 9.5 Intent to treat effects for full sample, postal and non-postal experiment

	N	Control group turnout	(1) Any campaign contact (leaflet, canvass + leaflet)			(2) Leaflet only			(3) Canvass + leaflet		
			Turnout	Effect (SE)	Covariate-adjusted (SE)	Turnout	Effect (SE)	Covariate-adjusted (SE)	Turnout	Effect (SE)	Covariate-adjusted (SE)
Full sample	6,525	–	–	3.5*	3.6*	–	2.5	2.8	–	4.4* (1.9)	4.5* (1.8)
Postal voter households	1,325	70.3%	69.0%	–1.3 (4.2)	–2.6 (3.9)	67%	–3.3 (4.7)	–4.8 (4.3)	71.1%	0.8 (4.6)	–0.3 (4.3)
Non-postal voters	5,200	25.0%	29.2%	4.2* (1.7)	4.6** (1.6)	28.7%	3.7+ (2.1)	4.3* (2.0)	29.7%	4.7* (2.1)	4.9* (2.0)

Robust standard errors (in parentheses) clustered on households. All tests two-tailed. **Significant p<.01, *p<.05, +p<.1.

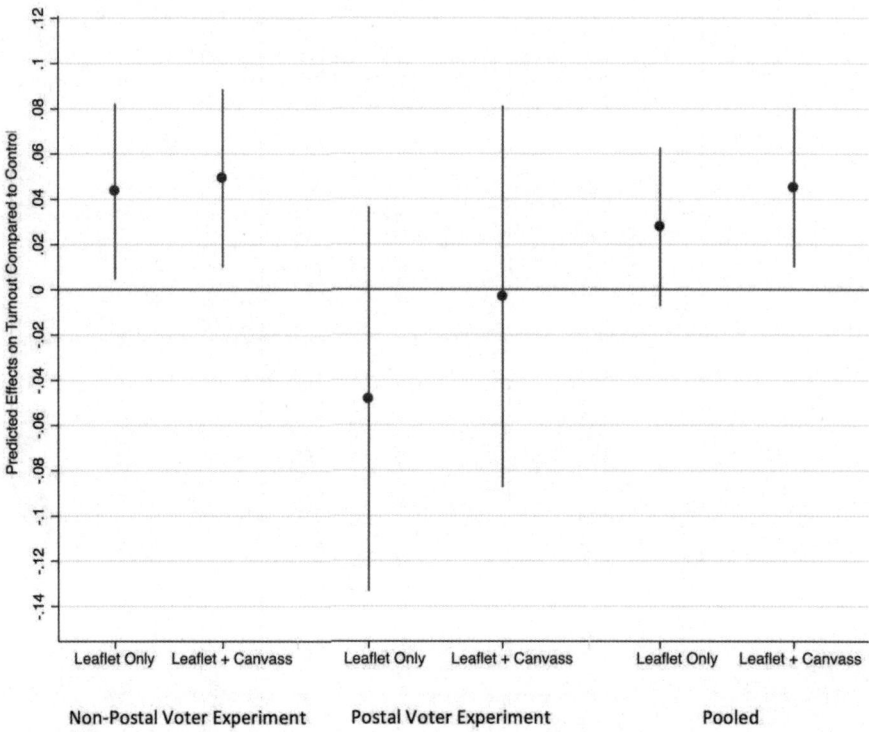

Figure 9.3 Predicted marginal effects of the treatments

the non-postal voter household experiment, the leaflet only treatment increased turnout by 4.3 percentage points. The effect of the leaflet plus canvass visit is larger – 4.9 percentage points. Among postal voter households, each treatment had negative and statistically insignificant effects.[7] The results suggest that the campaign affected postal voter households and non-postal voter households differently. As can clearly be seen from Table 9.5, there was no significant effect of campaigning on turnout among postal voters. Yet among non-postal voters, both leaflets and canvassing had statistically significant effects in boosting turnout. While postal voting households turned out at a far higher rate than non-postal voting households, this was not due to the Liberal Democrat campaign, which had no discernible impact on turnout.

Overall, our findings should give considerable heart to the Liberal Democrats and their longstanding emphasis on traditional place-based campaign techniques. Crucially, this experiment backs up survey evidence reported earlier in the chapter detailing the continued effectiveness of Liberal Democrat traditional, localised, personal campaign contact. Embedded in a real Liberal Democrat local campaign, our experiments show that leaflets and a combination of canvass visits and leaflets – the cornerstone of any Liberal Democrat campaign – both have positive effects on voter turnout at a local election. While this finding is not new, the 3.6 percentage point (ITT) effect of traditional party campaign contact (i.e. assignment to receive either of the treatment combinations) sits towards the higher end of other 'get out the vote' (GOTV) studies. This was driven largely by the effects among non-postal voter households rather than postal voting households. The results show that merely providing people with a party leaflet was enough to increase turnout among non-postal voting households, while only a limited further boost to turnout was provided by canvass visits. The effect of partisan leaflets (4.3 points among non-postal voters) is also towards the higher end of other reports and larger than those in US partisan studies (Barton *et al.*, 2013). It is worth noting that the leaflet contained partisan messaging but no specific behavioural or social pressure cues that have been shown to have powerful effects elsewhere (Green and Gerber, 2008). Reflecting how the Liberal Democrats construct their 'Focus' leaflets, the partisan leaflet was larger and contained more photographs and issue information than the Conservative leaflet that produced no overall effect in a comparable study in Somerset (Foos and John, 2016). It is worth reiterating that we were unable to run a canvass-only experiment, so gauging the effectiveness of Liberal Democrat doorstep canvassing is far more problematic. Nevertheless, the canvass visits in this study appeared to produce only limited additive effects, which supports the emerging thesis that door-to-door canvassing produces weaker turnout effects in Europe (Bhatti *et al.*, 2016).

The finding in the present experiment may not be surprising, given that the script echoed standard party scripts used at election time, which produce similarly weak turnout effects in Britain and Europe (Foos and John, 2016; Pons and Liegey, 2019. Given the low contact rate and high degree of uncertainty around the effect, the result should be treated with caution though. Without a third treatment group testing the impact of canvass visits alone, it is not possible to determine whether it was simply the initial partisan contact that prompted the effect, or whether the canvass reinforced the impact of the initial leaflet, and thus worked in tandem with it. Interestingly, the results also provide evidence that Liberal Democrat traditional campaign activities have particularly strong mobilisation effects among voters (most notably non-postal voters) who have a low or average underlying propensity to vote.[8]

Lastly, we analysed the turnout records of the voters participating in the election experiment to test whether the initial effects (in the May local election) persisted a month later (in the June general election). The goal was to identify evidence of any downstream effects of the original treatments. We find that across the full sample the ITT effects fall from 4.5 for the canvass/leaflet combination to 0.5 in June suggesting an enduring positive impact albeit the rate of decay in the effect of the original campaign contact between May and June was sizeable. With the May local election and the June general election only a month apart, given the higher saliency and turnout of the latter it is probable that the initial effects were predominantly drowned out by the noise.

Going digital: the great leveller?

So far we have shown that despite the Liberal Democrats' electoral woes post 2010, the party's emphasis on traditional modes and personalised methods was not misplaced. There were signs in 2019 that the intensity of these ground campaigns began to compare more favourably with opponents in the places that mattered. However, while the ground campaign remained a key arena of electoral combat, the digital electoral battlefield became increasingly pivotal. The advent of the 'fourth era' of campaigning has been an evolutionary development rather than a revolutionary break with the past. Professionalisation and the permanent campaign now coincide with increasing technological innovation, new campaigns tools and micro-targeting techniques emerging through the rise of 'big data' and the growth of social media (Roemmele and Gibson, 2020). Different advertising interfaces now provide opportunities for parties to run micro-targeted messages at highly localised audiences in key seats. Platforms such as Facebook and Google also offer parties unique advantages in terms of reach and connectivity. In addition to being a forum where parties can target content at key voters, these platforms also provide a vehicle for 'unofficial' material to be shared by digital party foot soldiers or organisations operating beyond party structures or control (known as satellite campaigns) (Dommett and Temple, 2018; Dommett *et al.*, 2021).

The digital sphere is now an integral part of election campaigning in Britain. It was initially envisaged as a great leveller for smaller parties like the Liberal Democrats, allowing them to better match their resource-rich opponents. Yet as the digital sphere has developed from one election to the next, this increasingly looks less likely. Here we gauge just how realistic this long-term ambition is, and whether the onset of digital campaigning has embedded offline electoral inequities. To address these 'big picture' questions, we use qualitative interviews from those on the frontline overseeing the Liberal Democrats' 2019 digital election campaign from party headquarters. This unique insight also contrasts with much of the literature, which, in the British case, predominantly focuses on the digital campaigns of the two main parties.

Assessing Liberal Democrat digital campaigning

From a party's perspective, digital activity for outreach and campaigning purposes comprises of 'organic' and 'paid' digital. Organic is primarily based on the followers the party has online across various social media accounts (Facebook, Twitter etc.) and broadly encompasses social networks of party support in these online communities. Individuals 'like' and share material with friends, family and associates and act as a digital army of volunteers who promote the party message on these different platforms. Paid digital, comprises the digital advertising programme, primarily on Facebook and Instagram, but also Snapchat and Google Search. For the party's digital campaign team, the paid side is the priority because it is how the party reaches people who do not already follow it. It is also where the party can actually control the content that goes out and how it is optimised for the platform in question, and – crucially – the party can target it to specific voters and areas. Organic and paid activity can and should complement one another, but the priority for political parties during elections is typically paid advertising online.

The Liberal Democrats' 2019 digital campaign primarily focused on paid online advertising with the simultaneous goal of adding to the national 'air war' and supporting the ground campaign. Within the party's online adverts programme, there were both national and local parts of the campaign plan. The national part focused on raising awareness of the party's core message and persuasion, while the local part incorporated most of these national messages, but also executed a strong squeeze message tailored to the individual seat. The objective of adverts in either case was to persuade and mobilise voters to support the party.

Gauging accurate causal attribution to digital activity is notoriously difficult, not least because areas of high digital investment tend also to be seats that receive more campaign activity overall. Nonetheless, the party's approach in 2019 focused on achieving a minimum, pre-defined audience penetration percentage across individual target seats, and then building to an average frequency of exposure to advertisements (how many times a user might see a Liberal Democrat advertisement) to give the best chance of raising awareness of the party's message. Additionally, the Liberal Democrats dedicated a small part of their digital resources on 'hard conversions' (donations, memberships) and some message testing run in split experiments on Facebook. For the Liberal Democrats, the digital advertising programme was more about objectives and supplementing other types of campaign activity. The main objective of the programme was to raise awareness of the Liberal Democrat message. The corresponding key performance indicators (KPIs) focused on reach and frequency across key areas. In an ideal world, digital campaigners conceded that a methodologically sound study would be run on this type of activity in order to develop statistically significant and causally sound results, but the short time frame and limited budget (compared with businesses and market research companies) meant this was not practical. Meanwhile, the organic aspect of the digital campaign (Twitter and Facebook accounts) was used to accentuate the national messaging, although it was very much a secondary consideration, after paid digital activity.

Based on interviews with digital strategists at party headquarters, there was a consensus that the Liberal Democrats ran a well-targeted and optimised campaign in 2019 target seats. Given the transparency of the Facebook Ad Library, the Liberal Democrats were able to see that while they launched clear advertisements specific to their target seats on a vast scale from day one of the campaign, the competition did not. The Conservatives and Labour really got their main campaign digital advertising machine live only in the final two weeks. It was at this stage when the Liberal Democrats started to see the number of live Labour and Conservative advertisements listed on the Ad Library begin to approach the level of their own. This 'number of live ads listed on the Ad Library' is indeed rather instructive because every time you split the audience with Facebook advertising, which you would have to do in order to carry out seat specific tactics, you increase the number of ads in your account, as shown by the Ad Library. The Liberal Democrats could therefore be confident that they were ahead of the competition in terms of the central digital advertising programme.[9] Put simply, in terms of building an intelligent, well-targeted, optimised digital advertising campaign, the Liberal Democrats felt confident that they led the field in 2019.[10] Yet at the local level it was far more mixed. Expertise in using the Facebook Ad Library is not uniform between local parties and therefore such digital activity varies considerably from seat to seat. However, strategists were quick to stress that there is little evidence to think that opposition local parties were actually any better than the Liberal Democrats on this front.

According to those working on the frontline, there were two issues which undermined the effectiveness of the 2019 Liberal Democrats' digital campaign. The first was creativity. Putting together creative digital content was organisationally challenging. With more time, digital strategists conceded that the creative quality would have been much higher. However, others point to longstanding structural challenges which hindered creativity. As our interviewees stated, one of the party's primary challenges for many years was simply having people who know what the party stands for – a challenge that long predated the Liberal Democrats' 2019 digital content output. The use of fairly punchy, simple messaging was arguably as effective a tactic that could be implemented, given the time and content constraints.

The second issue was the party's comparatively weak networking capabilities. In theory, networks offer the prospect of synchronicity between online and offline personalisation, where the digital can be joined up with the ground campaign. Networks can be crucial for sharing and amplifying key messages and content. Given the Liberal Democrats' emphasis on personalisation offline, one would assume that networks would be the vehicle that would allow the party to punch above its weight in the digital sphere. However, the key problem is that the party not only has a smaller army but also a quieter army of online supporters, dwarfed by followers of the one of the bigger 'tribes' (sometimes the Conservatives but usually Labour). Content is largely attacked and squeezed from both sides, making it difficult for the Liberal Democrats to post and amplify political content online. After 2015, for instance, the anti-Liberal Democrat agenda was prominent among online supporters of Corbyn. The Liberal Democrats were attacked as austerity enablers, which disarmed policy initiatives and manifesto promises. From those on the right, the party's openly pro-European and Remain ('People's Vote') stance also became the focus of organised online criticism. Yet when the party played an active and vocal role as part of a 'big tribe' – Remain versus Brexit during and after the EU referendum – the party's user engagement, shares and retweets shot up substantially. Reflective of their comparatively smaller online presence, Liberal Democrat strategists were quick to point to a 'shyness' or general anxiety among Liberal Democrat supporters online about sharing pro-Liberal Democrat content unless they felt confident that they were in a large group of like-minded people.

Other party digital strategists stressed the difficulty of measuring the impact of these networks on electoral outcomes. For instance, Labour's organic 2017 digital campaign of online foot soldiers and preference intermediaries such as Momentum and Grime4Corbyn contributed to them winning the digital war but not the election. As a Liberal Democrat digital campaigner at party head-quarters stressed, Labour dominated Instagram and Snapchat and had eight out of the 10 top UK Twitter trends on election day – but still lost heavily. Given that it is difficult to causally prove the effectiveness of various aspects of digital campaigns, it could equally be argued that without an online groundswell of support, Labour's 2019 defeat would have been worse. Leaving these caveats aside, the Liberal Democrats accepted that they would considerably benefit from having an army of volunteers to help make online content go viral, even if the efficacy of that activity on election outcomes is unclear. This kind of virality could be beneficial for a smaller party that struggles to gain national press attention. As one of the interviewees pointed out, the party achieved a version of this in the build-up to Jo Swinson's exclusion from the first 2019 televised election debate. The party managed to get #DebateHer trending on Twitter, which the press subsequently picked up. However, such examples were few and far between.

As regards digital advertising, even in an election with a small digital team at party headquarters (compared with Labour and the Conservatives) and a reasonable budget, the Liberal Democrats were at least able to go toe-to-toe with the competition during the campaign. However, when it came to organic (i.e. non-paid) digital activity, the Liberal Democrats struggled to gain online traction. The party's main noticeable increases in online audience were consist-ently linked to external news stories. Yet, Liberal Democrat digital campaigning was at a crossroads. The simple truth is that the party was already struggling to match the budget and resources of its opponents, and there is every indication that the gap will widen as time goes on. In 2019, data from Facebook and Google advertising archives revealed that parties spent just under £9 million in 2019 compared with £4.3 million in 2017 (Dommett and Bakir, 2020). On Facebook, the Liberal Democrats spent more than £1.3 million. This compared favourably to the Conservatives (£1.5 million) and Labour (more than £2 million), which were the largest spenders. However, on Google, the Liberal Democrats spent less than £250,000, while the Conservatives spent more than £1.7 million (Dommett and Bakir, 2020). A far larger number of Liberal Democrat advertisements emanated from the national party than was the case for other parties. This was not the case for Labour, where most came from candidates. As indicated by our interviewees, this probably reflected the need to coordinate scarce resources efficiently, but also indicated the variability in digital skills among Liberal Democrat candidates and the need to expand the use of digital advertising locally.

Among those involved in the 2019 digital campaign, there was a consensus that, going forward, the party's digital activity structure would not necessarily require a massive overhaul. The central party would retain control around who it was reaching with paid and organic digital, how often, and their engagement levels. This would then be aggregated to the seat level, although improvements would be dependent on resources. The Liberal Democrats needed more creative testing, beyond what was done in 2019, to remain competitive. This would involve testing a variety of content concepts and measuring their performance against a pre-defined KPI. This kind of message testing was carried out in 2019, but on a small scale. Message testing on a bigger scale, with more high-quality content, is increasingly the priority. Improving networks would also be beneficial going forward. Building an army of digital foot soldiers with access to party material who can organically reach out, build and permeate existing online (Facebook, primarily, but not exclusively) groups is crucial in the long term to shape an online personalisation element to the Liberal Democrats' digital campaign. In recent times, the Conservatives have been adept at organically spreading positive and negative messages through this route and currently have a distinct campaign advantage over other parties. It is a problem for the Liberal Democrats which cannot be solved in the short term but nonetheless needs to be addressed. However, the problem with network activity is the lack of control, transparency and reporting of clear, reliable metrics. Hence interviewees stressed the need for research to validate the impact online networks (voluntary digital activity by foot soldiers) have on persuasion and mobilisation, as well as the need to ensure that the right message is hitting the right people (as can be done with paid, targeted advertising). Resources therefore remain the key. With a skilled digital marketer and a sizeable budget, digital campaigning can help level the playing field. This is especially the case between election campaigns, when the role of digital activity is crucial for driving volunteer sign-ups, donations, membership recruitment and conversations to complement offline personalised activity.

Getting the campaign wrong … again!

So, with the ground campaign showing green shoots of promise and the digital campaign holding its own against better-resourced opponents, the big picture looks positive moving forward. However, to bridge existing campaign gaps between the Liberal Democrats and their opponents requires the national campaign to be in sync with the local and digital. Their campaign strategy needs to be coordinated, sure-footed and tactically sound. Given longstanding structural barriers, it has to be operationalised with ruthless efficiency. Worryingly, the party's national campaign strategy has come up short. Here we look at the 2019 general election – drawing on evidence from those at national headquarters who were involved in the campaign – which, despite some positives, was bedevilled by mistakes, oversights and failings. Put simply, it is possible to run highly effective localised campaigns backed up by targeted digital advertisements but if the overall strategy, tactics, communication and messaging are misjudged and inflexible then this can severely undermine the wider campaign effort.

Too many target seats and failings in the ground war

The wider miscalculation of the 2019 election campaign strategy stems in part from a YouGov multilevel regression and post-stratification (MRP) internal poll conducted in June that year. The results had the party ahead in 63 seats, tied in eight more and within five percentage points in a further 30. Of course, this internal poll was taken in the aftermath of successful local and European elections, when the Conservative vote was split and the Labour party under Corbyn was extremely unpopular, so much so that Liberal Democrats were challenging Labour for second place in the polls. While the party was not naïve enough to be taken completely in by the June wave of MRP polling, that polling did, alongside other factors – recent general and local election results as well as campaign and candidate activism in the seats – influence the categorisation of target seats. A 40/40/20 categorisation process was used to draw up the party's target seats. Seats were categorised as 'first 40', 'second 40', 'next 20' and 'other'. The first 40 were the top target seats, comprising held seats (e.g. Bath, Orkney and Shetland, and Westmorland and Lonsdale), non-held top targets like St Albans, and seats held by recent defectors (e.g. Luciana Berger's Finchley and Golders Green). The June MRP polling results largely lined up with the selection of target seats, with only six of the top-40 list – predominantly non-held targets like Totnes, York Outer, and Finchley and Golders Green – showing the Liberal Democrats in second place. The 'second 40' were also top targets for the party, but of a slightly lower priority. In practical terms, there proved to be a fair amount of overlap, with similar campaign materials and advertisements delivered in both categories. The second 40 included recently held seats – for example, Argyll and Bute, Eastleigh, Ross, Skye and Lochaber, and Taunton Deane – and a number of emerging target seats largely situated in London's large commuter belt – Hitchin and Harpenden, Mole Valley, and South West Surrey. These were seats that the Liberal Democrats did not hold and had not held for some time (or ever). However, demographic changes such as the growing influx of younger, Remain-voting professionals leaving the capital had begun to make these seats much more favourable to the party. Some of them were geographically congruent with first 40 targets, such as Esher and Walton (bordering the safe seats of Twickenham, and Kingston and Surbiton) and Hitchin and Harpenden (bordering top target St Albans). Finally, there were the so-called 'next 20' targets. These were largely seats in which the June MRP had put the Liberal Democrats within striking distance but conditions were not otherwise favourable enough for the party to mount a serious challenge (e.g. Welwyn Hatfield, Hendon, and Harrow East).

A second wave of MRP polling was conducted by the party in September 2019 and it made for more sobering and arguably realistic reading. The September wave had the party winning in just 23 seats and tied in four more. Among the first 40 target seats, a divide began to open up between held and non-held seats. The September MRP showed the party falling back in most of its non-held seats compared with June (e.g. South Cambridgeshire, Wimbledon, and Putney). Nevertheless, in the held seats (e.g. Twickenham, and Westmorland and Lonsdale), the party had maintained its winning margin. Heading into the general election campaign itself, the first 40 target seats by and large remained the same. After all, the September MRP had not drastically reordered seats across the country in terms of favourability – it had just defined the party's chances as much weaker. The first 40 were largely the 40 seats in Britain in which the party had the best chance of winning.

Based on evidence from those inside Liberal Democrat national headquarters, the length of the list of target seats was cause for concern, as it overstretched already tight resources. Crucially, many of the seats in the first 40 and second 40 had not been Liberal Democrat target seats before. As a consequence, there was a lack of historical canvassing data and enduring local activism. The fundamental components of the Liberal Democrat blueprint for winning seats – a longstanding local campaign machine built over many years, continuous campaigning outside of election time and a large team of activists embedded in the community – were absent. While the party sought to be ambitious, buoyed by favourable demographics and hardworking activists, it came at the cost of moving away from the tried and tested election-winning formula. This had inevitable consequences for how the campaigning was operationalised in practice. Firstly, the party delivered a direct mail campaign on an unprecedented scale. In some respects, the Liberal Democrats' ability to step up and deliver vast quantities of direct mail into its target seats is impressive. Yet, as noted in the party's 2019 *Election Review Report*, this ultimately did more harm than good (Liberal Democrats, 2019). Miscommunication between the local and national teams led to bitterness and ill-feeling, and resource limitations and logistical problems made it impossible to control what voters received and when they received it. Voters sometimes got more than one mailing at once and were inundated with national and local messages that were not always coordinated and were often contradictory. As the 2019 report stated, 'if the quantity was questionable, the quality and coordination were poor' (Liberal Democrats, 2019: 14). Secondly, the Liberal Democrat field team put in place 80 staff to support ground campaigning and voter contact. This National Field Organiser programme proved to be effective and provided vital support in seats less accustomed to the expectations of being a top target in a general election campaign. Vote share increases in many of these seats have been overlooked in the broader post-mortem of the 2019 campaign and in the long run may prove pivotal in forthcoming contests. However, despite the positives there were questions around timing and implementation. Based on insights from those involved in the campaign, it is beyond doubt that the party would have benefited from this team being assembled further in advance of the election, or – better yet – being a permanent presence in target seats over a number of years. In truth, despite these attempts to offset the campaign gap, with little historical canvass data in many of its new target seats, the party was largely flying blind.

Thirdly, during a campaign, target seats send canvass data to the national campaign team so they can evaluate changing voting patterns, assess the impact of particular messages and if necessary make the decision to redirect resources to contests where the party has the best chance of success. Yet in 2019 many of the target seats lacked any historical canvass data and the local capacity and resources to persuade voters through intensive doorstep exercises. Local parties instead focused on mobilising identified supporters and sidestepped particular demographic groups. The national campaign team was aware of these limitations and was reluctant to develop highly targeted messaging and to redirect resources based on the data. This meant that those seats which had collected high-quality data through intensive activism and fed this back to the national party did not get the support they needed. Such data were ignored and the opportunity to tailor messaging and redirect resources was missed. When the redeployment of resources was enacted during the final two weeks of the campaign, national headquarters judgements were jumbled and disorganised based on a less than satisfactory evaluation of the data. This contributed to seat losses and missed opportunities.

Ultimately, the party targeted too many seats that did not pass the basic viability test for a realistic Liberal Democrat target in a general election. For all the positives of hardworking activists on the ground, the 2019 Liberal Democrat campaign lacked a clear overarching strategy and leadership direction, while the national campaign was detached from the local one, which itself lacked resources, people on the ground and money. Messages lacked creativity and were haphazard, while not enough of them went to the right people (Liberal Democrats, 2019: 38–46). However, as the chapters in Part III of this volume illustrate, the failings identified in 2019 stem from a steady loss of experienced campaigners, their skills, insights and know-how, much of which was self-inflicted. These campaign organisers were the glue between the national, regional and the local. They were the sages who understood the political mood of the seat, the local community, the councillors and the minds of members, activists and voters. They possessed the local knowledge, campaign expertise and training assistance that local seats relied on, both outside and during the campaign period. Their removal during the early 2010s had not only left target seats with less support but severely undermined the potency of place-based community campaigning. Implementing an overstretched targeting plan in 2019 was always going to be unwieldy and impractical but with fewer skilled, experienced campaigners with local know-how on the ground to oversee and coordinate tailored messaging, intra-seat targeting, local data analysis, media work and so on, success outside of a few heavily resourced seats was nigh impossible. As 2019 reminded the Liberal Democrats, it takes time – longstanding continuous activism, enduring expertise on the ground and invariably a strong local council presence to build credibility – for the party to win a seat at a general election.

Miscalculating the air war

In previous chapters we stressed how the Liberal Democrats ran a presidential-style campaign ('Jo4PM') by putting Jo Swinson front and centre of the party's pitch to voters. Alongside the hard sell on Swinson was the party's 'revoke' policy on Brexit. Again, it originated at a time when the party was on the up and the opposition seemed vulnerable. Designed as an unambiguous appeal to Remain voters, it was envisaged as a cut-through message to Labour voters, with the explicit aim of exploiting Corbyn's travails with his parliamentary party and wider membership. Both these national messages backfired. The Liberal Democrat election review is unequivocal about how these messages departed from the party's established platform and brand, were blunt, unimaginative when compared with their opponents' messages, devised in a rush and not thought through or subjected to rigorous, robust testing with real voters (Liberal Democrats, 2019: 15–16). Additionally, no new messages had been created or developed and empirically tested. The complexities of the revoke policy led to the Liberal Democrats being stuck in the crossfire from both parties with the 'undemocratic label' hurting the Liberal Democrats' longstanding brand credentials. The party was consistently on the back foot, explaining the minutiae of the policy and as a consequence quickly lost the argument and voters' sympathy. The subsequent messaging shift to 'Stop Boris' to replace 'Stop Brexit' occurred far too late to have any noticeable impact.

As regards the presidential strategy, assumptions were made by party strategists that surges in support during the summer 2019 were in part due to Swinson being a viable alternative to the perceived unpopularity of Johnson and Corbyn. As the election campaign drew nearer there were already signs that this assumption was misguided, as the party's poll ratings started to turn. As we noted in Chapter 7, the wheels of the presidential campaign started to fall off during the campaign itself as the prospect of Swinson becoming Prime Minister became increasingly unrealistic to voters. Her approval ratings nose-dived and after some dithering the party sought to distance itself from its earlier 'your candidate for Prime Minister' national message; however, the damage was done, with the media frequently exposing the u-turn as an indication of Swinson's unpopularity. The Liberal Democrats were simply too slow to respond and any benefits from the sudden change in strategy were at best minimal. One of the consequences of focusing on Jo Swinson was that relatively high-profile MPs were sidelined in the national campaign. However, those inside the campaign were a little sceptical about whether a greater prominence for those MPs would have been beneficial. Many high-profile MPs were themselves embroiled in defending or winning their own seats. Outside of figures like Cable and defectors from Labour and the Conservatives, these MPs did not have a national presence and were unlikely to have garnered the same media attention. The Liberal Democrats were in a Catch-22 situation. Swinson had been front and centre of the campaign and was the driver of the national message. Taking a back-step was always going to be problematic, given that others did not have the national profile to fill the void.

So it was incumbent on Swinson to remain the focal point of the party's national message, yet her growing unpopularity meant that she was a source of the damage.

Strategically, the focus on the leader somewhat undermined the party's local DNA. The leader-orientated approach did not sit comfortably with the Liberal Democrats' established branding around the local champion and local issues. On the one hand, Swinson's unpopularity meant that the party's traditional local emphasis struggled to cut through. However, this should not in reality be an either/ or issue. With leaders becoming increasingly important and joined-up campaigning now established, local parties (with national help) can tailor their campaigns and messages to fit with the local context and champion salient local issues where necessary. Leader-focused campaigns can therefore complement rather than distract from these campaigns. The problem for the Liberal Democrats, though, is the capacity of leader unpopularity to neutralise the saliency of local issues, thereby undermining place-based efforts to persuade party leaners and potential tactical switchers. It can make local campaigns rudderless and weaken their ability to connect to voters. Of course, aside from when a local issue completely dominated a constituency campaign, other parties (particularly the Conservatives in 2015 and 2017) have been adept at deactivating the local focus of voters in national elections. However, this may be partly due to the dominance of 'big ticket' issues in recent elections, such as Brexit, where a local angle is more problematic to tease out. Campaign messages on issues such as the economy, the NHS and education, while national in orientation, can be strategically positioned through local experiences, allowing voters to judge performance through the local and apply this to the national situation. As such, there is scope for the air war and digital campaign to complement constituency-focused campaigning which joins up the local focus and the national focus for voters. That said, this requires the party to be creative in its messaging and different aspects of the party's campaign – from the leader's speeches to the manifesto – to be joined up in a harmonious manner. It was this lack of cohesiveness acknowledged by the Liberal Democrat in the 'air war' where it fell short in 2019 (Liberal Democrat Election Review: 14-17).

Summary

Nobody intended it to be how it was, but the outcome [of the 2019 general election] was catastrophic. We were poor performers in an election which we helped to call, and in which poor planning, leadership and decision making compounded to give us such a poor result. Disastrous as it was, however, it is the making not only of poor decisions in 2019, but the failure over many years to reform, properly plan and run our organisation with a culture focused on electoral success. The lessons were there before, with all their extenuating circumstances and they are here now without them. (Liberal Democrats, 2019: 17)

This honest appraisal sums up how the Liberal Democrats were knocked off their campaign pedestal and, as we have shown in this book, it is a story that pre-dates the 2010 general election but which snowballed in successive elections. Of course the Liberal Democrats cannot control the ability of opposition parties to up their game, draw on deeper resources and circumvent rules on local spending through highly effective national targeting. They can, however, control what they do. And the post-2005 period has been littered with strategic errors, miscalculations, repeated mistakes and an inability to reform failing practices.

Yet the big picture paints a rosier story. Not only are there signs that the intensity of face-to-face Liberal Democrat campaigning is beginning to outstrip its opponents' in the places that matter, any lingering doubt that the saliency of these traditional, more personalised modes are waning in their effectiveness seems premature. For a party that embraces the local and prioritises the personal, this is not only reassuring but encouraging for future electoral battles. Similarly, it is clear that resource issues and the absence of a critical mass of online foot soldiers scupper any prospect of a level playing field in the digital campaign sphere. Yet we find plenty of evidence that the party (particularly in the digital advertising field) is more than holding its own and with further innovation can seriously challenge its resource-rich opponents. In an ever-changing arena, the Liberal Democrats are well placed to do well. Put simply, the mechanics of the Liberal Democrat campaign machine still work. The ethos of community-based personalised campaigning remains relatable to voters. However, to be effective in a new era of campaigning, the party needs to embrace a long-term, coordinated strategic plan that harmonises the air, ground and digital campaigning around the party's brand credentials. Whimsical targeting plans like the one used in 2019 should be avoided in favour of the tried and tested incremental development of viable seats where the favourable brand appeal can be turned into brand loyalty through continuous activism and increasing local presence. For this, the party requires a comprehensive interwoven political and electoral strategy if it is to make a decisive electoral comeback.

Conclusion: the Liberal Democrats' identity crisis

At the outset of this book we identified seven themes that would run through our analysis of the Liberal Democrats. At the end of our account it is worth revisiting them. All seven themes are discrete but are interrelated in important ways. They culminate in an identity crisis for the Liberal Democrats – attention to which is long overdue if the party is to remain a viable entity. The themes for our analysis were:

- The credibility gap is the biggest obstacle to Liberal Democrat success.
- Quick-fix policy solutions have masked structural deficiencies and expose a vacuum in the political identity of the Liberal Democrats.
- Agency is crucial to the Liberal Democrats' electoral fortunes.
- Participation in the 2010–2015 coalition severely damaged the Liberal Democrats' reputation with British voters.
- The 'coalition shock' hampered the Liberal Democrats' ability to resist the process of Brexit, which in turn harmed the party's identity.
- The Liberal Democrats have lost their competitive campaigning advantage as rivals have appropriated and adopted their practices.
- The Liberal Democrats are not the masters of their own destiny and are reliant on the fortunes of other parties.

The credibility gap

The credibility gap is a function of the Liberal Democrats' place at the margins of British politics. Third parties in a system designed to sustain only two are frequently constrained by a lack of concentrated geographic support and natural electoral heartlands. Under-resourced financially and under-represented in the media the party feel they have to fight for every vote in every seat. The secret to bridging the credibility gap is to show that the party is a viable electoral choice to voters. This is why the Liberal Democrats tend to rally behind their campaign mantra of 'Winning here' – focusing on a local presence and personalised, intensive, all-year-round activism – to exploit opposition to one of the other mainstream parties in a pincer movement. Winning councils or achieving sizeable representation allows the party to establish a local culture of voting from which local electors can judge whether the party is viable option in first-order elections. However, it takes time for the Liberal Democrats to establish themselves as the main challenger in the constituency and build local representation to reinforce their credibility. Once credibility has been established, the local champions are difficult to stop and traditionally Liberal Democrat incumbents buoyed by a strong personal vote have proved to have enormous 'stickability' and extremely difficult to unseat (see Chapter 1).

This ability to retain hard-won seats was, however, undermined by the 2010–2015 coalition and its legacy, as well as the Eurosceptic turn in British politics. Going into coalition ripped out the heart from the Liberal Democrats' local infra-structure and, despite years of hard work, the personal vote of incumbents and evidence of effectiveness in such dire circumstances, the party could not prevent the electoral tsunami (see Chapter 4). The contradiction of the coalition came to bite the party hard. Going into the 2015 election, the majority of key Liberal Democrat local battles were against the Conservatives, who operationalised a highly successful 'black widow' electoral strategy, turning on their coalition allies in these competi-tive local contests. The legacy of coalition meant that the party ceased to be credible in places where it was previously strong. The slow decline of Nonconformism also ensured that the Liberal Democrats lacked core support in its traditional Celtic fringe heartlands, and so was unable to mount a quick recovery. Moreover, the paradox was that these traditional strongholds were bastions of anti-EU sentiment and yet consistently returned MPs for the most Europhile political party. Seats such as Devon North returned MPs like Nick Harvey, whose views on Europe seemed massively at odds with the party's national policy. Growing Euroscepticism, which culminated in the decision to leave the EU in 2016, meant that Liberal Democrats found it harder to stay credible locally and ignore the European issue. In Remain-leaning seats, where Labour was the main competitor, being labelled as 'Yellow Tories' by Labour opponents undermined efforts to bridge the Liberal Democrats' credibility gap after 2015. Put simply, solving the credibility puzzle still remains pivotal to the Liberal Democrats' future political and electoral prospects.

The quandary of quick-fix policies

The Liberal Democrats have often felt the need to develop novel and distinctive policies in order to capture the attention of the media and public, in order to counter the tendency for the party to be squeezed out of political discourse. The party repeatedly has to fight the claim that 'no one knows what they stand for' and policy innovation can be the most effective tactic in this venture. In truth, however, the policy arena needs to be carefully chosen. A party in perpetual opposition need not concern itself unduly with developing policies that are implementable but for a party desperately trying to overcome the credibility gap, and for whom participa-tion in government is not exactly a pipedream, the Liberal Democrats do need to appear a responsible electoral choice.

The pre-coalition Liberal Democrats found some policy positions that enabled them to prosper against incumbent governments of both flanks. Under Kennedy, the party had benefited from its stance against the Iraq war in 2001 but had supported the NATO bombing of Kosovo a few years earlier. This policy is a reminder of the importance of agency for the Liberal Democrats since an Ashdown-led party might not have cohered so easily against the Iraq invasion. Nevertheless, the Liberal Democrats had developed a track record of innovative approaches to policy formation. The hypothecated penny on income tax for health spending, opposition to identity cards, the pupil premium and in particular opposition to university tuition fees had given the Liberal Democrats an apparently distinctive and populist edge.

It is our contention that such policy stances tended to obscure structural difficulties and ideological splits within the party. They blurred the party's core identity and built transactional voter alliances which increased pressure on the party to deliver. Liberal Democrat opposition to tuition fees – and the immediate abandonment of the policy on entry to the 2010 coalition (far from being scrapped, fees actually tripled for students attending higher education in England) – is the epitome of the shortcomings of a short-term populist policy.

Opposition to tuition fees had been longstanding. The party had taken credit for the decision by the Labour–Liberal Democrat regime in the Scottish Parliament not to impose top-up fees for domestic students in 1999 and party personnel were happy to pose alongside anti-fee pledges throughout the 2010 election campaign. Despite being distinctive and popular with party members and voters, the leadership had already failed to dilute the official line and fees were not a red line for the Liberal Democrats in the 2010 coalition negotiations (to the surprise of their Conservative counterparts).

In his own account, Liberal Democrat leader and coalition Deputy Prime Minister Nick Clegg said the party leadership felt that opposition to tuition fees was unworkable: 'The tuition-fees furore is the clearest example of the dangers of taking policy decisions based solely on their merits, rather than their emotional impact' (Clegg, 2016: 27). For Clegg, the failure of the party to face down the party membership – and the campaigning power of the National Union of Students – was foolhardy, 'a communications disaster of epic proportions' (Clegg, 2016, 31). Events conspired to deal the Liberal Democrats a terrible hand according to Clegg: 'We had overstated what we could in practice deliver, and we compounded our woes by advocating a policy that many people at the top of the party did not believe in' (Clegg, 2016: 32). But the truth is that they managed to play that hand particularly badly and the reputational damage from undoing the pledge on tuition fees was incalculable.

The climbdown on tuition fees was an important moment for the party. Clegg could well be right in asserting that it offered the convenient excuse that many voters wanted to decouple from the Liberal Democrats after they had entered into coalition with the Conservatives. It is also correct that the Conservatives and Labour, especially, were able to deflect their own difficulties over tuition fees because of the hole the Liberal Democrats found themselves in. Nevertheless, the fact is that the Liberal Democrats were lightning conductors, and the abandonment of a key part of the party's identity came to symbolise the toxicity of the coalition combined with doubts over credibility and agency to rout the party's reputation.

Ironically, going into coalition gave the Liberal Democrats an opportunity to carve a distinctive policy space and become less reliant on quick-fix solutions (see Chapters 3 and 4). Nevertheless, after getting the coalition agreement and the allocation of portfolios wrong, the party found it impossible to walk the tightrope between defender and critic. Unable to control the agenda, the Liberal Democrats were neither blamed nor credited for the coalition's failures and successes. The party was outplayed by its Conservative partners and missed a golden opportunity to reinvigorate the brand, embed a core identity through policy ownership and subsequently rely less on short-term policy fixes to woo voters. This came back to haunt the Liberal Democrats after 2015, when the party, hamstrung by less airtime and the legacy of coalition, remained on the sidelines of British politics. Deemed an irrelevance in 2017, the party sought to break its Brexit shortcomings with the perceived populist 'revoke' policy but instead badly misread the room and blurred its policy identity as it sought borrowed support (see Chapter 7). The thin policy line between distinctive edge and debacle remains a hazard of the Liberal Democrats' quick-fix approach.

Agency matters

One of the consistent themes of the book has been how agency matters for the Liberal Democrats. As party loyalty weakens and volatility rises, voters are increasingly looking to leaders as a political cue. For third parties, confined by having few partisans, leaders provide a viable vehicle to circumvent the structural barriers they commonly face. Pre-coalition, the Liberal Democrats had developed a political strategy around the leader. Highly salient policy positions were synchronised with personal stances so voters attached these popular policies to the leader. Crucially, they became highly effective when contrasted with the unpopularity of those put forward by their opponents. For example, Kennedy's personal stance on the war in Iraq positioned the Liberal Democrats as the beneficiaries of antipathy towards Blair. With Clegg, like Kennedy before him, carefully constructed policy messages articulated through the leader were effective at appealing to less tribal voters and coalescing different sections of the electorate. Yet even when it worked, agency only got the party so far. And when it went wrong, inextricably positioning the leader as the fulcrum for party messaging and appeal, left the party, already hamstrung with a limited electoral base of support, little leeway for manoeuvre. As Clegg found in 2015, if the leader becomes the object of discontent, any attempt to control the policy agenda and get across party messaging becomes futile. The leaders of third parties (excluding the SNP) get a limited opportunity to make an impression on the electorate, given the intense focus on the two main parties. Getting the message and the campaign right from the outset is therefore imperative. From BlueKip to delusions of becoming Prime Minister, the Liberal Democrats have shown a consistent capacity to undermine agential attempts to circumvent both structural barriers and the ill-winds of the electoral context through leadership blunders, policy errors and strategic mistakes (see Chapters 6 and 7).

The toxic coalition

David Laws' account of the coalition neatly sums up how the combination of agency, populist policy errors and political naiveté led the Liberal Democrats into a vicious cycle of public outrage and political irrelevance after the formation of the 2010–2015 government (see Chapter 3). He says of the policy reversal on tuition fees:

> For Nick Clegg – a party leader who had promised 'no more broken political promises' – it proved to be a political disaster and an albatross forever hanging around his neck. No issue caused greater damage to the Liberal Democrats in the coalition government than university tuition fees. … While the policy might have been a success, the politics were not…. We had now handed our political opponents a massive stick to beat us with, and we had crafted a striking and simple totem of 'betrayal' for all those voters who never wanted us to go into coalition with the Conservatives at any price. (Laws, 2016: 50, 63)

Clegg himself admitted that the climb down on tuition fees damaged the party's reputation significantly. Yet while it 'became a lightning conductor … to symbolize the growing narrative … that our behaviour in the coalition was one of weakness and loss of principle' (Clegg, 2016: 33), it was actually going into coalition with the Conservatives that backfired politically with voters (see Chapter 4 – although Clegg maintained that it was the right thing to do). As we have asserted here, the sudden conversion to the austerity package of the Conservatives was the most notable feature of the Liberal Democrats' acceptance of the policy direction of the coalition: 'I don't think any of us foresaw at the time how much the narrative of austerity would blot out all other government ambitions' (Clegg, 2016: 130). For Clegg, the Liberal Democrats played a noble role in the formation of a new government at a time of unprecedented threat and financial insecurity. The conversion to austerity to prevent a Greek-style economic meltdown was the political equivalent of running a four-minute mile on the Road to Damascus but it may have been the honourable – and responsible – course of action:

> The Liberal Democrats played a thankless role, harangued non-stop from right and left, in ensuring that the government remained a moderate one. From the point of view of the party itself, the timing could not have been worse: finally making the transition from perpetual opposition into government at just the point where the whole of Europe was pitched into a prolonged bout of austerity. (Clegg, 2016: 255)

We find this argument unconvincing, considering that Britain's austerity package was further and deeper than many (including the Liberal Democrat manifesto of 2010) thought wise at the time, and subsequent analysis of the burden of austerity has revealed that the economy was further dislocated by the inequity of cuts, which disproportionately hit the poorest sections of the economy, society and the country rather than the most protected. Electorally, the party struggled to shrug off the label of 'austerity enablers' as many left-leaning Labour voters who had lent the Liberal Democrats their support in 2010 became rigidly determined not to make the same mistake twice.

Furthermore, the Liberal Democrats – the party that might have been expected to be the best-prepared for coalition negotiations – got them hopelessly wrong. The way in which the party was outmanoeuvred by the Conservatives is astounding given how many Liberal Democrat personnel had engaged with the academic literature on coalition formation and cabinet building. Agency played a key role here. Clegg makes an astounding admission in his own account:

> I didn't rule out the possibility of a hung parliament, but in 2009 when I asked Danny Alexander, David Laws, Chris Huhne and Andrew Stunnell to prepare for possible coalition negotiations, I expected it would remain a paper exercise. (Clegg, 2016: 175)

Going into coalition proved to be an unmitigated disaster. Through their own avoidable errors and mistakes they bred toxicity towards the party which still remains among some voters today. For others they became irrelevant. In the space of five years the Liberal Democrats took a huge step backwards from which they have struggled to recover and still remain highly vulnerable to circumstances outside of its control.

Brexit and beyond

After the 2015 electoral meltdown, the Liberal Democrats were dispatched to the margins of British politics. As Cameron's Conservatives, emboldened by their victory in 2015, set about facing down their own structural identity issues (and the challenge from UKIP) with the announcement of the 2016 Brexit referendum, the campaign to Remain in the European Union – and particularly the pro-Europe wing of the Conservative party – might have benefited from a higher-profile contribution from the Liberal Democrats under Tim Farron. However, the party was ostracised. It paid the price for coalition and the subsequent failure to hold onto their organisational strength in the country. The banishment of the Liberal Democrats from the public space of British politics had severe repercussions for the party and the nation as a whole.

The post-referendum phase of British politics seemingly promised a route back to relevance for the Liberal Democrats but this proved mostly illusionary. Under Vince Cable's leadership the party recovered significantly in local elections, and in the last ever European elections, but converting the 48 per cent to the Liberal Democrat cause at a general election would be a very different prospect. While both Corbyn and Johnson were 'Marmite'-like to many, perennial Liberal Democrat credibility problems – far more severe following the coalition shock – were almost insurmountable. When the coalition record of Swinson was weaponised by opponents, it underlined that that 2019 election would be less fertile ground for a Liberal Democrat revival than many had supposed. Yet the party also hurt itself (see Chapter 7). The serious political miscalculation of the 'revoke' policy; the spectacularly ill-judged presidential-style campaign around Swinson; and the decision to pivot back to the centre with anti-Labour sentiment as prevalent as anti-Conservative rhetoric from the leadership – all these factors once more demonstrated the restrictive power of structure and agency for the Liberal Democrats.

Losing the grassroots campaign advantage

The Liberal Democrats and their predecessors have often granted Svengali-like status to their campaign chiefs – from Trevor 'Jones the Vote' to Lord Rennard. In the post-Rennard era, the much-vaunted party campaign machine has been exposed as a myth. The super-local campaigns built on strong local performances from ward to ward and neighbouring areas, using *Focus* leaflets and other person-alised methods to establish presence and credibility. The Liberal Democrat voting then spread across regions and into parliamentary constituencies. This, though, was a strategy that could easily be copied. In fact, better-resourced parties could probably follow the pattern more efficiently and in target seats up and down the country the main parties perfected the Liberal Democrat template. Increasingly, opponents simply sought to do what the Liberal Democrats do, but to them better, and this nullified the Liberal Democrats' 'local pitch' and their tailoring of the 'local' more effectively to the national context. With growing professionalisation has come ever-increasing centralisation, allowing resource-rich rivals to target more efficiently and effectively, and to capitalise on a campaign advantage (see Chapter 5).

> Writing about the 2001 election campaign, the Director of Campaigns, Chris Rennard (then at the height of his influence in the party), revealed the limits to the targeting strategy for a party stretched to the limit in terms of resources. Spending in target seats had grown from 4 per cent of the campaign budget in 1992 to 40 per cent (£1 million) in 2001 but left the party struggling just to maintain its Westminster offices. 'Cash was still a major constraint on our capacity to expand the number of seats we could target through the ground war' (Rennard, 2018: 282).

There was also another ceiling to be hit with the expansion policy of the Liberal Democrats. Simply, the party ran out of viable targets. By the middle 2000s there was little juice left to extract from the fruit of campaigning. Local messages were increasingly exposed for their inconsistency with the national platform. Moreover, the televised leadership debates of the 2010 general election campaign and the excitement of Cleggmania pulled key activists out of the control of Cowley Street as local Liberal Democrats felt that hopeless seats were suddenly up for grabs. It is easy to see, therefore, why the Liberal Democrat model of expansion was exhausted. It is worth remembering that the 2010 general election was a major disappointment for the Liberal Democrats as vote share barely increased and the number of Westminster seats actually fell. The electoral performance in 2015 may have been a disaster borne from the coalition but the downturn in the Liberal Democrats' campaign advantage (also in 2017) and electoral fortunes had already set in beforehand (see Chapter 2). Despite saving the party from wipe-out, the weaknesses of the campaign machine became exposed in defensive situations and the party was slow to recover in the face of credibility issues and rivals' adoption of 'bottom up' tactics and techniques.

Reliance on the fortunes of other parties

The themes that run through our analysis of the Liberal Democrats are tied together in the realisation that the fortunes of the Liberal Democrats are tied explicitly to those of other parties. Credibility, record of achievement, policy formation, competitive advantages and events all come together to be magnified or reduced by the state of play in the other political parties. Recruitment and retention of Liberal Democrat activists, voters and elected officials are all contingent on what happens to the party's political opponents. Outsider status can boost the Liberal Democrats' protest vote, and being inside the tent can increase the party's credibility, but by and large these effects are contingent on how well placed others are to resist or encourage a Liberal Democrat surge.

It is also important to remember that Liberal Democrat fortunes might not turn out in the way currently expected. A change to the voting system, for instance, might give the Liberal Democrats increased electoral opportunities but it might also create space for other parties to enter the fractured space around the existing political system.

The analytical themes we have outlined throughout this book demonstrate that the Liberal Democrats remain surprisingly vague in terms of political identity. This is the existential crisis of the Liberal Democrats. The remaining task of this book, then, is to try to set out a range of possible strategies and tactics for the party as it comes to terms with the Liberal Democrat identity crisis.

Facing the future, learning from the past

The Liberal Democrats do not control their own destiny. The impact of party leadership upon overall level of support can be greater in negative rather than in positive contexts. Post coalition, Nick Clegg, Tim Farron and Jo Swinson could do little to stem the tide against the party, and Clegg's and Swinson's own personal records in government came under severe scrutiny from all sides in the general elections of 2015 and 2019. Since taking over in 2020, Sir Edward Davey has adopted an almost medical approach to his leadership of the party – like a doctor taking the Hippocratic oath – he seemed determined to *first, do no harm*. In fact, he signalled a willingness to let the party at large feel more independent from central control than was the case under his predecessor (whether by necessity or by design) and the party benefited from the unpopularity of the Johnson government in the form of three spectacular by-election victories. This led to much conjecture that an impressive Liberal Democrat recovery could be made on the back of Tory unpopularity, particularly in the so-called Blue Wall.

As our analysis shows (see Chapter 8), for all the bravado about knocking down the Blue Wall, the Liberal Democrats require seismic shifts in support to make serious progress. As Johnson made way for a new Prime Minister and the Conservatives turned first to Liz Truss, the government fell to even lower levels of voter satisfaction, and scarcely recovered when the Tories turned to Rishi Sunak 44 days later. Yet the Liberal Democrats stood to make ground in only a handful of seats according to the polls. Instead, a more fruitful strategy might concentrate on previous 'stomping grounds', particularly the so-called 'breakthrough 1997 seats' and constituencies where the party has recently lost but remains competitive. Put simply, relying on winning new Blue Wall seats is not a short-term recipe for revival but exploiting political geographies in places where the party did well in the past and uniting these with new geographies represents the best chance of making notable gains.

The truth of the matter, however, is that the Liberal Democrats' long-term prospects may depend on a slow realignment of the party vision rather than short-term electoral contingency. The Liberal Democrats benefit from, and suffer from, asymmetry of support. This has profound effects on the party's ability to recruit and maintain members, supporters and voters. Evidence over the past quarter of a century shows that the Liberal Democrats tend to perform better electorally when the party is to the left of the political spectrum on social issues. We have seen that proclaiming official equidistance from the two main parties in Britain harms the Liberal Democrats' ability to attract conditional support from the Labour party in particular (in seats where Labour cannot beat the incumbent Conservatives). Being perceived as too close to the Conservatives from 2015 and 2019 significantly contributed to the Liberal Democrats' underperformance in those elections.

In contrast, being on the left of the spectrum might persuade Labour sympathisers to lend their vote to the Liberal Democrats to oust Conservative incumbents. This is especially pertinent in Blue Wall seats, where demographic changes are slowly eroding the natural advantage for the Conservatives. Again, though, this relies on the performance of other parties. A Labour party that is far to the left can dissuade many from voting for the Liberal Democrats either because the Liberal Democrats are not radical enough to approximate a real protest to Conservative dominance or because centre-right voters fear that voting Liberal Democrat could let in a far-left Labour government. On the other hand, there is a constituency of

'One Nation' Tories who might vote Liberal Democrat if neo-liberal dominance in Conservative ranks persists. In 2019 this might have represented a tangible target group of voters for the Liberal Democrats but their overemphasis on reversing Brexit and the effects of a Corbyn-led Labour party undermined their campaign.

Davey's cautious approach to party management benefited the Liberal Democrats in the death-knell of the Johnson premiership. However, when faced with the Truss interregnum and the Sunak inheritance, the Liberal Democrat leader needed to express a more compelling vision of Liberal Democrat politics. It is hardly surprising that in November 2022 this vision was set out asymmetrically. According to Davey, the governments of Truss and Sunak had exposed the Conservatives as 'incompetent and morally bankrupt' while the legacy of the Johnson era had meant that the British homeowners in particular could not trust the Tories again. As a formal political strategy it all looked very similar to the ending of equidistance under Ashdown.

The halfway house position of the Liberal Democrats allows them to borrow votes from the supporters of both main parties if they see the Liberal Democrats as an effective safe haven if their natural electoral choice is a hopeless cause in their constituency. Naturally, the Liberal Democrats have often benefited from the 'plague on both your houses' anti-politics protest vote. As we, and others, have shown, the Liberal Democrats were somewhat of a receptacle for protest votes from across the spectrum in many elections. The weakness of this position is obvious. Primarily, it reinforces the fundamental fragility of the party: that it is defined in relation to the two main parties in British politics. While not entirely dependent on the fortunes of others for all of their own support, the Liberal Democrats tend to exist within the parameters set by the other mainstream political parties. Moreover, the party's standing can be knocked off course by actions of their own making and by those of their opponents. In other words, structure and agency both matter a lot to Liberal Democrat fortunes, setting the parameters of relative success and failure. If the Liberal Democrats were to be successful enough to join the establishment, they would likely lose some of the protest vote as a direct consequence. We have shown that this did indeed happen to the Liberal Democrats after they entered coalition with the Conservatives. Some Labour supporters refused to vote again for a Liberal Democrat party that they blamed for enabling and then upholding a Conservative austerity regime. Some of the Liberal Democrat vote went straight to the SNP in Scotland and even UKIP benefited after the Liberal Democrats entered government. The plague now fell upon the Liberal Democrat house as much as the Conservative and Labour houses.

To illustrate this, let us consider the position that the Liberal Democrats found themselves occupying in the autumn of 2022. Under the leadership of Ed Davey, the party had made steady progress and had re-established itself as credible force in local and Westminster politics on the back of improved local election results and some spectacular by-election victories. However, the potential for Liberal Democrat recovery was still set in reference to the other parties. Firstly, the unpopularity of Boris Johnson as Prime Minister might have given an artificial boost to Liberal Democrat standing in the early months of 2022. As Johnson's government became mired in allegations of sleaze and poor judgement, Davey's Liberal Democrats offered a trustworthy and reliable alternative in many seats where Labour could not feasibly challenge the Tories. The party was boosted in these circumstances and this, in turn, increased the pressure on the Johnson government. In July 2022, the Conservatives bowed to the inevitable and Johnson was forced to resign from office by a spectacular set of resignations from his own team of personnel.

The Conservatives then spent an excruciating summer of navel-gazing and disaster management before the party at large chose Liz Truss over Rishi Sunak as the new party leader and Prime Minister in September 2022. As a result, the Liberal Democrats were pushed off the political agenda. The death of the monarch days after Truss's elevation again squeezed the Liberal Democrats out of the picture. The Truss premiership might have afforded the Conservatives the chance to rehabilitate their brand with the British electorate. This did not happen. The unprecedented turmoil caused by the party's 'fiscal event' – a mini-budget of such moment that it seemed to combine extremely poor economic and political judgement in equal measure. Of course, the mini-budget's devastating effect on the economy was mirrored in the state of the Tory party too, as first the Chancellor, Kwasi Kwarteng, was sacked by Truss and then Prime Minister Truss was forced to resign in record time. After 45 days (during which most government activity was suspended due to mourning for the sovereign) Truss was replaced by the man she beat in the leadership contest the previous summer. As the sole candidate, Sunak was acclaimed as party leader and Prime Minister without the inconvenience of another ballot of the Conservative party membership, but there was no rapid turnaround in Conservative fortunes. Nevertheless, the fact remains that the Conservatives might have recovered from the damage inflicted on their image by the Johnson regime at the expense of the Liberal Democrats, and Davey and his team would have been unable to do the slightest thing about it.

In fact, the failure of Truss and Sunak to re-catch the fire of the Tory brand caused another problem for the Liberal Democrats. It threatened to sanitise the Labour party and proved a significant boost to the credibility of its leader, Keir Starmer. Throughout the Johnson regime, Starmer had looked an uninspiring, almost wooden leader. His Labour party might have seemed less threatening to previous Conservative voters but this had actually worked to Liberal Democrat advantage in many ways. With the mini-budget furore and the subsequent bail-out of pension funds by the Bank of England at the end of September 2022, and with notably good press from a well-run party conference for once, the Labour party was starting to look like the government in waiting and Starmer the next Prime Minister. At the end of September 2022 a YouGov poll published for *The Times* gave Labour a 33 percentage point lead over the Conservatives – a lead not seen since the heyday of New Labour and the disaster of the UK's exit from the

European Exchange Rate Mechanism. It is worth noting that the Liberal Democrats were on 7 per cent of the reported vote intention in the same September 2022 poll. As a party the Liberal Democrats could be forgiven for thinking that they had seen this film before – as the New Labour machine, and the unstoppable advance of Tony Blair led Labour to victory in 1997 with such a sizeable majority that all the talk of the *Blair–Ashdown Project* and new settlement of British politics was largely rendered obsolete before it had even begun.

To reiterate, the challenge for the Liberal Democrats is that it is almost impossible to strike the right balance of risk and reward. To gain ground, they require the Conservatives to be unpopular, but they also require Labour to be less toxic to potential voters in order to promote defections of voters from the Tories to the Liberal Democrats; a classic scare tactic of 'Don't let Labour ruin it' can be an effective rallying call for the Conservatives. If the Labour detoxification is too successful, however, many voters might switch straight to them from the Conservatives without stopping off at the halfway house of the Liberal Democrats. Furthermore, if Labour were to believe that they could go onto achieve an electoral landslide of 1997 proportions many of their strategists who had been talking openly of cooperation with others as part of an anti-Conservative common cause could now be encouraged to go it alone. In other words the Liberal Democrats mostly need to exist in a zone where both Conservatives and Labour retain some loyalty and mutual loathing in order for them to thrive in the hinterland. Furthermore, such events are way outside of the control of the Liberal Democrats – whose fortunes continue to be defined by the main parties' actions rather than by their own.

Long-term and short-term goals

The Liberal Democrats need both long-term and short-term strategies to solve the problematic space that they have occupied since 2010. Long term, the party could look for incremental growth of representation in elected chambers. In the short term, gains might be made through electoral strategies such as targeting seats and carving out a clear negotiation strategy for possible coalitions.

Re-empowering the local

Throughout this book we have demonstrated how the Liberal Democrats' longstanding commitment to community politics and activism sets it apart from its opponents. It is simply what the party is about. From an electoral standpoint, the party's emphasis on the local has parachuted the Liberal Democrats to record seat levels when times were good and saved the party from near electoral extinction when times were bad. Like all parties, though, the Liberal Democrats have had to adapt to changing times. As we have shown in Chapter 9, sustaining a local profile is becoming increasingly difficult when facing richer rivals that not only copy what works but have the resources to innovate further.

To recapture the electoral success of the past requires the Liberal Democrats to rebuild a ground game that is the envy of their opponents. The Liberal Democrats, though, do face a dilemma. Building a dedicated local team that is willing to embrace the 'work all year round' philosophy and the community politics ethos is often the easy part, but ensuring that intensive campaigning is sustained across the course of an electoral cycle can be far more difficult in practice, even with the best will of activists. Even longstanding, well-resourced local Liberal Democrat parties struggle to achieve these objectives and can occasionally lapse outside of election time. For newer local parties built around a couple of dedicated individuals and/ or elected local councillors who end up taking all the strain of 'flying the flag' year in year out, a lack of capacity hinders growth and development. While these face-to-face personalised tools embody what the Liberal Democrats are about, they are also incredibly labour intensive. With the Liberal Democrats so reliant on this local presence, an inability to fulfil the tasks of contacting residents or leafleting four times a year can stunt growth.

One obvious answer to this dilemma is digital campaigning. In Chapter 9, we talked about how digital campaigning has not led to the level playing field many envisaged. Yet nationally the party has consistently punched above its weight, despite creativity and network capability problems. Of course, here we are primarily judging digital activity coordinated and operationalised from the centre. What about bottom-up digital campaigning? On the face of it, this seems to the logical evolution of the ground campaign and potentially provides a good fit with the Liberal Democrats' grassroots activism. Moreover, it has numerous benefits both during and outside an election campaign. If run creatively and operationalised effectively, a vibrant local digital presence can provide the en- trenched community focus equivalent to that of leaflets and other offline tools. While national headquarters can provide valuable support, it cannot provide the 'lived in' experience and local voice that emanates from the ground. Not only does a highly professional local digital presence complement existing per- sonalised tools by providing up-to-date local content, it can fly the flag of party activism and residents' campaigns on local issues, provide an interactive focal point for residents' concerns, act as a recruiting tool for candidates, activists and members, and deliver a space to tailor national messages to a local context. From an electoral standpoint, it can be a valuable source of data for the local party. During the election it can be the centrepiece of the local campaign – from presenting the local candidate to promoting party issue standpoints – and a forum through which a local party can reach out to a new audience and cement support from sympathisers. Given its ability to reach a wide audience, a strong digital presence has the potential to override offline access shortfalls and make up for few activists on the ground. Outside of the election campaign, a lively interactive digital presence allows the local party to retain its local voice and maintain contact with residents on a continuous basis. Just in the way offline activism nurtures support, a local digital presence can be a way in which the party builds and sustains a profile by trumpeting and constructing local empowerment on community issues.

This is hardly news to the Liberal Democrats. The national party has encouraged local digital activity, particularly in target seats, and has provided content, training, templates, links to Facebook groups, visual assets such as 'squeeze bar charts' and party logos and general expertise and knowledge exchange with local parties. Yet as we mentioned in Chapter 9, anecdotal evidence of a skills gap, haphazard local quality emanating from deficient training and a significant disconnect between the national and the local persists. More broadly, there is fairly consistent evidence from the surveys of electoral agents that Liberal Democrat e-campaign intensity at the constituency level tends to lag behind their main opponents. On the positive side, it is much higher in target seats than others and it remains the case that, at the grassroots level, none of the major parties are dominant. The potential for the Liberal Democrats to steal a march on their opponents and own the local digital arena remains open.

Buoyed by the role of digital campaigning in recent by-election successes and the implementation of internal digital innovations, it is clear that the new Liberal Democrat leadership team is embracing the online sphere to complement the existing offline tools and capabilities. Getting the right people trained in the right way is certainly a sizeable hurdle to overcome. Then the balance needs to be right between national oversight and local autonomy if the party is able to portray itself as the genuine local voice. Using a vibrant local digital presence across different social media platforms will allow the party to tap into local gatekeepers through which messages can be tailored and capacity can be built. The potential benefits of a highly networked profile will, over time, weaken credibility issues. However, this needs to be bottom up, to ensure authenticity and build local support. While target seats are already in receipt of national assistance (albeit their local digital presence and effectiveness do vary and invariably need upgrading) it is in places where the party is seeking to establish a presence and garner interest and support that such a strategy of re-empowering the local digital sphere could have the greatest short-term impact. More broadly, it could be the secret weapon to partially offset the structural hurdles against the party while simultaneously proving the antidote to the national campaigns and messaging which the Liberal Democrats struggle to compete against. Put simply, it would embolden the ethos of community-orientated politics and activism, and thereby re-establish the party's relevance as the one which gives the 'local' a voice.

A socially liberal party

Flirtations with economic liberalism have not been good for the party's fortunes. An electoral strategy as part of an anti-Conservative alliance could be a long-term winner and help set the party's sustainable identity in the minds of members and voters. One of the main themes of our analysis of the road to – and recovery from – the coalition years for the Liberal Democrats is that, politically, it seems that the party ought to be able to settle on its ideological identity fairly safely. The party's electoral fortunes have been better served by the Liberal Democrats pitching a socially liberal rather than an economically liberal stance. The party's growth from inception to the vote-share, seat-share record of 2005 demonstrated this and the post-2005 electoral retreat and the road to and back from coalition confirmed it. It is tempting to suggest that a distinctive electoral identity should focus on social liberal themes and distinctive policies. The evidence from the fallout of the scandal-ridden Johnson premiership and the economic mismanagement of its successors seems to suggest that the Liberal Democrats under Davey were keen to embrace this social liberal identity and move away from any form of equidistance. The party, however, is at the mercy of events and a massive rehabilitation of Labour could wipe out the marginal advantage that the Liberal Democrats might otherwise find on the back of Conservative failings.

Such a move, to a permanent socially liberal identity rather than an economically liberal profile might make sense electorally but it may also help the Liberal Democrats to push through in the medium to long term. The Liberal Democrats could use social liberalism as a motif through which they could influence and set the political agenda rather than being seen as a purely electoral machine.

Future-proofing the Liberal Democrats

In response to the existential crisis for the Liberal Democrats, the party needs to finally resolve what it is for. Put simply, it must decide on its own vision statement. Do the Liberal Democrats want to be a rational, standard, vote-maximising/seat-maximising electoral entity, or do they want to be part of a more fundamental movement challenging the way in which British politics is conducted?

For the former, the party may struggle to avoid the trapdoors and rabbit holes of placing too much emphasis on context-specific tactics and policies at the expense of long-term identity. We have argued that this was the case both in 2010, when the party allowed itself to be defined by a single policy on tuition fees that the party leadership knew was not sustainable, and in 2019, when the ownership of a particular policy (stopping Brexit) overestimated the potential for the party to cash in on transactional and conditional sympathy for the Liberal Democrat position.

For the latter, the Liberal Democrats will have to be more relaxed about ceding power and influence to others. The party could see its role as influencing the long-term direction of British politics without necessarily being the benefactors of such a change. The contemporary Liberal Democrats might benefit from owning the mainstream space on environmental policy, for instance, but a change in the electoral system (commonly thought to work to the favour of the Liberal Democrats) might actually allow the Greens more freedom to operate in a looser party system framework and challenge Liberal Democrat dominance of that space. Moreover, the Liberal Democrats might have to face up to the fate of many minor parties across Europe, namely, being the agenda-setters but not necessarily being the beneficiaries of political change. Policies and issues promoted by the Liberal Democrats could be appropriated by larger parties. The Liberal Democrats need to carve out an identity that not only manages to survive such appropriation but actually celebrates the ability of the party (either in or out of power) to influence the direction of British politics. The Liberal Democrats might be able to control the thermostat but still rely on mainstream parties to fire up the generator.

The Liberal Democrats as a movement?

One of the most curious features of researching the Liberal Democrats is that the more certain we become about the party's patterns of electoral support and sources of strength, the less definite we can be of the future direction of the party. This is the nub of the problem for the Liberal Democrats. They exist as a party but with weak organisational ties and low levels of automatic support. Their electoral appeal can be built on their campaigning strength – a local base, a proven record of breaching the credibility gap so that incumbent Liberal Democrat MPs often seem to stick around for longer than expected – but the party can also be blown off course by events outside of its control or by sea-change occurrences such as the 2010–2015 coalition or a change of leadership direction in other parties.

David Steel famously told the Liberal conference of 1979 that the Lib–Lab pact had shown the nation that a small number of MPs had influenced the political agenda to a greater extent than the numbers should have delivered. Strange as it might seem, it might be time to see the Liberal Democrats not so much as a vote-maximising electoral machine but as the driver of change in British politics, influencing the agenda of the country but not necessarily being the political party that benefits the most from the change.

As well as Steel's example of the Lib–Lab pact, we might agree with the assertion that Liberal Democrat by-election victories in Eastbourne in 1990 and the Ribble Valley in 1991 precipitated both the fall of Margaret Thatcher and the end of the poll tax, respectively (Rennard, 2018). Furthermore, it is possible to see that the coalition agreement of 2010 owed much to the vision of Liberal Democrat thinking, and set the course for the ways in which British politics was conducted for a sustained period of time. We might see a role for the Liberal Democrats in driving social change through a liberal agenda that is likely to be adopted and appropriated by the mainstream – and indeed more fringe – parties. A case in point here could be the role that the Liberal Democrats might play in the intersection between constitutional change and environmental politics.

The Liberal Democrats might be buoyed by the recent evidence from the British Social Attitudes survey of unprecedented support for a change to the electoral system, despite the heavy defeat of the 'alternative vote' option in the 2011 referendum. This chimes neatly with the familiar Liberal Democrat complaint about the inequity of the first-past-the-post system, but the Liberal Democrats should be reminded that electoral reform would increase the opportunities to vote for other parties too.

At the same time, the Liberal Democrats have been able to stake out some distinctive policy ownership on environmental protection. Ed Davey himself served as Secretary for State for Climate Change in the coalition government and arguably enabled the Liberal Democrats to set the agenda on issues such as renewable energy, increased carbon capture and energy efficiency and the strengthening of carbon trading requirements. As such, Liberal Democrat strategists might look at the prospect of a fairer voting system as an opportunity to further the party's ecological credentials and reputation. Nevertheless, the harsh truth might be that the very same delivery system for electoral reform might benefit parties other than the Liberal Democrats. The party that currently loses out to both Conservatives and Labour due to its geographically dispersed support and the 'wasted vote' syndrome might actually be better placed to cash in on tactical voting with first past the post than its smaller rivals. A change to the electoral system might benefit the Liberal Democrats generally but specifically fairer votes might benefit others more in the policy realm of environmental issues. The Liberal Democrats might be the driver of change in this and other areas but they might also need to be comfortable with not necessarily being the benefactors from the change they are able to engineer.

In conclusion, this book has shown that the Liberal Democrats are faced with a set of unique problems of structure and agency. The party is locked in place by its positioning in relation to other parties and is not the master of its own destiny. The Liberal Democrats face structural challenges as a third party in a system designed to sustain only two, and frequently gets shot from both sides if it is seen as the halfway house between left and right. Structurally, the party found the limits on its growth in the 2000s were set by the reality of national politics and organisationally the party was too weak institutionally to roll out a national identity. Political agency allowed the party to develop and prosper, culminating in its entry into government, albeit through coalition, in 2010 at the national level. Nevertheless, this was not the game changer that the Liberal Democrats might have hoped. In truth, the Liberal Democrats got the coalition wrong, were outplayed by their Conservative partners and party support suffered significantly in the aftermath.

The long road to recovery since the coalition for the Liberal Democrats has been painful and the future prospects for the party continue to be constrained by issues of structure and agency. The party's focus as an electoral entity helps to set the parameters for Liberal Democrat future success. Short-term fluctuations in the party's fortunes (often dependent on how the Conservative and Labour parties are performing) frame the frontiers for the party's future electoral performance. Nevertheless, the party should not be seen as a purely electoral machine and the long-term future of the Liberal Democrats might depend more on the party's ability to shape the direction of politics than on it being the partisan beneficiary of the agenda change. An elective professional political party with the outlook of a social movement; investing in the potential of technological innovation in local campaigning but running the risk of seeing those innovations appropriated by other parties; influencing the agenda but not necessarily being part of the government machine: this might be the fate of the party for many years to come. Indeed, it might be the lasting legacy of the party – the change agents rather than the electoral victors.

Appendix

Chapter 4

Table A4.1 Logistic regression model of voting Liberal Democrat in 2011 (vote intention): 2010 LD voters only

Variables	β	SE
Constant	−5.94*	0.58
LD switchers 2010: non-tactical voters	−1.49*	0.16
LD switchers 2010: tactical voters	−1.66*	0.28
Positive about the Coalition Government	−0.66*	0.10
Approve of European Union	0.19*	0.06
Approve public expenditure cuts	0.16*	0.07
Approve of tuition fees increase	0.08	0.07
Trust Nick Clegg	0.76*	0.06
Socio-demographics		
Male	−0.08	0.15
Own home	0.26	0.18
Professional and managerial class	−0.07	0.15
Non-white	0.13	0.33
Age	0.00	0.01
Model fit		
Wald (chi = <0.05)	399.84*	
Log likelihood	−827.38	
McFadden R^2	0.35	
AIC	1,680.77	
N	2,100	

*Significant $p<0.05$. Model uses 2011 AV referendum and BES Cross-sectional Pre–Post election survey – 2011 post-sample weight used.

Table A4.2 Linear regression model of change in the feelings towards the Liberal Democrats 2010–2011 (all voters)

Variables	β	SE
Constant	−0.22	0.15
Feelings towards the LDs 2010 (lag)	−0.51*	0.01
Authoritarian–libertarian (crime–rights)	0.05*	0.01
Economic left–right (tax–spend)	−0.06*	0.02
Approve of EU	0.19*	0.03
Tuition fees	0.44*	0.02
Fairer taxes	−0.13*	0.03
Trident renewal	−0.05*	0.02
LD strength of partisanship 2010 (base: not LD PID)		
LD PID: not very strongly	0.70*	0.15
LD PID: fairly strongly	0.85*	0.15
LD PID: very strongly	1.75*	0.35
Model fit		
F (P = <0.05)	201.06*	
R^2	0.27	
N	8,277	

*Significant p<0.05. Model uses 2011 AV referendum and BES Pre–Post election survey – 2011 post-sample weight used.

Table A4.3 Multinomial logistic regression of party vote intention, pooled January 2012 – December 2013 CMS (cumulative file)

Variables	Vote LD		Vote Cons		Vote Labour	
	β	SE	β	SE	β	SE
Constant	–3.14*	0.55	–3.98*	0.45	–3.95*	0.47
Government handled crisis well	0.18	0.11	0.66*	0.06	0.03	0.11
Subjective economic evaluation	–0.23*	0.04	–0.24*	0.03	0.04*	0.03
Party best on most important issue: Base: None						
Conservative	0.47*	0.12	1.43*	0.06	0.41*	0.13
Labour	0.70*	0.14	0.15	0.21	2.10*	0.07
Liberal Democrat	2.26*	0.14	0.31	0.27	0.75*	0.20
Other Most Important Issue	–0.91*	0.16	–0.69*	0.09	–0.19*	0.01
Leader						
Cameron	–0.05*	0.02	0.57*	0.02	0.57*	0.02
Miliband	–0.05*	0.02	–0.13*	0.02	0.42*	0.01
Clegg	0.53*	0.02	–0.01	0.01	–0.04*	0.02
Partisanship: Base = No party						
Conservative	–0.64*	0.15	1.85*	0.07	–0.24	0.13
Labour	0.09	0.15	–0.25	0.15	2.37*	0.07
Liberal Democrat	2.43*	0.10	–0.15	0.14	0.58*	0.10
Other	–0.12	0.15	–0.45*	0.12	–0.55*	0.10
Socio-demographics						
Male	0.31*	0.08	0.04	0.06	0.14*	0.06
Own home	0.10	0.10	0.15	0.08	–0.08	0.07
Married	–0.01	0.09	–0.04	0.06	0.21*	0.06
White British	0.12	0.13	0.15	0.10	–0.13	0.08
Age	–0.04*	0.02	–0.01	0.01	0.00	0.01
Age^2	0.01*	0.00	0.01*	0.00	0.00	0.00
In FT education	0.31	0.19	0.00	0.17	0.06	0.13
Working class	–0.28*	0.12	0.05	0.08	–0.18*	0.07
Unemployed	0.12	0.19	–0.15	0.17	–0.05	0.13
Income < £20,000	0.05	0.10	–0.12	0.08	–0.01	0.07
Scotland	–0.27	0.14	–0.29*	0.11	–0.27*	0.10
Wales	–0.45*	0.19	–0.11	0.13	0.19	0.12
Model fit						
Log likelihood	–11,665.54		–11,665.54		–11,665.54	
R^2	0.63		0.63		0.63	
AIC	23,487.08		23,487.08		23,487.08	
BIC	–39,226.74		–39,226.74		–39,226.74	
N	24,950		24,950		24,950	

*Significant *p*<0.05. Reference category is None, Don't Know and Other vote intention

Table A4.4 OLS regression model of feelings towards Clegg in 2015 general election (2010 Liberal Democrat voters only)

Variables	β	SE
Constant	4.52*	0.45
Parties deliver on promises	−1.22*	0.05
Difficult who to blame	0.05	0.05
Stay in the EU	0.60*	0.10
Left–right	0.10*	0.03
Tuition fees gone too far	−0.30*	0.06
National cuts gone too far	−0.20*	0.06
LDs best party on most important issue	1.26*	0.14
Subjective economic evaluation	0.07	0.05
National economic evaluation	0.12	0.07
Change in economy	0.41*	0.07
Partisanship: Base = No party		
Conservative	−0.07	0.17
Labour	−0.28*	0.12
Liberal Democrat	1.96*	0.11
UKIP	−0.88*	0.27
Green	−0.13	0.20
Other	−0.05	0.38
Socio-demographics		
Male	−0.53*	0.08
Own home	0.01	0.09
Married	0.06	0.09
Non-white	−0.27	0.26
Age 60 plus	0.06	0.09
Unemployed	−0.32	0.26
Degree or more	−0.09	0.09
Model fit		
F ratio	82.66*	
R^2	0.32	
N	3,603	

*Significant $p < 0.05$. Source: 2015 BEPS – 2015 w6 core weight used

Table A4.5 Logistic regression models of Liberal Democrat voting in 2015 general election

Variables	Model 1		Model 2	
	β	SE	β	SE
Constant	−5.76*	0.38	−5.56*	0.40
Liberal Democrat prior vote	−		2.34*	0.12
Parties deliver on promises	0.05	0.04	0.02	0.04
Authoritarian–libertarian	−0.04	0.06	−0.05	0.07
Redistribution (economic)	0.02	0.02	0.02	0.02
Stay in the EU	0.44*	0.09	0.31*	0.09
Left–right economic values	0.10	0.06	0.10	0.07
Tuition fees gone too far	−0.03	0.05	−0.03	0.05
National cuts gone too far	−0.10	0.05	−0.07	0.06
LDs best party on most important issue	1.47*	0.17	0.97*	0.21
Subjective economic evaluation	0.11*	0.05	0.09	0.05
Change in economy	0.06	0.04	0.05	0.05
LDs responsible for policy	0.10*	0.04	0.09*	0.04
Cameron	−0.08*	0.02	−0.08*	0.02
Miliband	−0.07*	0.02	−0.06*	0.02
Clegg	0.30*	0.02	0.28*	0.02
Likelihood of Lib Dems winning the seat	0.28*	0.01	0.23*	0.02
Tactical voting	0.95*	0.13	1.00*	0.14
Partisanship: Base = No party				
Conservative	−0.88*	0.13	−0.67*	0.13
Labour	−0.38*	0.12	−0.38*	0.12
Liberal Democrat	1.64*	0.11	0.98*	0.13
Socio-demographics				
Male	0.12	0.08	0.04	0.08
Own home	0.12	0.09	0.09	0.09
Non-white	−0.37	0.21	−0.47	0.24
Age	0.01*	0.00	0.01*	0.00
Degree (or more)	0.31*	0.08	0.30*	0.09
Scotland	0.01	0.11	0.05	0.12
Wales	−0.18	0.14	−0.08	0.15
Model fit				
Wald chi-square <0.05	1,901.40*		1,977.52*	
Log likelihood	−2,696.86		−2,448.18	
R^2	0.38		0.43	
AIC (used by Stata)	5,447.71		4,952.36	
BIC (used by Stata)	5,653.78		5,166.05	
N	15,244		15,244	

*Significant p<0.05. Model 1 and 2 weighted using w6 core weight. Source: 2015 BEPS

Chapter 5

Table A5.1 The 'short' campaign: logistic regression of Liberal Democrat support in the 2015 general election (Liberal Democrat–Conservative battlegrounds only)

Variables	β	SE	AMEs
Constant	−1.88	1.07	–
Prior Intention to Vote LD	3.15*	0.33	0.26*
Campaigning			
Liberal Democrat	0.46	0.34	–
Conservative	−1.04*	0.33	−0.09*
Labour	−0.02	0.30	–
UKIP	0.10	0.30	–
Party identification			
Liberal Democrat	1.47*	0.38	0.12*
Conservative	−1.04*	0.41	−0.09*
Labour	−0.89*	0.36	−0.07*
UKIP	−2.23*	1.09	−0.19*
Party Leader			
Clegg	0.25*	0.05	0.02*
Cameron	−0.06	0.06	–
Miliband	0.01	0.05	–
Farage	−0.20*	0.05	−0.02*
Political Attitudes			
Left–Right	0.01	0.08	–
Coalition Difficult to Deliver	−0.13	0.12	–
Immigration Most Important Issue	−0.01	0.41	–
Cuts Gone too far	−0.00	0.16	–
Tuition Fees Gone too far	−0.12	0.17	–
Stay in the EU	−0.19	0.28	–
Tactical Decision			
Tactical Voting	3.10*	0.32	0.26*
Socio-economic			
Female	0.39	0.24	–
Age	0.02*	0.01	
UG/PG degree	0.16	0.25	–
Non-white	0.05	0.71	–
Model fit			
Chi square <0.05	313.32*		
Log likelihood	−417.60		
R^2	0.57		
AIC	885.20		
N	1,346		

*Significant p<0.05. Weighted using (combined W4 and W6 weight) Voters only

Chapter 7

Table A7.1 Logistic regression models of 2010 Liberal Democrat voters who supported Labour in the 2017 general election

Variables	Model 1		Model 2	
	β	SE	β	SE
Constant	0.84*	0.31	−2.22*	0.35
Redistribution (economic)	−0.10*	0.02	−0.03	0.02
Left–right political values	−0.43*	0.03	−0.18*	0.03
Tuition fees gone too far	0.33*	0.05	0.09	0.06
Anti-austerity factor	0.31*	0.05	0.24*	0.06
Subjective economic evaluations	−0.07	0.05	−0.00	0.05
Like Corbyn	–		0.45*	0.02
Voted Remain	–		−0.12	0.10
Model fit				
Wald chi-square <0.05	709.15		1,039.80*	
Log likelihood	−2,145.31		−1,682.70	
R^2	0.18		0.32	
AIC	4,302.63		3,381.39	
BIC	4,341.72		3,433.31	
N	4,991		4,866	

* = Significant p<0.05 – w13 new weight

Table A7.2 Logistic regression models of 2015 Liberal Democrat voters who supported Labour in the 2017 general election

Variables	β	SE
Constant	−3.26*	0.64
Redistribution (economic)	−0.01	0.04
Left–right political values	−0.13*	0.05
Increases in tuition fees gone too far	0.12	0.11
Anti-austerity factor	0.22*	0.10
Subjective economic evaluations	0.07	0.09
Like Corbyn	0.43*	0.04
Voted Remain	−0.26	0.17
Model fit		
Wald chi-square <0.05	294.25*	
Log likelihood	−643.10	
R^2	0.24	
AIC	1,302.20	
BIC	1,346.56	
N	1,892	

* = Significant p<0.05 – w13 new weight

Table A7.3 Multinomial logistic regression on those who switched from Liberal Democrat in 2017 to the Conservatives or Labour in 2019

Variables	LD17 to Cons19		LD17 to Lab19	
	β	SE	β	SE
Constant	−2.69	1.47	−1.32	1.34
Authoritarian–libertarian	0.06	0.10	0.06	0.09
Left–right (economic)	−0.20*	0.08	−0.08	0.09
Revoke (cancel Brexit)	0.38	0.42	0.79*	0.39
Like Swinson	−0.18*	0.08	−0.12*	0.06
Like Johnson	0.37*	0.07	−0.21*	0.08
Like Corbyn	−0.06	0.10	0.15*	0.06
Liberal Democrat partisanship	−0.68	0.50	−0.62	0.37
LD likelihood of winning seat	−0.12	0.07	−0.21*	0.07
Wasted vote	0.15	0.17	0.28	0.18
Female	0.35	0.31	0.01	0.33
Age	0.02	0.02	−0.01	0.01
Degree	0.33	0.41	−0.17	0.35
Social grade (class)	−0.13	0.12	0.08	0.12
Full-time employment	0.27	0.44	−2.75*	0.27
Model fit				
Log likelihood	−1,124.66			
R^2	0.28			
AIC	2,369.33			
BIC	−5,046.53			
N	6,107			

*= Significant $p<0.05$. Model base category = voted Liberal Democrat in 2015 and 2017. Coefficients for All other voters; LD switch to Other Parties are not shown.

Table A7.4 Logistic regression of voting Conservative in 2019 (2016 Remain voters only)

Variables	β	SE
Constant	−2.95*	0.46
Redistribution (Economic)	0.07*	0.03
Left–right political values	0.17*	0.05
National economic evaluations	0.18*	0.07
Revoke (cancel Brexit)	−0.76*	0.16
LD likelihood of winning seat	−0.15*	0.02
Like Swinson	−0.23*	0.03
Like Corbyn	−0.30*	0.03
Like Johnson	0.53*	0.03
Party best on most important issue (base: none)		
Conservative	1.03*	0.13
Labour	−1.24*	0.43
Liberal Democrat	−1.67*	0.55
Partisanship (Base = No/DK partisanship)		
Conservative	0.65*	0.16
Labour	−1.03*	0.19
Liberal Democrat	−0.60*	0.19
Nationalist	−4.04*	0.86
Green	−2.60*	0.50
Other	−0.05	0.70
Socio-economic variables		
Female	0.29*	0.12
Degree	0.13	0.13
Social Class	−0.09*	0.04
Age	−0.00	0.00
Model fit		
Wald chi-square <0.05	1,444.20	
Log likelihood	−1,170.64	
R^2	0.71	
AIC	2,385.27	
BIC	2,544.79	
N	10,414	

* = Significant p<0.05 – w19 new weight.

Notes

Introduction

1   Russell and Fieldhouse (2005). Other exceptions to this gap in the literature include Cyr (1977), Bogdanor (1983), Crewe and King (1995) and MacIver (1996). Others have focused on a particular aspect of party politics – these include: Whiteley *et al.* (2006), Evans (2011), Pack and Maxfield (2012) and Brack *et al.* (2015).

Chapter 1

1   At their 2002 party conference, the Liberal Democrats passed a resolution outlining certain conditions that had to be met for the party to support the war. Such reservations were reiterated by the party's Federal Executive four months later. The Liberal Democrats therefore did not unconditionally oppose the war. When party leader Charles Kennedy spoke at the 'Stop the War' rally, he was speaking in a personal capacity.

2   See the 2003 Stop the War rally video at https://www.theguardian.com/politics/video/2015/jun/02/charles-kennedy-speaks-2003-stop-the-war-rally-video.

3   A YouGov poll (19 April 2010) in the days following the first leaders' debate found 27 per cent of respondents chose Clegg as the 'best Prime Minister', compared with 28 per cent for Cameron and 23 per cent for Brown. Towards the end of the campaign (YouGov Poll 3 May 2010) support for Clegg had fallen to 22 per cent but this is still extremely high for Liberal Democrat leaders.

4   See https://youtu.be/wEYMIagoGgm (0:38-48 s).

5   The key correlations are as follows: voting for the Liberal Democrats in 2005 and percentage working in education = 0.31**, and percentage students = 0.18**; voting for the Liberal Democrats in 2010 and percentage working in education = 0.31**, and percentage students = 0.17**; switching vote to the Liberal Democrats from 2001 to 2005 and percentage working in education = 0.17**, and percentage students = 0.30**; switching vote to the Liberal Democrats from 2005 to 20010 and percentage working in education = 0.01, and percentage students = −0.02.

6   We use the 2005 BES pre-campaign/post-election panel and for 2010 we use the BES rolling campaign panel (pre and post) because it contains the four policy stances on taxation and the question on Trident renewal.

7   The 'fairer taxes' variable is derived from a principal components analysis. From the three variables, one factor was extracted using orthogonal rotation (eigenvalue 1.36 with 45.3 per cent of the variance explained). Scores for the factor were: tax threshold = 0.69; mansion tax = 0.75 and tax relief on pensions = 0.57.

8   For a more detailed account, see Pack (2014), who examines the evolution of Liberal Democrat campaigning over time and provides a critical assessment of the Rennard strategy.

9   The survey of electoral agents contains cross-sectional data on local constituency

campaigning from the 1992 election onwards and is used to measure and assess the changing character of local campaigns on turnout and party choice (Denver and Hands, 1997; Fisher and Denver, 2008).

10   Much of the information presented here stems from an interview with Chris Fox on 26 May 2010. We wish to thank Chris Fox for his assistance and time.

Chapter 2

1   Panel data are more reliable because they are less reliant on respondents remembering how they voted at the prior election, because responses are collected in the immediate aftermath of that election.

2   Using the 2010 rolling panel, the Liberal Democrat recruitment in all 57 seats was as follows: Liberal Democrats 62 per cent; Labour 21 per cent; Conservatives 6 per cent; other 6 per cent; did not vote 6 per cent. In the Liberal Democrat–Conservative held seats in the south-west region: Liberal Democrats 64 per cent; Labour 22 per cent; Conservatives 6 per cent; other 2 per cent; did not vote 6 per cent.

3   In order to capture tactical voting, we combine those who said they were tactical voters with those who said the party they really preferred could not win.

4   These seats were: Camborne and Redruth, Cornwall South East, Harrogate and Knaresborough, Hereford and Herefordshire, Montgomeryshire, Newton Abbot, Oxford West and Abingdon, Richmond Park, Romsey and Southampton North, Truro and Falmouth, Winchester, and York Outer.

Chapter 4

1   The Continuous Monitoring Survey (CMS) was conducted from July 2008 to December 2012 with the goal of tracking trends in public opinion and voting. It was the third element of the 2010 BES and was latterly used to examine shifts in opinion preceding and after the May 2011 AV referendum. The AV referendum survey was therefore a part of the CMS which in turn was a component of the 2010 BES study. Full details of the study design can be found in Whiteley et al. (2013: 284–285).

2   Fieldhouse et al. (2021) run a similar model examining the change in feelings between 2010 and 2015 and combining 2010 and 2015 predictors. Our model focuses on the first year of coalition and contains the same respondents in both the 2010 BES and 2011 AV referendum datasets. This enables us to include variables that reflect Liberal Democrat policy positions in 2010 – Trident renewal, the mansion tax, tuition fees, eco taxes – so that we can capture changes in feelings on these redistribution measures, left-leaning policies (Trident) alongside traditional economic left–right and authoritarian–libertarian scales. We can also establish whether the patterns shown by Fieldhouse et al. (2021) were evident during the early days of the coalition which has obvious implications for other explanations of Liberal Democrat decline.

3   All the BES data are weighted using the 'w6core' weight. The BES team defined a smaller core sample, of around 21,000 respondents in each wave, that established a cross-sectional group which is more representative than the full sample. They recommend using this core sample for cross-sectional work. Here we are examining the 2015 vote from the wave 6 (general election) cross-section and using a variable that records their 2010 vote based on previous responses. We use this w6core weight for all our cross-sectional analysis when using the panel data in this chapter.

Chapter 5

1   For the 2015 general election (on 7 May), the 'official' campaign or 'regulation period' began on 19 December 2014. From this date, candidates' spending was subject to legal limits. From 19 December 2014 to the dissolution of parliament is known as the 'long campaign'. The period from 30 March 2015 to polling day is known as the 'short campaign'. Before 19 December 2014, candidates' spending was not limited (the 'non-regulatory period').

2   The 2015 local elections occurred on the same day as the general election. The Liberal Democrats lost around 400 seats, leaving them with 1,808 council seats (8.9 per cent seat share) compared with 3,940 (19 per cent seat share) in 2010.

3   These 37 Liberal Democrat–Conservative seats do not include Eastleigh, where UKIP came second in the 2013 by-election and demoted the Conservatives to third place.

4   Three of these 14 seats are in Cornwall, where independents have a strong record of standing and winning, which slightly skews the drop in the Liberal Democrat local base across the south-west of England. If these Cornish seats held by the Liberal Democrats are excluded, the overall drop in the party's local base across the remaining 11 seats is still only 5.8 per cent.

5   Data from the two surveys are commonly reported separately, even if they are from different constituencies. In actual fact, the trends in the various aspects of campaign preparation and organisation recorded in the agent survey mirror those reported in the main body of the text for directly comparable seats: election address prepared, 39 per cent (2010), 29 per cent (2015); electoral register 70 per cent (2010), 58 per cent (2015); building a database 57 per cent (2010), 47 per cent (2015); identifying supporters by canvassing 57 per cent (2010), 47 per cent (2015); street stalls (pre-election) 33 per cent (2010), 25 per cent (2015); resident surveys (pre-election) 71 per cent (2010), 54 per cent (2015).

6   Here we combine non-held marginal seats (less than a 10 per cent majority) and held seats in the sample. The sample sizes in 2010 and 2015 are 27 and 28 seats respectively.

7   These are the same factors (derived from the same socio-economic variables) as we used in Chapter 2, where full details of how the models were constructed are given.

8   The Liberal Democrats performed better against both their rivals where it had a stronger local presence: bivariate relationship (–0.03* in the Con–LD model; –0.05* in the Lab–LD model). When accounting for prior vote but excluding other variables (–0.02* in the Con–LD model; –0.02* in the Lab–LD model).

9   We ran a simple OLS model of 2015 Liberal Democrat vote share which included this 'local council decline' variable, party incumbency, campaigning and previous Liberal Democrat vote share. The coefficient was –0.79 with a standard error of 0.30 and was significant at the 5% level.

10 These seats were Carshalton and Wallington, Ceredigion, Leeds North West, Sheffield Hallam, and Westmorland and Lonsdale. Orkney and Shetland, Norfolk North and Southport had not selected at this point.

11 We exclude non-voters from the analyses of voter choice and examine only those respondents with a validated vote. We ran the same models including non-voters (where non-voters were a category in a multinomial logistic model) and there were no substantial differences in the findings.

12 Across all 57 incumbent seats, the probability of voting Liberal Democrat if electors were contacted by the party during the 'short' campaign is six percentage points higher than for those not contacted. This implies that during the short campaign the Liberal Democrats were more successful in shoring up party support in Scotland and where it was fighting Labour rather than the Conservatives.

Chapter 6

1 These included: the former Liberal Democrat seats of Richmond Park, St Ives, Cheltenham, North Devon and Cheadle (lost to the Conservatives); Sheffield Hallam and Leeds North West (lost to Labour); Ceredigion (lost to Plaid Cymru); and North East Fife (lost to the SNP).

2 Cable revealed in his political memoir *Partnership and Politics in a Divided Decade* that he had suffered a mini-stroke while leader, which had severely affected his ability to deliver speeches in parliament and other political events (such as this 2018 conference speech).

3 In 2019, the Liberal Democrats stood in 611 seats. It stood aside in 17 seats as part of the Unite to Remain pact with Plaid Cymru and the Greens, as well as Beaconsfield, Broxtowe and Luton South. It also did not stand in the Speaker's seat (Chorley).

Chapter 7

1 In the 2015–2017 BEPS, the redistribution variable runs from 0 to 10, where 0 = Government should try to make incomes equal; 10 = Government should be less concerned about equal incomes. The findings from the linear regressions are as follows: in 2015, $\beta = 0.06$ (0.01), which is significant at the 5% level. Two years later, $\beta = -0.121$ (0.01), also significant at the 5% level.

2 In the 2015–2017 BEPS, the national security variable runs from 0 to 10, where 0 = Fight terrorism; 10 = Protect civil liberties. The findings from the linear regressions are as follows: in 2015, $\beta = 0.02$ (0.02), two years later, $\beta = 0.188$ (0.01), both significant at the 5% level.

3 To examine views on austerity we combined responses to whether cuts in national spending, local services and the NHS had gone too far. We ran a factor analysis and obtained one factor (C1 = 2.02; initial eigenvalue 67.33 per cent of the variance) with the following loadings: National cuts 0.85; Local cuts 0.85; NHS cuts 0.79.

4 We use perceived likelihood of a party winning the seat from the pre-election campaign wave. Given that support for Labour got stronger throughout the campaign, it is probable that respondents' expectations would have increased as polling day grew closer. Similarly, respondent-perceived likelihood of the Liberal Democrats winning in these Remain seats would presumably have decreased as expectations of Labour being successful increased.

5 The exact figure (24 per cent) is obtained when the data are weighted using the new wave-13 weight. The unweighted figure is 15.4 per cent, which compares with 4 per cent for both May and Corbyn.

6 From April to June 2016 (post-EU referendum wave), Cameron's mean likability rating rose from 3.5 to 3.9, while Corbyn's declined from 3.9 to 3.4. Farron remained consistent at 3.7. In wave 10 (November 2016), May recorded a 4.9 mean likeability rating, compared with 3.5 for Corbyn and 3.7 for Farron. Over the 2017 election campaign, May's mean likeability fell from 5.0 to 3.9, while Corbyn's rose from 3.5 to 4.6. Farron's mean likeability rating fell from 3.5 to 3.4.

7 All data are weighted using wave-17 and wave-19 weights.

8 Deltapoll (www.deltapoll.co.uk/wp-content/uploads/2019/12/Deltapoll-MOS191207.pdf) found that only 22 per cent of women felt that Swinson was doing well at her job, compared with 28 per cent of men. Similar numbers were recorded for both men and women regarding those who said Swinson was doing badly (Deltapoll, 5–7 December 2019). Of course, this is only a snapshot and the linear model reported in the text suggests women became less favourable over the course of the campaign.

9   We use cross-sectional weights to derive these figures. The unweighted figures show a slow decline from March to early November (27 per cent to 25 per cent) and then a steep fall during the campaign period (25 per cent to 12 per cent).

10 Support for a referendum on a deal remained stable, while support for leaving with a deal with no referendum (Johnson's policy) climbed by eight percentage points. Support for leaving without a deal also dropped by four points (from 21 to 17 per cent) over the campaign. All data are weighted using the panel weight wave 17 – wave 19.

11 We did not use the BEPS 'anti-austerity sentiments' to assess 2019 Liberal Democrat/ Swinson performance because the questions were asked of only on a sub-sample of the BEPS respondents and the smaller number would have compromised statistical power. The austerity measure instead used in the model is a factor representing three variables – National/Local/NHS cuts on a 1–5-point Likert scale, from 'not gone far enough' (1) to 'gone too far' (5). These three variables loaded on one factor – National cuts 0.89; Local cuts 0.88; NHS cuts 0.85 – with an eigenvalue of 2.28 and explaining 76.1 per cent of the variance.

12 For brevity, the equivalent model for the whole of the BEPS sample (wave 19) did show a positive relationship between austerity cuts and supporting Labour (0.28, SE 0.15) but this was not significant at the 5 per cent level. In the model (with variables equivalent to those in Table 7.3), excluding those who voted Liberal Democrat in 2010, there is clearly no significant relationship between austerity and voting Labour in 2019 (0.21, SE 0.18).

Chapter 8

1   Across the south of England, Liberal Democrat vote share increased from 9.9 per cent in 2015 to 10.5 per cent in 2017 and to 16.5 per cent in 2019.

2   In 2015, incumbents in Inverness, Badenoch and Strathspey, Argyll and Bute, and Caithness and Sutherland all recorded single-digit drops in support. However, in West Aberdeenshire, and Ross, Skye and Lochaber support ebbed away at levels above the UK national average. Christine Jardine (Gordon) bucked the incumbency trend as party support dropped by only 3.3 points.

3   In 2017, the Liberal Democrats were relegated to fourth place in Inverness, Berwickshire, Roxburgh and Selkirk, and West Aberdeenshire, while in Ross, Skye and Lochaber, and Gordon the party trailed in third, behind the SNP and Conservatives.

4   Sometimes local government boundaries do not correspond with constituency boundaries, making such estimations less reliable. Since the local electoral cycle is four-yearly, there is only ever partial congruence with the parliamentary cycle, so a number of constituencies did not have local elections. Baston and Thévoz (2015) provide a far more comprehensive analysis than we do here. Our findings generally concur but there are some slight differences given the problems of dealing with multi-member wards, incomplete local party slates and so on. Go to www.socialliberal.net/lib_dem_seats_ in_2010_5_where_did_the_votes_go_part_2_of_2 for their findings.

5   There is 0.33 correlation between per cent degree and per cent working in education, compared with 0.49 between per cent full-time students and per cent working in education. Here, the latter is used to define a 'university' seat.

6   The 26 seats (under 2019 electoral boundaries) are: Buckingham, Chelsea and Fulham, Chesham and Amersham, Cities of London and Westminster, Epsom and Ewell, Esher and Walton, Finchley, Golders Green, Henley, Hitchin and Harpenden, Islington North, Islington South and Finsbury, Kenilworth and Southam, Maidenhead, Mole Valley, North East Hampshire, South Cambridgeshire, South East Cambridgeshire, South West Surrey, Streatham, Tunbridge Wells, Vauxhall, Wantage, Wimbledon, Windsor, Woking and Wokingham.

7   It is worth noting that the Liberal Democrats were less than 20 percentage points behind the incumbent in Kensington and around this figure in Ceredigion but in both cases came third in 2019.

8   Only two of the 'Red Wall' seats (Redcar and Leigh) that Labour lost to the Conservatives had a 2017 majority of more than 20 per cent. In 2015, the Liberal Democrats lost six of the 12 seats where they had majorities of 20 per cent or more: Bath, Bristol West, North East Fife, Ross, Skye and Lochaber, Twickenham, and Yeovil.

9   These 'Blue Wall' seats match the YouGov classification but are different from Steve Akehurst's (2021) classification (Wantage and South East Cambridgeshire are not included).

10 Classifying seats always come with some caveats. Of the seven 'non-Blue Wall' seats won post 1997, Cheadle is the closest to being regarded as either a 'traditional' or a 'breakthrough' seat. Not only did the party win it in 2001 but it has had the most consistent Liberal vote over time, with the party actually winning the seat in 1966.

Chapter 9

1   The Traditionalism index includes the following variables: Number of regional or national leaflets delivered; Number of local leaflets delivered; Percentage of electorate canvassed on the doorstep; Number of campaign workers; Number of polling-day workers; 'Good Morning' leaflets delivered; 'Knock-up' voters on polling day; Proportion of electorate covered. The Face to Face index includes the following variables: Pre-election doorstep canvassing; Pre-election campaign street stalls; Pre-election campaign resident surveys; Percentage of electorate doorstep canvassed; Campaign effort – canvassing to identify supporters; Campaign effort – canvassing to introduce candidate; Number of campaign workers; Voters 'knocked up' on polling day; Number of campaign helpers on polling day.

2   The polling-day index includes the following variables: 'Good Morning' leaflets delivered; 'Knock-up' voters on polling day; Proportion of the constituency covered on polling day; Number of campaign helpers; Number of volunteers sent to the constituency.

3   This adjustment involves multiplying the factor score by 33.3 and then adding 100.

4   A detailed version of this study is published in Political Science and Methods (Townsley, 2018).

5   Some minimal spillover between postal voters and non-postal voters in the households that contained both could not be ruled out. Those households that contained a mixture of postal voters and non-postal voters were assigned to the postal voter experiment. All households in the non-postal voter experiment contained non-postal voters only, and most participants (76 per cent) in the postal voter households were postal voters.

6   In total, 1,012 of the 1,325 voters in the postal voter experiment were registered postal voters (396 of the 515 in the canvass group; 410 of the 541 in the leaflet group; and 206 of the 269 in the control group).

7   We report the 'complier average causal effect' (CACE) estimator to account for one-sided non-compliance in the canvass treatment group. We follow the procedure laid out in Gerber and Green (2012). Across the pooled groups, the CACE is 6.2 percentage points, with a 95 per cent confidence interval (95% CI) of –8.2 to 20.6. Among postal voter households, the CACE is 16 points, with a 95% CI of –10.4 to 42.5. Among non-postal voter households, the CACE is 2.3 points, with a 95% CI of –15.1 to 19.7. The low contact rate (28 per cent) alongside the sample size contributes to the uncertainty surrounding the CACE of the canvass treatment. Therefore, reliable inferences of the

additional effect of canvassing cannot be made because of the lack of statistical power, which is reflected in the lack of statistical significance of the effects.

8 We can interpret the findings as a ceiling effect in the mobilisation effect of contact among postal voters, given they had turnout rates of 70–85 per cent in Britain. In this experiment, the turnout of individuals living in households containing postal voters was similarly high. Given this, it follows that any mobilising effects that might come from additional campaign contact would meet a ceiling.

9 Facebook/Meta remains the go-to channel not just in the UK but across the world. And with the implementation of the General Data Protection Regulation (GDPR) it is even more important in the UK than in North American countries.

10 This was validated by positive industry press at the time, the Facebook Ads Library data, and the party's own post-election review.

References

Adams, James, Jane Green and Caitlin Milazzo (2012) 'Has the British public depolarized along with political elites? An American perspective on British public opinion', *Comparative Political Studies* 45(4): 507–530.

Adams, James and Samuel Merrill (2006) 'Why small, centrist third parties motivate policy divergence by major parties', *American Political Science Review* 100(3): 403–417.

Adams, James, Samuel Merrill and Bernard Grofman (2005) *A Unified Theory of Party Competition*, New York: Cambridge University Press.

Akehurst, Steve (2021) '"The Blue Wall" or the Great aWoking-ing and the swing seat we're not talking about', Strong Message Here, https://strongmessagehere.substack.com/p/the-blue-wall (accessed 20 March 2022).

Ashcroft, Michael (2013) 'What are the Liberal Democrats for?', Lord Ashcroft Polls, https://lordashcroftpolls.com/wp-content/uploads/2013/03/LibDem_Poll.pdf (accessed 5 August 2017).

Ashdown, Paddy (1989) *Citizens' Britain: A Radical Agenda for the 1990s*, London: Fourth Estate.

Axelrod, Robert (1970) *Conflict of Interest*, Chicago: Markham.

Bale, Tim (2010) *The Conservative Party from Thatcher to Cameron*, London: Polity.

Bale, Tim (2011) 'I don't agree with Nick: retrodicting the Conservative–Liberal Democrat coalition', *Political Quarterly* 82(2): 244–250.

Bale, Tim (2012) 'The black widow effect: why Britain's Conservative–Liberal Democrat coalition might have an unhappy ending', *Parliamentary Affairs* 65: 323–337.

Bara, Judith (2006) 'The 2005 manifestos: a sense of déjà vu?', *Journal of Elections, Public Opinion and Parties* 16(3): 265–281.

Bartels, Larry (2002) 'Beyond the running tally: partisan bias in political perceptions', *Political Behavior* 24(2): 117–150.

Barton, Jared, Marco Castillo and Ragan Petrie (2013) 'What persuades voters? A field experiment on political campaigning', *Economic Journal* 124: 293–326.

Baston, Lewis and Seth Thévoz (2015) 'Lib Dem seats in 2010–5: where did the votes go (Part 2 of 2)?', Social Liberal Forum, https://www.socialliberal.net/lib_dem_seats_in_2010_5_where_did_the_votes_go_part_2_of_2 (accessed 4 May 2017).

BBC News (2011) 'AV referendum: Ashdown attacks Tory "breach of faith"', https://www.bbc.co.uk/news/uk-politics-13303862 (accessed 7 August 2017).

BBC News (2013) 'Vince Cable attacks "ugly" Conservative politics', https://www.bbc.co.uk/news/uk-politics-24103857 (accessed 15 July 2017).

BBC News (2019) 'Sir Vince Cable to quit as Lib Dem leader in May', https://www.bbc.co.uk/news/uk-politics-47577739 (accessed 23 August 2020).

Beech, Matt (2011) 'A tale of two liberalisms', in Steve Lee and Matt Beech (eds), *The Cameron–Clegg Government: Coalition Politics in an Age of Austerity* (pp. 267–279), Basingstoke: Palgrave Macmillan.

Bennett, Asa (2014) 'Barely anyone knows what the Liberal Democrats' policies are', Huffington Post, https://www.huffingtonpost.co.uk/2014/10/13/libdems-nick-clegg-policies_n_5976254.html (accessed 14 August 2017).

Bhatti, Yosef, Jens Dahlgaard, Jonas Hedegaard and Kasper Hansen (2016) 'Is door-to-door canvassing effective in Europe? Evidence from a meta-study across six European countries', *British Journal of Political Science* 49(1): 279–290.

Blagden, James and Will Tanner (2022) 'Another brick in the wall: where is the battle-ground at the next election?', Onward, https://www.ukonward.com/wp-content/uploads/2022/02/blue-wall.pdf (accessed 5 August 2022).

Bogdanor, Vernon (1983) *Liberal Party Politics*, Oxford: Oxford University Press.

Brack, Duncan, Richard Grayson and David Howarth (2007) *Reinventing the State: Social Liberalism for the 21st Century*, London: Politicos.

Brack, Duncan, Robert Ingham and Tony Little (2015) *British Liberal Leaders*, London: Biteback.

Browne, Eric and Mark Franklin (1973) 'Aspects of coalition payoffs in European parliamentary democracies', *American Political Science Review* 67(2): 453–469.

Buelens, Jo and Airo Hino (2008) 'The electoral fate of new parties in government', in Kris Deschouwer (ed.), *New Parties in Government: In Power for the First Time* (pp. 157–174), London: Routledge Taylor and Francis.

Callander, Stephen and Catherine H. Wilson (2007) 'Turnout, polarization, and Duverger's law', *Journal of Politics* 69(4): 1047–1056.

Campbell, Angus, Phillip E. Converse, Warren E. Miller and Donald E. Stokes (1960) *The American Voter*, London: Wiley.

Channel 4 News (2014) 'Nick Clegg: Osborne's cuts to welfare a "monumental mistake"', https://www.channel4.com/news/george-osborne-budget-economy-2014-hard-truths-video (accessed 17 July 2017).

Clarke, Harold, Matthew Goodwin and Paul Whiteley (2017) *Brexit: Why People Voted to Leave the European Union*, Cambridge: Cambridge University Press.

Clarke, Harold, David Sanders, Marianne Stewart and Paul Whiteley (2004) *Political Choice in Britain*, Oxford: Oxford University Press.

Clarke, Harold, David Sanders, Marianne Stewart and Paul Whiteley (2009) *Performance Politics and the British Voter*, Cambridge: Cambridge University Press.

Clegg, Nick (2016) *Politics: Between the Extremes*, London: Bodley Head.

Copus, Colin (2007) 'Liberal Democrat councillors: community politics, local campaigning and the role of the political party', *Political Quarterly* 78(1): 128–138.

Crewe, Ivor (1985) 'Great Britain', in Ivor Crewe and David Denver (eds), *Electoral Change in Western Democracies: Patterns and Sources of Electoral Volatility* (pp. 100–150), London: Croom Helm.

Crewe, Ivor and Anthony King (1995) *The Birth, Life and Death of the Social Democratic Party*, Oxford: Oxford University Press.

Curtice, John (1996) 'Who votes for the centre now?', in Don MacIver (ed.), *The Liberal Democrats* (pp. 191–204), Hemel Hempstead: Harvester Wheatsheaf.

Curtice, John (2021) 'Is there a Conservative "blue wall"?', *Progressive Review* 28(2): 194–203.

Cutts, David (2006a) 'Continuous activism and electoral outcomes: the Liberal Democrats in Bath', *Political Geography* 25: 72–88.

Cutts, David (2006b) '"Where we work we win": a case study of Liberal Democrat local campaigning', *Journal of Elections, Public Opinion and Parties* 16: 221–242.

Cutts, David (2014) '"Local elections as a stepping stone": does winning council seats boost the Liberal Democrats' performance in general elections?', *Political Studies* 62(2): 361–380.

Cutts, David and Edward Fieldhouse (2009) 'What small spatial scales are relevant as electoral contexts for individual voters? The importance of the household on turnout at the 2001 general election', *American Journal of Political Science* 53(3): 726–739.

Cutts, David, Edward Fieldhouse and Andrew Russell (2010) 'The campaign that changed everything and still did not matter? The Liberal Democrat campaign and performance', *Parliamentary Affairs* 63: 689–707.

Cutts, David and Matthew Goodwin (2017) 'Is the balance of power in the southwest really tilting toward the Lib Dems?', *The Times* (Red Box), https://www.thetimes.co.uk/article/is-the-balance-of-power-in-the-southwest-really-tilting-toward-the-lib-dems-mlpd7kz8p (accessed 20 September 2018).

Cutts, David, Matthew Goodwin, Oliver Heath and Caitlin Milazzo (2019) 'Resurgent Remain and a rebooted revolt on the right: exploring the 2019 European Parliament elections in the United Kingdom', *Political Quarterly* 90(3): 496–514.

Cutts, David, Matthew Goodwin, Oliver Heath and Paula Surridge (2020) 'Brexit, the 2019 General Election and the realignment of British politics', *Political Quarterly* 91(1): 7–23.

Cutts, David, Ron Johnston, Charles Pattie and Justin Fisher (2012) 'Laying the foundations for electoral success: Conservative pre-campaign canvassing before the 2010 UK General Election', *Journal of Elections, Public Opinion and Parties* 22(3): 359–375.

Cutts, David and Andrew Russell (2015) 'From coalition to catastrophe: the electoral meltdown of the Liberal Democrats', *Parliamentary Affairs* 68(1): 70–87.

Cutts, David and Andrew Russell (2018) 'The Liberal Democrats: green shoots of recovery or still on life support?', *Parliamentary Affairs* 71(1): 72–90.

Cutts, David and Andrew Russell (2020) 'Relevant again but still unpopular? The Liberal Democrats' 2019 election campaign', *Parliamentary Affairs* 73(1): 103–124.

Cutts, David and Andrew Russell (2021) 'Orpington all over again: why the North Shropshire electoral earthquake means the Liberal Democrats have turned the corner on the road back to recovery', LSE Blog, https://blogs.lse.ac.uk/politicsandpolicy/north-shropshire-libdems (accessed July 2023).

Cutts, David, Andrew Russell and Joshua Townsley (2021) 'Will Chesham and Amersham kick-start a Liberal Democrat revival? Not until the party unites its old and emerging electoral geographies', LSE Blog, https://blogs.lse.ac.uk/politicsandpolicy/chesham-and-amersham-byelection (accessed July 2023).

Cyr, Arthur (1977) *Liberal Party Politics in Britain*, Richmond: Calder.

Dahlgreen, Will (2015) 'Public view of Lib Dems is as bleak as ever', YouGov, https://yougov.co.uk/topics/politics/articles-reports/2015/07/16/futures-bleak-lib-dems (accessed 12 June 2019).

Dathan, Matt (2015) 'Budget 2015: even Lib Dems didn't care about Dany Alexander's alternative Yellow Budget', *The Independent*, https://www.independent.co.uk/news/uk/politics/budget-2015-even-lib-dem-mps-didn-t-care-about-danny-alexander-s-alternative-yellow-budget-10120623.html (accessed 12 August 2017).

de Swaan, Abram (1973) *Coalition Theories and Government Formation*, Amsterdam: Elsevier.

Debus, Marc, Mary Stegmaier and Jale Tosun (2014) 'Economic voting under coalition governments: evidence from Germany', *Political Science Research and Methods* 2(1): 49–67.

Denver, David and Gordon Hands (1997) *Modern Constituency Electioneering*, London: Frank Cass.

Dommett, Katharine and Mehmet Bakir (2020) 'A transparent digital election campaign: the insights and significance of political advertising archives for debates on electoral regulation', *Parliamentary Affairs* 73(1): 208–224.

Dommett, Katharine and Luke Temple (2018) 'Digital campaigning: the rise of Facebook and satellite campaigns', *Parliamentary Affairs* 71(1): 189–202.

Dommett, Katharine, Luke Temple and Patrick Seyd (2021) 'Dynamics of intra-party organisation in the digital age: a grassroots analysis of digital adoption', *Parliamentary Affairs* 74(2): 378–397.

Dorling, Daniel, Colin Rallings and Michael Thrasher (1998) 'The epidemiology of the Liberal Democrat vote', *Political Geography* 17(1): 45–70.

Downs, Anthony (1957) *An Economic Theory of Democracy*, New York: Harper Row.

Duch, Raymond and Randolph Stevenson (2008) *The Economic Vote: How Political and Economic Institutions Condition Election Results*, Cambridge: Cambridge University Press.

English, Patrick (2021) 'Conservative vote share down 8pts in "Blue Wall", with party potentially losing up to 16 seats', YouGov, https://yougov.co.uk/topics/politics/articlesreports/2021/07/30/conservative-vote-share-down-8pts-blue-wall-party (accessed 20 March 2022).

Evans, Elizabeth (2011) *Gender and the Liberal Democrats: Representing Women?*, Manchester: Manchester University Press.

Evans, Elizabeth and Emma Sanderson-Nash (2011) 'Sandals to suits: professionalisation, coalition and the Liberal Democrats', *British Journal of Politics and International Relations* 13: 459–473.

Evans, Geoffrey and Jon Mellon (2016) 'Working class votes and Conservative losses: solving the UKIP puzzle', *Parliamentary Affairs* 69(2): 464–479.

Evans, Geoffrey and Anand Menon (2017) *Brexit and British Politics*, Cambridge: Polity Press.

Farron, Tim (2016) 'Tim Farron's conference speech', https://timfarron.co.uk/en/article/2016/1187219/tim-farron-s-conference-speech on (accessed 23 March 2019).

Fieldhouse, Edward and David Cutts (2005) 'Steady progress or a failure to seize the moment? The Liberal Democrats' 2005 General Election performance', in A. Geddes and J. Tonge (eds), *Britain Decides: The UK General Election 2005*, Basingstoke: Palgrave Macmillan.

Fieldhouse, Edward and David Cutts (2009) 'The effectiveness of local party campaigns in 2005: combining evidence from campaign spending, agent survey data and individual level data', *British Journal of Political Science* 39(1): 367–388.

Fieldhouse, Edward and David Cutts (2018) 'Shared partisanship, household norms and turnout: testing a relational theory of electoral participation', *British Journal of Political Science* 48(3): 807–823.

Fieldhouse, Edward, David Cutts and Andrew Russell (2006) 'Neither north nor south: the geography of Liberal Democrat voting in 2005', *Journal of Elections and Public Opinion* 16(1): 77–92.

Fieldhouse, Edward, Jane Green, Geoffrey Evans, Jonathan Mellon, Christopher Prosser, Hermann Schmitt and Cees Van Der Eijk (2021) *Electoral Shocks: The Volatile Voter in a Turbulent World*, Oxford: Oxford University Press.

Fisher, Justin (2010) 'Party finance: normal service resumed?', *Parliamentary Affairs* 63(4): 778–801.

Fisher, Justin, David Cutts and Edward Fieldhouse (2011) 'The electoral effectiveness of constituency campaigning in the 2010 British General Election: the "triumph" of labour?', *Electoral Studies* 30: 816–828.

Fisher, Justin and David Denver (2008) 'From foot-slogging to call centres and direct mail: a framework for analysing the development of district-level campaigning', *European Journal of Political Research* 47: 794–826.

Fisher, Justin, David Denver and Gordon Hands (2006a) 'The relative electoral impact of central party co-ordination and size of party membership at constituency level', *Electoral Studies* 25(4): 664–676.

Fisher, Justin, David Denver and Gordon Hands (2006b) 'Party membership and campaign activity in Britain: the impact of electoral performance', *Party Politics* 12(4): 505–519.

Fisher, Justin, Edward Fieldhouse and David Cutts (2013) 'Members are not the only fruit: volunteer activity in British political parties at the 2010 General Election', *British Journal of Politics and International Relations* 16(1): 75–95.

Font, J. (2001) 'Dangerous coalitions (for small parties): the electoral consequences of government in Spanish regions and municipalities', *Southern European Society and Politics* 6: 71–96.

Foos, Florian and Peter John (2016) 'Parties are no civic charities: voter contact and the changing partisan composition of the electorate', *Political Science Research and Methods* 6(2): 283–298.

Ford, R. (2022) 'UK local election results were messy now Boris Johnson's future is on the line', *The Guardian*, https://www.theguardian.com/politics/2022/may/07/uk-local-election-results-were-messy-now-boris-johnsons-future-is-on-the-line?CMP=Share_AndroidApp_Other (accessed 7 May 2022).

Fortunato, David (2019) 'The electoral implications of coalition policy making', *British Journal of Political Science* 49(1): 59–80.

Fortunato, David and James Adams (2015) 'How voters' perceptions of junior coalition partners depend on the prime minister's position', *European Journal of Political Research* 54(3): 601–621

Fortunato, David and Randolph Stevenson (2013) 'Perceptions of partisan ideologies: the effect of coalition participation', *American Journal of Political Science* 57(2): 459–477.

Fox, Chris. (2010) Interview with the authors, 26 May 2010.

Gamson, William (1961) 'A theory of coalition formation', *American Sociological Review* 26: 373–382.

Gerber, Alan and Donald Green (2000) 'The effects of canvassing, direct mail, and telephone contact on voter turnout: a field experiment', *American Political Science Review* 94(3): 653–663.

Gerber, Alan and Donald Green (2012) *Field Experiments: Design, Analysis and Interpretation*, New York: W. W. Norton.

Gibbon, Gary (2011) 'Tory backbenchers "spoiling for a fight" with Lib Dem partners', Channel 4 News, https://www.channel4.com/news/by/gary-gibbon/blogs/tory-backbenchers-spoiling-for-a-fight-with-lib-dem-partners (accessed 25 July 2017).

Grayson, Richard (2007) 'Analysing the Liberal Democrats', *Political Quarterly* 78(1): 5–10.

Grayson, Richard (2010) 'The Liberal Democrat journey to a Lib-Con coalition – and where next?', Compass, http://clients.squareeye.net/uploads/compass/documents/Compass%20LD%20Journey%20WEB.pdf (accessed 15 May 2017).

Grayson, Richard (2013) 'Why I'm not renewing my Liberal Democrat membership', Compass, https://www.compassonline.org.uk/why-i-am-not-renewing-my-liberal-democrat-membership (accessed 12 May 2017).

Greaves, Bernard and Gordon Lishman (1980) *The Theory and Practice of Community Politics*, Association of Liberal Councillors, Campaign Booklet Number 12, http://www.rosenstiel.co.uk/aldc/commpol.htm (accessed 12 February 2017).

Green, Donald and Alan Gerber (2008) *Get Out the Vote: How to Increase Voter Turnout* (2nd edition). Washington, DC: Brookings Institution Press.

Green, Donald, Bradley Palmquist and Eric Schickler (2002) *Partisan Hearts and Minds: Political Parties and the Social Identities of Voters*, New Haven: Yale University Press.

Green, Jane (2007) 'When voters and parties agree: valence issues and party competition', *Political Studies* 55(3): 629–655.

Green, Jane (2015) 'Party and voter incentives at the crowded centre of British politics', *Party Politics* 21(1): 80–99.

Green, Jane and Sara Hobolt (2008) 'Owning the issue agenda: party strategies and vote choices in British elections', *Electoral Studies* 27(3): 460–476.

Green, Jane and Will Jennings (2017) *The Politics of Competence: Parties, Public Opinion and Voters*, Cambridge: Cambridge University Press.

Grice, Andrew (2010) 'I want to push this all the way, declares Clegg', *The Independent*, https://

www.independent.co.uk/news/uk/politics/i-want-to-push-this-all-the-way-declares-clegg-1950668.html (accessed 2 August 2017).

Guardian, The (2001) 'Lib Dem manifesto changes the spectrum', https://www.theguardian.com/politics/2001/may/16/election2001.liberaldemocrats (accessed 14 May 2016).

Guardian, The (2002) 'Voters say no to Iraq attack', https://www.theguardian.com/politics/2001/may/16/election2001.liberaldemocrats (accessed 18 May 2016).

Guardian, The (2003) 'Guardian opinion poll', http://image.guardian.co.uk/sys-files/Politics/documents/2003/03/18/17303ICM_poll.pdf (accessed 18 May 2016).

Gurling, James (2011) 'Liberal Democrats consultative session: election review May 2011', http://d3n8a8pro7vhmx.cloudfront.net/libdems/pages/2008/attachments/original/1390839676/Liberal_Democrats_Election_Review_.pdf?1390839676 (accessed 25 August 2017).

Harvey, Nick (2015) 'From the rose garden to the compost heap', *Journal of Liberal History* 88: 35–38.

Hayton, Richard (2014) 'Conservative Party statecraft and the politics of coalition', *Parliamentary Affairs* 67: 6–24.

Heath, Anthony, Roger Jowell and John Curtice (1985) *How Britain Votes*, Oxford: Pergamon.

Heppell, Tim (2019) *Cameron: The Politics of Modernisation and Moderation*, Manchester: Manchester University Press.

Heppell, Tim and David Seawright (eds) (2012) *Cameron and the Conservatives: The Transition to Coalition Government*, Basingstoke: Palgrave Macmillan.

Hjermitslev, Ida (2020) 'The electoral cost of coalition participation: can anyone escape?', *Party Politics* 26(4): 510–520.

HM Government (2010) *The Coalition: Our Programme for Government,* London: Cabinet Office, http://www.cabinetoffice.gov.uk/media/409088/pfg_coalition.pdf (accessed 1 June 2017).

Huntbach, Matthew (2015) 'Coalition: a difficult situation made worse', *Journal of Liberal History* 88: 40–43.

Johnston, Ron, David Cutts, Charles Pattie and Justin Fisher (2012) 'We've got them on the list: contacting, canvassing and voting in a British General Election campaign', *Electoral Studies* 31: 317–329.

Johnston, Ron and Charles Pattie (2006) *Putting Voters in Their Place: Geography and Electors in Great Britain*, Oxford: Oxford University Press.

Johnston, Ron and Charles Pattie (2011) 'Where did Labour's votes go? Valence politics and campaign effects at the 2010 British General Election', *British Journal of Politics and International Relations* 13(3): 283–303.

Kanagasooriam, J. (2019) 'How the Labour Party's "red wall" turned blue', *Financial Times*, https://www.ft.com/content/3b80b2de-1dc2-11ea-81f0-0c253907d3e0 (accessed 18 June 2021).

Kellner, Peter (2011) 'Is there really a progressive majority?', YouGov, https://yougov.co.uk/topics/politics/articles-reports/2011/05/16/there-really-progressive-majority (accessed 15 June 2017).

Kentish, Benjamin (2019) 'Jo Swinson "absolutely categorically" rules out working with Corbyn even to deliver new Brexit referendum', *The Independent*, https://www.independent.co.uk/news/uk/politics/jo-swinson-corbyn-general-election-brexit-referendum-coalition-a9185896.html (accessed 12 March 2020).

Laws, David (2016) *Coalition*, London: Biteback.

Laws, David and P. Marshall (eds) (2004) *The Orange Book*, London: Profile Books.

Leiserson, Michael (1968) 'Factions and coalitions in one-party Japan: an interpretation based on the theory of games', *American Political Science Review* 62: 70–87.

Liberal Democrats (1997) *Liberal Democrat Manifesto 1997: Making the Difference*, London: Liberal Democrats.

Liberal Democrats (2001) *Liberal Democrat Manifesto 2001: Freedom, Justice and Honesty*, London: Liberal Democrats.

Liberal Democrats (2010) *Liberal Democrat Manifesto 2010: Change That Works for You*, London: Liberal Democrats.

Liberal Democrats (2019) *2019 Election Review Report*, London: Liberal Democrats.

Lodge, Milton and Charles Taber (2013) *The Rationalizing Voter*, Cambridge: Cambridge University Press.

MacIver, Don (ed.) (1996) *The Liberal Democrats*, Hemel Hempstead: Harvester Wheatsheaf.

MacKinnon, David (2008) *Introduction to Statistical Mediation Analysis*, New York: Taylor and Francis.

Martin, Lanny and Randolph Stevenson (2001) 'Government formation in parliamentary democracies', *American Journal of Political Science* 45(1): 33–50.

Marshall, Paul and David Laws (2004) *The Orange Book: Reclaiming Liberalism*, London: Profile Books.

Mattes, Kyle and Caitlin Milazzo (2014) 'Pretty faces, marginal races: predicting election outcomes using trait assessments of British parliamentary candidates', *Electoral Studies* 34: 177–189.

Meadowcroft, John (2001) 'Community politics, representation and the limits of deliberative democracy', *Local Government Studies* 27: 25–42.

Merrick, Rob (2019) 'Question Time debate: Jo Swinson admits "getting it wrong on austerity and won't say she can become PM"', *The Independent*, https://www.independent.co.uk/news/uk/politics/election-debate-jo-swinson-become-prime-minister-regret-austerity-a9214526.html (accessed 23 March 2020).

Meyer, Thomas and Daniel Strobhl (2016) 'Voter perceptions of coalition policy positions in multiparty systems', *Electoral Studies* 41: 80–91.

Nagel, Jack and Christopher Wlezien (2010) 'Centre-party strength and major-party divergence in Britain, 1945–2005', *British Journal of Political Science* 40(2): 279–304.

Nickerson, David (2008) 'Is voting contagious? Evidence from two field experiments', *American Political Science Review* 102(1): 49–57.

Opinium (2019) 'Political polling 10th December 2019 – final poll', https://www.opinium.com/resource-center/political-polling-10th-december-2019-final-poll (accessed 7 April 2020).

Pack, Mark (2014) 'The Liberal Democrat approach to campaigning', *Journal of Liberal History* 83: 6–14.

Pack, Mark and Edward Maxfield (2012) *101 Ways to Win an Election*, London: Biteback.

Parker, George and Kiran Stacey (2015) 'Clegg dismisses any coalition deal with Labour involving SNP', *Financial Times*, https://www.ft.com/content/fd3b7bec-ea97-11e4-8c7e-00144feab7de (accessed 29 September 2017).

Pattie, Charles and Ron Johnston (2009) 'Still talking, but is anybody listening? The changing face of constituency campaigning in Britain, 1997–2005', *Party Politics* 15(4): 411–434

Pons, Vincent and Guillaume Liegey (2019) 'Increasing the electoral participation of immigrants: experimental evidence from France', *Economic Journal* 129(617): 481–508.

Pring, Coralie (2011) 'Disloyal Lib Dems', YouGov, https://yougov.co.uk/topics/politics/articles-reports/2011/05/16/disloyal-lib-dems (accessed 19 June 2017).

Quinn, Thomas, Judith Bara and Jon Bartle (2011) 'The UK coalition agreement of 2010: who won?', *Journal of Elections, Public Opinion and Parties* 21: 295–312.

Rapoport, Ronald and Walter Stone (2005) *Three's a Crowd: The Dynamic of Third Parties, Ross Perot and Republican Resurgence*, Ann Arbor: University of Michigan Press.

Rennard, Chris (2018) *Winning Here: My Campaigning Life – Memoirs, Volume 1*, London: Biteback.

Riker, William (1962) *The Theory of Political Coalitions*, New Haven: Yale University Press.

Roemmele, Andrea and Rachel Gibson (2020) 'Scientific and subversive: the two faces of the fourth era of campaigning', *New Media and Society* 22(4): 595–610.

Russell, Andrew (2010) 'Inclusion, exclusion or obscurity? The 2010 General Election and the implications of the Con–Lib coalition for third-party politics in Britain', *British Politics* 5: 506–524.

Russell, Andrew and Edward Fieldhouse (2005) *Neither Left Nor Right? The Liberal Democrats and the Electorate*, Manchester: Manchester University Press.

Russell, Andrew, Edward Fieldhouse and David Cutts (2007) 'De facto-veto? The parliamentary Liberal Democrats', *Political Quarterly* 78(1): 89–98.

Sanderson-Nash, Emma (2012) '*The Orange Book*: turning right or changing gears?', *Economic Affairs* 32(2): 11–15.

Scott, Kirsty (2001) 'Kennedy vows to scrap tuition fees', *The Guardian*, https://www.theguardian.com/politics/2001/may/23/uk.highereducation (accessed 10 January 2017).

Seawright, David (2013) '"Yes the census": the 2011 UK referendum campaign on the alternative vote', *British Politics* 8(4): 457–475.

Sened, Itai (1996) 'A model of coalition formation: theory and evidence', *Journal of Politics* 58(2): 350–372.

Strøm, Kaare (1990) *Minority Government and Majority Rule*, Cambridge: Cambridge University Press.

Strøm, Kaare, Wolfgang Muller, Torbjorn Bergman and Benjamin Nyblade (2008) 'Conclusion', in Kaare Strøm, Wolfgang Muller and Torbjorn Bergman (eds), *Cabinets and Coalition Bargaining: The Democratic Life Cycle in Western Europe*, Oxford: Oxford University Press.

Survation (2019) 'Survey archive', https://www.survation.com/archive/2019-2 (accessed 7 April 2020).

Telegraph, The (2017) 'Who's Tim? More than half of voters don't know who Tim Farron is', https://www.telegraph.co.uk/news/2017/05/26/tim-half-voters-do-not-know-tim-farron (accessed 19 June 2019).

Thornton, Daniel and Tess Kidney-Bishop (2018) 'Ministers reflect: Nick Clegg' (pp. 1–18), Institute of Government, https://www.instituteforgovernment.org.uk/ministers-reflect/wp-content/uploads/2018/07/Nick-Clegg.pdf (accessed 12 September 2017).

Timmins, Nicholas (2012) 'How the Coalition carved up the NHS', *The Independent*, https://www.independent.co.uk/news/uk/politics/how-coalition-carved-nhs-7924971.html (accessed 25 September 2017).

Townsley, Joshua (2018) 'Is it worth door-knocking? Evidence from a United Kingdom-based Get Out The Vote (GOTV) field experiment on the effect of party leaflets and canvass visits on voter turnout', *Political Science Research and Methods*, 1–15.

Verzichelli, Luca (2008) 'Portfolio allocation', in Kaare Strøm, Wolfgang Muller and Torbjorn Bergman (eds), *Cabinets and Coalition Bargaining: The Democratic Life Cycle in Western Europe* (pp. 237–267), Oxford: Oxford University Press.

Wager, Alan, Aron Cheung and Tim Bale (2021) 'Breaching the blue wall', UK in a Changing Europe, https://ukandeu.ac.uk/working-paper/breaching-the-blue-wall (accessed 18 June 2021).

Warwick, Paul (1994) *Government Survival in Parliamentary Democracies*, New York: Cambridge University Press.

Watt, Nicholas (2011) 'Rethink on managing coalition after Nick Clegg rejects No 10 report', *The Guardian*, https://www.theguardian.com/politics/wintour-and-watt/2011/nov/08/liberal-conservative-coalition-nickclegg (accessed 25 May 2017).

Whiteley, Paul, Harold Clarke, David Sanders and Marianne Stewart (2013) *Affluence, Austerity and Electoral Change in Britain*, Cambridge: Cambridge University Press.

Whiteley, Paul, Patrick Seyd and Anthony Billinghurst (2006) *Third Force Politics: Liberal Democrats at the Grassroots*, Oxford: Oxford University Press.

Wilson, Des (2014) 'I'm sorry to report the political death of my disastrous leader: Nick Clegg', *Daily Mail*, https://www.dailymail.co.uk/debate/article-2638398/Im-sorry-report-political-death-disastrous-leader-Nick-Clegg-A-damning-critique-Deputy-PM-DES-WILSON-founder-Lib-Dems.html (accessed 4 September 2017).

Wintour, Patrick (2010) 'Coalition talks: Labour revolt may scupper deal with Liberal Democrats', *The Guardian*, https://www.theguardian.com/politics/wintour-and-watt/2010/may/11/coalition-talks-libdem-labour-deal (accessed 17 May 2017).

Wintour, Patrick (2014) 'Cameron and Clegg square off as coalition rift grows', *The Guardian*, https://www.theguardian.com/politics/2014/dec/07/cameron-clegg-argue-economy-deficit-coalition-splits-grow (accessed 5 August 2017).

Wintour, Patrick and Helene Mulholland (2012) 'Nick Clegg apologises for tuition fees pledge', *The Guardian*, https://www.theguardian.com/politics/2012/sep/19/nick-clegg-apologies-tuition-fees-pledge (accessed 15 August 2017).

Wintour, Patrick and Nicholas Watt (2015) 'The Clegg catastrophe', *The Guardian*, https://www.theguardian.com/politics/2015/jun/24/the-nick-clegg-catastrophe (accessed 2 October 2017).

YouGov (2015) 'YouGov leader tracker', https://d25d2506sfb94s.cloudfront.net/cumulus_uploads/document/nh4tayipg2/YG-Archives-Pol-Trackers-Leaders-Approval-180415.pdf (accessed 18 April 2018).

YouGov (2019a) 'If a party stood on a manifesto of staying in the EU and won a majority in a general election, do you think it would or would not be legitimate for them to keep Britain in the EU?', https://yougov.co.uk/topics/politics/survey-results/daily/2019/09/16/b11b3/1 (accessed 7 April 2020).

YouGov (2019b) 'YouGov/The Sunday Times survey results', https://d25d2506sfb94s.cloudfront.net/cumulus_uploads/document/3e6ngxeco2/TheSundayTimes_VI_Results_191129_w.pdf (accessed 7 April 2020).

Index

Fox, Chris. 42, 43, 51, 283
Franklin, Mark 78

Gamson, William 71
Gerber, Alan 236, 240, 243, 287
Gibbon, Gary 82
Gibson, Rachel 244
Goodwin, Matthew xi, 152, 153
Grayson, Richard 20, 63, 64, 65, 66, 74
Greaves, Bernard 36, 37
Green Party 56, 105, 106, 111, 118, 119, 156,
    158, 170, 177, 181, 193, 194, 269, 276,
    281, 285
Green, Donald 104, 236, 240, 243, 287
Green, Jane 19, 21, 23, 104
Green, T. H., positive liberty 65, 75
Grice, Andrew 78
Grimond, Jo (MP 1950–1983; Liberal leader
    1956–1967) 37, 63
Guardian, The 20, 25.
Gurling, James 88
Gyimah, Sam 157, 160

Hands, Gordon 35, 36, 283
Harvey, Nick (MP 1992–2015) 74, 76, 205,
    256
Hayton, Richard 71, 72
Heath, Anthony 46, 47
Heppell, Tim 71, 72
Hino, Airo, 73
Hjermitslev, Ida 73
Hobhouse, Leonard 75
Hobson, John 75
Howard, Michael 24, 31, 86
Hughes, Simon (MP 1983–2010) 148
Huhne, Chris (MP 2005–2013) 75, 76, 80,
    82, 260
Huntbach, Matthew 81
hypothecated taxation ('penny on income
    tax to pay for education/NHS') 4, 20,
    21, 23, 63, 66, 152, 257

identity cards 78, 257
Iraq war 21, 22, 24, 25–26, 28–32, 40, 41, 44,
    111, 209, 212, 257, 258

John, Peter 243
Johnson, Boris 158, 163, 164, 165, 168, 185,
    187, 252, 261, 281
    and 2019 election campaign, 158–163,
    185–195
    fading popularity 163–165
Johnston, Ron 2, 35, 36, 60

Kanagasooriam, James 223
Kellner, Peter 66

Kennedy, Charles (MP 1983–2015; leader
    1999–2006) 20, 22, 23–30, 31, 32, 40,
    42, 43, 47, 51, 52, 64, 65, 96,111, 166, 211,
    212, 224, 257, 258, 282, 296
Kentish, Benjamin 158
Kidney-Bishop, Tess 76, 80, 82
King, Anthony 282
Kosovo (NATO bombing of) 257

Lamb, Norman (MP 2001–2019) 148, 149
Laws, David (MP 2001–2015) 65, 75, 76, 77,
    80, 81, 259–60
leader debates 25, 88, 89, 150, 261
Leiserson, Michael 72
Liberal Democrat manifestos, 5, 20, 22, 43,
    63, 152, 156, 238, 246, 253
    1992 *Changing Britain for Good* 63
    1997 *Making the Difference* 20
    2001 *Freedom, Justice and Honesty* 20
    2010 *Change That Works for You* 23, 43,
        57, 65, 66, 78, 81, 82, 86, 93, 260
    2017 *Open, Tolerant and United* 152
    2019 *Stop Brexit: Build a Brighter Future*
        161, 246
Liberal Democrat seat types
    breakthrough 127, 196, 205, 206, 208, 222,
        224, 263, 287
    legacy heartland 16, 127, 136, 203, 205
Liberal Democrats
    2019 *Election Review* report 250, 252, 253,
        288
    'identity' of party 1–8, 19, 20, 23, 34,
        37, 40, 43, 46, 47, 56, 57, 58, 63, 64,
        73, 74, 78, 81, 84, 85, 93, 95, 119, 217,
        255–272
    as a movement? 2, 154, 270–272
libertarian–authoritarian axis 100, 112, 115,
    117, 172, 182, 183, 274, 277, 283
Liegey, Guillaume 243
Lishman, Gordon, 36, 37
Lloyd, Stephen (MP 2010–2015, 2017–2019)
    153, 162
local elections 36 37,42, 88, 89, 121, 133, 142,
    150, 154, 155, 156, 165, 166, 207, 208,
    236, 238, 284
Lodge, Milton 104

MacIver, Don 37, 282
MacKinnon, David 129
Marshall, Paul 65
Martin, Lanny 72
Mattes, Kyle 238
Maxfield, Edward 282
May, Theresa 79, 97, 150, 155, 179, 285
Meadowcroft, John 37
Mellon, Jon 152